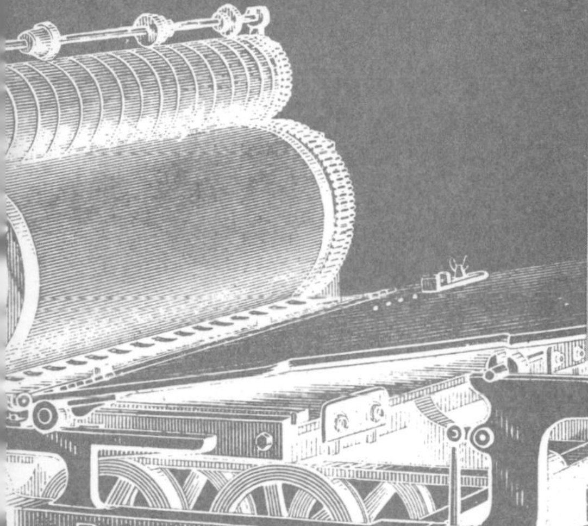
R. HOE & CO.
NEW-YORK & LONDON.
TUTTLE-N-Y

ENDLESS FRONTIERS

BOOKS BY ROGER BURLINGAME

You Too

Susan Shane

High Thursday

The Heir

Peace Veterans

Cartwheels

Three Bags Full

March of the Iron Men

Engines of Democracy

Whittling Boy: The Story of Eli Whitney

Of Making Many Books

Inventors behind the Inventor

Backgrounds of Power

General Billy Mitchell

Machines That Built America

Benjamin Franklin

Henry Ford

The American Conscience

Endless Frontiers: The Story of McGraw-Hill

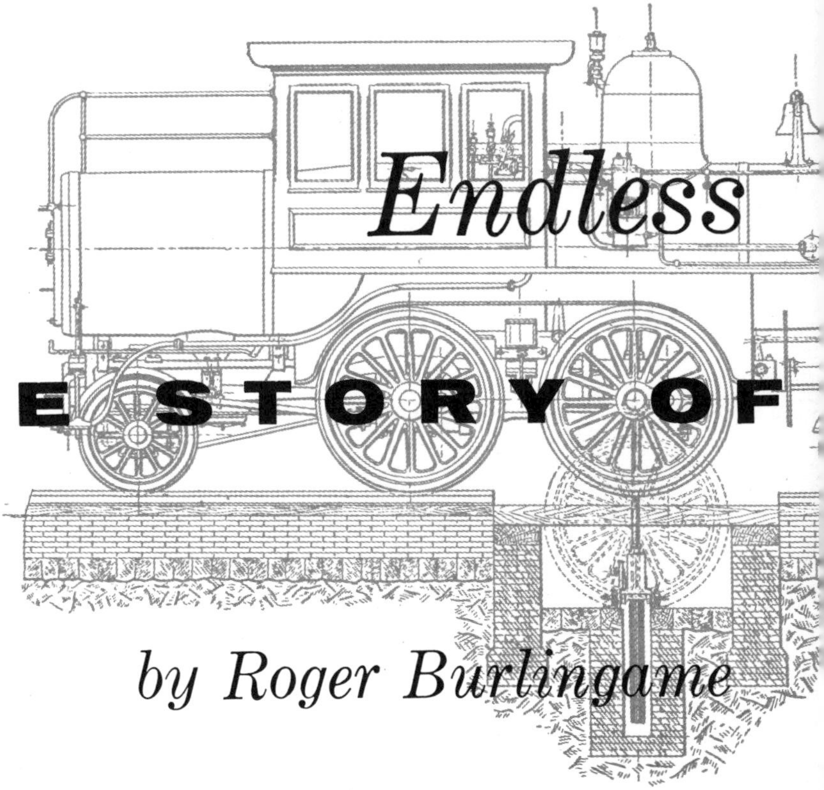

Endless

THE STORY OF

by Roger Burlingame

McGRAW-HILL BOOK COMPANY, INC.

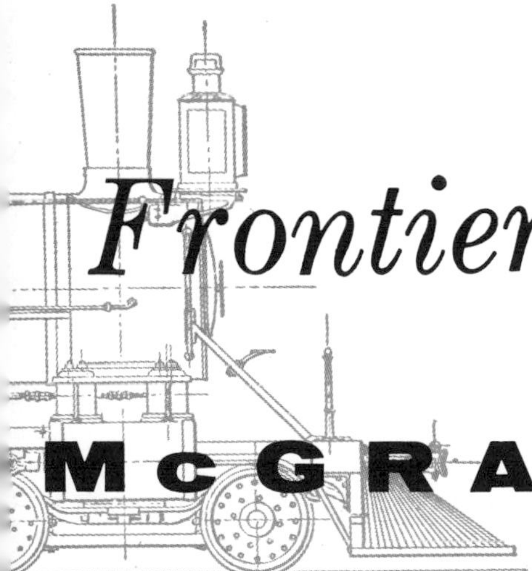

Frontiers

McGRAW-HILL

NEW YORK TORONTO LONDON

About the Author

Roger Burlingame, distinguished writer on Americana and the economic scene, was born in 1889 in New York City. He attended preparatory school in Morristown, New Jersey, and in 1913 received an A.B. degree from Harvard College. He worked for a year on the staff of *The Independent,* and for twelve years with Charles Scribner's Sons. Since 1926 he has been a free-lance writer, with time out only for service from 1942–1943 in the Office of War Information. In 1945 he was a correspondent in the European and Mediterranean theatres. His previous books include *Inventors Behind the Inventor, Backgrounds of Power, Engines of Democracy, General Billy Mitchell, Machines That Built America, March of the Iron Men,* and *Henry Ford.* In all, he is the author of twenty books.

Endless Frontiers: THE STORY OF MCGRAW-HILL

LIBRARY OF CONGRESS CATALOG CARD NUMBER: 58-12992

First Edition

To Willard Chevalier
with gratitude

Preface

First of all I want to explain what this book is not. It is not company history in the accepted sense. It is not even what publishers like to call a definitive biography of McGraw-Hill. Readers will look in vain for posed portraits of successive company executives. Except for the founders and a few of the men—no longer in the picture—who set the standards, this story is not concerned with personalities. As far as possible I have tried not to interrupt the narrative with statistics. For purposes of reference, a detailed chronology has been set apart in an appendix.

From my first thinking, I have conceived this undertaking as the preservation of an era: the era in which the power of print was called into the service of industry. In those years there has been enacted one of the greatest dramas in the history of civilization. In it were evolved most of the technics that have wholly changed the face of the world we live in. To today's children these things are commonplaces. The generation, transmission, and application of electric power, automotive transportation, electronic communication, and machine computation are taken for granted. It is only when we come to know the awful birth agonies of these things, when we explore their slow gestation that goes back to the very dawn of science that we arrive at a sense of humility before the transcendent facts.

Actually the fruitful era falls nearly within the lifespan of McGraw-Hill and its progenitors. As I came to study the publications of these organizations I realized that they gave an interpretation of most of the phases of growth in the period. As a whole they form a body of contemporary documents that is of great value to the historian who is attempting to give clarity to the otherwise incredibly complex and fast-moving sequence of events.

With this discovery I realized what the pattern of my book must be. It must be a sort of historical motion picture with a protagonist or, as a dramatist would say, a hero, appearing in every scene, sometimes as an interpreter but often taking part in the action. This protagonist or interpreter would be McGraw-Hill.

My concept naturally led me away from the conventional company-history blueprint. In it the focus was no longer exclusively on the company. In it the company was seen simply as a reflective or, at times, a catalytic agent. Its printed pages not only mirrored industrial and business progress through the years; they often gave it stimulus. At the same time they helped develop a new and necessary kind of journalism.

It is because the background of the world outside the Green Building has seemed so important to me that I have given so little space to the company's internal mechanics. That is, of course, a fascinating story, but it is not this story nor can it be written by this author.

To the McGraw-Hill Publishing and Book Companies, I am an outsider. I know the Green Building only as a visitor. I have had to explore it from the outside in. That is why I cannot write the inside story of McGraw-Hill. That work must be undertaken by someone who has lived and grown with the organization.

I am not, however, unfamiliar with the era upon which I believe McGraw-Hill to have had an impact. I have lived through most of it. I have for many years been a close student of technological and industrial history and I have written books on both. I have also been exposed to magazine and book publishing and I once wrote a book about that.

The experience of writing my story of McGraw-Hill has been, on the whole, a happy one. My first introduction to McGraw-Hill was by my old friend Edward C. Aswell, then in the Book Company. When I agreed to undertake the project, I was given total freedom by a liberal contract to write as I pleased. The whole picture has been put before me without reserve. Everywhere I have encountered humility rather than boasting. Company executives, publishers, and editors have leaned over backward to give me an objective view. Occasionally, even, when some of my enthusiasms have carried me away, these people have brought me down to earth with the caution that perfection has always been a goal rather than an accomplished fact.

Notwithstanding this sympathetic help, however, I have maintained the pattern of excluding reference by name to individuals now active in the company except in connection with their recorded interviews. From these I have quoted liberally and given credit in footnotes. And let me say here that these oral reminiscences made with the aid of one of Columbia University's expert interviewers have been of substantial assistance. I have made use of this tape-recorded oral history—originated, I believe, at Columbia—in other work, and I am convinced that it must be a part of the future historian's equipment.

Although the kindness I have been shown has been universal, I have room to thank only a few who have given me constantly of their time and energy. At the top of the list is Col. Willard Chevalier, one of the most engaging gentlemen I have ever met; the privilege of having been his companion is one of the happier experiences of my life. His attention to my work has been unremitting from start to finish. And, I may add, he has greatly lightened whatever burdens it may have presented by his gently humorous and ironic views on what have seemed to me at first glance to be dreary matters. It is a rare quality in the Colonel that has let him maintain a certain detachment, a certain invariable relation of inside things to outside things. Neither engineering nor McGraw-Hill has confined him. The most engrossing moments will evoke from him a classical quotation or an illustration from the vast amount of reading he has somehow absorbed in the interstices of a fabulously busy life.

Then there is Mr. Henry G. Lord whose first talk with me opened the whole vista down which I was to travel. He was ninety years old then and after three hours showed no hint of fatigue. Another door opener was Mr. Paul Montgomery who first showed me the magazine panorama. Mr. Nelson Bond has offered me a view from the top of the sales staff and the training it undergoes, and Mr. Ralph Smith has done the same for the editorial side. Mr. Curtis Benjamin has kept me informed about the Book Company of which he is President. Mr. Harold McGraw, Jr., and Mr. Edward Kuhn, Jr., have been indispensable in the work of putting my manuscript into print and between covers.

For conversations outside the organization, I want to thank Mrs. Joseph Quirk, daughter of John Hill, Mr. Harold Rudd, Mr. Donald Baldwin, Mr. Fred Colvin, Mr. Edgar Kobak, Dr. Jerome Hunsaker, Mr. Edward Mehren, Mr. James Thompson, and Dr. Harlan B. Phillips.

Mrs. Angelyn Corcoran gave me almost daily assistance for two years. She was able to find every needed document, to check on dates, and to do much of the exacting spadework connected with my research.

I have been fortunate in getting firsthand reminiscences of James H. McGraw, Sr., from his son, Mr. Donald C. McGraw, now president of the parent company, with whom I have had several valuable conversations; from Mr. George C. Tenney, the founder's close friend, from Mr. James A. McGraw, his nephew, from Mr. Kobak, and from Mr. Mehren. For firsthand reminiscences of John Hill I am indebted to Mrs. Quirk and Mr. Colvin.

I am especially grateful to Miss Rose Boots, librarian of the excellent company library, and to her staff for expert aid at all times.

I thank all these people and I hope that in some measure I may have justified their patience and their confidence.

ROGER BURLINGAME

Contents

PART ONE • ORIGINS

PART TWO • GROWTH

1 • ORIGINS

CHAPTER ONE

The Power of Print

The way of industrial history is beset with roadblocks. The history of business is even more difficult. To the explorer of old byways and alleys in both realms the greatest obstacle is scarcity of contemporary record. The printed word that has revealed so much to us of literature, philosophy, religion, the arts, and pure science is simply not there when we try to learn the origins of some of the vital industrial and business enterprises.

The upshot of this is that historians are forced to rely on what they call *artifacts:* relics of old machinery, old buildings, factories, millraces, abandoned mines—a hundred kinds of silent monuments to the vast undertakings that built the foundations of our life today. Occasionally there are account books, bills of lading, invoices yellow with age, inventories, lists of a ship's cargo, or confidential letters to friends or customers or banks, or the notebooks of an inventor like the great Leonardo da Vinci, or the wonderfully lucid manuals of our own first experimenter in automation—Oliver Evans.

Oddly enough the United States is especially weak in such material. In France the encyclopedists produced a quantity of valuable descriptions of machines, of all the progress in technology, in fact, as far back as the sixteenth and seventeenth centuries. In England there are the three-volume detailed *Lives of the Engineers* compiled by Samuel Smiles and the voluminous papers of the Newcomen Society. The Germans have written of great commercial enterprises. But in the United States, where industrial and commercial achievement has brought us far into the van of the world, there is only the scantiest record. In any American library we will be supplied with exhaustive accounts of wars, elections, rises and falls of political parties, debates, social movements, and the lives of presidents, generals, judges, and orators. But when we ask for source material about the origins of the great American machine-tool industry, or the evolution of the first assembly line, or the fascinating stories of the organization of communications, the librarian is puzzled.

When the Winchester Repeating Arms Company in New Haven took over the business that had been maintained by three generations of the Whitney family, the buildings were ransacked for some revealing record of the great Eli who had founded the dynasty. Only one was discovered—an artifact. It was an old, rusty, broken milling machine designed—invented from scratch—by Eli Whitney. Yet the inventor of this machine had also been the inventor of the entire pattern of interchangeable parts on which modern mass production is largely based. In his early mills he must have had enough machines for the quantity production of muskets by a new method: the manufacture of parts in series. As Denison Olmsted, his first biographer, wrote:

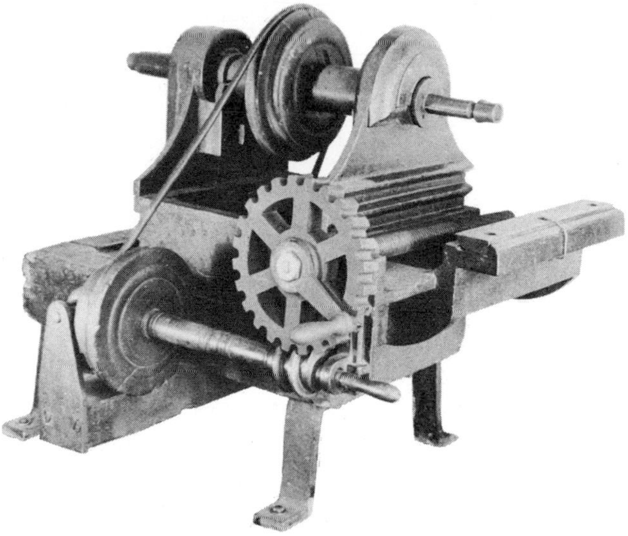

First milling machine built by Eli Whitney about 1797.

The several parts of the musket were, under this system, carried along through the various processes of manufacture, in lots of some hundreds or thousands of each. In their various stages of progress, they were made to undergo successive operations by machinery, which not only vastly abridged the labor, but at the same time so fixed and determined their form and dimensions, as to make comparatively little skill necessary in the manual operations. [1]

We may guess at the extensive sequence of machines in that novel gunmaking factory. Yet a century later only one survived! And only a handful of papers or records telling of the man's work: letters, a few sketches, and Olmsted's brief magazine article outlining his life! Today some industrious historians—Prof. Joseph

[1] Denison Olmsted, "Memoir of Eli Whitney, Esq.," New Haven, 1846, reprinted from Benjamin Stillman's *American Journal of Science and Arts* where it appeared in 1832. *Silliman's Journal,* as it is usually called, was the first "class paper" published in America.

Wickham Roe, Miss Jeannette Mirsky, and Prof. Allan Nevins among them—have finally, but only after years of research, been able to put together the life story of this pioneer of mass production. And, happily, the magazine *American Machinist*[2] has done much to compensate for the absence of contemporaneous records.

2 There are reasons for this deficiency. For one thing, Americans were making history so fast and in so many directions in the formative years that there was little time to write it. Those who did write it thought of History with a capital H as dignified literature dealing with laws and men, not stooping to recognize the noisy machine shop, the dirty, smoky factory, or the stuffy office where men engaged in the vulgar activity of making money. The Battle of Bunker Hill, the trials of Washington at Valley Forge or, later, the Missouri Compromise, the Dred Scott decision, the rise of the Populists, and the change in senatorial elections—these were dignified matters. Even Eli Whitney was mentioned in the older histories—not because he began mass production but because his cotton gin was one of the indirect causes of the Civil War!

The physical things, the very basic factors of life, were not thought worthy of print. Food processing, building, spinning, weaving, and sewing, the vital mechanics of water supply, of sewage disposal, of transportation by land and water, of road making, of the manufacture of shoes or hardware: these were part of the daily activity; they were not things to read about. The great physical achievements incidental to conquering the continent, from the digging of the Erie Canal to the building of railroads across the Rockies, had no dominating part in the history books; and generations of school children grew up taking American industrial growth for granted. It was a shocking defect in our education that these things were kept out of what anthropologists call our *cultural stream* in America. Happily this condition is being reversed and in new histories boys and girls are finding the stories of great engineering or business enterprises as exciting as fiction.

[2] A McGraw-Hill publication founded in 1877.

3 Recognition of the power of print came slowly in American factories and offices. In industry it took us a long time to graduate from the old apprentice system. Before the days of Frederick W. Taylor, Frank Gilbreth, Henry L. Gantt, Frederick A. Halsey, and the other pioneers of scientific management, each skilled worker had his own ideas of how a job should be done. He had learned his ways as a boy apprentice; the master had learned them in his own apprenticeship. Thus all the skills were passed down from one generation to another without benefit of written words. There was no standard practice in machine work or in the use, or even the maintenance, of tools. In the old days, in fact, it was customary for the worker to bring his own tools to work. With the coming of elaborate and heavy machinery this custom changed, yet it changed gradually; the smaller tools were still the worker's. His skills were all his own and he was jealous of them; he was reluctant to explain to anyone how he worked. Even when the factory developed a fairly intricate pattern, foremen respected a man's private possession of craftsmanship and let him go his way.

Management [wrote Frederick W. Taylor in 1903] is still looked upon as a question of men, the old view being that if you have the right man the methods can be safely left to him.[3]

Henry G. Lord, a McGraw-Hill director for thirty years, gives a picture of these conditions in the textile industry in the late 1880s:

All the superintendents and the overseers of the departments had learned their trade, so to speak, from their predecessors, their fathers. A dyer had probably been of a family of dyers for generations. He treasured his recipes for the dyeing of certain colors. He wouldn't even disclose them to his employer. You hired a man for his individual knowledge.[4]

In some industries the old apprentice system endured into the twentieth century. The workers in glass factories, for instance,

[3] *Scientific Management,* Harper & Brothers, New York, 1947, p. 18.
[4] Henry G. Lord, recorded interview in McGraw-Hill Archives, pp. 18, 19.

were extremely reluctant to abandon the tradition of secrecy begun in Murano in the fourteenth century when men were imprisoned lest the mysteries of their skills leak out. As late as the early 1900s when the manufacture of glass was being mechanized, it was a rule of the American window glassmakers' union that none but the nearest of kin to a blower or gatherer could ever become apprentice to either.

At the turn of the century, Taylor found such customs completely out of tune with the times. In large industrial establishments in which there was necessary division of labor, lack of uniformity in the performance of various functions caused long delays between departments. Unplanned time sequences caused costly interruptions. As each worker used his own methods, variations in the length of time required for each operation created a kind of syncopated movement throughout the factory. As Taylor wrote:

> Instead of having one way which is generally accepted as a standard, there are in daily use, say, fifty or a hundred ways of doing each element of the work. And a little thought will make it clear that this must inevitably be the case since our methods had been handed down from man to man by word of mouth, or have, in most cases been almost unconciously learned through personal observation. Practically in no instance have they been codified or systematically analyzed or described. [5]

In short, Taylor saw the pressing need for record. He saw that analysis would have to be made of every industrial operation, put into words and figures, and kept on file in the factory. The rule of thumb was no longer possible. Once this was done, every worker must forget all that he had learned from the long line of his ancestors or predecessors and learn the standardized methods that Taylor had put into writing. The result was speed, synchronization, increased production, and a uniform quality of product.

4 A business office in the old days was what Horace M. Swetland called a "citadel of individual secrecy in methods and

[5] *Op. cit.*, pp. 31, 32.

operation." It was supposed that any information leaking out of an industrial plant would be snapped up by a rival with disastrous results. Meetings of industrial competitors for the discussion of common problems and the exchange of information vital to the industry as a whole were virtually unknown. The large industrial convention so universal today would have aroused horror among the executives of the 1870s and 1880s.

> Fifty years ago, [wrote Swetland in 1923] each manufacturer, ignorant of the value of coordinate information, guarded his formulae, processes and methods as individual property. He did not realize that in exchange for the results of his individual experience he might receive the full research and combined knowledge of the entire industry. [6]

These customs were deeply entrenched. They were part of business tradition. They composed the force that for so long kept manufacturing companies family institutions. In New England factories, especially, the owner-boss who called his workers by their first names and whose children went to the same school as those of his artisans or laborers used to be proud of carrying the whole business "in his head." He had no prying bookkeeper to balance his accounts. Usually part of a dynasty, he used to boast that "the way Dad did it" was good enough for him. There is something appealingly leisurely and intensely personal about all this; the stories of it are as nostalgic as yarns of moonlight sleigh rides or fireplace cooking. But unhappily for the old-time manufacturer, the world was passing him by.

Almost every day, as the nineteenth century drew toward its close, there was some new scientific discovery or technological invention. At the same time in the United States, the tremendous demand for manufactured goods boiled down to three words: More! Faster! Cheaper! Americans believed in the equality concept: each man was as good as the next. Thus every man was entitled to the best. If he could not afford it today he could tomor-

[6] *Industrial Publishing,* New York Business Publisher's Association, Inc., New York, 1923, p. 3. Swetland was an early associate of James H. McGraw.

row. Tomorrow he would have more money *or* the thing he wanted would cost less. The wisest of the American businessmen could see this vast potential market in a country where men were equal—or thought themselves so. The wisest manufacturers had already produced for that market, applying the basic principles of mass production which in the early days had compensated for American labor shortage. They had produced farm machinery, sewing machines, clocks, watches, and guns on these principles, in quantities undreamed of anywhere else in the world.

The new inventions—new tools, new metals, new chemicals, new techniques of all kinds—made this production easier. They also made it harder. They scrapped the old customs. To satisfy the demand which grew in direct ratio to the enormous, rapid population increase, industries had to organize labor, management, and techniques on a uniform basis. Every operation in every process had to be synchronized with every other. As new, complex machine tools were evolved, work was divided and subdivided until each worker performed only a fraction of what he had done before. As the operations were timed and standardized to eliminate lost motion and material waste, the function of management took on new magnitude and vast complexity. Old easygoing ways were no longer possible. Systematic cost accounting could not be done in the boss's head. As more and more of a worker's skill was taken over by machines, his old-time secret methods, learned in an apprenticeship, were of little use.

This change, introducing scientific in place of rule-of-thumb management, has been called the second industrial revolution. It was halting at first, staggered, syncopated, uneven. Taylor and his associates had an uphill fight against conservatism. Success alternated with failure. Many industrialists fiercely resented the changes. Others were unable to keep up with the new ideas. But the revolution seemed to be swept on by an irresistible, impersonal, and invisible force that no individual could defy. Many old-timers fell by the wayside, but the men of the younger generation knew that there was one great crying need: education. Education, information, some means of knowing what was going on in the world, of learning of each new step, of being competent to adopt each innovation from wherever it started: this, suddenly, was essential—at least to American industry. And as education came in the door, secrecy was forced out.

Fortunately a framework for one of the answers to this need had long been building in America. As a whole, it was neither finished nor particularly well designed by the time the new phase of the industrial revolution began. But it was there to be used and improved. It was not a new thing in the world when Americans constructed it, but for Americans it had a peculiar appeal.

5 From the beginning the citizens of our democracy have had a greed for print. They may have been slow to appreciate the art of literature but they insisted on printed news. As the frontier moved westward after the Republic was founded, there was almost always a printing press in the van of settlement. The epidemic of newspapers that Benjamin Franklin started in colonial times spread rapidly into the West. Nothing astonished foreign visitors to the United States more than the ubiquitous American newspaper. In England the newspaper had been a luxury read by the upper classes. In America it was a necessity, even, as one Englishman observed, to the bootblack who read his paper between shines. As early as the 1830s there were 1,200 newspapers in the nation; by the time of the Civil War, 3,000. Of those 3,000, 400 were daily; the rest were weekly, biweekly, and monthly. Accustomed to periodical print, Americans became avid magazine readers.

As the average American's daily work was always accompanied by this sort of reading, it was natural for him to want to read about his business or his job. As industries took definite shape, certain industrialists wanted to write, not about a particular company, but about an industry as a whole—its philosophy, economics and techniques. Both these impulses grew with the enlargement of the national industrial complex. About the middle of the nineteenth century we see a sort of groping toward this kind of expression. Here and there appeared a periodical devoted to railroads, another to mining, one to shoemaking, several to banking and general commerce. In the decade of the fifties there were papers in the fields of photography, telegraphy, printing, iron, pharmacy, dentistry, carriage and harness manufacture, hardware, and illuminating gas.

As we look over copies of some of these first, uncertain steps toward what became the large, coordinated enterprise of industrial publishing, we can see that their evolution from that point would be an uphill fight. The editors of those early gazettes were obviously confused. Many of them seemed to feel that a magazine must have a literary flavor. They printed poetry, for instance, that had nothing to do with the subject. Editorials, written in a turgid style, dealt with broad generalities. There were personals and quips. It is hard to find anything resembling an editorial policy. It is evident that the editors were intimidated by old prejudices, by traditions of secrecy, jealousy, and the prevailing atmosphere of cutthroat competition.

Yet these struggling papers were building the framework that would answer the urgent later need for education in the form of cooperative knowledge, the exchange of information, and open discussion of common industrial and business problems. As we shall see, the structure grew more solid as industry defined itself and the "second industrial revolution" brought new order out of the old disarray.

Incidentally, even the rickety framework of early industrial publishing began to make the task of the industrial historian easier. Sometimes unreliable, usually inadequate, the little papers at least supplied useful pieces of source material.

Given the volume of print in our industrial press of today, the job of the future historian will be one of selection from what is truly an embarrassment of riches.

CHAPTER TWO

Ancestors of the Business Press

The search for the earliest ancestor of the business press takes us to Europe in the stormy days when the first Elizabeth sat on the English throne. It is surprising to those of us who think high-powered, far-reaching business is a modern phenomenon to know of the vast extent of certain commercial houses in the sixteenth century. The great German house of Fugger with headquarters at Augsburg had acquired by the middle 1500s interests ranging from China to Peru and, for a time, seemed to hold the fate of the very monarchs of Europe in the hollow of its hand.

To the modern eye [writes a historian of the enterprise] the Fugger business can only be compared to a vast financial concern. It works mines in the Tyrol, Carinthia, Hungary and Spain; in its hand is an immense spice trade; cloth weaving is carried on at high pressure, and financial transactions of great scope strain the resources of the firm to the utmost. [1]

Loans fom the Golden Counting-House, as the Augsburg offices were called, kept governments from bankruptcy. Fugger money brought about the election of Charles V as Holy Roman Emperor. The variety and extent of this business would seem to require every medium of modern communication. Yet none of these media was present.

In a world without telegraph or newspapers, it was imperative for the House of Fugger to be kept informed of the trend of events, because, whether of a political, financial, or even of a local nature, these might seriously affect that business. They therefore appear to have established a kind of news-reporting agency in all the chief cities, such as London, Paris, Antwerp, and Venice, and by the series of regularly written letters from each important agent or foreign partner, their famous Golden Counting-House in Augsburg became cognizant of all the happenings of the known world. [2]

In some ways these laboriously handwritten letters seem the very opposite of today's business papers. Most of them were top secret and, had their contents become known to certain political potentates, they might have changed the course of history. Had the letters been read by rivals of the Fugger dynasty, they would certainly have changed the face of the mercantile world. They were instruments of business in a world torn by war, honeycombed with international intrigue, racked by religious controversy with its accompaniment of bloody persecution—a world in which business had to contend not only with normal intricacies of law and politics but with piracy and privateering as well. And being confined to the operations of a single firm they seem more like the forebears of the house organ than of the independent business paper.

[1] Victor von Klarwill (ed.), *The Fugger News-letters,* ser. 2, John Lane, London, 1926, pp. xvi–xvii.

[2] *Ibid.,* ser. 1, 1924, p. iii.

Ancestors of the Business Press

Yet the techniques of receiving, interpreting, and analyzing the news that are common in the business press today are basically similar to those of the Fugger system. Letters would come from Italy, Spain, South America, or India. These would be read and compared at Augsburg. From there other letters would go out to the far-flung agents containing conclusions reached about coming events or some devious intrigue; thence they would be sent out again in the language of the country.

A letter from Seville in the winter of 1569 read:

> I have heard exactly what the English have been doing in Spain. A Fleming who has been acting as interpreter to them there writes that they have sailed into all the harbors in the mainland, have sold all their wares, in part amicably, in part by force . . . . They are said to have carried off property to the value of 600,000 ducats. [3]

To the Golden Counting-House such a letter would suggest that there would soon be good customers in England and the English agents were notified accordingly. While predatory operations no longer belong to business news, information is acquired and analyzed in much the same way today. A glance at such a business letter as is issued daily by Platt's Oilgram Service shows that correspondents are watching straws in the wind in Lebanon, Syria, and Saudi Arabia.

A Fugger newsletter from Lisbon in 1585 gives a complete inventory of ships from India with the value of each item. A 1956 Oilgram gives a summary of petroleum imports into Argentina from various specified ports of the world from Curaçao to Odessa. One report came to Augsburg headquarters by longhand letter through weeks of travel; the other came instantaneously by teletype to McGraw-Hill in New York. Both fitted into the world tempo of their time and both were essential to large-scale business.

The difference shows the progress of business through the centuries. Telegraphy, newspapers, news services, radio, and fast presses have broken down the secrecy. Competitive enterprise has

[3] *Ibid.*, ser.2, p. 2.

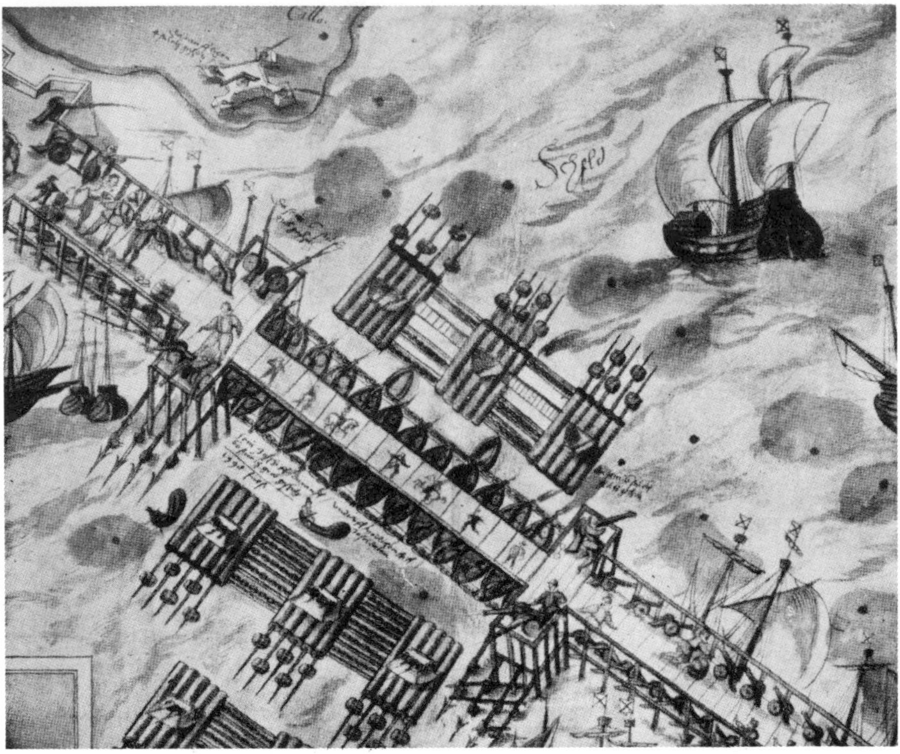

A water color showing a Palisade at Antwerp, from the following Fugger Newsletter, dated August 21, 1585, which describes the taking of Antwerp:
"On the 17th day of this month the treaty of the handing over of this city was concluded and on the 20th day of this month it was read in public. No particular joy nor jubilation on account thereof was manifested by the populace; only the Italians and some Catholics burnt bonfires. The Town Council made but little ado about the reading. Everything is quiet here. The troops display inexpressible home-sickness; the reformed preachers will these days travel by ship to Holland and Zeeland. Nothing has as yet been seen of the waggons with provisions, wine, and beer, which, according to rumour, are said to be in the camp. In the Parma's camp wine costs half a thaler the pint. According to information given out here, the Prince of Parma is not to enter until the 1st day of September, which is his birthday. It is said that he has kept for this occasion a special favour not included in the treaty, which he will bestow upon the town. It will then be seen with what affection he regards it."

Platt's OILGRAM News Service - New York Edition - February 7, 1956

ARGENTINE IMPORTS UP

Buenos Aires 2/6—Argentina imported 20.9% more crude and products in December than in November, but total, 667,050 tons, was far short of all-time record of 845,327 tons set last October.

Item	December 1955	November 1955	December 1954
Crude	380,817	307,043	355,285
Residual	268,765	289,159	170,810
Aviation gasoline	---	8,157	7,500
Diesel	5,065	13,609	10,949
Gas oil	8,588	33,912	38,447
Motor gasoline	2,139	---	---
Kerosine	1,676	---	19,520
Total	667,050	551,880	602,511

Crude was lifted at Mina al Ahmadi, 146,400 tons; Puerto La Cruz, 141,200; Punta Cardon, 30,000; Las Piedras, 16,800; La Libertad, 16,150; Curacao, 11,320; Los Organos, 10,830; Lobitos, 5,500 (amounts are approximations).

Fuel oil came chiefly from Curacao, Odessa and Caripito, with lesser shipments originating at Aruba and Las Piedras. Gas oil, kerosine and gasoline came from Punta Cardon, the diesel from Curacao.

'SIGNIFICANT' ALTA. FIND TOLD BY UNION

significant" discovery of c
River, Alta., where its sh
12-17 flowed oil on three
30 bbl. an hour of 38 grav
Union has a 100% inter
rounding the discovery, ne
erected to permit a full ga
Well hit top of granite
between 4,740 and 4,745 ft
Three drill-stem tests
made of the interval 4,740
was from 4,762-4,771 ft. f
4,797 ft. for 40 min.

TAPLINE SEEN AMENAB

Line Co. informed Syria to
of increase in transit payn
Minister. Official added th
eight weeks time before sta

"Platt's Oilgram News Service," February 7, 1956.

broken monopoly. Business news is out in the open, available to everyone. Even in the areas of production of such critical materials as petroleum and uranium, the truth is extremely difficult to conceal.

2 The printing press brought books before periodicals. Long before the industrial revolution there were some fine books on the industrial arts, many of them adorned with lucid and beautiful engravings of elaborate mechanical devices. While to a modern reader these machines may suggest the inventions of a Rube Goldberg, they represent signal achievements in an age with no prime movers except windmills, water wheels, and beasts of

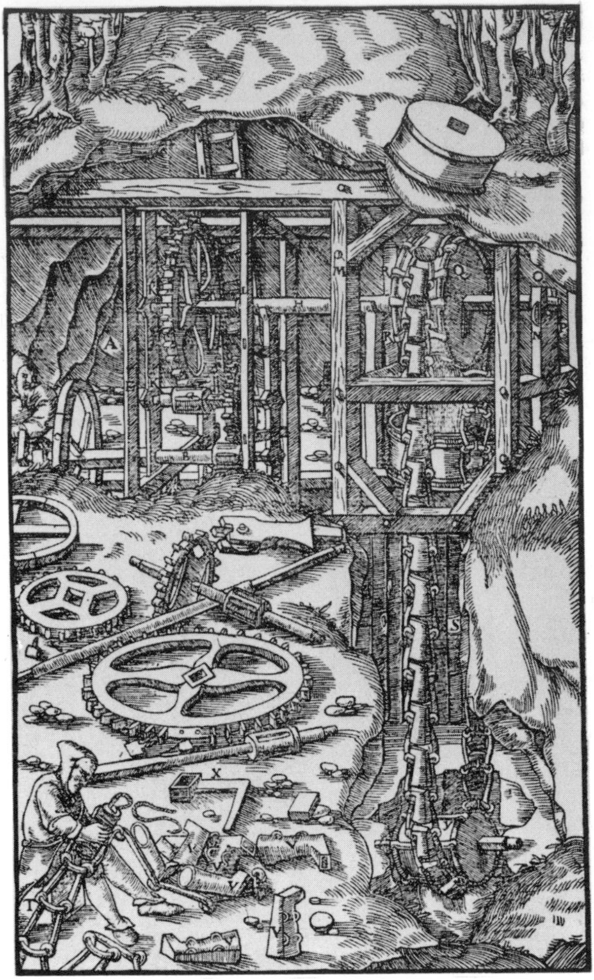

A miner fitting together a chain pump. (Woodcut from Agricola's "De Re Metallica.")

burden and when human labor was expendable. Books of this sort have been dug up by a new school of historians, writers deeply interested in the materials of our modern industrial world. And they are well worth looking at by any explorer of the history of technical literature.

As early as 1530, all that was known of mining and metallurgy was contained in a book by the German, Georgius Agricola. The title was *De Re Metallica* and the text was in Latin. It was translated in 1912 by no less an authority than Herbert Hoover, assisted by his wife. The book thus comes twice into the history

The art of pump-making. (Woodcut from Agricola's "De Re Metallica.")

of the printed word applied to technics: first as one of the earliest engineering works; second because its translation appeared in a technical paper, England's *Mining Magazine.* The original was abundantly and superbly illustrated, "lest," the author explains, "descriptions which are conveyed by words . . . not be understood by men of our own times." [4] In the text and woodcuts we find boring devices and pumps. One illustration shows a miner putting together a pump mechanism in which a chain of buckets

[4] Quoted by Greville Bathe, *An Engineer's Miscellany,* published by the author, Philadelphia, 1938, p. 3.

and a sequence of large cogwheels are used. On the ground about him lie all his tools so that we may learn precisely how the work was done.

Mr. Bathe tells us about the copperplate engravings in the books of another German, Jacob de Strada, published in 1629, showing a water-powered tilt hammer in operation and other devices "some of which are so fanciful that they could have had no bearing in fact."[5] Perhaps, like many designs in the notebooks of the great engineer Leonardo da Vinci, they were ideas for which the time was not yet ripe. There may, for example, be more fancy than truth in the extraordinary preview of automation in a little book by Thomas Powell in mid-seventeenth century:

> In *Dantzick* in *Poland* there was set up a rare invention for weaving of four or five webs at a time without any humane help; it was an Automaton or Engine that moved of itself and would work night and day . . . .[6]

No one could check on this author for he adds that "the invention was suppressed because it would prejudice the poor people of the town," but at least the book reveals that such ideas were in existence at least two centuries before automatic machine sequences came ino use.

3 Our story has more concern with the printing press than with any other invention. As we shall see, the whole industrial and commercial world we know today is dependent on it. Remove it and the entire slowly, painfully built civilization we enjoy would collapse. It makes no difference how many other communication media you retain; without printing society must fall apart. The picture in art or on film can never take its place. The reason is that although a picture conveys an immediate emotional and intellectual message, it never imposes that message upon the memory as the printed word must do. Between the written or printed word and the mind occurs a separate mental process—the process of

[5] *Ibid.*, p. 4.

[6] *Humane Industry of Most Manual Arts*, London, 1661, p. 85.

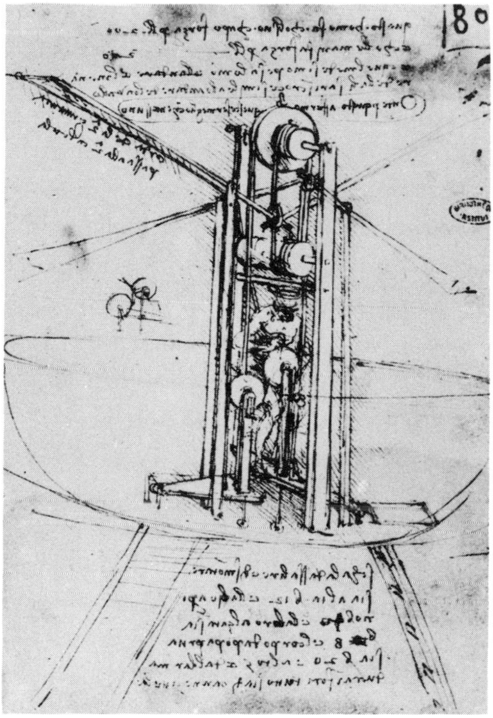

This machine should be tried over a lake, and you should carry a long wineskin as a girdle so that in case you fall you will not be drowned.

It is also necessary that the action of lowering the wings should be done by the force of the two feet at the same time, so that you can regulate the movement and preserve your equilibrium by lowering one wing more rapidly than the other according to need, as you may see done by the kite and other birds. Also the downward movement of both the feet produces twice as much power as that of one: it is true that the movement is proportionately slower.

The raising is by the force of a spring or if you wish by the hand, or by drawing the feet towards you, and this is best for then you will have the hands more free.

("Mechanism of the Flying Machine" from "The Notebooks of Leonardo Da Vinci," with an explanation by the artist.)

translating the little black marks into ideas; and this process engraves the meaning on the memory. Reading is work; looking at pictures is not. It is the work of the reader that makes the print indelible on his brain.

The spoken word, recorded on tape, film, or wax, remains ephemeral. The printed record traps it for keeps. The new historical method of oral reminiscence is of the greatest value to this and many other histories, but until the oral record is transcribed, its value is not complete. You may run back your tape a hundred or a thousand times; you may attach it to an amplifier, so that a hundred or a thousand people may hear it, but until it gets into the inked word on paper it has no finality. The unreported voice is the instrument of demagogues and dictators and all who appeal to mob psychology. The voice can do what the lettered word cannot; but the spoken thought cannot be analyzed for truth until it is caught on paper. There is great emotional power in the spoken word and great aesthetic value: it has a hundred subtle shadings of meaning. What would we not give for a record of the Gettysburg Address made while Lincoln spoke! Yet the total power of that speech comes only as we read and reread it in quiet, weighing each meaningful syllable.

It is true that the printing press furnishes the basis of our modern civilization, but it also is the instrument that built that civilization. It began by dissolving superstition. No doubt superstition survived the printing of the Bible, but the interesting fact is that those who read the Book for themselves were less subject to fears of dark magic and supernatural menaces than those who had it read aloud to them. For that reason the churches whose power depended upon those fears tried to keep the printed Bible out of the hands of their congregations. Even in early American Protestant churches ministers encouraged their flocks to have the Bible read to them in church and interpreted to them there. The thought that someone might shut himself up in a room alone with the Bible frightened them. Who knew what heresy one might evolve if he were allowed to juggle the printed words at will and at length?

But for our story perhaps the most important effect of printing came in enlarging the reader's world. As Lewis Mumford says:

> More than any other device, the printed book released people from the domination of the immediate and the local. [7]

The whole trend of business and industry was away from the local. To bring about the world spread of today, transportation and electrical communication were necessary; but the press began it, and it was largely the needs of the press that brought the other developments. The other developments in turn made the press more than ever necessary. The business papers, for example, were scarcely necessary in an era of local self-sufficiency. As Charles T.

[7] *Technics and Civilization,* New York, Harcourt, Brace and Company, Inc., 1934, p. 136.

Root, in one of his lectures on the history of industrial journalism, summed up the whole evolution:

Ancestors of the Business Press

> The business paper, that is, broadly speaking, the periodical devoted to the production or distribution, or both, of some class or related classes of merchandise, is the product of a highly evolved commercial system. When transportation and communication were slow and difficult and each community supplied its own wants and formed its own market, there was no need for this adjunct of modern trade. The seed of the business journal, indeed, existed in commerce, but in order that this seed might sprout the ground had first to be plowed by the locomotive and fertilized by the electric telegraph.[8]

We have come full circle, then, from the printing press to the printing press. Between Gutenberg in 1450 and the immense production of the printed word five centuries later, lies the whole expansion and centralization of commerce and industry in our Western society.

The focus of our story is the power of print. We shall refer back to that focus at every point. Newspapers and magazines demonstrate it not only in their text but in their advertising. The power of sound, the power in the spoken word is tangential. The graphic arts are aids but they are incomplete in themselves.

The substance of our story must be the integration of print and industry. The two have not always kept together. Print may have led us into that larger world in which industrial development was possible. But in a large part of our history, between print and industry, there was what engineers call a *hysteresis.* Print lagged behind. In our glance at the industrial revolutions, we shall see why.

[8] "The History and Development of Industrial Journalism," in *Lectures in the Forum in Industrial Journalism at New York University,* 1915, under the Auspices of the New York Trade Press Association, *Advertising and Selling* Magazine, Inc., New York, 1915, p. 10. Other lecturers in the series were James H. McGraw and E. A. Simmons.

CHAPTER THREE

Industrial Revolution

Science and business met in England near the close of the eighteenth century. Of the meeting was born the industrial revolution. Till then science had been locked in an ivory tower. It was too pure to be understood by vulgar people interested in making money. Scientists were horrified at the idea of its becoming sullied by the smoke and grime of the factory.

The battering ram that cracked the ivory tower of science wide open was the steam engine designed by James Watt. It was over this engine that science and business met. Early in the century another engine had been invented by Thomas Newcomen which pumped water out of coal mines by atmospheric pressure working against a vacuum created by condensing steam. With its aid miners could go deeper into the earth in search of their coal. The trouble with Newcomen's engine was that it used nearly as much coal as it helped to mine. The wastage of fuel was said to be over 99 per cent. Here, then, science scarcely helped business. It did prove, however, that man could be assisted in his work by a force other than wind, water, or animal power—the only agents of prime movers known before. To our story Newcomen's main contribution was that he inspired the establishment of the English Newcomen Society whose publications added the power of print to the power of steam and mechanics.

But by Watt's time big business had grown, in England, to enormous proportions. The great textile mills had been equipped with the productive machinery of Hargreaves, Kay, Crompton, and Arkwright. There was not enough water power in England to take care of the industrial expansion. There was a crying need for improved transportation. And there was a fast-growing, wealthy, and powerful middle class behind the factories that would soon hold Parliament in the hollow of its hand.

The noise of all this reached the ears of a pure scientist who sat in the ivory tower of Glasgow University. Joseph Black had assisted Watt with his engine that used the expansive power of steam. Whether or not Black had heard the dictum of the practical American, Benjamin Franklin, that "a discovery which can be applied to no use, or is not good for something is good for nothing," he had come to believe its truth. And with the vista of steam power with all its benefit to society stretching before his imagination, he came to have contempt for scientific snobbery.

Watt and his business partner Matthew Boulton wanted to sell Watt's engine. But the industrialists, knowing only of the wastefulness of the Newcomen pump, thought that a steam prime mover must be inefficient.

"If you can guarantee," they said, in effect, to Watt and Boulton, "the economical operation of your machine and tell us in advance precisely what its maximum coal consumption will be, we will buy it."

Romanticized drawing of the propeller steamboat invented by John Fitch.

Oliver Evans's "Orukter Amphibolos," about 1804.

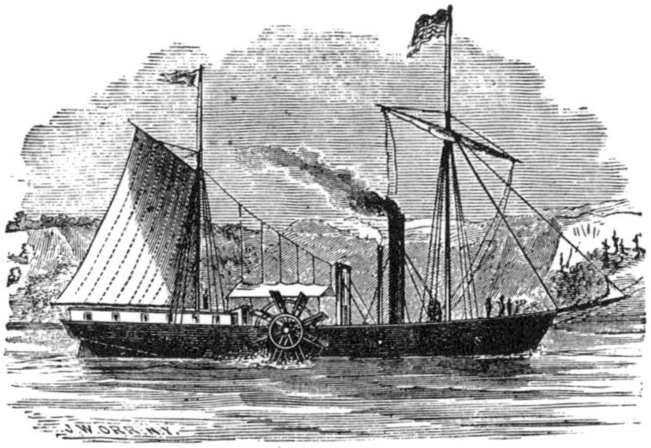

Romanticized drawing of Fulton's "Clermont."

When Black heard this, the question and the promise clicked in his mind with a set of theories he had been working on. His subject, as a professor, was heat. He had evolved new theories about heat—theories which later constituted the basis of thermodynamics. He now saw the chance to prove his theories by Watt's engines and at the same time, if the theories were correct, to put Watt in business. Thus, as Lancelot Hogben has written:

> Watt's engines were at once the offspring and the parent of scientific knowledge which Newton and his contemporaries did not share.[1]

Black's researches established the principle of thermal equilibrium and there evolved "a balance-sheet between the source of heat and the use of heat."[2] Watt was then able to answer the mill-owners' questions and by 1800 there were 500 Boulton and Watt engines in service, 62 per cent of which supplied power for mills and furnaces.[3] Less than a decade later one was installed in Robert Fulton's *Clermont*, the vessel that started the steamboat era in America.

From the time of Watt and Black the partnership between science and business became closer with every passing decade and, as the union came to be recognized, the power of print welded it into an inseparable connection.

2 In the year that the British colonies of North America declared their independence of Britain, a great book appeared on a new subject. Business had been regarded as beneath the dignity of literature. Although a few essays had been written on what was coming to be called "political economy," any extensive work which should deal with money, markets, exchange, demand, and supply lacked appeal to a publisher. It was a brave one, therefore, that brought out, in 1776, *An Inquiry into the Nature and*

[1] Lancelot Hogben, *Science for the Citizen*, W. W. Norton & Company, Inc., New York, 1951 (revised), p. 594.

[2] *Ibid.*, p. 594.

[3] Richard S. Kirby, Sidney Withington, Arthur Burr Darling, and Frederick G. Kilgour, *Engineering in History*, McGraw-Hill Book Company, Inc., New York, 1956, p. 172.

Causes of the Wealth of Nations by a Scot named Adam Smith. Perhaps even the strong endorsement of the book by the celebrated philosopher David Hume did not convince Smith's publisher that here was the curtain raiser of the capitalistic age. Certainly he could not foresee that it would become the Bible of the champions of free private enterprise throughout the world.

The book plotted the direction industry would take with the division of labor, the departmentalizing of operations, and the increasing productivity per worker. The book also dealt with the origin and use of money, the prices of commodities, the wages of labor, and the profits of stock and of rent. After its publication businessmen could discuss openly in polite society the subjects they had talked of only in the shelter of their offices. No longer need they feel the stigma of being "in trade"—the phrase used by the English aristocracy to show their scorn of commerce.

But as usual the printed page was a mirror of the times. The change in England from an agricultural to an industrial economy was nearly complete. So was the change from mercantilism to

The "De Witt Clinton," first locomotive

capitalism. The transition was accompanied by abuses. The "dark satanic mills" of the English Midlands became notorious in the Western world and the reports of them that drifted overseas, and shocked Americans in the new Republic may have delayed the industrial revolution in America. At the same time the philosophy of Adam Smith sent down deep roots into the American soil, and when large industrial and business activity did start here, Americans became more completely dedicated to Smith's doctrine of *laissez faire* than any other people in the world.

Industrial Revolution

It has been said that there is a symbolic meaning in the coincidence of Smith's *Wealth of Nations* with the Declaration of Independence. Surely the Smith economics made as clean a break with the past as did Jefferson's document. Also the political philosophy in the *Wealth of Nations* assumed the sort of government Americans wanted most—the government that should govern least. This was heralded by one of the greatest of American philosophers before Smith's book appeared. In 1764 Benjamin Franklin wrote:

run on the Mohawk Valley Railroad.

In time perhaps Mankind may be wise enough to let Trade take its own Course, find its own channels and regulate its own Proportions. . . .[4]

Two years later he stated:

It seems contrary to the Nature of Commerce, for Government to interfere in the Prices of Commodities. Trade is a voluntary Thing between Buyer and Seller, in every Article of which each exercises his own Judgment. . . .[5]

Franklin was the first American prophet of free private enterprise—free, that is, from government interference. He was also the first American to write extensively about business. But also, in Franklin, business, science, and journalism first met in America. He saw his scientific discoveries in the light of their practical everyday values.

No history of publishing can ignore Franklin. He started a chain of newspapers. He was, in addition to his other vocations, a publisher par excellence. He was the first American to understand that a periodical could be supported by its advertising. None was, in his day, because advertising was so little developed. But Franklin understood the value of advertising and for his time he was an expert in promotion.

Looking back, it seems as if Joseph Black, James Watt, Adam Smith, and Benjamin Franklin had opened the doors on a new age. In it the discipline of engineering would be born. In it theory and practice, science and industry would come together and the result would change the face of the world. And the catalyst of the change would be the printed word: first in the static book; then, as tempo quickened, in the more fluid journalistic exchange.

3 In America with its vast agricultural potential, the industrial revolution came slowly. The Napoleonic Wars which closed the gates to imports from Europe gave the first boost to manufac-

[4] *The Writings of Benjamin Franklin,* Albert H. Smyth (ed.), The Macmillan Company, New York, 1907, vol. 4, 243–244.

[5] *Ibid.,* p. 469.

turing industry in the United States. With the westward migration when the pioneering Americans cleared the wilderness and established the surplus farms, there came a demand for manufactured goods that the new Eastern industrial centers could not meet with the scanty man power at their disposal. Salvation came through the invention of labor-saving machinery.

The invention was done quietly and under severe handicap. The men who did it—mainly in such New England towns as Windsor, Vermont; Springfield, Worcester, and Chicopee Falls, Massachusetts; Hartford, Collinsville, Plymouth, and New Haven, Connecticut; and Providence, Rhode Island—had little science. In the early years of the nineteenth century British law forbade the exportation of machinery and all information about machines as well as the emigration of skilled workers. Materials available to American artisans were scarce and of poor quality. In communities whose main preoccupation was farming there was no traditional apprentice system for mechanics and the geniuses who designed productive machines were mainly self-taught. Yet in the first half of the century nearly all the foundations were laid for America's eventual industrial triumph.

Ever more insistent were the cries of "more" and "faster" from the quick-growing, home-settling, and migratory population. Under the pressure, such commodities as firearms and clocks were no longer "built" or "fabricated"; they were "produced." Eli Whitney established a factory tooled for the departmentalized manufacture of muskets by the thousand. Terry and Jerome took contracts for the turnout not of dozens, or even hundreds, but thousands of clocks whose gears were cut by powered machines. Oliver Evans designed the forerunner of automation in the form of mills that ground meal into superfine flour without the intervention at any point of a human hand. And all this was done so quietly, with so little fanfare, and especially with so little printed publicity, that when in 1851 a reaper and firearms with interchangeable parts were exhibited at the Crystal Palace Exhibition in London, Britons whose science, skill, and workmanship were,

Eli Whitney from a painting by Samuel F. B. Morse. (Yale University Art Gallery.)

in general, far ahead of ours were suddenly amazed at a Yankee ingenuity they had not suspected. And some two years later when England was on the verge of war, the British ordnance department sent a commission to America to buy 157 machine tools and with them set up a new plant for the quantity production of Enfield rifles.

Occasionally there would be a newspaper story about some of these steps toward the mass production that would be the top achievement of American democracy in the material sphere. The *Chicago Daily Journal* of March 31, 1851, ran a vivid description of the production line at the McCormick reaper factory in Chicago. An article in the English magazine, *Household Words,* by Charles Dickens told of Colt's London revolver factory where

The Colt Armory at Hartford.

machine sequences produced parts in series and there was random assembly. In 1851 the *Journal of the Royal Society* contained an eyewitness account of the English field trial of Cyrus McCormick's machine. Oliver Evans gave a full account of his "automation" in his *The Young Mill-Wright and Miller's Guide,* one of the first American books to be illustrated with well-executed mechanical drawings, and of his important work with steam engines in *The Young Steam Engineer's Guide.* But we had to wait until the twentieth century for the full story of this continuous American progress in quantity production that answered the demand for "more, faster, cheaper" and brought the United States into leadership of the industrial world. It came, then, in the technical press.

Certain industrial periodicals have led the way in recounting industrial history. In this they have done a signal service to education. At a time when the only American history Americans knew was almost wholly concerned with war, politics, and diplomacy, these papers discovered what, from a physical, material point of view had made the nation tick and wrote about it.

As we have seen, the shadow of the cotton gin obscured Eli Whitney's greater achievement until Prof. Joseph Wickham Roe wrote of his interchangeable-parts system in the *American Machinist* in 1914. In addition to this, Roe wrote a series of *Ma-*

Oliver Evans

chinist articles reviewing the evolution of machine tools not only in America but in England. He wrote, for example, a full description of the brilliant galaxy of London tool builders in the early 1800s—of Henry Maudslay, John Wilkinson, Joseph Bramah, Joseph Clement, Richard Roberts, James Nasmyth, and Sir Joseph Whitworth—and of the machine sequence that produced the ship's blocks for the British Navy at the time of the Napoleonic Wars. He told, too, of the mechanical inventions of such Americans as Oliver Evans, Elisha Root, Thomas Blanchard, Stephen Fitch, and Frederick Howe, and accompanied his articles with

Industrial Revolution

Oliver Evans's flour mill. Grain was emptied from a wagon at one end and flour in barrels came out at the other. There was no human intervention at any point.

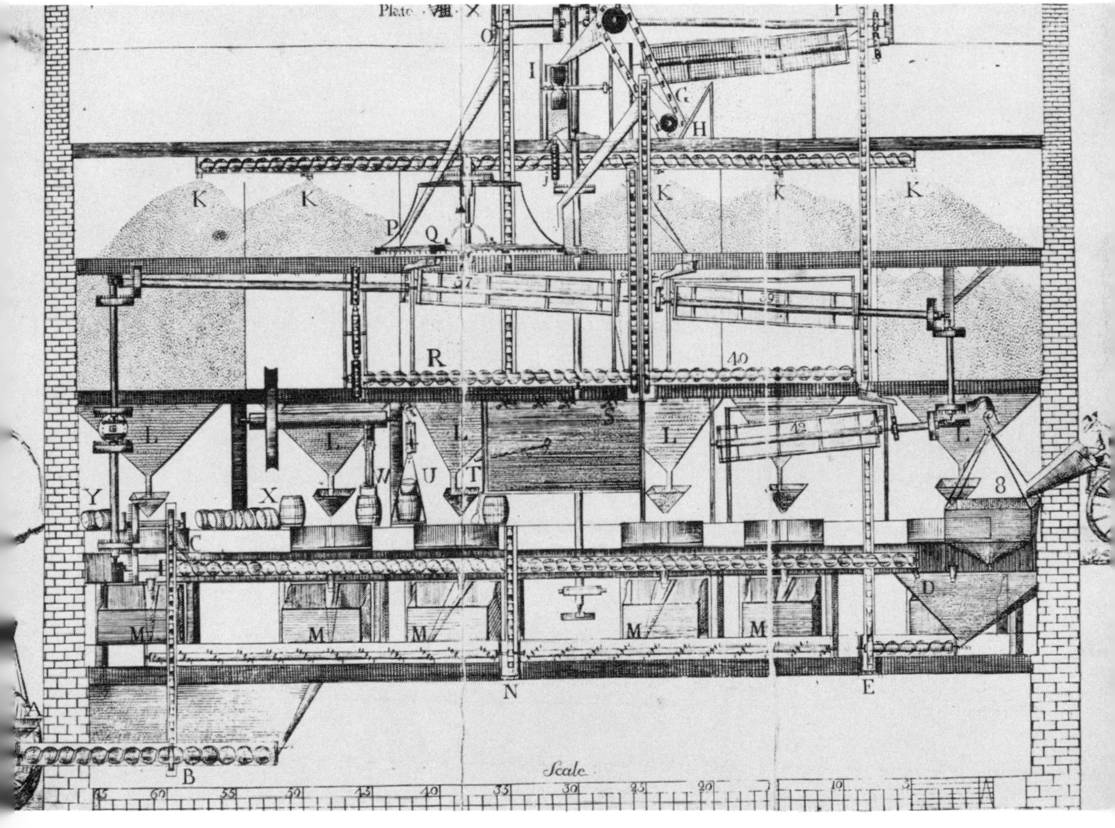

ORIGINS

illustrations. The articles were not written in language that would be comprehensible only to the engineer or technician; they were done in simple English for the layman's understanding. Later they were assembled into a book [6] that has become a classic of industrial history.

In 1923 another series appeared in the same magazine on the "Development of Machine Tools in New England" by Guy Hubbard, himself the descendant of a Yankee toolmaker. The twenty-three pieces in this series went into the most remote places of origin of those tools, jigs, and fixtures that became the very foundations of American manufacture. One tells the fascinating story of the boy genius, Richard Lawrence, who made the rifles for the London exposition, of Christian Sharps, designer of the famous breech-loading rifle, of the visit of the British small-arms committee to the Yankee shops, of the founding of the Weed Sewing

[6] *English and American Tool Builders,* Yale University Press, New Haven, 1916; republished, McGraw-Hill Book Company, Inc., New York, 1926.

Genealogy of the Interchangeable System. ("American Machinist," June, 1914.)

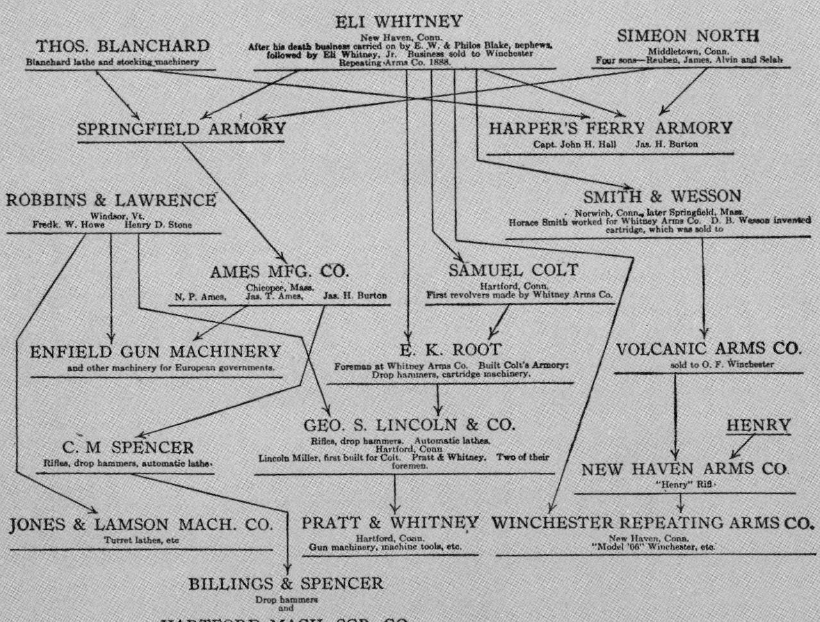

Machine Company, the Hartford Machine Screw Company, the Pope Manufacturing Company, Brown and Sharpe, and Pratt and Whitney.

Later this magazine carried detailed illustrated articles on machine-tool history from the 1870s to the 1950s.[7] Another comprehensive historical article was "The Story of Power" in the 50th Anniversary issue of *Power* which gave the sequence from antiquity through animal, wind, water, steam, gas, and electric prime movers. As the earlier phases of this story could not be illustrated by photographs, artists recreated the techniques in a series of paintings and drawings based on many months of research.

Other publications of the industrial press soon followed the McGraw-Hill lead. *Iron Age* published a history of a hundred years of machine tools in 1955.[8] In *Abrasive Industry* in 1929 an

[7] Vol. 66, no. 20, pp. 826–878, May 19, 1927; 75th Anniversary Issue, vol. 96, no. 24, November, 1952, *passim.*

[8] Vol. 175, no. 27, pp. E2–E7, June, 1955.

Robbins and Lawrence miller built in 1853. ("American Machinist," October, 1914.)

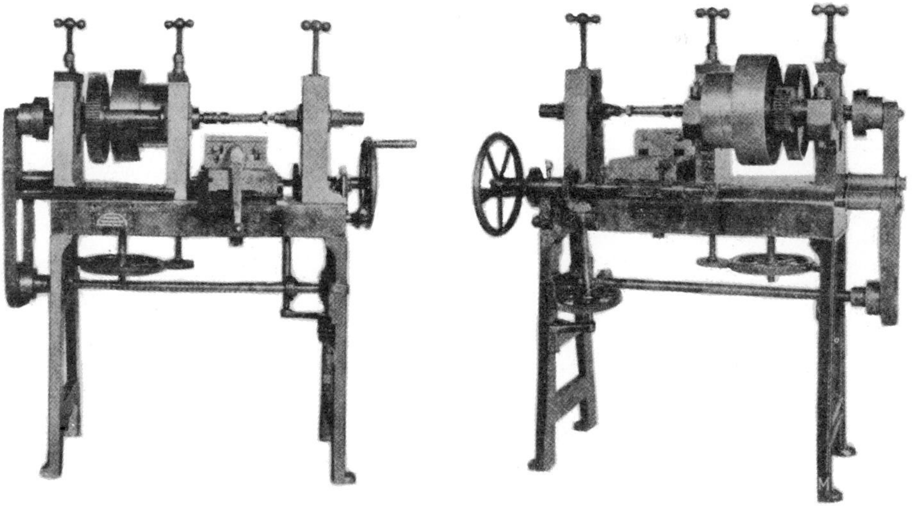

article whose roots were deep in the story of American continental conquest was entitled "100 Years of Ax Making" by Herbert R. Simonds.[9]

Thus through industrial journalism the lost pieces of the picture puzzle of the American industrial revolution were found and put together. It was an evidence that modern industrialists are interested in the background of their industry. The accusation has often been made that the people of late generations are inclined to take for granted the miracles of applied science, assuming that they came upon us full-blown without the centuries of preparation, without the long, slow, patient, often heartbreaking work of countless minds. Thus the Spanish philosopher José Ortega y Gasset writes of the "mass man" living only in today, ignorant of the history of technics and therefore unfit to use its products.

Against this kind of ignorance the industrial press has taken the lead in America and has provided the historian with an abundance of material.

[9] Vol. 10, no. 2, p. 74, February, 1929.

CHAPTER FOUR

American Pioneers

There was a railroad magazine in America before there was a railroad. Vehicles had run on rails, to be sure, wooden rails, but they had moved by gravity or been hauled by horses. One steam locomotive had been imported from England but it had proved too heavy for its track; engines had been put on wheels and these strange contraptions had actually hauled cars with brave passengers in them, but boiler explosions, derailments, fires, and other accidents interrupted the attempts to establish schedules. Nevertheless, in January, 1832, there appeared the *American Rail-Road Journal and Advocate of Internal Improvements* published in Wall Street, New York, by D. Kimball Minor who presented himself as editor as well as publisher.

RAIL-ROAD JOURNAL

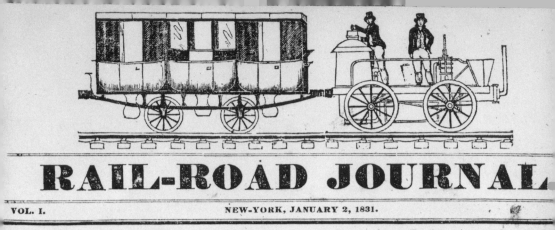

VOL. I. NEW-YORK, JANUARY 2, 1831.

AMERICAN RAIL-ROAD JOURNAL.

The subscriber proposes to publish a weekly Journal, commencing about the first of January, ensuing, to be called the **AMERICAN RAILROAD JOURNAL.** A principal object in offering the proposed work to the Public, is to diffuse a more general knowledge of this important mode of internal communication, which, at this time, appears to engage the attention of almost every section of our country.

THE AMERICAN RAILROAD JOURNAL will be printed on a sheet of the largest size, (mammoth) and put up in a convenient form for binding, each number to contain sixteen large octavo pages of *three* columns each. The selections, upon the subject of railroads and other works of internal improvement, will be from the best authors, both of Europe and America, and will be occasionally illustrated by engravings. A part of this Journal will be devoted to the subject of internal improvement—giving a history of the first introduction of railroads into England and their improvements to the present day. It will also notice the meetings, in different sections of the country, upon the subject of railroads. The remaining part of the paper will contain the LITERARY, MISCELLANEOUS AND NEWS matter of the **NEW-YORK AMERICAN**, *as prepared for that paper*, omitting *all political* subjects, except such as are of general interest.

The terms of the American Railroad Journal are THREE dollars per annum, *payable in advance;* and will not be sent without. Any person who will obtain eight subscribers and remit the amount, shall have a copy gratis: and to companies of ten subscribers, who associate and remit twenty-five dollars, it will be sent for $2,50 each per annum. The Journal will be sent for *any* length of time desired, if paid in advance. It will be published on *Saturdays*.

Letters upon the subject of the AMERICAN RAILROAD JOURNAL may be addressed, free of postage, to the publisher and part proprietor,

D. K. MINOR,
No. 35 Wall-Street, New-York.

TO THE PUBLIC.

In offering the AMERICAN RAIL ROAD JOURNAL to the public at this time, when so much and such general interest is felt on the subject of Rail-roads in different sections of the United States, no apology is deemed necessary. The importance of some other mode of internal communication in this country, where the canals and rivers are for about one third of the year closed by frost, renders it highly desirable that a fair experiment should be made of the utility of Rail roads. Such experiments are now in progress in several States; and all information, therefore, upon the comparative value of Rail-roads and Canals, which may be generally diffused amongst the people, must be valuable, as it may prevent a premature and useless expenditure of capital upon works concerning which sufficient data for a correct judgment are not possessed. Further investigation may lead to the construction of new Canals, of the value of which, for a part of the year, we are fully aware; or it may confirm the opinion, fast gaining ground in this country, that Rail-roads will, in a great measure, supersede Canals, and therefore hasten the construction of a few important lines, through those parts of the country where the amount of business will warrant the undertaking. It is the object of this Journal to disseminate as extensively as possible, accurate statements, drawn from European publications, little known, and less read in this country; to record the observations and suggestions of gentlemen of experience in the construction and use of rail-roads here; and to afford the whole at so cheap a rate, as to be within the reach of every person taking an interest in the subject.

It is intended to give a concise history of the introduction of Rail-roads into England, (which appears to have been as early as between the years 1602 and 1649, in the vicinity of Newcastle-upon-Tyne,) with the various improvements, down to the present time; and to trace their introduction into, and peculiar adaptation to the business and climate of this country. It will also be the aim of the publisher to show, what *he* thinks may be shown conclusively, that for practical purposes, Rail-roads are far superior to any other mode of internal communication; and that they must, in a few years, entirely take the place of of Canals, where new works are to be constructed. "The great advantage of Rail-ways," says Tredgold, a writer upon the subject, "will consist in their affording the means of transporting *heavy* goods with speed and certainty; and, recollecting that Rail roads are in an imperfect state, while the united efforts of our civil engineers have been chiefly devoted to canals for about a century, we may confidently hope that there is scope for improvement; and we may fairly infer that for new works Rail roads will in nine cases out of ten, be better adapted for public benefit than canals." Entertaining these views, and aware of the general movements making in different sections of the country for the purpose of adopting measures for the construction of Rail-roads, he is induced to believe that a publication more acceptable, at this time, to a large portion of the intelligent community, could not be offered; and to that class of readers he looks with confidence for a liberal patronage, meaning, as he does, to merit it by untiring zeal to serve them.

Gentlemen engaged in constructing, or superintending Railroads; and others in possession of information upon the subject, which may serve to give a more correct and general knowledge of the *disadvantages* as well as benefits resulting from them, will serve the community by contributing to the columns of the *Rail-road Journal*; and they ... invited to do so.

A part, only, of the Journal will be devoted to the subject of internal communication and improvements. The larger part will be occupied with *literary* and *miscellaneous* selections from foreign Journals, with the review of new publications, as prepared for the *New-York American*, and the general news of the day,—excluding *all political* matter, excepting what may be deemed of *general* interest. It will, in fact, contain most of the interesting and important matter published in the New-York American.

With this expression of his views and intentions, the publisher submits the AMERICAN RAIL-ROAD JOURNAL to an intelligent community for its decision.

D. KIMBALL MINOR.
No. 35 Wall street, New-York.

The following extract from a treatis[e] ... roads, by NICHOLAS WOOD, ESQ., will g... of the first attempts, of which we hav... count, to introduce Rail-roads into Engla[nd]...

HISTORY AND PROGRESS OF RAIL-...

It is very difficult to trace the precise ... Rail-ways were first introduced into Gre[at Britain]... When the traffic consisted of various art[icles]... conveyed in numerous directions, the e... forming a road suitable for all parties, ... pense of branching it off to all the diff... where the goods were to be carried, wo... to prevent the introduction of Rail-road... cies of general communication.

The more probable supposition is, tha... tion of these artificial roads first took p... the goods were of a certain description, ... be conveyed to one place only; and whe... tity also was considerable. Continually pa... the same road, when perhaps the mater... holding it and keeping it in repair were... might induce them to seek out som... and, it is not unlikely, that the laying do... ber, in the worst parts of the road, migh[t]... introduction of wooden rails the who[le]... Such is the practise in Russia, and it app... been as ancient as civilization in that co[untry]...

At the coal-works in the neighborho[od of New]castle-upon-Tyne, the expense of con... coals from the pits to the places where ... be shipped by sea, would be very great ... the year 1600, the only mode appears to h... carts, on the ordinary roads; and in som... by "panniers" on horseback. A record i... of one of the free companies of Newc... 1602, states, "That from tyme out of m... been accustomed that all cole-waynes ... carry and bring eight baulls of coles to ... thes upon the ryver of Tyne, but of late ... brought only, or scarce, seven baulls." ... transporting such a heavy article as coal ... mon roads, which may be supposed wou... the best description, in carts containi[ng]... eight bolls, would operate very powerful[ly]... rating the introduction of some improve[d]... mode of conveyance, to lessen the expe[nse]...

In a work published at Newcastle, ... 1649, by a Mr. Gray, called "A Chor[ographia]... survey of Newcastle-upon-Tyne, the fo... count of the Coal Trade is given: "Ma[ny]... people are employed in this trade of co... live by conveying them in wagons an... the river Tyne," &c. And in p. 31 of th... he states, "Some south gentlemen hath ... losse of benefit, come into this countr... their monies in coale pits. Master Beau... tleman of great ingenuity and rare parts ... into our mines with his 30,000*l*., who b... him many rare engines not known th... parts, as the art to boore with iron rod... deepnesse and thicknesse of the Coale; ... to draw water out of the pits; waggo[ns]... horse to carry down coales from the pits ... thes to the river, &c.; within a few y... sumed all his money, and rode home up... horse."

Considering that the carts employed i... the coals were, in 1602, called "wayn... carriages introduced by Master Beau... gons;" and also, that ever since that pe... riages employed upon Rail-roads have ... nated by that name; we may infer, tha... gon" of Mr. Beaumont was applied upon

There was, in fact, an epidemic of railroad fever in 1832. Those in favor fought angrily with those opposed. Several roads existed on paper. They had been chartered and first spikes had been driven, accompanied by festivals with speeches, the firing of cannon, brass bands, and champagne. There was, therefore, a public for the journal. Its main function was propaganda. But the editor was hard put to it to find any substantial material for his paper and in his leading editorial was forced to announce:

> A part, only, of the Journal will be devoted to the subject of internal communication. . . . The larger part will be occupied with *literary* and *miscellaneous* selections from foreign Journals, with the review of new publications . . . and the general news of the day. . . .

He was able to dig up enough on his subject for three pages; the other thirteen contained poetry, dramatic criticism, the doings of the English Parliament and the American Congress, and prices on the New York Stock Exchange. The railroad matter included three columns of English railway history going back to the seventeenth century when rails were used in the coal mines. Yet the paper persisted for some eighty years under various editors, one of whom was the celebrated Henry Varnum Poor of *Poor's Manual* who held the *Journal's* chair from 1849 to 1863. Bought in 1911 by the Simmons-Boardman Publishing Corporation, it is still published today by them under the title, *Railway Locomotives and Cars.*

Other railroad papers had brief lives. For the most part they were organs of promotion in those feverish years when mad, haphazard, greed-inspired building was covering the East with a network of useless rails—tracks that ran from town to town as instruments of local politics. Most of the journals at mid-century were pressing for the transcontinental span. They were concerned with future enterprise rather than with the facts of the existing industry. Two survived: *Western Railroad Gazette* (later *Railroad Gazette*), born in 1856 and *Railway Age,* twenty years later. They married in 1908 and are now living happily as *Railway Age,* published today by the Simmons-Boardman Publishing Corporation.

First issue of the "Rail-Road Journal," January, 1832. (The date on the photographed page is a typographical error.)

It was through railroad papers that both the leading figures in our story came into publishing. The first of these magazines, *The American Journal of Railway Appliances,* appearing in the summer of 1883, announced a thoroughly down-to-earth purpose.

We aim [read the publishers' Salutatory] to give the practical railroader, be he manager or mechanic, a paper dealing with the actual workings of all branches of this vast and growing interest.

No literature here! No poetry, essays, or propaganda! No gazing into a crystal ball to divine futures! This paper would deal with actual workings, with car construction, passenger-car furnishing, running gear, machinery and shops, track, station, and office methods, and even the lowly horse-drawn streetcar. The paper was also a new departure in arrangement. It was divided into departments, each dealing with an aspect of railroad business or technique. In each department the advertisements applying to that phase were to be grouped with the text. When the *Journal* was two years old, James Herbert McGraw was on its staff. Three years later he owned it.

At about the same time, the contribution of the printing press to railroading was luring John Alexander Hill out of the cab of a locomotive on the Denver and Rio Grande. His series of practical letters and articles appearing in *American Machinist* brought him to the attention of the men who started a journal called *Locomotive Engineer.* We shall return in a later chapter to the details of these entrances upon our scene.

2 While the railroads were laying out the great skeleton of the nation, other businesses and industries were becoming self-conscious and bursting into print. Some of them were ancestors of McGraw-Hill papers. Some whose descendants found other homes were nonetheless important to the background of our story, for they played essential parts in the history of American business.

Perhaps the earliest of these others was the *American Journal of Pharmacy.* This grew out of a paper started in 1825 as the organ of the Philadelphia College of Pharmacy. The Introduction in the first issue suggests that the American apothecary had never attained the respectability of his European brother. He sold paint and varnish as well as medicines. If the editor who wrote this could look into the window of one of today's drugstores, he would find that it could be reasonably respectable even if it sold cameras and underwear in addition to drugs. The editorial further implied that a journal might help the trade's standing as it had done, for instance, in France, where the *Journal de Pharmacie* was some thirty years old.

There was no paid advertising in the *Journal of Pharmacy* until 1850 except of medical books. Then, when announcements of medical preparations finally appeared, they were of the most exemplary character, contrasting sharply with the fraudu-

First paid advertising in "American Journal of Pharmacy," May, 1850.

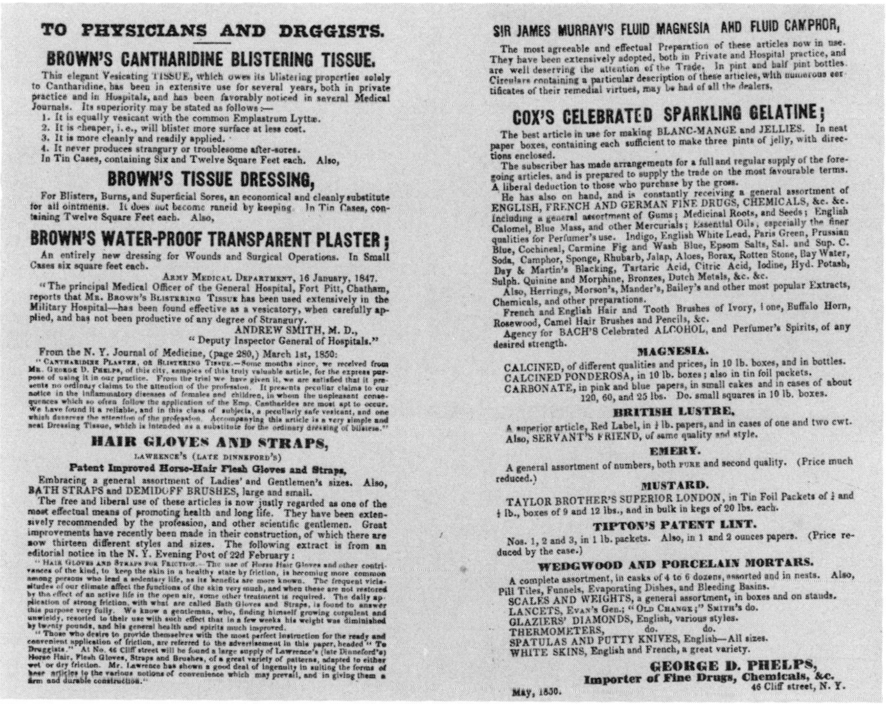

TO PHYSICIANS AND DRGGISTS.

BROWN'S CANTHARIDINE BLISTERING TISSUE.

This elegant Vesicating TISSUE, which owes its blistering properties solely to Cantharidine, has been in extensive use for several years, both in private practice and in Hospitals, and has been favorably noticed in several Medical Journals. Its superiority may be stated as follows:—

1. It is equally vesicant with the common Emplastrum Lyttæ.
2. It is cheaper, i.e., will blister more surface at less cost.
3. It is more cleanly and readily applied.
4. It never produces strangury or troublesome after-sores.

In Tin Cases, containing Six and Twelve Square Feet each. Also,

BROWN'S TISSUE DRESSING,

For Blisters, Burns, and Superficial Sores, an economical and cleanly substitute for all ointments. It does not become rancid by keeping. In Tin Cases, containing Twelve Square Feet each. Also,

BROWN'S WATER-PROOF TRANSPARENT PLASTER;

An entirely new dressing for Wounds and Surgical Operations. In Small Cases six square feet each.

ARMY MEDICAL DEPARTMENT, 16 January, 1847.

"The principal Medical Officer of the General Hospital, Fort Pitt, Chatham, reports that MR. BROWN'S BLISTERING TISSUE has been used extensively in the Military Hospital—has been found effective as a vesicatory, when carefully applied, and has not been productive of any degree of Strangury.

ANDREW SMITH, M. D.,
"Deputy Inspector General of Hospitals."

From the N. Y. Journal of Medicine, (page 280,) March 1st, 1850:

"CANTHARIDINE PLASTER, OR BLISTERING TISSUE.—Some months since, we received from MR. GEORGE D. PHELPS, of this city, samples of this truly valuable article, for the express purpose of using it in our practice. From the trial we have given it, we are satisfied that it presents no ordinary claims to the attention of the profession. It presents peculiar claims to our notice in the inflammatory diseases of females and children, in whom the unpleasant consequences which so often follow the application of the Emp. Cantharides are most apt to occur. We have found it a reliable, and in this class of subjects, a peculiarly safe vesicant, and one which deserves the attention of the profession. Accompanying this article is a very simple and neat Dressing Tissue, which is intended as a substitute for the ordinary dressing of blisters."

HAIR GLOVES AND STRAPS,

LAWRENCE'S (LATE DINNEFORD'S)

Patent Improved Horse-Hair Flesh Gloves and Straps,

Embracing a general assortment of Ladies' and Gentlemen's sizes. Also, BATH STRAPS and DEMIDOFF BRUSHES, large and small.

The free and liberal use of these articles is now justly regarded as one of the most effectual means of promoting health and long life. They have been extensively recommended by the profession, and other scientific gentlemen. Great improvements have recently been made in their construction, of which there are now thirteen different styles and sizes. The following extract is from an editorial notice in the N. Y. Evening Post of 22d February:

"HAIR GLOVES AND STRAPS FOR FRICTION.—The use of Horse Hair Gloves and other contrivances of the kind, to keep the skin in a healthy state by friction, is becoming more common among persons who lead a sedentary life, as its benefits are more known. The frequent vicissitudes of our climate affect the functions of the skin very much, and when these are not restored by the effect of an active life in the open air, some other treatment is required. The daily application of strong friction, with what are called Bath Gloves and Straps, is found to answer this purpose very fully. We know a gentleman, who, finding himself growing corpulent and unwieldy, resorted to their use with such effect that in a few weeks his weight was diminished by twenty pounds, and his general health and spirits much improved.

"Those who desire to provide themselves with the most perfect instruction for the ready and convenient application of friction, are referred to the advertisement in this paper, headed "To Druggists." At No. 46 Cliff street will be found a large supply of Lawrence's (late Dinneford's) Horse Hair, Flesh Gloves, Straps and Brushes, of a great variety of patterns, adapted to either wet or dry friction. Mr. Lawrence has shown a good deal of ingenuity in suiting the forms of these articles to the various notions of convenience which may prevail, and in giving them a firm and durable construction."

SIR JAMES MURRAY'S FLUID MAGNESIA AND FLUID CAMPHOR,

The most agreeable and effectual Preparation of these articles now in use. They have been extensively adopted, both in Private and Hospital practice, and are well deserving the attention of the Trade. In pint and half pint bottles. Circulars containing a particular description of these articles, with numerous certificates of their remedial virtues, may be had of all the dealers.

COX'S CELEBRATED SPARKLING GELATINE;

The best article in use for making BLANC-MANGE and JELLIES. In neat paper boxes, containing each sufficient to make three pints of jelly, with directions enclosed.

The subscriber has made arrangements for a full and regular supply of the foregoing articles, and is prepared to supply the trade on the most favourable terms. A liberal deduction to those who purchase by the gross.

He has also on hand, and is constantly receiving a general assortment of ENGLISH, FRENCH AND GERMAN FINE DRUGS, CHEMICALS, &c. &c. Including a general assortment of Gums; Medicinal Roots, and Seeds; English Calomel, Blue Mass, and other Mercurials; Essential Oils, especially the finer qualities for Perfumer's use. Indigo, English White Lead, Paris Green, Prussian Blue, Cochineal, Carmine Fig and Wash Blue, Epsom Salts, Sal. and Sup. C. Soda, Camphor, Sponge, Rhubarb, Jalap, Aloes, Borax, Rotten Stone, Bay Water, Day & Martin's Blacking, Tartaric Acid, Citric Acid, Iodine, Hyd. Potash, Sulph. Quinine and Morphine, Bronzes, Dutch Metals, &c. &c.

Also, Herrings, Morson's, Mander's, Bailey's and other most popular Extracts, Chemicals, and other preparations.

French and English Hair and Tooth Brushes of Ivory, Bone, Buffalo Horn, Rosewood, Camel Hair Brushes and Pencils, &c.

Agency for BACH'S Celebrated ALCOHOL, and Perfumer's Spirits, of any desired strength.

MAGNESIA.

CALCINED, of different qualities and prices, in 10 lb. boxes, and in bottles.
CALCINED PONDEROSA, in 10 lb. boxes; also in tin foil packets.
CARBONATE, in pink and blue papers, in small cakes and in cases of about 120, 60, and 25 lbs. Do. small squares in 10 lb. boxes.

BRITISH LUSTRE.

A superior article, Red Label, in ¼ lb. papers, and in cases of one and two cwt. Also, SERVANT'S FRIEND, of same quality and style.

EMERY.

A general assortment of numbers, both PURE and second quality. (Price much reduced.)

MUSTARD.

TAYLOR BROTHER'S SUPERIOR LONDON, in Tin Foil Packets of ¼ and ½ lb., boxes of 9 and 12 lbs., and in bulk in kegs of 20 lbs. each.

TIPTON'S PATENT LINT.

Nos. 1, 2 and 3, in 1 lb. packets. Also, in 1 and 2 ounces papers. (Price reduced by the case.)

WEDGWOOD AND PORCELAIN MORTARS.

A complete assortment, in casks of 4 to 6 dozens, assorted and in nests. Also, Pill Tiles, Funnels, Evaporating Dishes, and Bleeding Basins.

SCALES AND WEIGHTS, a general assortment, in boxes and on stands.
LANCETS, EVAN'S Gen.; "OLD CHANGE;" SMITH'S do.
GLAZIERS' DIAMONDS, English, various styles.
THERMOMETERS, do. do.
SPATULAS AND PUTTY KNIVES, English—All sizes.
WHITE SKINS, English and French, a great variety.

GEORGE D. PHELPS,
Importer of Fine Drugs, Chemicals, &c.
46 Cliff street, N. Y.

May, 1850.

lent and often obscene quack and nostrum advertising that sullied the pages of nearly every daily and weekly newspaper, including the religious press. Such things crept, too, into the industrial press; the *American Journal of Mining,* for example, in 1866, announced Winchester's hypophosphates, "the Specific Remedy for Consumption, Nervous Debility and all Disorders of the Lungs, Nerves and Blood Systems," the "Golden Tablet" for catarrh and diphtheria, and a "Specific Pill" for afflictions which even today are rarely mentioned in print. It was difficult, however, for any periodical in those days to survive without such concessions. Actually, quack advertising disappeared from business papers long before it dropped out of general publications. This was, perhaps, due less to a change in morality or taste than to the fact that as trade papers became more and more dedicated to specific interests, the nostrum advertisers found them less profitable.

The *American Journal of Mining,* by the way, is the oldest ancestor of a McGraw-Hill paper. It arrived in 1866 soon after the Comstock Lode in the Sierras had opened a new golden era. In its first issue some four packed columns are devoted to these wonderful Nevada mines—evidently written by a correspondent on the spot. Meticulous and highly technical descriptions are given of the famous mines in their early days: of Ophir, Gould and Curry, Savage, Hale and Norcross, and Chollar-Potosi. But the correspondent was not above getting in a few personal digs delivered with acrid irony; and these suggest the general atmosphere of sharp dealing in this high, wide, and handsome time and place. Occasionally he would meet an honest man minding his own business and not trying to rob either his company or his competitors. One such inspired this sarcastic outburst:

> Not long ago I met the Superintendent of the Gould and Curry a-foot in a snow storm, far distant from the mine, attending to the business of the company. He keeps no fast horses at the expense of the company, and what is more reprehensible, he has changed the mine from a non-paying mine to a dividend paying mine, and from what we see,

Mine locomotive (Jeffrey Electric Motor Car), about 1886.

has the welfare of the mine at heart. This will never do. It is vulgar. Other officials will have to do the same thing. . . .

Mining in California, Montana, Colorado, Arizona, and seven other states as well as British Columbia and New Granada is as fully covered. The second issue shows the extent of the petroleum fever only seven years after the drilling of the first American oil well by listing some 570 petroleum companies. What a wealth of source material for the historian of that exciting era! He will need good eyes for the microscopic print, but there is both truth and color here that may not exist elsewhere.

But the *American Journal of Mining*, like nearly every other paper of its kind in that day, could not resist an occasional advertisement disguised as news. Despite the declaration of George Francis Dawson in his Salutatory editorial that

. . . puffery is my special abhorrence and so long as I conduct the JOURNAL nothing of the kind shall be seen in its editorial columns, . . .

the front page of that very issue presents some two and a half columns with a picture praising a certain rock drill advertised on another page and calling the reader's attention to the advertisement. Whether the advertiser paid extra for this we have no means of knowing. But if he did he was only following the accepted practice of the day. In general, puffs invaded editorial as well as news columns and Mr. Dawson's abhorrence marked him as a rare editor.

Unlike many other business papers, this magazine in its ninety-year career suffered only one radical change of name. Three years after its founding it became the *Engineering and Mining Journal.* John Hill added it to the list of the Hill Publishing Company in 1906 and thus it became, eleven years later, a part of the McGraw-Hill group. In the course of its long life, it absorbed eight mining and metallurgical papers and spawned three others. It flourishes today in the Big Green Building in close proximity to its eldest child, *Coal Age.*

3 Throughout this complex history we shall see papers changing their names again and again, absorbing lesser, duplicating papers in the same field, and reproducing by splitting in two like the ameba. This is true not only of McGraw-Hill but in the whole field of industrial or business journalism. To the outsider this behavior is a source of wonder, sometimes of irritation, that the innumerable changes in name, character, subject matter, and rate of publication have so involved the careers of the magazines. It seems as if there could be no stability in this business of eternal fission and flux.

The fact is that in the hurtling first century of its existence no orthodox stability has been possible for the business press. Almost from day to day the country's restless industry has changed size and color. Every change has brought a new subdivision in each field, an obsolescence of earlier materials and techniques. Constantly we have gone from specialization to specialization. It is industry itself that has divided like the ameba. Where a single paper could once cover the whole electrical area, for example, that area soon split into communication, light, and power. When new transmission techniques brought the "subdivided" current into the home, new problems arose of distribution, of wholesale and retail selling. Finally, down a future vista appeared in all their glory the infinite possibilities of electronics. Each of these sectors required a special kind of information exchange, hence, a new paper.

Again, when the technics to which they were dedicated became obsolete, the papers had either to fold their tents or seek new objectives. Thus, when the trolley replaced the horsecar, the *Street Railway Journal* had to become the *Electric Railway Journal;* and that, in turn, had to be replaced by *Transit Journal* and *Bus Transportation.*

There has gradually evolved, however, over all this apparently kaleidoscopic era, a set of principles applying equally to every publication. As we watch new papers forming today, there is a striking similarity in the aspects of gestation, whether a paper is concerned with food or mechanics, flying or digging in the earth. This uniformity and economy of method have come about largely through the big publishing companies in which an over-all policy can be formed through executive control. There may be superficial differences in the ways of Haire, Simmons-Boardman, Fairchild, or McGraw-Hill, but certain management, editorial, and ethical reference points serve them all.

4 Some early business papers established landmarks. As we look back over the list we find a sort of guide to the great events of the century. The *American Telegraph Magazine* came only eight years after Samuel Morse had tapped "What hath God wrought?" over the line between Baltimore and Washington. Professor Morse, indeed, wrote to the editor that he saw no reason why the magazine should not be "*quite as permanent* as THE TELEGRAPH ENTERPRISE ITSELF"—sentiments that the editor, bursting into italics and capitals, quoted in an editorial. The magazine's only advertising, however, was the promotion by that odd character Henry O'Rielly (sic) of a line to the Pacific—evidently insufficient for the thirty-two pages of fine-printed text, for the ambitious little paper folded within the year.

That the manufacture and distribution of textiles was well under way, but also that their retail sale was beginning to be a national interest, was suggested in 1846 by the appearance of the *Dry Goods Reporter and Commercial Glance.* The sequence of name changes through which this journal has passed in more than a hundred years is an index of changes of climate in American commercial opinion. We see the coming, for instance, of a broad national consciousness in the proud second title: *United States Economist and Dry Goods Reporter.* Evidently this later seemed too flamboyant to its publishers—or perhaps it was difficult to draw checks to—so it was condensed to *Dry Goods Economist.* Finally under the influence of Stewart and Wanamaker, the field enlarged, it became *Department Store Economist,* under which sensible twentieth-century title it is published by the Chilton Company today.

In 1915 Charles T. Root, the former publisher of the paper, told some amusing reminiscences before the Forum in Industrial Journalism at New York University. "A generation ago," he said, the paper's

> . . . advertising canvas was tinged with apology and involved the consumption of more shoe leather than brain tissue. Its advertising rate was a "movable feast" and as the solicitor, not the paper, commanded the business, the commissions it paid would have been ruinous had the expenses of getting out the publication amounted to anything comparable with those of the present day.[1]

This was typical of the seventies and eighties. The salesman usually asked a favor of the advertiser. Sometimes he would ask the advertiser to take space as a charitable act to support a

[1] *Lectures in the Forum in Industrial Journalism at New York University,* 1915, under the Auspices of the New York Trade Press Association, Advertising and Selling Magazine, Inc., New York, 1915, p. 12.

trade paper. Again, the advertiser would buy a quarter-page to get rid of the salesman.

One story told by Root shows the attitude of merchants toward advertising. He heard one day that a certain dry-goods merchant had just acquired an extremely attractive new line and he called on the gentleman to display the fine qualities of these goods in the paper. The merchant was horrified.

"What," he said, "put that in the paper and let everybody know what I've got?"

He was willing to put his card in the paper, yes. But until he got the customer into the privacy of his office, he would never reveal any details about his merchandise! Under the circumstances it is not surprising that the mortality rate of the journals that depended almost wholly on subscriptions to defray the costs of publication was extremely high.

As the practice of depending on advertising rather than circulation became common, the character of certain papers began to change. The *Engineer and Surveyor,* a McGraw-Hill ancestor, for instance, appeared with an ambitious prospectus in April, 1874. It was published and edited by a surveyor, George H. Frost, in his spare time.

> Frost depended [wrote Henry H. Norris] on subscriptions from the land surveyors of the country to support his enterprise at the start. This was a mistake. Few of them felt as he had done the need of engineering information.

Anyone who has been a surveyor knows that the day's long treks and straining eye work leave little time or strength for reading. Moreover,

> . . . Frost overlooked the fundamental publishing axiom that to be self-supporting a publication must serve readers who control reasonably large expenditures for supplies in its field. Surveyors were not in this class.[2]

[2] H. H. Norris, *The Story of the "Engineering News,"* unpublished manuscript in McGraw-Hill Archives, p. 3.

Mr. Norris, of course, was writing from hindsight. In 1874 what he states as an axiom was scarcely self-evident to many publishers. Benjamin Franklin had realized it more than a century before, but in many fields Franklin was thinking at least a hundred years ahead of his time. However, when Frost, on the advice of his engineer friends, shifted the emphasis from surveying to construction and changed his paper's title to *Engineering News,* it began to pick up. Under the management of Arthur Mellen Wellington, editor 1887–1895, it prospered. John Hill bought it in 1911 and its happy marriage in 1917 with its rival, James McGraw's *Engineering Record,* made it one of the most successful and revered papers on the McGraw-Hill list.

And what of the *Record's* pedigree? Here again was a landmark. In the twentieth century the United States has become celebrated for its plumbing. In central heating, in the number and efficiency of its bathrooms, in its management of water supply and sanitary engineering, it has come into world leadership. But less than a century ago interest in these things was just beginning. In 1877 when the urban trend was already under way and along the railroads and waterways huge cities seemed to grow like weeds in the night, some farsighted men were seeing into the future. At this point the American Plumber Publishing Company put out the first issue of *The Plumber and Sanitary Engineer* which announced that it would deal with Water Supply, Drainage, Heating, and Lighting. (Lighting, of course, in the days when illuminating gas traveled through pipes, was a branch of plumbing.) The text of the first issue is not animated but it is practical. It explains, for the comfort of the householder who has just installed the new gadgets, what the alarming "grating," "buzzing," and "rumbling" noises mean and why boilers explode. But the advertising copy with its pictures of the "luxurious" conveniences of the 1870s is fascinating.

Like the *Engineer and Surveyor,* though its advertising value was greater, the *Plumber* continued until it became obvious that the field had grown large and dignified and extended vitally into construction realms. In 1880 it dropped the limited term *plumber* and from *Sanitary Engineer* it eventually graduated into *Engineering Record,* a feverish rival of the *News.* How these rivals joined forces is a story that must come later.

The same evolution came to many other papers. A gay little sheet called *The Operator*—spiced, when it first appeared, with poetry, gossip, and quips—was dedicated to the impecunious young men at the telegraph keys who could hardly be expected to buy anything. This, too, was a product of 1874. The nostalgic Edison, perhaps remembering his own operating days, helped it out with some advertising of his recording instruments. As Mr. Norris tells us:

An advertisement from "The Sanitary Engineer," April, 1881.

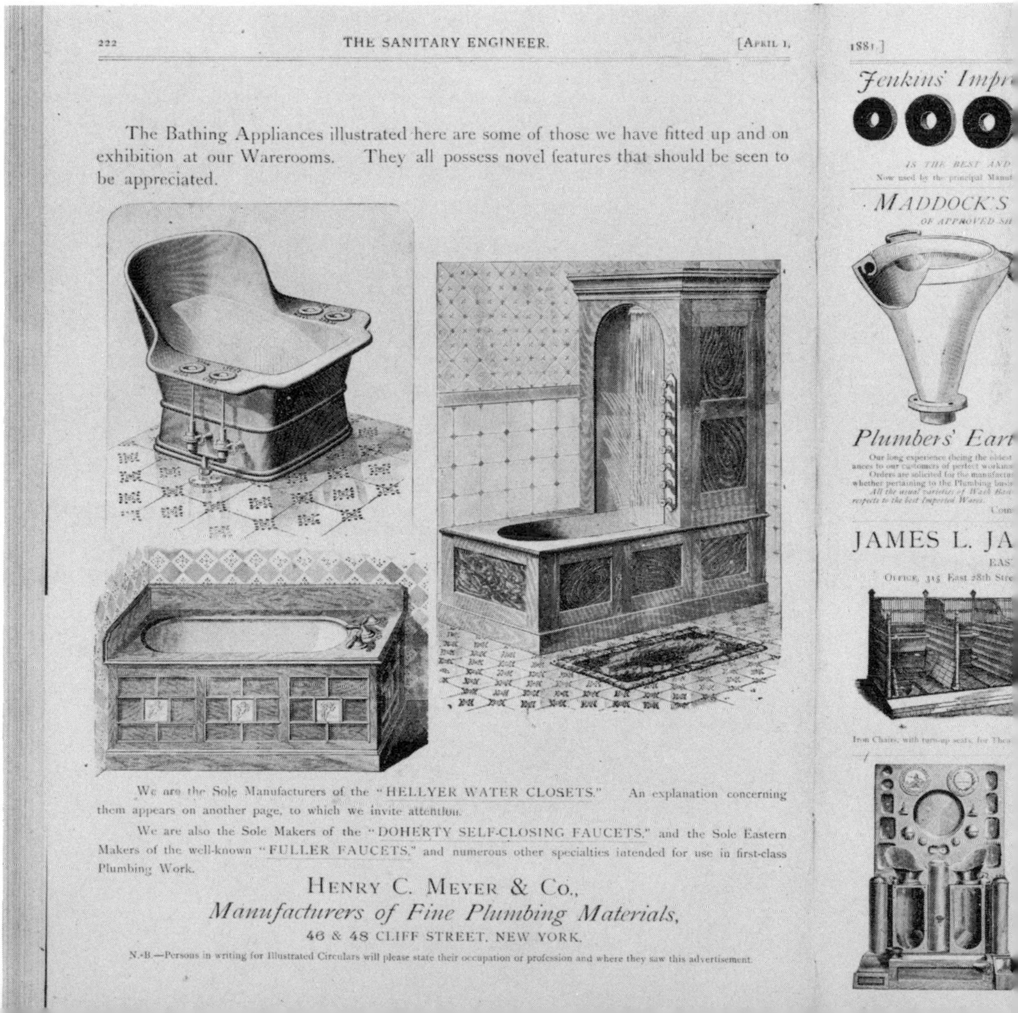

. . . the pages contained many curiosities of advertising, as judged by present day practices and standards. For some time . . . there were full pages devoted to patent medicines, accordions, etc. The advertisements included watches, printing outfits, toys, jewelry, silverware, musical instruments, hair tonics, and even a manual of knitting, crocheting, and lace making. . . .[3]

Perhaps the boys and their wives bought these things but the advertisers would have reached a larger audience in a general magazine. Yet *The Operator* was a logical publication in 1874, for communication dominated the whole electrical field. In the 1880s change began. The tremendous electrical development of that decade brought the enlargement of *The Operator* to the *Electrical World.* As such it was able to play an active part in industrial history until James H. McGraw bought it in 1899, since when it has become one of the most important of the McGraw-Hill publications, giving birth, as we shall see, to several more specialized offspring.

5 Through the gropings of these early journalistic efforts toward a place in the growing industrial parade of the era, we may learn of the very beginnings of the huge industrial complex that surrounds us and nourishes us today. As each found its position in the line of march, it becomes evident that industry from then on would depend more and more on the power of print. Many unfortunates dropped out. Some faded because of stupid or venal editorship or management; a few succumbed to changing times. Others astutely adapted themselves, as when the *Street Railway Journal,* at first dedicated to horsecars, saw the trolley coming before it came.

As industry matured so did journalism. The more mellowed general newspapers gave up the vituperations against their rivals which at one time had seemed the very lifeblood of their editorial bodies. The separation of advertising from editorial departments

[3] H. H. Norris, *The Story of the "Electrical World,"* unpublished manuscript in McGraw-Hill Archives, pp. 12–13.

An advertisement from "The Operator," June 1, 1874.

L. G. TILLOTSON & CO.,

8 DEY STREET, NEW YORK,

MANUFACTURER-, IMPORTERS, AND DEALERS IN

TELEGRAPH MACHINERY

AND SUPPLIES OF EVERY DESCRIPTION.

SOLE AGENTS FOR JOHNSON'S CELEBRATED **Line Wire.**

nerican Compound Telegraph Wire.

uvet's Patent Screw Insulators.

shop's Insulated Wires and Cobbles.

'ooks' Paraffine Insulators.

le Agents for LOCKWOOD PATENT BAT-Y, which is acknowledged to be the most ect and Economical Telegraph Battery in world.

le Agents for the LECLANCHE PATENT TERY, now universally adopted for Hotel nciators, Burglar Alarms and Bell Circuits erally.

gents for HILL & CALLAND'S PATENT TERY.

le Agents for the PATENT NITRO-ROMIC BATTERY, for Electro-Motors, Gold Silver Plating, and for any purpose where t quantity of current is required.

Agents for KENOSHA INSULATORS, PATENT WATERPROOF OFFICE WIRE, ELECTRICAL BLASTING APPARATUS, ELECTRICAL BELLS, HOUSE AND HOTEL ANNUNCIATORS, BURGLAR AND FIRE ALARMS, &c., &c.

The largest Stock, the greatest variety, and the best quality of Telegraph Goods in the country, at Lowest Prices.

Instruments, Office Fixtures, Line Wire and Material, Insulators, Office Wires, Battery Material, Chemicals, Tools, in any quantity always on hand. Equipment for Long Lines, Short Lines, or any kind of Telegraph Line ready to ship at a moment's notice.

Although doing a wholesale business we fill promptly any orders from a Battery Clamp upward. Don't be afraid to send in your orders, however small, they will always receive our best attention. We aim to supply every want known to the telegraph world, and are constantly adding to our stock.

If you want anything appertaining to Telegraphy send to us at first and save time and money.

e wish to call attention to our new 3 Pony Sounder, which is made in best manner, finely finished and is ounced by old telegraphers to be st the thing." Although a first-class rument, we have fixed the price at ow figure of *Five Dollars and Fifty s.* Main Line Pony Sounders for s from one to ten miles in length, 0 to $7.50. Relays finely finished ame style of lines, $7.50. fact we keep *anything* required by dents of Telegraphy, Amateurs and

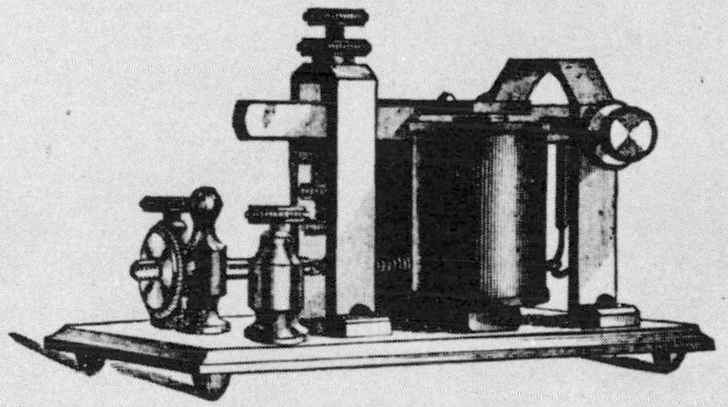

(No. 3 Pony Sounder.)

Telegraphers. Anything for experimental purposes not in the market we will make to order at living prices.

Come to head quarters at once for your Telegraph Material and save time, money and trouble.

L. G. TILLOTSON & CO.,

8 DEY STREET,

NEW YORK.

We make a Specialty of Instruments and Material for Students, Amateurs and Short Private Lines, d can offer the very best at exceedingly Low Prices, considering the quality of the goods.

THE EXCELSIOR TELEGRAPH INSTRUMENT.

his is the best Low-Priced rument ever put on the ket, and will work well on s from a few feet to several s in length. We are in ession of many voluntary mmendations from parties have purchased them and surprised by their excel-e. We respectfully request interested to call and see n and be convinced that ing they can buy in any r place for the same money approach them in dur-

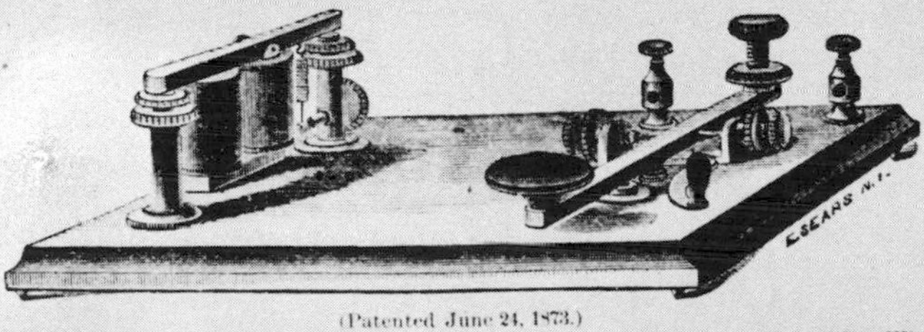

ability, finish and good working qualities. Owing to the simple construction of this instrument it is not liable to get out of order in any part, and we are enabled to make them of the best Material and Workmanship for the exceedingly Low Price of *Six Dollars and Fifty Cents complete*, full-size Pony Sounder and Trunnion Lever Keys, finely finished and mounted on finished Mahogany Base.

(Patented June 24, 1873.)

Student's Outfit consisting of: 1 Instrument Complete, 1 Cell Hill Patent Battery and Chemicals, 8 Feet Office Wire, 1 Complete Instruction Book taining besides Cuts and Prices of all the regular Telegraph Instruments in general use), all for *Seven Dollars and Fifty Cents.* Same outfit, including ntning Arrester, cut out and ground Switch, $8.50. SEND FOR CIRCULAR.

L. G. TILLOTSON, 8 Dey Street, New York.

became more and more rigid. After a few fights the advertisers themselves welcomed the change. Advertising was the main support of publications but the advertisers came to realize that the best media were those that played fair with their readers.

The value of advertising to business seems to have been realized by financial people ahead of publishers. At any rate, when the bankers John B. Murray and Company started the *American Gas-Light Journal* back in 1859, largely as a means of promoting illuminating company securities, there appeared on the front page of the first issue this somewhat sententious collection of metaphors:

ADVERTISING is the lever, with which resting on Enterprise as the fulcrum, Commerce moves the world.

CHAPTER FIVE

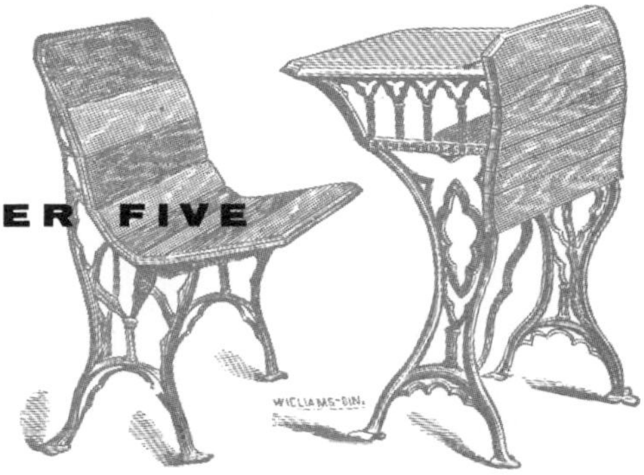

Schoolteacher into Publisher

Farthest west in New York State, bounded by a corner of Pennsylvania and by the waters of Lake Erie, lies Chautauqua County. The town of Chautauqua on Chautauqua Lake has become celebrated as the center of a cultural movement. Thousands have gone there year after year to expose themselves through lectures and conferences to a sort of semi-intellectual sun bath at which the higher highbrows have often looked down their noses. But there was little "culture" of any sort in the rich farmlands of the country in 1860 except what may have been brought in the buggies of the book agents. Men, women, and children worked hard with cows and corn.

Farmhouse of Patrick McGraw.

West of the lovely town of Jamestown lies the township of Harmony and in its midst is the tiny village surprisingly named Panama whose population of 650 in 1860 had dwindled to 374 a century later. This decrease seems to have begun by 1873, according to the *Gazetteer and Business Directory of Chautauqua County, N.Y.*, published in that year.

It [Panama] was once a thriving village, but its isolation from railroad communication has effectively checked its growth.[1]

Both the railroads were 5 miles away from the village—an apparently insuperable distance for the farm wagons! However, in 1873 there were still three churches, a Union School, eight stores, three shoeshops, two carriage factories, a cheese factory, a gristmill, sawmill, two planing mills, a cooper shop, harness shop,

[1] Hamilton Child, *Gazetteer and Business Directory of Chautauqua County, 1873–74*, Syracuse, 1873, p. 132.

and four blacksmith shops. The *Business Directory* lists one Patrick McGraw and we know that on his farm near Little Broken Straw Creek in 1873 a sturdy lad of thirteen—one of nine McGraw children—was doing his share of the farm work and attending the district school.

School-teacher into Publisher

James Herbert McGraw was a serious boy with steady blue eyes that reflected intensity of purpose. Like all the McGraw children he worked on his father's dairy farm which produced some 600 pounds of butter a year. The winters were long and tough; the snowfall was heavy and frequent, and the ground was seldom clear from November to May. The hard work gave the boy broad shoulders and a powerful frame but even in his early adolescence his mind reached beyond the cornfields. In his restless mental energy the jobs with the cows and corn must have irked him. Perhaps that was why later in his life he often sought release from physical effort.

King's Corner District School, Clymer, New York. First school attended by James H. McGraw.

But we know little about his childhood. If there were play and pranks and wickedness, he remained close-lipped about them. We know that he came of the solid Irish stock that settled much of New York State from Cherry Valley westward. In the earnest teacher and the powerful publisher little Jamie was lost. As he looked back on himself, the little Jamie must have seemed insignificant, provincial, and remote. It is a pity that he closed that early book because we are always curious about the beginnings of spacious careers. But we must be content with the view of the emerging adult in which we see scant trace of what we associate with the Irish: the fey humor, the gaiety, and the poetic inconsistency. These were rarely visible in the mature James Herbert McGraw.

The boyhood memories he later communicated centered around schools and teachers. He went back once to Panama in the years after his success. The first thing he looked for was the red schoolhouse. It was still there but he was saddened to find it empty and boarded up. As we all do with the most vivid scenes of our past, he half-consciously expected it to be alive and noisy with the boys he had known, impressed with the presence of a remembered instructor. It was in this district school that his mind first jumped from learning to teaching, that he felt that intense desire to impart knowledge to others, to build the minds and wills of others, that never left him. Fortunately the opportunity was close at hand; there was a State Normal School in nearby Fredonia.

In one of his rare reminiscent moments, he recalled the turning point:

> I chose Fredonia in common with a number of boys from the Panama school because I was ambitious to teach. Just at the time that a number of us were ready to go away to school Dr. Palmer came to Panama to preach on Sunday morning in the Baptist Church. The following day he visited our school and the boys met him through the principal of the school, H. M. Swetland. I think our visit with Dr. Palmer brought

Panama Union Free School attended by James H. McGraw prior to 1880.

PANAMA UNION
FREE SCHOOL

about the final decision to go to Fredonia. . . . We liked the idea of the State Normal School with no tuition and with books furnished. . . .[2]

To the farmers' sons of Panama, the appeal of "no tuition" must have been compelling. The more ambitious of them were already seeking ways to augment their meager pocket money. Jamie's way was to contribute school news and local gossip to the weekly newspaper edited by the town druggist. He wrote, too, for a monthly magazine, *The Countryside* (which paid five dollars a column) and was a book agent for *Heart of the World.* He also sold subscriptions. He did not know it then, but these activities posed a threat to his deeper ambition which would one day be conclusive.

2 It has often been said of James H. McGraw that teaching was the true direction of his genius and that everything he did was a kind of teaching, that everything he established was a kind of school. Even when material needs led him away from his first love, he retained the schoolteacher's attitude toward men and language; stubbornly he worked to turn every field he entered into educational pastures.

During the four-year course at Fredonia, he seems to have spent part of the time actually teaching at an elementary school. The time off did not interfere with his graduating from the Normal School in 1884 as valedictorian of his class. The address has been lost; it may have been no better or no worse than countless other such speeches, as formulated and as ephemeral. It undoubtedly pointed to a glorious future—a crescendo of scholarly inspiration to the young mind—yet there are reasons to doubt whether, in the mind of that young Jamie, he was sure that future was to be his.

One reason is revealed in a letter he received about the time of his graduation. It was from the principal of his old school,

[2] From a letter printed in *The Leader,* 1938, student publication of Fredonia State Normal School. Editor's Note: "from James H. McGraw of the McGraw-Hill Publishing Company, Inc."

James H. McGraw at the time of his graduation from Fredonia State Normal School.

Horace Monroe Swetland. Swetland had suddenly thrown pedagogy out the window and gone to seek another kind of fortune. It is likely that Swetland had been led away by his friend Emerson Harris, a venturesome lad with a pocketful of money to invest. The lure had been the publishing business, first in Boston, then in New York.

The upstate promise was, after all, not bright—not, at least, in teaching. The money rewards were virtually subsubsistence. They offered little scope for the restless mind, for the inquiring urgency of boys, then as always, expressed in the colloquial American: to go places and see things. And it was the time of the new trend away from the land to the teeming foci of business and industry. For upstate New York young men, the city at the mouth of the Hudson, wicked and dangerous as it was, was Mecca.

The farmers' sons as schoolboys and young teachers had nearly all eked out difficult livelihoods by selling subscriptions to periodicals. A local newspaper or a household magazine was part of the farmers' lives. The religious press penetrated every village with some sort of print; and these papers gave commissions on the subscriptions for which, in those days of meager advertising, they were eternally hungry. In America, as we have seen, folk lived on print as well as bread.

3 On June 19, 1884, Swetland wrote:

Friend James

I am in receipt of yours containing commencement cards for which I wish to make a special acknowledgement for your kind remembrance. . . .

Regarding your work for the future, no one but yourself can decide the question. Only the one old item of advice can be repeated:

"Select that profession to which you think your-self best adapted, and which is most pleasing to your taste, and having decided, *stick,* till you get into that cosy corner on the top shelf . . . ."

Regarding the Journal of R'y Appliances as a money making scheme, every thing would depend on your adaptability and the *offer you get from the Co.* And the territory you are to work. Business will come slow, & you will need some experience. An A 1. ad solicitor having experience and acquaintance among business men will get from $2,000 to 6 or 8,000 per year. . . .

Even the lower figure must have been tempting to a farmer's son in 1884! But Swetland's letter makes it evident that the two had talked or corresponded before about the technical paper, the *American Journal of Railway Appliances.* Swetland and Harris had already acquired some editorial and publishing experience. They had written and sold advertising for the *Boston Journal of Commerce.* Now Harris had bought the American Railway Publishing Company; he and Swetland had put out the appliances

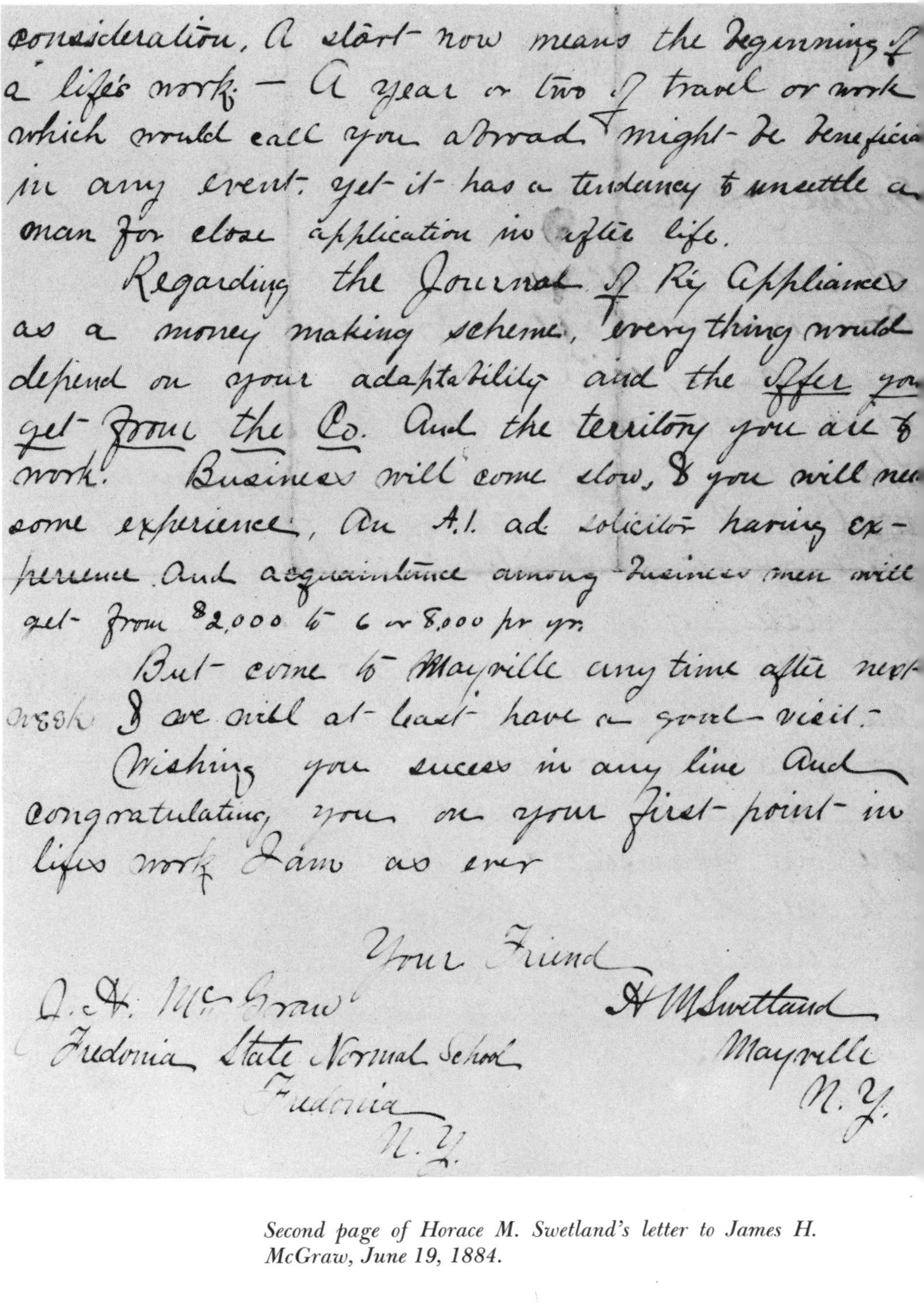
consideration. A start now means the beginning of a life's work. — A year or two of travel or work which would call you abroad & might be beneficial in any event, yet it has a tendancy to unsettle a man for close application in after life.

Regarding the Journal of Ry Appliances as a money making scheme, everything would depend on your adaptability and the offer you get from the Co. And the territory you are to work. Business will come slow, & you will need some experience. An A.1. ad solicitor having experience and acquaintance among business men will get from $2,000 to 6 or 8,000 pr yr.

But come to Mayville any time after next week & we will at least have a good visit.

Wishing you success in any line And congratulating you on your first point in lifes work I am as ever

Your Friend

H M Swetland
Mayville
N. Y.

J. H. McGraw
Fredonia State Normal School
Fredonia
N. Y.

Second page of Horace M. Swetland's letter to James H. McGraw, June 19, 1884.

paper and were angling for other periodicals. To Friend James these men must have seemed well on their way toward bright horizons.

At the same time the hope of becoming a teacher was hard to give up. James had loved the Fredonia school. Many years later he remembered with affection the men and women who had first "taught him to think": Dr. Palmer, Professor Dana, Miss Richardson, Miss McKinstry, and Professor Freeman. Many years later, too, he wrote, "I believe I would have loved teaching better than publishing." He did not realize then, perhaps, that in the eyes of his associates he had never wholly left the classroom. Listening to him talk in meetings and conferences—stern, looking always like the bearded professor, shaking his "nine-inch forefinger" (as they said) at them while he talked—the people of his company had felt themselves back in school and college days.

Through the summer vacation of 1884, young McGraw sold subscriptions for Harris's *Journal of Railway Appliances*. He must have done some extensive traveling. Yet over and above his expenses, he made more than $40 a week—a very considerable sum in 1884. In contrast stood the $700 a year that was usually paid to teachers in the district schools. The temptation must have been overwhelming to put the stuffy classrooms with their overheating stoves forever behind him and to move on to fortune in the city.

But it was not in James McGraw's character to be suddenly overwhelmed by such lures. He had already signed a contract for a year's teaching at Corfu, New York, for $700. It never occurred to him to break the contract. But during the winter he rationalized the situation and came to the conclusion that he was not sufficiently educated for the teaching profession. As we think back, knowing his natural gifts, to the fact that he had completed with honor a course at a state teacher's college, and balance these things against what we may imagine to have been the caliber and equipment of the country schoolteachers of the day, this conclusion seems farfetched to say the least. It is probable, however, that it was fetched thus far to meet the approach from New York.

In any case, he tells us that "when the year was over I hastened back to New York and joined the American Railway Publishing Company."

4 About equidistant from Fredonia and Panama at the head of Chautauqua Lake lies the village of Mayville. Here lived the Swetland family. Bennett and Augusta Swetland had moved there from Le Boeuf in Erie County, Pennsylvania, after the birth of their son, Horace Monroe Swetland, in 1853.

Horace graduated from Mayville High School in 1870. He taught district school for four years and then was made principal of a school at Findley Lake. After three years there he came to Panama as principal. This was in the winter of 1878 when James McGraw was just eighteen. Some of his later associates were sure that Swetland had been to college, so impressed were they with his apparently extensive education. That he was impressive even at twenty-five is beyond doubt. His heavy eyebrows gave his face a stern, austere look; this had been deepened by the years of keeping discipline in classrooms. He was persistent to the point of stubbornness, following his carefully thought-out ideas with ruthless indifference to opposition.

There were other Swetlands in Chautauqua County. They had migrated there from Massachusetts where they were one of the old families, coming originally from Wales. Benjamin Swetland, living in Portland on the shore of Lake Erie, was a physician celebrated enough to have his portrait in the *Biographical and Portrait Cyclopedia of Chautauqua County.*[3] As this was an honor never accorded to a McGraw, we may assume that, socially, in the Chautauqua hierarchy, the Swetlands were a cut above the McGraws.

This was not, however, the reason for the somewhat patronizing tone of Horace's note to "Friend James." He was seven years older and had become a man of the world. He had been the principal of a school where Jamie had been one of the boys. Obviously the young man looked to him for guidance, not be-

[3] Published in Philadelphia, 1891, p. 359.

Horace M. Swetland, about 1884.

cause he was a Swetland but because he had been a teacher; now that he had taken the plunge into the great world of commerce, he was the lodestone to draw the farmer's son away from the sticks.

When McGraw had finished his contracted year of teaching at Corfu, his immediate reason for hastening to New York was that Swetland had made him an offer of $1,200 a year as a member of the business staff of his railway journal. Just how Swetland thought he was going to pay this princely sum must have been figured in a long dream of futures. Already he and Harris were overextended. They had reached well beyond the practical little railroad paper. In their early work on the *Boston Journal of*

Commerce they had been fascinated by a department of that paper dedicated to steam engines. In the autumn of 1884 they had bought a moribund enterprise called *Steam* and made it the basis for a new publication, *Power.* As if that were not enough load for their shoestring company, they had made another paper out of a column on horsecars in the *Journal of Railway Appliances* and called it *The Street Railway Journal.*

At the time that McGraw arrived in New York, the finances of the little publishing company had become critical. An installment of $500 was due on the printing plant which the partners had bought for $2,500, and $1,500 was owed for paper. The paper man was on the point of closing in on the company and taking over its property. The only thing that had dissuaded him from doing this was the fact that the property was worth so little.

McGraw knew nothing of this and was sent off as Philadelphia representative. Then Swetland got to work and tried to revive the company. He had been away looking after the Boston branch and the decay had set in during his absence. Swetland was a strong dynamic person and there was something about his look and manner that inspired confidence. The story is that when, with his back to the wall, he asked the bank for $500 to pay his last installment, the bank refused, but the cashier had such faith in him that he let him overdraw his account for the sum. Thus he kept the company going until the summer of 1886.

Meanwhile McGraw, in Philadelphia, had been working to sell subscriptions to the railroad journal. All this time, however, he had received no pay. Suddenly he got a call to come to New York. He discovered, then, how precarious the company's finances had become. Before he could complain of the year's unpaid salary, Swetland said, "James, is there any possible way you can raise money?"

5 McGraw had not the faintest idea how he could raise a single dollar. But he had faith in the paper for which he worked. He had formed ideas of what such a paper should be and he

STEAM

RECORD OF THE WORLD'S WORK PERFORMED BY STEAM POWER, AND A POPULAR SCIENC[E]
ENGINEER MONTHLY DEVOTED TO THE INTEREST OF STEAM USERS.

[Vo]l. I. Entered at Chicago Post Office as second-class matter. CHICAGO, NOVEMBER, 1882. All rights reserved. PRICE EIGHT CENTS. No. 2

WHY THE FIRE BURNS.

[Th]e process of combustion is one of the mys[terie]s of nature. For thousands of years chem[ists o]f all countries explored the hidden recesses [of na]ture under the [som]e desire for [maki]ng gold and [silv]er by some [mystica]l method, for[gettin]g that as soon [as it] was easily and [cheap]ly made, it [woul]d lose its val[ue]. Abandoning [the] attempt, the [ch]emists next [turn]ed their atten[tion] to the full un[derst]anding of the [...] phenomena [of b]urning bodies. [W]ith all the re[searc]hes of the past [...] hundred years, including the [...] of latest sci[ence] bearing upon [the] subject, it is too much to [say] that the sub[ject] has some as[pect]s which yet re[main] sealed against [hum]an grasp. The [...] difficulty in [...]ring upon the [ques]tion before us, [cons]ists in the in[vis]ibility of the el[emen]ts which enter the process of [com]bustion or bur[ning]. This is an [obst]acle which the [tea]cher meets. He offers all [the] glories of the [unse]en world with [eloq]uent words, and [...] no response. [The] following is of[ten] ridiculously [...]. Not seeing, [...]de don't be[lieve]. But, on the [othe]r hand, a rail[road] contractor advertises two dollars a day for [men] to go into some malarial district, and thou[sand]s are more than ready to engage themselves, [beca]use the results are easily measured and out[ward]ly tangible.

[T]here are in nature two kinds of bodies, one [elem]entary and the other compound. Thus iron [—pu]re iron—is an elementary body; gold, silver [and] copper are other examples; but brass and similar metals are compounds. The elementary bodies are few, but the compound bodies are infinite in number. In understanding the subject of combustion, let us carefully consider what elementary substances enter into the process, and how they are at first and afterward combined.

In passing let us remark that, while the elements of combustion in the main are invisible, they are now so thoroughly understood that they are as easily handled as though they were solid bodies.

The ordinary act of making a fire is to strike a match, add light fuel in small quantities, and as the heat and flame increase, add coal and other combustible bodies. The heat, flame, hot gase[s], smoke and ashes are the external signs of th[e] chemical action which results from the sepa[ra]tion and the combining in new forms of th[e] elementary bodies previously held togethe[r]. The oxidizing [or] rusting of iron e[x]posed to the weat[h]er, and the wasting away and absor[p]tion of an uncare[d] for building, at o[ne] extreme, and th[e] fire of a blacksmi[th's] forge and the bur[n]ing down of a cit[y] are one and th[e] same process [of] combustion; in t[he] one case rapid, [in] the other, slow.

The chemic[al] process of comb[us]tion is thus descr[ib]ed by a high [au]thority: "C[oal] thrown on a fi[re] evolves, amon[g] others, two prin[ci]pal combustibl[es], CARBON and H[Y]DROGEN, whi[ch] uniting with the [OX]YGEN of the ai[r], an incombusti[ble] yet a necessary s[up]porter of a fir[e], produces heat a[nd] light at the sa[me] time. Simple as [the] process may [ap]pear, its analysi[s is] yet a complica[ted] chemical proble[m]. The chief age[nts] operating in [a] furnace are carb[on], hydrogen and o[xy]gen, and their u[nion] in certain prop[or]tions produces [oth]er bodies, as w[ater] or steam, carb[onic] acid, besides ot[hers] of less practical [im]portance." L[et us] more clearly d[efine] what these principal agents are.

OXYGEN is an invisible gas. The reader [will] remember that common illuminating gas a[s we] use it in shops and dwellings is an invisible [gas]. Steam in a boiler is also invisible, although [a] gas; and these illustrations indicate how pos[sible] and real a substance can be and yet not be vi[sible] to the eye. Oxygen has no smell, and rem[ains] permanently in receptacles, unchanged by [...]

GEORGE STEPHENSON.

wanted to keep his hold on it, tenuous as it was. It was characteristic of him to say "yes" to Swetland. There was no hesitation. Seldom in the life of this quick-thinking man was there hesitation over a decision. He saw things whole and at once that others had to spell out for themselves. On that August afternoon in Swetland's dark little office with its roll-top desks and gaslight, James McGraw saw the *Journal* stretching out into other journals, into a publishing complex that could be molded by his own hands. The single word he said to Swetland marked the start of a career from which he would never swerve.

"Yes," he said, put on his hat, walked out of the office and up Broadway, wondering how he could ever keep this sudden promise. Then he passed the building of the New York Life Insurance Company and the answer came. Young, robust, without a physical defect, he presented the safest possible risk and he was able to buy a $2,000 life-insurance policy with the little money in his pocket. For the beneficiary, he named James Knapp, a rich farmer he had known in schoolboy days back in Chautauqua County. Then, with what was left in his pocket—there always seems to have been something—he took a train.

Knapp had probably been asked for loans before by young men whose families were his old friends. So when James McGraw asked him for $1,000 he replied, quite naturally, with a question about security.

"I have nothing," said McGraw, "but my note and this policy. It is made out in your name, so if I die, two thousand dollars will go to you."

The young man probably never in his life looked less like dying than at that moment. And the old farmer appeared unlikely to survive him. As McGraw looked at him, then, there must have been something of that insistent quality that men later always saw in his eyes. You could not refuse James McGraw what he asked because always behind his request was a compelling reason. As William Bolitho wrote in his remarkable study of dynamic characters in history, *Twelve Against the Gods*, there is no

An early issue of "Steam."

such thing as luck with certain determined men. What they demand they *must* have, not for themselves but because they are the instruments of some larger design, and their unspoken will carries across in just those terms.

There was, however, a note of special kindness in Knapp's reply and a reflection of the quiet faith that transcended notes and policies.

"Jamie," he said, "if you will make this a debt of honor, I will loan you the thousand dollars."

James McGraw may be pardoned his exulting exaggeration as, many years later, he recalled the subsequent event.

"The next day," he wrote, "I laid a check for that amount on Mr. Swetland's desk. The poor treasurer promptly fell in a faint."

The check, however, had strings tied to it. It was less a gift than a weapon.

"I took stock for the thousand dollars as well as for the fifteen hundred dollars due me, and became a vice-president of the little publishing house. That marked a turning point. Two years later we paid a 10 per cent dividend."

The little publishing house turned out to be too small for two such powerful wills as those of Swetland and McGraw. It is doubtful, indeed, if any equal partnership could ever have endured with James McGraw as one of the partners. We only know that none ever did.

Yet in his lifetime there was a place in the growing industrial and business world for just such an individual force. It is probable that that time has passed. Today organization is so vast, so diverse, so complex, involving so many interlocking economic, social, and political, as well as technical problems, that no single person, genius though he may be, can sit at the top and, with all the strings in his hand, manipulate them all.

To his statement about the dividend, then, James McGraw added that "it wasn't long before there was a disagreement in the firm and we split on the rock of industrial progress."

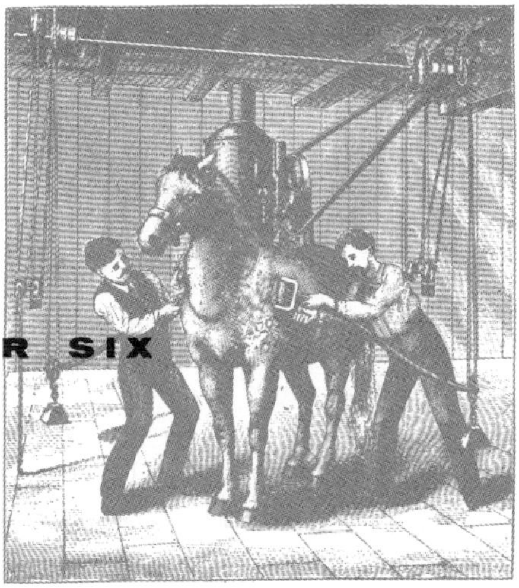

CHAPTER SIX

Reader First

To most Americans the word *power* immediately suggests that great beating heart of all industry, the electric generator, forever pumping out the lifeblood of the industrial body through thousands of miles of arteries that reach and animate every member, every extremity. To all of us, too, it is a warm and intimate thing answering the touch of a finger on light switch or household machine: something we cannot do without but happily an accessible commodity, cheaply purchasable by every American. And power is also a thing by itself, separately marketable, bringing business to corporations concerned only with its manufacture, not with its application. We think of it, then, as both goods and service, a commodity bought and paid for in measured units and at the same time as a utility, a means to an end. Thus the mystery has gone out of it. Electric power is tangible, as budgetable as paper, as available as a bank account.

It was shrouded in mystery in 1884. Power was scarcely thought of in terms of electricity. The world's first central station had opened in New York two years before. Edison's famous Pearl Street installation used his pattern of distribution—an invention greater, perhaps, than that of the incandescent lamp itself—and people were still talking about his "miracle." In October, 1882, a technical journal had given forth the news that

> . . . the throng of people that pass in the evening down Fulton Street, on their way to Brooklyn, observe with interest that in place of the usual gas lights in several of the stores . . . the little glowing horseshoes of the Edison Electric Illuminating Company, each in a small pear-shaped globe of glass, pendant beneath a porcelain shade, shed an exquisitely soft light upon the goods that formerly were but poorly illuminated. [1]

In the years when Swetland and Harris were thinking of a new magazine to bolster up the struggling *Journal of Railway Appliances,* the dynamo and the motor were just emerging from the experimental stage. Current was direct only. Edison was making great strides in the distribution of this current for lighting, but transmission over long distances and adjustment to motors large and small in industry had to wait on the inventions and development of Nikola Tesla, Charles P. Steinmetz, and George Westinghouse. The alternating-current and the polyphase motor were still in the future. The few establishments that used motors generated their current on the spot. Power in 1884 meant steam power and when, in November of that year, Harris and Swetland brought out the first issue of their new paper, they attached to it the cumbersome title *Power with which is incorporated Steam.*

The curious little Chicago publication thus incorporated must have cost the partners little enough. As we look over the rare extant issues, it is hard to imagine anyone reading it. Erudite articles such as "Why the Fire Burns"—attempting to expound what was then known of the chemistry of combustion—were inter-

[1] *The Electrician,* vol. 1, no. 10, p. 208, New York, October, 1882.

spersed with execrable verse and flowery essays having nothing whatever to do with steam. The trivia disappeared after the incorporation; eventually the name *Steam* dropped from the masthead, and the magazine appeared with the single, dignified, and arresting name *Power.* From the days of the steam engine known as the "Corliss Wonder" to the days of atomic energy no basic change of name was ever needed.

Reader First

Offhand one would be inclined to credit these publishers with vision into the future in the use of this word which means to us so many things. In fact, the vision came later. As we shall see, both Harris and Swetland were limited in their understanding of the possibilities of electric power, whereas James McGraw, who had little to do with the purchase and promotion of the power magazine, saw further than either into an electric-power future.

2 In June, 1934, the fiftieth-anniversary issue of *Power* ran a picturesque description of the world in which the paper began publication.

Eighteen hundred eighty-four. Chester A. Arthur in the White House; Grover Cleveland impatiently awaits nomination. Thirty-eight states form the Union; in some . . . troops still fight Indians. In the cities, horse cars, omnibusses and victorias dot the cobbled streets. Silk-hatted or square-derbied business men talk with side-whiskered professional men.

Niagara Falls roars in solemn grandeur, untapped for power except for one or two puny waterwheels on a toy canal. The Centennial Corliss is still an object of awe, the steam turbine little more than a fascinating toy. Wheezy steam engines are served by long lines of little horizontal boilers, stoked hour after hour by sweating men stripped to the waist. Engineers are hard-bitten practical men; scientific knowledge is only for professors. . . .

Offices [for *Power*] are set up in the old Stone Building at 32 Liberty St., with flickering gas lights in flossy fixtures, one sided heating from a coal stove, no telephone, two rackety typewriters. . . .[2]

[2] *Power,* vol. 78, no. 6, p. 309, McGraw-Hill Publishing Company, New York, June, 1934. Though *Power* traces its beginnings back to 1882 this fiftieth-anniversary issue was not published until 1934.

To this office two years later James McGraw brought his check for $1,000 causing Swetland's legendary fainting spell. By this time Harris and Swetland had also acquired the *Street Railway Journal.* As we look back this publication seems the very antithesis of *Power.* A comparison of the two with an occasional side glance at the *Journal of Railway Appliances* will give as sharp a picture of that age of transition as any contemporary documents can.

It is usually forgotten, even by those who remember the era, the enormous part played by the horse in American industry. Except for the performance of locomotives and steam vessels, all transportation depended on this noble animal. Industrial equipment—boilers, engines, machines, fuel—went from the railroad to the factory on trucks drawn by massive Percherons. Horses brought building materials to new construction projects and pulled the earth out of excavations. They helped make the farm self-sufficient. They were its power plant: they planted the grain that was their fuel, they fertilized it, and they harvested it. But not only did they transport goods over the country's rough roads and cobbled streets, they also pulled cars on rails. And it was over this last equestrian function that, according to the story, the partners in the American Railway Publishing Company—publishers of the *Street Railway Journal*—split on the "rock of industrial progress."

3 In the meantime, James McGraw, working on various phases of the shoestring operation, had begun to form some convictions of his own about the technical press. At best the industrial press was a sort of moon, dimly reflecting the sun of industry. Its articles caught up with the rapid sequence of events long after the facts. Usually it was conservative and cautious, fearful of promoting novel trends, preferring to play safe with the old and tried ways. Almost never could a technical paper be found out in front leading down some new path. Its publishers wanted it to be a mirror or an echo, and to the young McGraw an industrial paper seemed a sort of scrapbook of stale clippings.

I found the industrial editor [he remembered] a rather insignificant figure. In most cases the publisher was chiefly concerned with getting advertising enough to pay the printer. . . . The editor was an item of expense and his department was not lavishly supported. Paste-pot and scissors were his principal tools and write-ups from his advertisers were an important source of material. In fact, no matter how seriously the editor might take himself, it was a common saying, outside his sanctum, that he was a wholly necessary evil required by the postal authorities to enable the publisher to send his paper through the mails at second-class rates.[3]

Reader First

Seeing these things he reached a conclusion that seems to us scarcely arguable but was evidently not accepted in industrial publishing in the eighties: namely, a magazine is meant to be read and to be interesting primarily to its readers. And only when it becomes so interesting that it is a real necessity to readers, something they cannot do without, can it be of any value whatever to its advertisers. In short, advertisers will gladly support an interesting, an original, or a necessary paper, but they have to be

[3] G. D. Crain, Jr. (ed.), *Teacher of Business: The Publishing Philosophy of James H. McGraw,* Advertising Publications, Inc., Chicago, 1944, pp. 26, 27.

A horsecar of the 1880s.

goaded, wheedled, prodded, and cajoled into paying for space in a dull, stale copybook. This fact is accepted as an axiom today in the business publishing world but it was the McGraws, the Swetlands, the Hills, the Haires, and the other pioneers of the business press who made it so.

There was a reason why this extremely primitive truth was not understood in the nineteenth century. The general press—daily and weekly newspapers—and the general magazines dealt with politics, foreign affairs, crime, social movements, science, education, literature, and the arts—matters of universal interest divorced from questions of dollars and cents. The business press, however, had to treat of commodities, of buying and selling, of manufacture for sale, of profitable transactions, of matters always concerned with commerce. There was, therefore, a confusion in the minds of these publishers between editorial and advertising content, between reader and advertiser. The dominant belief was that a business paper existed, however you might disguise or conceal the fact, primarily for the advertiser. The larger concepts of commercial activity, of cheap quantity production, distribution, and consumption as implements of democracy and calculated to raise living standards—were just beginning to dawn, and the idea that new inventions, techniques, processes, or machine sequences were interesting in themselves apart from immediate cash values was just beginning to take hold.

We cannot be sure that all this was formulated in James McGraw's mind in, say, 1888. But we do know that he was restless, fully aware of the flies in the publishing ointment. We know that he was feeling for something new, eager to strike a tangent from the rotary thing in which he found himself.

It has been said by those who knew him then that his first visible talent in business was that of a salesman. Presumably the term is used in the modern sense, meaning not merely a man who exchanged goods or services for profit but one who could persuade in any direction. In any case it is probable that he induced more people to subscribe to and advertise in the Railway Publishing Company's papers than any of the other three. His calls in the interests of sales took him into the offices of many industrial leaders. One of these was Frank Julian Sprague, the pioneer in electric traction. In 1887 in Richmond, Virginia, Sprague had made the first complete electrification of a street railway system ever known and in the next year or two had installed more than a hundred similar systems in various cities of America and Europe.[4] But McGraw had also followed the work of Van Depoele, John C. Henry, Elihu Thomson, and Leo Daft. The story of this immense development must have stood in sharp contrast in McGraw's mind to the jangling horsecars that were part of his daily life in Manhattan. According to his own account, electric traction was the specific "rock" on which he and his partners split. From this point on, the mysterious fluid that had captured the minds of Franklin, Faraday, Joseph Henry, and a host of others fascinated James McGraw more than any other industrial factor. It fascinated him, however, not in its technics but in its colossal business potential.

Reader First

4 The "more than 100,000 horses and mules" that in the eighties were "engaged in pulling 18,000 streetcars on 3,000 miles of track in cities all over the United States"[5] represented a considerable investment. Also these animals provided a lucrative by-product. "In a single year, for example," John Miller tells us, "the Third Avenue Railroad in New York realized $13,750 from the sale of manure.[6] If cable or trolley cars replaced the horsecar, this commodity would cease to exist. All these considerations influenced the conservatives, the cautious, the reactionaries among street-railway men. These

. . . looked with suspicion on all attempts to employ electricity as a means of providing local transportation service. Horse-cars had proved themselves able to do a satisfactory and efficient job. There might be a field for the cable-car under special circumstances, they thought, but

[4] Manuscript collection of Frank Julian Sprague in New York Public Library.

[5] John Anderson Miller, *Fares, Please! From Horse-Cars to Streamliners*, copyright, 1941, by Appleton-Century-Crofts, Inc., New York, p. 32.

[6] *Ibid.*, p. 29.

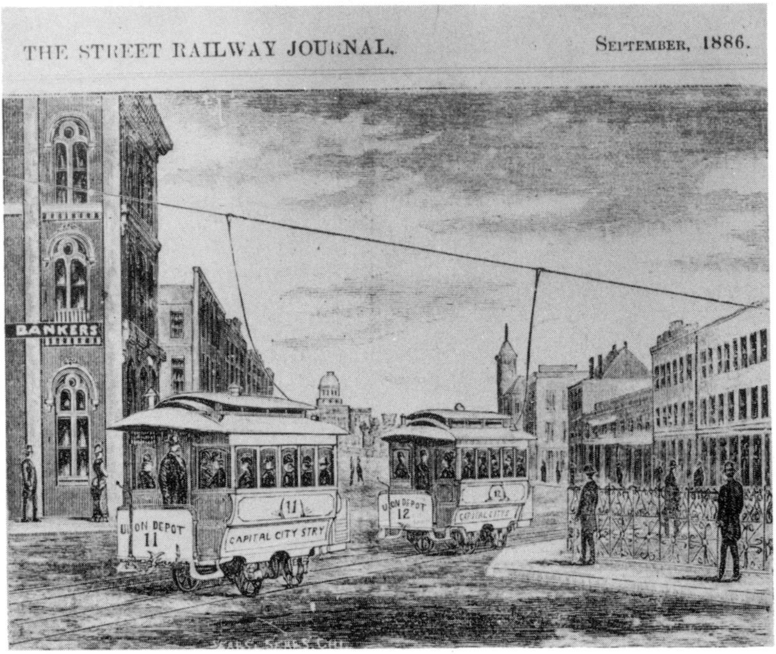

Electric railway at Montgomery, Alabama—Van Depoele system, 1886.

a majority of them agreed that "no self-propelled car could meet the conditions to be found on American tramways."

"If you want to pull a car," said one of them, "you must put something in front of it." [7]

According to McGraw's reminiscence, the *Street Railway Journal* shared this view and the editor would not listen to his warning of "the impending doom of the horsecar and of the cable car." Certainly the early issues of the magazine devoted page after page to the care, feeding, grooming, shoeing, stabling, and medical treatment of the horse. The advertising was of horses, mules, harness, and horseshoe nails. The correspondence discussed the horse versus the mule and whether the salt used to melt ice on

[7] *Ibid.*, pp. 59, 60.

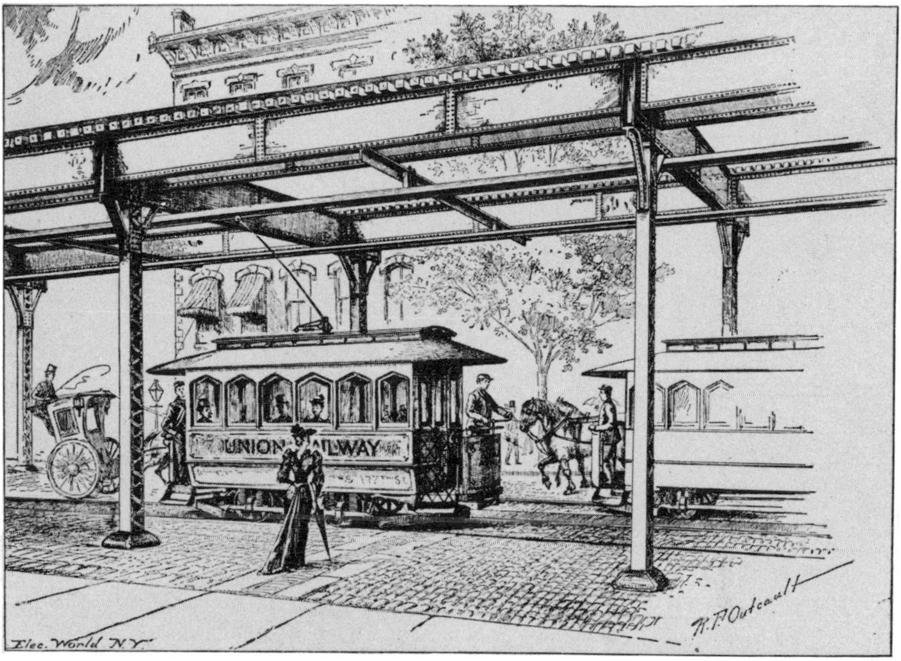

New York's first trolley line, 1891.

the tracks would hurt the animals' feet. Mr. McGraw wanted the emphasis shifted and space devoted to the revolution he foresaw so clearly. Especially he wanted an editor who knew about electricity.

So [he wrote] the firm broke up, Mr. Swetland, the treasurer, buying *Power.* The rest of the property, including the composing room, came to me.[8]

Here the old man's memory seems to have skipped a page. The record shows that the *Street Railway Journal* was retained by Harris. It was true that Swetland bought *Power,* paying Harris $16,000 for the property. But McGraw joined Swetland for a

[8] G. D. Crain, Jr. (ed.) *op. cit.,* p. 28. The reminiscence was published in 1944 when James McGraw was eighty-four.

THE SONG OF THE TROLLEY

I am coming, I am coming, hark you hear my motor humming,
For the trolley's come to conquer, so you cannot keep it back;
And "Zip!" the sparks are flashing, as the car goes onward dashing
While the wheels are whirring smoothly along a perfect track.
'Tis vain then to delay me, for you cannot stop or stay me,
Though old fogies fought against me, for I "went too fast," they said;
And they talked of death and danger to the native and the stranger—
Oh! a frightful state they were in from my wire overhead.
Yes, it seems the trolley shocked them—for right and left I knocked them,
And I made them grow much wiser in their day.
So, at last, they've learned their folly and stopped fooling with the trolley;
Now when they hear me coming its a case of clear the way.
I have harnessed nature's forces, I've freed the mules and horses,
I have helped the toiling thousands to new ways to earn their bread;
Then, as civilization's factor, I will laugh at each detractor
And keep on doing business at the same old stand instead.
Hear me whizzing through the highways—see me brightening up the byways,
Annihiliating distance as I merry speed along;
I bring new life and faces to old sleeping towns and places
And a million homes are brighter for the music of my song.
The business world's my debtor, 'twill ne'er find servant better,
For I've wakened up a nation and prosperity's at hand;
See the future thats before me, 'tis in vain you would ignore me,
For the voice of the trolley is heard all through the land.
I've no palace car or sleeper, but I carry people cheaper,
And I bring the breath of country to the toilers of the town;
I increase the mail facilities—freight carrying abilities
Are among my many virtues and I cannot be kept down.

I laugh to scorn resistance and all thoughts of time and distance,
The embodiment of Progress, hear me hustling near and far
In the van of civilization, and a most apt illustration
Of how commerce has successfully hitched its wagon to a star.
Yes, I'm coming, I am coming, dont you hear my motor humming?
For the trolley's here to conquer and you cannot keep it back;
And "Zip"! the sparks are flashing as the car goes onward dashin
Yes the trolley's come and conquered, so look out! and clear the track!

Roy L. McCardell.

[WRITTEN EXPRESSLY FOR THE STREET RAILWAY JOURNAL.]

brief period and the short-lived partnership of Swetland and McGraw published *Power* and the old *Journal of Railway Appliances.* What rock this partnership split on is not recorded, but it was obviously foredoomed by the conflicting ambitions of the two men. This left McGraw with only the railway-appliance paper on which he had started.

Reader First

It is evident that even while the dispute was going on much electric traction material infiltrated the *Street Railway Journal.* There was hardly an issue without some discussion about the new motive power. As far back as December, 1885, there was a full-page advertisement of the Van Depoele electric railway system and in the same issue appeared a two-page article by John Bruns highly favorable to electric streetcars. Before the break in 1888, Harris asked Frank Sprague to send him an illustrated article on the electrified Richmond road. The piece was the feature of the *Journal's* June number, occupying five pages and with a fold-out map. And a bold editorial in the May issue stated that "the utility of electricity as a motive-power for the propulsion of street-cars is no longer a matter of question."

Office of Richard Felton Outcault, staff artist of "Street Railway Journal."

So we may suspect that there were other motives behind the dissolution of the American Railway Publishing Company beside the dispute over the doomed horse. But the fact remains that James McGraw was the first of the three pioneers to see the dominant part electric power was to play, not only in transportation but in all kinds of industry. And, after he had lost the *Street Railway Journal* to Harris, it was obvious that he would never rest until he got it back. Thus, early in 1889, he managed to raise the first payment on $22,000, and Harris, who at that time was beginning to dream of other horizons, was happy to have the paper taken off his hands. From then on, horses, mules, and stables began to disappear from its pages and to be replaced by motors, overhead wires, and underground conduits, until, in October, 1894, a souvenir issue was introduced by a full-page illustrated poem called "The Song of the Trolley," composed by Roy L. McCardell in the Kipling manner. The pictures, done by no less an artist than the celebrated Richard Felton Outcault, creator of the "Yellow Kid" and "Buster Brown," show the wistful mule and the tired horse on the way out. By this time the new electrically minded editor Henry W. Blake had been installed and the *Journal* had achieved international fame.

After the sale of the *Journal* to McGraw, Harris in a wave of nostalgia withdrew from New York and publishing and went back to Chautauqua County where he engaged in the gentler pursuit of grape culture. In dynamic contrast Swetland and McGraw moved with full vigor on their separate ways into the great twentieth-century American industrial revolution.

CHAPTER SEVEN

Locomotive Engineer

Three years before the start of the Civil War a boy was born to George and Margaret Hill in the little farming community of Sandgate, Vermont. They might have named the baby after the father of his country for his birthday was the same as Washington's, but the parents preferred to call him John Alexander. If, in 1858, John showed promise of the handsome features and finely proportioned body that characterized his later years, George and Margaret Hill must have been proud indeed to show him off to the neighbors.

John was still a young child when the family moved west. Moving west was the fashion in the more rugged parts of New England where short, cool summers and stony soil made farming

John A. Hill, about 1888.

hard. The hills around Sandgate in the southwest corner of the state, the southern beginnings of the Green Mountains, added to the difficulties. George Hill had to supplement his farming with the trade of a wheelwright in which he did business with wagon owners in nearby Bennington. So John's earliest memories were of a shop and tools, a forge and an anvil.

The family settled in the village of Mazomanie, Wisconsin, on the main line of the Milwaukee and St. Paul railway, and in John's school days, the tracks of this road were extended to join Chicago with the twin cities of Minnesota. The boy must have spent fascinated hours watching the balloon-stacked wood burners come and go, for the locomotive was one of the great loves of his life. The other, the printing press, he met when he was fourteen.

In the meantime the war had come to an end. The proud state of Wisconsin had sent 90,000 men to the Union armies out of a population of some 800,000. With the war over new swarms of immigrants came and population passed the million mark by 1870. By then industry had begun to infiltrate the state which had been dedicated to wheat and sheep.

Even in his early years John must have been a responsible and conscientious boy. We know little about those years for John Hill was as tight-lipped as James McGraw about his growing time. It is said that at eight he was given sole charge of a flock of 300 sheep—a large order for a child even in the sixties when children matured faster than they do today. But we know that at the start of his adolescence he moved forever away from farming and became an apprentice in a printing shop. He remained there for six years—from fourteen to twenty—and in addition to the work of compositor and pressman, he used his mechanical flair in the maintenance and repair of press machinery. From 1875 to 1878 he was foreman of the shop—a foreman in his teens.

In 1878 the country's eyes became focused on the center of Colorado just as a decade before they had been focused on western Nevada and twenty years before that, on the valley of the Sacramento in California—and for the same reason. Silver and gold had been found in the lead ore in the mines around Leadville, Colorado. Within a year, Leadville, from a handful of mean shanties, had become a thriving city whose population was to grow to 35,000 by the end of 1879. In it much of the earlier romance of Virginia City was reenacted with claim jumping, shooting, and blood mingled with champagne in its gay bars and gambling halls. News of the hysterical silver rush had reached John Hill by the time of his twentieth birthday and "Leadville fever" drew him back toward the first great love of his life.

Some of his later friends said that he talked about prospecting during 1878 but there is no evidence that he made any fortune at it. We know that before the year was out he was firing a locomotive on the Denver and Rio Grande Railroad. There was more security, no doubt, in such a job, even at a dollar a day, than in the speculative mining, but any job on that particular railroad was dangerous. John Hill has told us enough of the failures of a tricky signal system, of wildcat trains running the wrong way on a single track, of landslides falling on the little shelves where the road ran thousands of feet up around the edges of canyons, of jumps from the cab only seconds before disaster, to convince us that railroading in the Rockies was an adventure of large proportions. But besides all these things there was a war, often fought with pistols and dynamite, between the Denver and Rio Grande and the Atchison, Topeka, and Santa Fe railroads that lasted through Hill's first year or so. Whether he was involved in the battles he has not said, but he probably did plenty of thinking about the conflict.

From the delicate task of setting type to the rough job of keep-

A Denver–Rio Grande double-header on Veta Pass in southern Colorado, early 1880s.

ing up steam in a locomotive boiler, the change seems radical indeed, even for those fluid days. Yet curiously enough, in Hill's uncommon mind the two things were not mutually exclusive. From his six years—and they were the formative years—in the printing shop, the young man emerged with a feeling for words, an understanding of their values, a desire to express in words his own experience, or to give body to the words of others. And in the long night hours in the cab, he must have been making up stories out of the rich material of his daily life.

His talent for writing was undoubtedly native. The rough work of railroading contributed direct and salty language to his expression. In a day when writing was usually turgid and pseudoliterary, his words seemed to come like a smashing blow of truth, unmistakable and uncompromising. But his constant association with all conditions of men—crooks and square shooters, reprobates and sober workers, liars, philosophers, and heroes—gave him abundant chance for character estimates. John Hill might have had a successful career as a writer of fiction but the charm of the iron road held him to the throttle.

He broke once. In 1882 he married Emma Carlisle of Mazomanie. After they were married, her husband's long absences must have made life worrisome for Emma Hill. Perhaps it was she who made him quit in 1885 and try his hand at journalism. Settling down in Pueblo, he started a paper there, the *Daily Press*. But the venture held him for less than a year. He was an experienced engineer by then, familiar with all the railroad mechanics. He had worked in roundhouses and shops and the offices of master mechanics. It seemed to him that he was wasting his time handling news and editorials and local gossip that had nothing to do with a railroad. So he went back into the cab.

Yet even in the cab there was conflict. There in the cab he kept pursuing one of the strangest hobbies a locomotive engineer ever rode. There in the cab he wrote and wrote and wrote. He wrote about all the things that were wrong on the road. He wrote about men and signals and headlights, switches, ornery bosses, lying conductors, piston packing, injectors, and jumps in the dark. As the eighties drew toward their close it was inevitable that he should choose a career that would resolve the conflict. In 1888 in faraway New York, the chance came.

2 During the Civil War the invention, design, and building of machine tools took a long jump forward. With the large sudden demand in the 1860s every device that could speed production became important. Firearms, uniforms, shoes, and wheat were needed in a hurry and in huge quantities. Labor shortage made it necessary that these things be produced by more or less automatic machines. Sewing machines, agricultural machinery, gun borers, and the elaborate sequence of the shoe factory answered the demand. To produce these, there must be precise and productive powered tools.

In the postwar boom in the North almost countless factories sprang up, making everything from Waltham watches to Pittsburgh steel rails. For a time this mushroom expansion was halted by the panic of 1873. But once that depression was over, it became evident to the wiser industrialists that the business of making the powered tools was becoming a large independent industry. The time was past when a manufacturer could design and build his own tools, as rifle producers such as Robbins and Lawrence of Vermont could do in the fifties.

A signal focus of this industry was Hartford, Connecticut, where the firm of Pratt and Whitney had become a leader. From its shops the old rule of thumb was already disappearing by the mid-seventies and artisans were becoming engineers. The need for a new kind of education for tool designers, patternmakers, foundrymen, and machinists—one which should include mathematics as well as shop training—was becoming evident. Print must complement the old vocal instruction; men must learn theory along with practice. A foreseeing machinist at Pratt and Whitney—one of the early promoters of the milling machine—realized that in the rapid transition of the age, books were not enough. There must be something more flexible, more current: something that would give quick news of quick changes. To John J. Grant of Pratt and Whitney a magazine was the answer.

Grant found two journalists, Jackson Bailey and Horace B. Miller, who were able to carry out his idea. How they did it is a mystery for those who contemplate launching a new publication in the mid-twentieth century. Jackson and Bailey had no capital. They had peculiar ideas about advertising, believing it secondary to reading matter. Yet in 1877 they founded a journal that has endured for eighty years and has become recognized throughout the world as one of the great technical papers of all time. This journal was the *American Machinist.*

Before printing they built up a paid circulation of 5,000. Even without advertising this gave them a start. On the masthead page of the first issue Miller gave expression to his views on advertising. First, he announced in italics:

Positively we will neither publish anything in our reading columns for pay or in consideration of advertising patronage.

In the leading editorial, also in italics, appeared the statement:

We are not specially interested in the sale of machinery or other merchandise.

Following this disinterest in practice, the publishers set a rigid limit of sixteen pages per issue. This was to include both text and advertisements. Pages were allotted first to editorial matter. After that was filled, whatever space might be left was sold to advertisers. If there were more advertisers than space, the advertisers were told they must wait and there was, from the start, an advertisers' waiting list! This practice was characterized by a later editor of the magazine as "unique in publishing history."

The subtitle of the *American Machinist* was "A Journal for Machinists, Engineers, Founders, Boiler Makers, Pattern Makers and Blacksmiths." The subtitle suggests that the appeal was intended to bypass the highbrows. The editors did not hold fast to this intention. Some exceedingly erudite articles on the condensation of steam and the "science of machines" appeared in the earliest issues, written by professors in the new discipline of engineering. But evidently the publishers wanted to keep the paper from wandering too far from the shop and from machine-tool practice. In the third number an editorial emphasized this:

The present high standard of our machinery is due entirely to [the] system of making special tools for each part, *by which they are made interchangeable,* thereby producing an article of uniform quality in indefinite numbers, and without the slightest variation in style or finish. In no branch of our manufacture is this system so thoroughly understood and practiced as in the machine shop for it is there that all the machinery which sets in motion the other branches of industry is designed and manufactured.[1]

By June, 1879, sixteen pages per month had proved inadequate for the material that kept pouring in. The publishers, however, refused to relax their rule. Instead they changed the magazine from a monthly to a weekly. In the first years after the change, it tried to cover the entire field of mechanical engineering. Not only powered tools but the steam engine became the subject of elaborate articles. In the mid-eighties there was a preponderance of railroad material. A long, heavy series on locomotive construction was interspersed with "Letters from Practical Men" on every subject from train-flagging to snowplowing.

These pieces make dull reading for the modern reader. Printed in fine type on pages of monotonous uniformity, they lacked the directness and vitality that we expect in this day when so many other activities compete with our reading time. In the eighties there was less pressure. Thus we may imagine even the locomotive engineer and fireman poring over the pages of the *American Machinist* between duties in the cab. Perhaps they sighed with relief when the reading was over. But then in 1885 came something new.

Out of the blue came a letter on oiling a locomotive. The let-

[1] *American Machinist.* vol. 1, no. 3, p. 8, January, 1878.

ter had no style. It told about the oil holes in the wrong places. It told about the men who wasted oil. It was forceful, pugnacious, and full of humorous exaggeration. It appeared in the May 23 number. No place name was attached. It was signed simply J. A. Hill—a name no one on the *American Machinist* had ever heard.

Two years later letters from the same source came flooding in. One was given the dignity of a full-dress article on page 1. It was entitled "Shall the Head-Light Go" and the by-line John A. Hill appeared on top. It began with a withering attack on some superintendent who had said there was "no use of a headlight on a locomotive."

> Now I very much doubt [the piece went on] if this superintendent has ridden behind a headlight watching every inch of ground it cleared up, for as many years as I have. Perhaps he has not seen it disclose the misplaced switch, the obstruction, the snows, the wash-outs and the wash-ins, the cattle, the drunken men and the fallen trees, has not had his neck saved by seeing the glare of a head-light of a wild train "off its base" or on his time. . . .
>
> I . . . . recall how upon two occasions a good head-light has let me see a huge pile of rocks on the track in one of our rocky mountain canons, just in time to let myself and fireman strike *terra firma,* about three seconds before the head-light went out forever against the cold stone.[2]

In another communication there was a condemnation of the seniority system of promotion by which lazy, stupid, incompetent firemen became engineers. Another told of a habit of lying about accidents that had grown up among railroad men because men had been discharged for trivial offenses. Now it had come to be accepted that no accident report by an engineer or conductor could be true. Hill told the story of a young engineer who, on his maiden trip, "made a fly run into a siding through four feet of snow, and telescoped six empty box cars." When the frightened youth started to write his report of the accident,

[2] Vol. 10, no. 16, p. 1, April 16, 1887.

two older engineers counseled him to say that he had "coupled into the cars and pulled them to pieces trying to get them out of the siding."

One good single-handed liar on a division of a railroad can make a master mechanic distrust every plug puller from the "pony" to the pay car engine. . . . It makes a man hate his mother to make out a true report of an accident and know that his superior officer will only read it as a matter of form, and all the time is thinking, What a gifted liar the cuss is.[3]

Through 1887 the copy came thick and fast: letters signed John A. Hill from Pueblo, South Pueblo, or Denver, until before the year was out there was one of the breezy pieces in practically every issue. To the editors and publishers of the *American Machinist* here was a writer to be conjured with. And, as 1888 arrived, a niche opened in the American Machinist Publishing Company that seemed just about perfect for a first-rate practical locomotive engineer who could write.

3 The paper by 1888 had outgrown its sixteen-page dress. At the same time its conservative publishers refused to enlarge it. To them its strict formula gave it dignity. The answer must be, therefore, to limit its material, to concentrate it more precisely on a single subject, that of machine tools. By this time Horace Swetland's *Power* was thriving and the *Machinist,* in its articles on steam engines, was overlapping or duplicating *Power's* field. It was decided to leave steam engineering for *Power.* But the railroad material which was taking up most of the space was too popular to let go. Also there was no railroad magazine which appealed mainly to the grimy-handed runners and firemen. So the *Machinist's* publishers decided to start a new magazine called *Locomotive Engineer* to catch all the overflow railroad material from the older paper. This was one of the first of these ameba-like splits that would characterize industrial publishing from now on as industry became more and more specialized.

[3] *Ibid.,* vol. 10, no. 1, p. 7, January 8, 1887.

"Locomotive Engineer," vol. 1, no. 1, January, 1888.

LOCOMOTIVE ENGINEER.

DEVOTED TO
THE SPECIAL INTERESTS OF
LOCOMOTIVE ENGINEERS AND FIREMEN
AND TO
LOCOMOTIVE MAINTENANCE AND REPAIRS.

I. NO. I. NEW YORK, JANUARY, 1888. $1.00 per Year. or 10c. a copy.

m the Publishers' Standpoint.

it very many railway master mechan-
id executive officers were once loco-
e engineers and firemen is well
 among railway men. Such officials,
ore, have a personal, as well as a
sional concern in matters relating
 locomotive.

t many of the enginemen of to-day
tep from the heroisms and responsi-

es of the cab, to places of mechanical
executive control, is as certain as any
e event can be. To such, also, the
ods and appliances of the repair shop
ss a double interest. Taking the
notive as a complete machine at the
 of the designer and builder, it is
nt, therefore, that there is, or should
 intimate relation existing between
en who run it (many of whom have
nore or less shop experience), and the
 house and repair shop employes, and
r mechanics with whom they co-op-
in the task of keeping it in condi-
o run. That this army of workers
nown in railway circles to wield
fluence in those circles, none the
otent because not fairly estimated
outside, may be stated with entire confidence.

Unhampered by exclusive connection with either of the grand divisions of this army, the aim of this journal will be to indicate a common ground, upon which earnest workers in all can meet in the interest of progress, and to claim for all the meed of recognition which is their due. The editor, John A. Hill, who has been for several years connected with the motive power department of the Denver and Rio Grande R. R. as fireman and engineer, with corresponding shop experience, introduces himself upon another page. We bespeak for him the good will and co-operation of all.

Naming Engines.

The old time practice of naming engines is coming into vogue again on some roads that long ago abandoned it as foolish. There is no doubt that the public like the idea, and a hundred people will talk about the feats of the "Quickstep" that would never remember the 194 for four days. For passenger service we believe it pays.

Vreeland's Transfer Jack for Removing and Replacing Locomotive Drivers and Trucks.

It is often desirable or necessary in railroad repair shops to remove a pair of drivers or a truck from under a heavy engine. The usual method is to raise the engine up by four hydraulic or screw jacks, placed under each corner, until the wheel can be rolled out. This required the

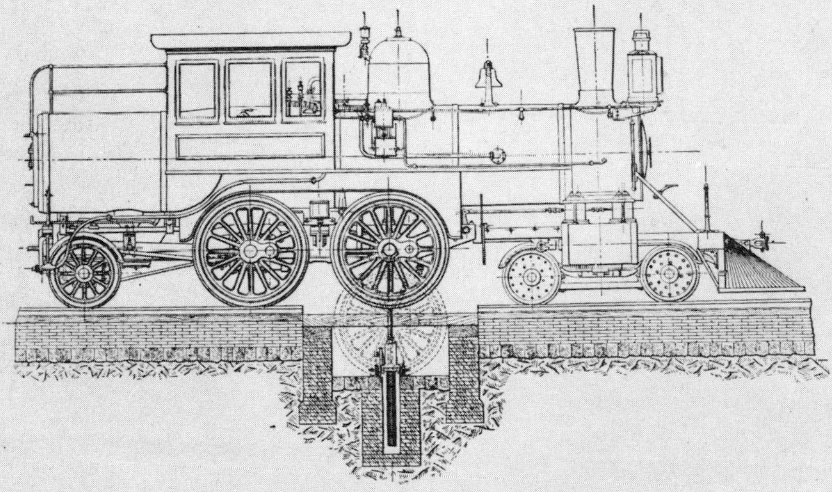

APPLICATION OF TRANSFER JACK.

lifting of the whole machine from fifteen to twenty-four inches. It not only makes the engine too high to work on without staging, but, as the jacks must be used elsewhere, the ponderous boiler is blocked up and left there—a dangerous and unhandy arrangement. Some very large shops have "drop tables" and "steam lifts" to do some of this work, but these are cumbersome, expensive, and occupy valuable floor space.

Endless annoyance of this kind induced J. H. Vreeland, master mechanic of the eastern division of the New York, Lake Erie and Western Railroad, to invent and build at his shops in Jersey City the jack here described and illustrated.

By reference to the cut of the tool itself

The first task was to find an editor. The publishers knew an expert in every phase of practical railroading. There was, for example, an ex-engineer, Henry Colvin, now manager of the Rue Manufacturing Company in Philadelphia. The publishers knew Colvin because the Rue company had advertised its railroad equipment in the *Machinist.* They asked him to recommend an editor and were not surprised when he said the ideal man was a Pueblo fellow named Hill, *if* he could be induced to leave his engine.

"Of course," said Miller. "He is our most regular contributor. And one of our best writers."

That was how John Hill came into the publishing business: one of the most astonishing changes of career in American history.

CHAPTER EIGHT

Machine Tools

A glance at the first issue of *Locomotive Engineer* in January, 1888, suggests that John Hill wrote the whole of it. If others contributed, he must have revamped the contributions. The language is consistently direct, hard-hitting, and colloquial—quite free from the "literary" style that makes parts of the parent paper such hard going for today's reader.

On page two is a fictional piece entitled "Fighting Against Nature" with the thinly disguised by-line of John Alexander. Its argument is that you should not try to make a boy who wants to be a locomotive engineer into a doctor or lawyer. All Alexander's boys are eager to become engineers. The eldest, Harry, is already a fireman. This idea that a white-collar job is more honorable than that of a skilled mechanic is hurting many boys.

I am proud of my calling [Alexander concludes] and if my boys want to follow in it and excel their father, I am not going to fight against their natures as I know many an engineer is doing today.

Here is the signal that *Locomotive Engineer,* in addition to its other functions, is to be the vehicle for Hill's creative impulse. Nearly every issue from this beginning would carry something by John Alexander. Eventually he would do a series of short-short stories whose hero, Engineer Jim Skeevers, would run the gamut of railroad experience. As we read these sketches today, they bring to us the charm of an era forever past—prestreamlined—when human judgment was not bolstered by any electronic device and the lives of passengers and crew depended almost wholly on the eye and hand of the runner. But to the reader of the 1890s, the little tales pointed up hundreds of practical hints; they may well have prevented wrecks as well as stepped up efficiency in cab, roundhouse, and shop.

John Alexander's dinner pail.

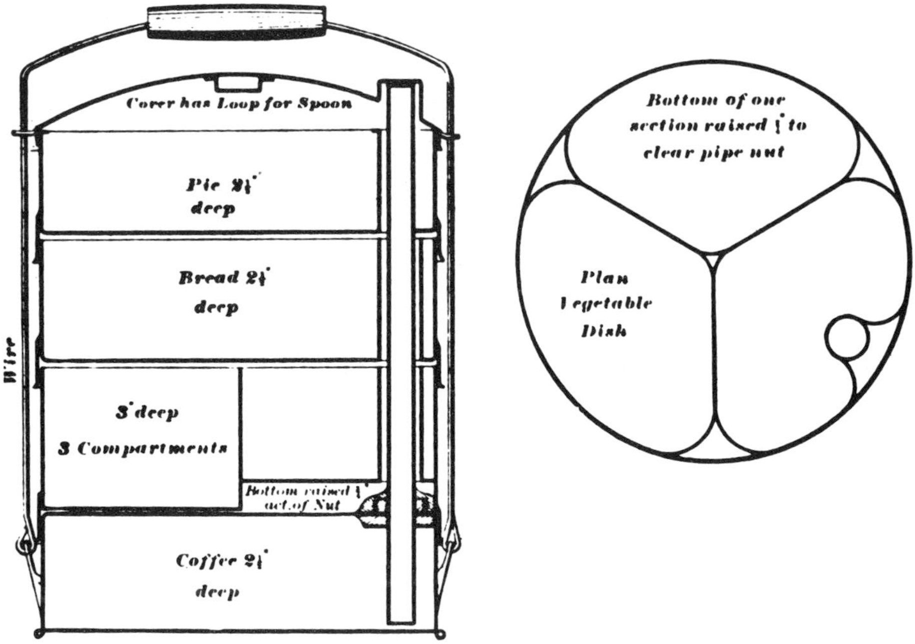

When John Alexander wrote a letter to the editor describing an ideal dinner pail for an engineer to carry in his cab—a single container for pie, bread, meat, vegetables, and coffee—he started an avalanche of correspondence. In May, 1889, the paper took note of this.

> Ever since John Alexander [wrote John Alexander Hill] gave a description of his ideal dinner pail, we have been receiving letters asking if they could be purchased, if we had a picture of one, would we please give Mr. Alexander's address, and one man sent $2 and said, "Get me one, if it costs $10."

Hill told Alexander about this and Alexander replied with an elaborate description, a diagram, and an account of how he once got a tinsmith to make the pail but it was immediately stolen. "I wouldn't care so much," he added, "but I had left a quarter section of cream pie . . . and the deep-dyed villain took that, too."

In another early issue an anonymous article, "The Jack of All Trades," establishes a landmark.

John Alexander's Dinner Pail.

Ever since John Alexander gave a description of his ideal dinner pail, we have been receiving letters asking if they could be purchased, if we had a picture of one, would we please give Mr. Alexander's address, and one man sent $2 and said, "Get me one, if it costs $10." We wrote to our festive correspondent, and depicted our woes to him, and he answered as follows:

Editor The Locomotive Engineer:

"Uneasy lies the head that is a clown's." This is the eleventh letter from you about dinner pail. Can't a fellow say what he wants, without all the people in the land rising up as one man, and saying they want it too? Did I tell everybody from Dan to Bersheba that I had dinner pails to sell or give away? I had one of those pails made, as near as a country tinner could build it, with no other facilities than a soldering iron and a piece of rosin, and it looks a little (not very much) like the sectional sketch sent you herewith. I don't know which is the worst, the drawing or the pail, as I have no means of comparison—some fiend in human form nipped the pail the second trip out—I wouldn't care so much, but I had left a quarter section of cream pie to top off on after I registered, and the deep-dyed villain took that, too.

Well, here are directions for building and operating the device, such as it is. The bottom is 2½ deep by 8 inches across, and the brass nut is soldered into it and tinned over, to keep it clean. The pipe is ½ inch copper, and tinned or nickel-plated, outside and in; this makes it easy to clean It extends to top of pail, so that a man can drink without taking the pail apart or getting cinders stuck in the lariax, or something, of his Adam's apple. The next story is partitioned off into three compartments, as shown in the separate sketch. These are for vegetables, and when the pail is put on a stove or the boiler head to get the coffee hot, it gets the whole lunch warm. I would place the hole for pipe in one of the partitions, but for the fact that one of the sections has to have its bottom raised to clear the pipe nut, corners are rounded.

The other sections are shown and sizes marked on, in sketch; any one that knows enough to eat a lunch can see that he could open one of these sections without the other, by raising up and swinging on the pipe. I did think the bail should snap around the pipe, but the plan shown works O. K. It would be better if the pipe extended through the cover and had a cap on it, but I preferred the style shown, because it was easier made and kept clean. If there is as much talk as all this about a jim-crow dinner pail, it would seem to a man up a gooseberry bush as if it would pay some outfit to make a few and dispose of them to the meek and hungry car hands who read the L. E. Should any tin peddler come to you with propositions tending to make him the bloated monopolist and millionaire manufacturer of John Alexander's great and only fodder can, inform him that I seek the good of all mankind, and will therefore sell, barter or bequeath all my right, title and interest in the aforesaid dyspepsia dispenser for a small consideration in the current coin of the realm.

JOHN ALEXANDER.

> He used to be the mechanical oracle of every community, great and small [this piece begins]. He could patch up a machine that the machinist swore wasn't worth the rivets in the patch. . . . He could repair a watch, grind skates, put rivets into bladeless knives, make humming tops and botch up good work. . . . He was attached to the machine shop and roundhouse about the same as a liveried fool was to the court of foolish kings. His work is over and his days are numbered. This is . . . the age of specialties.[1]

With so much lightness and gaiety interspersed among the practical articles on steam gauges, oil cups, coupling, switch keys, headlight wicks, valves, signals, and throttles, it is not surprising that *Locomotive Engineer* became exceedingly popular. To business-paper journalism, Hill had brought something wholly new. Although its circulation was supposed to be mainly among railroad workers, it soon carried extensive advertising including that of the principal locomotive works. In a few years it was making more money than the *American Machinist,* whose bills it helped pay.

2 In the 1890s John Hill, restless, ambitious, and energetic, was no longer content to be an editor only. Furthermore, he was not happy about the ultraconservative policies of the publishers of the paper that he had built from scratch. He wanted even more than the princely salary of $2,800 a year to which he had been raised. He wanted a share in the ever-increasing profits of *Locomotive Engineer.* He wanted greater control over the advertising. He wanted, in short, to be the publisher rather than the editor; he wanted ownership instead of a salaried job. But this would require money and John Hill had not saved enough from his salary to meet even the lowest price Miller and Moore might consider.

He happened, however, to have a friend and neighbor in East Orange, New Jersey, where he had settled, who was both a rail-

[1] *Locomotive Engineer,* vol. 1, no. 2, p. 2, Feb., 1888.

road man and a capitalist. Angus Sinclair, Scottish born, was a university graduate, a specialist in locomotive engineering, an editor, and a writer who had published two books on technical subjects. Although he had once been a roundhouse foreman, he was more versed in theory than in practical railroad work. In its early years he had been a constant contributor to *American Machinist* and had even served for a year or so on its editorial staff.

Investing the money he had made in these activities, Sinclair had played in luck. He had known enough to see the high potential of the Westinghouse air brake. It is probable that even this scarcely brought him a real fortune in modern terms, but there was enough to liberate John Hill's paper. In addition, Sinclair was earning some $5,000 a year as editor of the *National Car and Locomotive Builder,* so the risk was not formidable. If the owners could be induced to sell for a reasonable price, Sinclair would be willing to supply the cash and take Hill's note for his share. So Hill talked to Horace Miller and Lycurgus Moore.

These owners were reluctant to lose so lucrative a property. At the same time they knew that John Hill *was* the *Locomotive Engineer.* Without him the paper would be like the play of *Hamlet* with Hamlet removed. He had become irreplaceable. There was an intensely personal relationship between the editor and his readers. His personality had jumped across from the printed page to the hearts of both subscribers and advertisers. Now unless Miller and Moore would let him buy the paper, he would resign from its editorial chair. Furthermore—and this was the argument which has closed so many deals in the publishing world—Hill would start a competing paper. So the price agreed upon was only $6,000 cash. Sinclair paid it and took Hill's note for a half interest.

The transaction was completed in October, 1891, nearly four years after *Locomotive Engineer* first started on its brilliant career. Sinclair thought its title narrowed its interest to runners and he wanted the magazine to appeal also to men on a more theoretical level—engineers in the larger sense. So the name was changed to *Locomotive Engineering,* and perhaps this was the start of Hill's waning interest. Also, Sinclair wanted to be an editor. He suggested to Hill that he manage the paper.

"Hell!" John Hill is supposed to have remarked, "I don't know anything about the business end!"

"You know more than I do," replied Sinclair. "I don't know a check from a draft. So if this paper is going to be successful, you've got to be the business manager and I'll handle the editorial policy."

This was Hill's entry into publishing. From then on he was as skillful a publisher as he had been an editor. But from then on, too, his eyes began to move over wider and wider horizons.

3 While all these things had been happening, the parent paper, *American Machinist,* was going through troubled times. From the start policy about its editorial content had wavered. Beginning strictly in the machinist field, devoting most of its space to machine tools, it had branched out, first into the stationary engines that furnished power to the tools, then into foundries, blast furnaces, engines for locomotives, steamships, agricultural machinery, and all sorts of manufacturing machinery. It had extended finally into the entire area of the mechanical engineer's interest.

That area in the 1880s was large and vaguely defined. Mechanical engineering as a profession was still young. Specialization had not yet arrived. A mechanical engineer, holding a degree from a university or technical school, was expected to understand the embryonic electrical power, steam power in all its phases, productive machinery, powered metal-working tools, and materials. And the editors and publishers of the *American Machinist* felt that the paper must follow the engineer wherever he went.

One reason for this was an event of major importance that occurred in the paper's third year. Between 1877 when the magazine began and 1879, the paper had brought together through its columns all sorts of people interested in machinery. They came to think of the paper as the first meeting place they had found.

Local engineers' clubs existed in towns but there was no national society. These readers and contributors from all parts of the country came to feel that some sort of common focus of assembly should be set up so that they could meet each other in the flesh and exchange ideas. A Cornell professor of engineering, John Edson Sweet, put this feeling into words in letters to Alexander Lyman Holley who had introduced the Bessemer steel process to America, to Robert Henry Thurston of the Stevens Institute of Technology, and to Jackson Bailey, the *Machinist's* editor. Bailey and Lewis Lyne, the paper's mechanical engineer, were immediately enthusiastic about Sweet's suggestion and offered the *Machinist's* cooperation.

Sweet then wrote to a carefully selected list of engineers.

> It having been suggested [his letter read] by several prominent engineers that a national association of mechanical engineers would be desirable, and a meeting for the purpose of taking steps to organize such a society being in order, your presence is hereby requested at the office of the *American Machinist,* 96 Fulton Street, New York, the sixteenth day of February, 1880, at 1 o'clock sharp, at which time the necessary steps for organizing such an association should be made. . . . [2]

Thirty came. The list includes the leading American engineers of the time. They represented many phases which afterward became distinct specialties. Charles W. Copeland was a marine engineer; Charles E. Emery was interested in large central-power stations; William P. Trowbridge was a professor at the Columbia School of Mines; and Henry R. Worthington was the designer of the celebrated Worthington pump. There were also editors of technical papers and a Federal government man. Perhaps it is not surprising that disagreement grew into dispute and, when the meeting broke up, it looked as if the project had been lost. At this point, however, Horace B. Miller, the *Machinist's* business manager, stepped into the breach with genial hospitality.

[2] Quoted by Henry H. Norris, *The Story of the "American Machinist,"* unpublished manuscript in McGraw-Hill Archives, p. 14.

"We are all tired," he said in effect, "and this little office is confining. I invite you all to be my guests for dinner at the Astor House where we can continue our conversation under more congenial circumstances."

It happened the Horace Miller, in addition to being a publisher of some talent, was a wine expert. When the guests arrived, therefore, at the Astor the conversation turned from engineering to the remarkable selection of vintages Miller had picked to accompany the many courses of the dinner. By the time the liqueurs arrived, everyone had forgotten the differences that had caused the conflict. An organization meeting was agreed upon, the time and place set, and thus began the American Society of Mechanical Engineers, one of the world's leading professional societies. Nothing could have given the *American Machinist* more enduring prestige.

The event, however, may have been a factor in the paper's temporary financial decline. The interest of engineers of so many different stripes with which, in a sense, the *Machinist* had now become identified, led it into such a variety of fields that readers began to complain. We have seen how the overloaded railroad department was taken over by another magazine in 1888. But readers and advertisers were confused. What public was the paper really aimed at? The machine-tool people who thought they had been its original inspiration were losing interest and dropping off.

A conflict was precipitated by the presence on the staff of a man with a machine-shop background—another Miller no relation to Horace—who was insistent on narrowing the paper's scope and focusing on a highly specialized circulation. There was no doubt in Fred Miller's mind that the machine-tool industry had grown large and important enough to have a magazine of its own. Here was another early case of that process that would go on endlessly in those pregnant years of multiplying technics when the growing industrial and business papers would be forced to divide and subdivide in adjustment. But Fred Miller had his troubles. The *American Machinist's* owners were fearful of changes. With dignified horror they recoiled from any concession that might be made

Offices of "American Machinist" where the American Society of Mechanical Engineers was founded, 1880.

to advertisers. Advertising was still looked upon, even in the nineties, as a slightly disreputable necessity—and no wonder, considering its historical background!

4 It is probable that John Hill, in those transitional days, looked with interest over the head of *Machinist's* fat child at the slimmer and paler parent. The *Machinist,* after all, had been the first vehicle of his talent. Sitting in his cab during smooth runs or long stops, he had read every word of every issue. From the beginning, he had been aware of its enormous potential. He had, too, admired its honesty. A paper which in those days would state its circulation on its masthead, in figures too conservative to be doubted, was rare indeed. A paper which repeated in every issue, in italics, that it would never accept pay for anything printed in its "reading columns" shared the reputation of Caesar's wife! And quixotic as their restriction of advertising space might be, the publishers certainly were displaying the policy of Reader First—a doctrine in which Hill had almost a religious faith.

Like all dynamic men, John Hill in his prime in his mid-thirties, was restless, looking always for new roads down which he might venture. The cab of a locomotive, even when it had been transmuted into an office in downtown New York, had grown too small for him. Now that he had learned the business end of *Locomotive Engineering,* the publishing virus was in his blood. For a publisher one paper was not enough. With the experience he had gained in the Sinclair partnership, the things he could do with such a magazine as *American Machinist* would put it on the sure way to success.

At the same time, Fred Miller, a close friend of Hill's, knew that his editorial aims would prosper under Hill as they had never done with the old publishers. By 1895 he had become editor of the *Machinist,* but by then the paper seems to have reached its all-time low financially. Horace Miller and Lycurgus Moore had sold their interests. Under the new owners who were unfamiliar with machinist interests and were thought to have bought it as a speculation, the paper had gone from bad to worse in spite of the high quality of its editorial staff, which now included Frank Richards, a practical expert, and the celebrated mechanical engineer, Frederick A. Halsey. So Fred Miller worked on Angus Sinclair as well as Hill, and in 1895 a deal was consummated by which the controlling interest in the American Machinist Publishing Company passed to the owners of *Locomotive Engineering.* On January 2, 1896, the old magazine appeared transformed with new format, new bulk, new paper, new typography, and a breeziness on its editorial page that was like a breath of fresh air from Colorado.

Announcing the new 9-by-12-inch dimensions, the fact that the type was for the first time machine-set, and a new electrical department, the new owners added that there had been a break in the old advertising policy—yet not a clean break. As there was now double the quantity of reading matter, advertising pages could likewise be increased. However, the advertising pages were "so attached that they may be taken off when the numbers are to be permanently bound, thus reducing the bulk of the bound volume, which we think very desirable. Advertisements are things of today"! The historian must think otherwise and he is grateful that a few wise possessors of business-paper volumes did not heed this editorial's advice.

5 Of the next phase we have little record. Businessmen in those days kept no memoranda of their private conversations. From what we know of John Hill's character, we may suspect that even in his thirties he was, like James McGraw, uneasy in any equal partnership. But if there were disagreements between him and Sinclair, embellished perhaps by the celebrated picturesqueness of Hill's language, the sound of them has long been hushed.

We must rely, then, on the story told by one who knew both men well.

Angus Sinclair, it must be admitted [wrote Fred H. Colvin], was something less than a zealot about machinery, being more interested in a hunting lodge in Scotland while Hill carried on alone with the bulk of the work. Angus did not get on well at all with Fred Miller, particularly after Fred had become editor-in-chief of the *Machinist.* These and other sources of friction soon led to a dissolution of the Hill-Sinclair partnership.

John made Angus a give-or-take offer when they were about to split up. Each member of the original partnership would take either the *Machinist* or *Locomotive Engineering* but not both; and would run it independently of the other from here on out. Angus, who had been the *Locomotive's* angel, surprised everyone by choosing the *Machinist,* about which he knew decidedly little; it was thought that he did so only because he wanted the satisfaction of sending a cable to Fred Miller, who was in Europe at the time, telling him that he was fired! He was finally persuaded that the railroad paper was his best bet, for it was in this field in which he was best known and in which he had made his reputation.

Sinclair must have realized that he could never have handled the *Machinist,* and would probably have run it into a fair-sized hole in a couple of years.[3]

So Sinclair sold Hill his rights in *American Machinist,* Hill sold Sinclair his rights in *Locomotive Engineering,* and both went their separate ways. It is suggestive of Hill's confidence in his own convictions that he not only bought the *Machinist* at its all-time low but bought it in a bad depression year. But he knew precisely what he wanted to do, and with the control of the company in his hands he started the business on its upward climb within two years. In 1899 the net profit of the American Machinist Press was about $28,000; in 1900 it was nearly $60,000. Two years later the American Machinist Press, Inc. had become the Hill Publishing Company. This, in the next fifteen years, would prove to be one of the top leaders in American business publishing and would have, perhaps, only one rival worthy of its steel.

[3] Fred H. Colvin, *60 Years with Men and Machines,* McGraw-Hill Book Company, Inc., New York, 1947, p. 103.

CHAPTER NINE

Electrical Revolution

In the twenty years from the mid-seventies to the mid-nineties, the electrical revolution changed the face of the world. In 1875 there had seemed to be no use for the elusive electric force except the telegraph. It was true that scientific giants like Michael Faraday and Joseph Henry had discovered important truths and worked out theories of high potential, but so, a century before, had Benjamin Franklin. It was true that the poverty-stricken inventor, Thomas Davenport, had made a motor by tearing his wife's precious silk wedding dress into shreds to insulate his wire as Henry had prescribed, but his motor did little except revolve. It was true that various Englishmen, all the way from Humphry Davy in 1809 to Joseph Swan in 1877, had produced both arc

Pearl Street Station.

lights and incandescent lamps of a sort, but none was of any practical value. All these things were mere experiments, and even Bell's telephone in 1876, which promised such miracles, was still in the realm of communication: in effect only a refinement of the telegraph.

In 1878 the motor was still a toy. An editorial in the *American Machinist* for May of that year stated:

> Electro-motors have been made to develop more than a horse-power, though we have never seen one work well above a dog-power—indeed, they appear to best advantage at less than a cat power.

Then, following Edison's demonstration of his incandescent lamp in 1879, new practical applications of electricity came so thick and fast that everything seemed to be happening at once.

In 1881 Werner Siemens built the first permanent electric railway in Germany. In 1882 came the Pearl Street Station in New York, distributing current for lighting through the city. In 1883 the first course in electrical engineering was given at Cornell. The year 1884 saw the first electric passenger elevator. In the next two years came electric welding, the electrolytic process for the extraction of aluminum, and the first alternating-current power plant. By 1890 the induction motor, electric freight locomotives, the telautograph, power transmission, the electric sewing machine, and wireless telegraphy had appeared, and in cities all over the United States electric trolley cars were replacing horsecars and cable cars. The next year saw the first electric automobile. By 1893 a large Connecticut manufacturing plant was using electrically driven machinery, and in 1895 Frank Sprague perfected his multiple-unit control, opening the way to all the elevated and subway railway development of the future as well as to the electrification of the steam railroad. And in the same year the great hydroelectric power plant at Niagara Falls started its three 5,000-horse-power generators.[1]

In a score of years we had gone from the dim gaslit world of the seventies to a brilliantly illuminated scene alive with a new kind of power. Visibly ahead lay the vista in which mass production, mass distribution, and mass communication would redesign society.

2 For ten of those years a young man just entering on a career of industrial publishing watched the kaleidoscopic changes with growing fascination. From the time he came to New York and met some of the entrepreneurs who were electrifying the advertising pages of the *Street Railway Journal,* James H. McGraw had been aware that the revolution had begun. More and more closely he watched the developments as the eighties merged into the nineties. The *Journal* had come wholly into his hands. His personal interest in it had become undivided. His other railway appliance paper seems to have been sold although the record is not clear.

[1] A useful chronology of inventions and technological developments is in *American Machinist,* vol. 96, no. 24, pp. 3–18, November, 1952.

But as he built the *Street Railway Journal* into a paper entirely dedicated to electric traction, he watched the growth of other electrical papers. He and his editors read a monthly called the *Electrical Engineer* and a weekly called *Electrical World.* Perhaps the editors read the text while he concentrated on the advertising pages. McGraw's interest in the electrical revolution was not a technical interest. He knew and cared little about volts, amperes, and ohms; what fascinated him was the vast business complex that would grow out of them. But he was perceptive enough to know that the only way a periodical could participate fully in that business was by appealing to the industrial leaders with newsy, authoritative, and readable text.

Make a paper interesting, he said again and again, and the advertisers would flock to it. He proved his theory in his own *Street Railway Journal.* In its first decade the *Journal's* number of advertising pages grew from 310 in the first volume to 2,700 in the tenth. There were 476 advertisements in volume 1 and 3,852 in volume 10. It is true that the street-railway business had greatly expanded in that period; yet there were competing papers in the

Lanterns in front of the Plaza Hotel and the entrance to the Manhattan Athletic Club. (Outcault drawings.)

field whose growth did not approach that of the McGraw *Journal.* How, then, did he make his paper interesting?

The answer to that question takes us beyond the *Street Railway Journal* into a field outside it but surrounding it, for the men he chose to make the *Journal* interesting were men familiar not merely with traction but with every phase of electrical development over which the country's greatest industries were becoming concerned. Henry W. Blake and Edward E. Higgins had both graduated from the Massachusetts Institute of Technology as electrical engineers. Both had served practical apprenticeships with the Sprague Electric Railway and Motor Company. An editor with less formal technical education but with a strong mechanical and inventive bent was Charles B. Fairchild, who by wide travel and intensive field work brought the *Journal* and its industry together and thus carried out McGraw's second basic aim: to make the paper essential to its readers. None of these men could ever be wholly confined within the street-railway realm. If you rode a streetcar to the end of the line you found yourself in a power plant and, once there, the hum of the generators drew

Two views of the Chicago elevated. (Outcault drawings.)

your imagination into the farthest Elysian fields of the electrical future.

But in 1891 the *Street Railway Journal* was further enriched by a manager who was familiar with the business aspect of every electrical industry. The hiring of this man was the first signal of a future event of unprecedented significance to our story. The man was Clarence Stump. James McGraw found him in the offices of the paper which at the time covered the whole electrical field more completely than any other. The paper was *Electrical World* and Stump was its business manager. McGraw made him vice president of the Street Railway Publishing Company and business manager of the *Street Railway Journal.*

But what, in 1891, was *Electrical World?* We caught a glimpse of this journal when we were spotting journalistic landmarks of American technological history. We saw it grow out of the gay little telegrapher's *The Operator* when the operators proved too poor to support a magazine whose purpose was mainly recreational. To follow the evolution of the paper is to follow the change and growth of the American mind, individual and social, under the impact of the colossal new force.

3 The charm of *The Operator* had been in its intimate personal appeal to a relatively small group of skilled men whose life and trade were new enough to keep it a sort of fraternity. Their pleasures and hardships were the same and their understanding of a code that was mysterious to others set them apart. In 1874 there was still romance in the sending and receiving of messages through night and storm, floodtime and snowfall. The operators were in a position to know a thousand secrets of love, business, and crime. Daily and nightly they tapped out words of life and death. They were superior folk in a world still surprised by magnetic communication.

In its second issue *The Operator's* editor announced that "all literature of a heavy or scientific character has been purposely eschewed, and nothing has been permitted in its columns but that which is pleasant, mirthful and often facetious." The result was an assortment of personal gossip written in a jargon that was quite unintelligible to anyone outside the fraternity. Its outbursts of "mirth" and "facetiousness" suggest that telegraphers of the seventies must have had extremely juvenile risibilities. Nevertheless, the little paper had a substantial following of readers, contributors, and correspondents.

In 1875 the paper was bought by a dynamic Irishman, William J. Johnston, and its character changed slightly. Even before he assumed full control, but while he was an editor, he had got into an animated scrap with the Western Union Telegraph Company from which he had emerged victorious. An operator himself, employed by Western Union, he had edited *The Operator* in his spare time. In its columns he had criticized his employer and the company had sent him an ultimatum. Either he must give up the paper or quit his job. His decision was instantaneous. By the same messenger who brought him this message he returned his resignation from Western Union. This was on December 20, 1875. On January 1, 1876, as sole proprietor, he spread on his paper's editorial page the full story of the controversy with the comment that Western Union's attempt to "suppress" *The Operator* had been an outrage on liberty of the press, intolerable in free America.

This demonstration of courage gave *The Operator* a new lease on life. But to Johnston its function was not purely recreational. It was time, he thought, that his readers grew up. Edison had gone from the telegrapher's key into the vast, mysterious realms of electrical science. Why should not other operators do the same? Johnston knew that many of them were avid for technical learning. He therefore interspersed the juvenile contents of his paper with more serious articles. And he changed the subtitle from "The Telegraph Operator's Journal" to "A Journal of Scientific Telegraphy."

In the next six years Johnston's altered magazine attracted some thoughtful contributors. One of these was a French Canadian, Cyprian Odilon Mailloux, who had migrated as a boy to Massachusetts, had studied medicine under Oliver Wendell Holmes, and had been dissuaded from a physician's career by the portents of the coming electrical revolution. The other was Thomas Commerford Martin, an Englishman who had turned to electricity from the ministry and had come to America to work with Edison. Both men had a flair for writing and both had found *The Operator* a vehicle for their talents—Mailloux as contributor, Martin as editor. The articles by Mailloux on electric lighting, beginning in October, 1882, soon became celebrated for their clarity. Still today they could be read as an elementary course of instruction for the electrical beginner. Thus we see, even in the old *Operator,* that educational germ that seems to have existed in so many of the ancestors of the McGraw-Hill publications.

These scientific additions, however, turned that formerly folksy paper into a sort of bastard publication. The old readers complained that it was no longer either fish or fowl. Members of the operators' fraternity were bored or bewildered by the serious trend. More advanced readers were contemptuous of the old gossipy and facetious relics that Johnston would not let go. But the deciding factor was the concert of opinion of Mailloux and Martin. These men were far more aware than he of what was happening in the world outside. They were constant readers of technical papers, foreign as well as American. They not only sensed the vision of Edison but they knew also of the experiments of Sir William Thomson, of Camille Faure, of Josiah Gibbs and Lucien Gaulard, of Werner Siemens and, nearer at hand, of Charles Van Depoele, Leo Daft, and Charles F. Brush. This, they told Johnston, was the psychological instant in which to start a leader among American technical publications—a paper with the dignity of England's *Electrician* or France's *L'Electricien.* They had trouble weaning Johnston away from his commitments to the telegraphers. But he compromised at last and out of his compromise came the *Electrical World.*

The compromise combined the old title with the new. In the first issue of the new weekly, *The Operator and Electrical World,* an editorial maintained that inasmuch as *The Operator* had "grown to be an epitome of the electrical world we should take pride in announcing that fact in its title." There was, nevertheless, an immediate howl from the old guard. In vain they searched among the ponderous articles for the "pleasant, mirthful and often facetious" items. Even the poetry (which continued) was no longer rollicking but had taken on a heavy and dignified meter. The dear old *Operator* had been swallowed! What solace was this erudite reading after a weary day at the telegraph key?

So, after almost four months, Johnston made a second concession which must have made everybody happy. We can almost hear the gasp of relief coming from Martin and Mailloux as the word *Operator* was dropped from the head, leaving *Electrical World* unencumbered by shadows from the past. And the nostalgic fraternity brothers were delighted to see their old organ reappear—a separate paper, all their own, and wholly unscientific.

An editorial entitled "Sub-Dividing the Current"—a figurative use of a popular technical term of the time—spoke almost weepingly of "our old telegraphic friends—those who were the stronghold of *The Operator* in the days of its struggling infancy—who miss the old paper with its fund of entertainment, of airy professional gossip, and of fraternal good-fellowship." In the revived *Operator* "it will be our aim to provide a medium for recreation from the toil of the office and the exchange where the existence of such troublesome things as induction, resistance, electromotive force, algebraic formulae and geometrical symbols may, for the time, be ignored; where the daily life and personal gossip of the fraternity may be set forth, the latest amusing incidents of the profession enjoyed, confidences exchanged, old times recalled, and grievances discussed and righted, undisturbed by the rumble of the dynamo or the glare of the electric light."

Despite all this sentiment, however, the revival was too late. The old-timers did not realize it but in less than ten years the fraternity had dissolved. Hundreds and thousands of new men, and even women, had entered the field. These mediocre persons, as the old-timers thought them, looked upon telegraphy as a humdrum job. New routine performance had taken away the glamour of the perilous days. Telegraphy was no longer mysterious; it was the merest commonplace. Thus, as a periodical can hardly be supported solely by the nostalgia of aging men, *The Operator's* twilight was brief. It died in September, 1885, and was buried in a general publication entitled *Johnston's Journal: An Illustrated Magazine for the People*—a venture far from our concern.

Meanwhile *Electrical World* went on to glory. To its staff came Nathaniel Keith, founder of the American Institute of Electrical Engineers, and Joseph Wetzler, the first graduate of Stevens Institute to win an electrical engineer's degree. By midsummer, 1887, the paper had increased its size in four and a half years from eight pages of text and six of advertising to twenty-one of text and thirty-five of advertising—an exact quadrupling of overall volume. The changes in the advertising are as revealing as those in the reading columns of the progress of the electrical revolution. By 1887 the watches, ornamental clocks, parlor organs, furniture, jewelry, and best-selling novels had been replaced by dynamos and motors, lighting systems, storage batteries, transformers, wire, and cables.

Then, in the next three years, while the prosperity continued, there were internal troubles. It has been said of Johnston that "his inflexibility of purpose at times gave rise to friction in his relations with men."[2] The nature of the disagreements is unrecorded and the principals are dead. There was, after all, a happy ending in the events that occurred as the century closed. It is probable that the causes were financial, as the rupture followed Johnston's incorporation of his business and the apportionment of stock. In any case, editors Martin and Wetzler and business manager Stump, the men who had been largely responsible for the paper's rise, quit abruptly in the first months of 1890. And the worst of it was that the editors joined the staff of the *World's*

[2] From the obituary of William J. Johnston in *Electrical World*, vol. 19, no. 5, p. 312, May, 1907.

bitterest rival, the *Electrical Engineer*. The next year Stump joined McGraw.

At this point let us follow Martin and Wetzler and discover what sort of journal they moved to and what they did with it when they moved. This will not be a digression from our theme for it, too, the *Electrical Engineer*, was a McGraw-Hill ancestor.

4 The *Electrical Engineer* was the offspring of a little paper called *The Electrician* after the London journal of that name. *The Electrician* arrived nearly simultaneously with Edison's Pearl Street station and, as we saw, ran a pretty story about the horseshoe filaments glowing in the stores.

The word *electrician* in January, 1882, meant anyone who was interested in electricity. At the same time the term was beginning to be applied also to the overall-clad men who fixed short circuits. By 1884 the editors were apparently uneasy about the new application of the term for they changed the title to *Electrician and Electrical Engineer*. By 1888 *Electrician* was dropped from the title entirely.

Before Martin and Wetzler joined the staff of the *Electrical Engineer* in 1890, it was still a monthly and was not, therefore, a dangerous rival of the *Electrical World*. The first thing Martin and Wetzler did, however, was to persuade its publisher to make it a weekly. There began then a keen competition between the two papers and Johnston had to use all his skill and experience to keep his paper in the lead.

His first move was to replace the renegade editors with a man of top rank, Dr. Louis Bell. Bell was young, energetic, brilliant, and had as good a technical education as was available in America. A graduate of Dartmouth at twenty, he had earned his Ph.D. at Johns Hopkins while still in his early twenties. He was only twenty-six when he joined Johnston.

The main effort of Bell and his immediate successors was to lighten the paper and so increase its contrast with its more erudite rival. These men were human beings first and engineers afterward and they believed their readers were as human as they. They cared about the social as well as the technical effects of electricity. They knew, too, that even the most studious and disciplined minds could do with a little amusement occasionally. One of the additions to the staff proved their beliefs. This was the cartoonist, Richard Felton Outcault, who made drawings to go with the electrical news. He went to every exposition, every important power plant. With accuracy he drew the machines; with charm he drew the silk-hatted, bewhiskered, cane-carrying gentlemen who moved among them. The delicacy, the economy of line and shading, the balanced composition, and the general animation of his sketches in *Electrical World* set the pace for the illustrative art of the time and gave the welcome sense that machines never wholly dominated people.

Indeed, as we look back over the history of the industrial and business press right up to the present, the most successful ventures seem to have been those that kept a balance between men and mechanisms. Even in such highly technical fields as automation, electronics, and nuclear energy, the best magazines keep reminding us that in the most completely mechanistic complex there is always somewhere a man, and that in any ultimate crisis he can and must be master.

5 We come now to the first great roundup of separate enterprises in the business-paper field, the consolidation that resolved the problems besetting the publications we have been exploring. In 1896 James McGraw's period of watchful waiting bore fruit. He had seen and analyzed the competition between *Electrical World* and *Electrical Engineer* and he was seeing more and more duplication despite Johnston's strenuous efforts to make his paper complementary rather than overlapping.

Furthermore, he saw that neither paper could reach the "man down the line"—the man in that fast-growing trade who by 1896 was frankly labeled *electrician.* The men who arrived at a perilous instant to avert disaster with wrenches and screwdrivers, the "sons

The Chicago World's Fair, 1893. (Outcault drawing.)

of Martha," as Kipling called them: men who worked underground to "piece and repiece the living wires," did not they, too, need a paper? Many of these men, after all, would, in the American tradition, soon be on their way: foremen, superintendents, managers, designers, perhaps presidents of some vast enterprise in this fabulous field. Twenty-seven years before, a tousle-headed boy had fixed a stock-exchange ticker on Black Friday when men were going mad because of its malfunction, and that boy today was the Wizard of Menlo Park. A dozen companies bore his name. How many young Tom Edisons might there be in 1896 who could use a paper candidly called *Electrician* as a first school?

In Chicago there was a struggling little paper called *Electrical Industries*. Probably some people wondered what so astute a publisher as McGraw could want with a picayune property like that. But when he had bought it and changed its name to *American Electrician,* they found out.

The purpose of the *American Electrician,* the salutatory editorial announced, "will be primarily to supply practical information for practical men—in such form and in language so simple that all may understand without necessarily having previous knowledge on the subject treated."

The outsider whom McGraw had taken into his confidence on this venture was a man whose qualities proved that McGraw was a judge of editors. This was William Dixon Weaver, one of Johnston's staff. He clicked immediately with McGraw's thought on the need for a practical man's paper. So he left Johnston and came over to the American Electrician Company. He became in time one of the dominant figures in the McGraw-Hill drama. Years later James McGraw used to say Weaver was the best editor he ever had and he would hold him up to others, sometimes to their exasperation, as a model.

But as we look through the bound volumes of the *American Electrician* we see that it was not all Weaver. In every issue we feel the presence of the schoolteacher from Chautauqua County. One department was entitled "Lessons in Practical Electricity." It began at the bottom with EMF, current, and resistance. Another department was "Electrical Catechism." Here the reader was asked questions about what he had learned in the "Lessons." We may imagine that hundreds of young men after the day's work was over were eagerly turning the pages with roughened fingers until they came to these departments and asking one another "What is an alternator?" "What is meant by step-up and step-down transformers?" "What is to be done if the brushes suddenly begin to flash or spark excessively?" Some half-dozen questions in every number were calculated to keep these young readers on their toes and lead them on to higher levels.

It is mysterious, even to men who knew him, precisely how James McGraw indoctrinated his editors in this educational direction. Perhaps they simply felt, half-consciously, after listening to him for a time, that they had to go out, then, and be schoolteachers themselves. Perhaps he, again half-consciously, had picked men who knew how to teach. In any case, we know that this sort of adult education was one of the things that gave the papers their appeal and that eventually a large part of the industrial press followed the example they set. In the autobiographies of most of the men who have had to replace formal education with home study, we find that they did it by reading technical magazines in the night hours.

Having indoctrinated his editors, however, McGraw spent much of his own time traveling. He went to many conventions and talked with the men who knew precisely how the *business* which had grown out of the tremendous new inventions and technologies was progressing. He saw the competition that was going on between the companies that were destined to become giants. By 1898 he had seen that the rivalry, now grown bitter, between *Electrical World* and *Electrical Engineer* was beginning to hurt the industry as a whole. Advertisers thought they must buy space in both papers; therefore their appropriations were diluted. McGraw came to realize that one strong paper could do the job of two. So he bought the two and combined them.

With three papers now in his hands—*Street Railway Journal, Electrical World and Engineer,* and the *American Electrician*—he had become identified with the American electrical industry. To consolidate and tighten his control and to demonstrate that the enterprise had become solidly his, he established, in 1899, the McGraw Publishing Company. Perhaps he already envisioned the time when the electrical merger would be extended still further. In the meantime many things would happen. He would reach out toward other industries and other professions, into the realms of civil engineering and chemistry. His ambition in these years was not merely to acquire new publishing properties. It was to mold these properties into the shape determined by his basic ideals. These later became a definite, clearly stated code for his business, but they had probably crystallized in his mind by the time he started his company. As he eventually articulated them:

> First among these ideals is independence—the determination of a journal to be its own master, to have no other guides for its opinions and policies but truth and the sound interests of the field it serves. . . . The right-minded publisher holds that he has a covenant with his subscribers—a covenant to be honest with all and to do harm to no one who is pursuing an honest course. From that covenant he will not depart.
>
> An industrial journal so controlled at once commands respect. If it is to exert influence as well, it must also command ability of a high order. Managerial skill, necessary as it is, will not alone suffice. There must be that rare editorial power, compounded of knowledge, alertness and foresight, that can keep its finger on the pulse of an art and an industry, analyze achievements and comprehend tendencies, that . . . mistakes neither charlatanism for genius nor genius for charlatanism. Not even the editor of an industrial paper, of course, can be infallible, and when he is in doubt he does right honestly to say so; but it is his part to bring to his task of interpretation and guidance all that industry, application and constant contact with his field can supply.[3]

In the course of some sixty years, McGraw editors and McGraw-Hill editors have made mistakes; so has their chief; but the obligation to admit and repair them, to express their doubts and when in doubt, "honestly to say so" seems to have been a prevailing compulsion, on the peaks as well as in the valleys.

[3] James H. McGraw, "Ideals of Industrial Journalism," *Electrical World,* vol. 50, p. 559, September 20, 1924.

CHAPTER TEN

Disaster: Analysis and Reporting

Late on a midsummer afternoon in 1907 eighty-five skilled workers were finishing the day's work on a bridge that had been designed to be the longest of its kind in the world. The 5:30 whistle had just blown, warning the men that work would stop in fifteen minutes. Then suddenly the flooring under their feet began to sink; the men ran frantically toward a shore they never reached; in half a minute 20,000 tons of steel lay in the river and among the twisted girders lay the dead and injured men.

The bridge was the Quebec Bridge: a cantilever spanning the St. Lawrence a dozen miles upriver from the city. It was designed to carry two railroad tracks, two trolley tracks, two roadways, and two footpaths. The span was to be 1,800 feet—90 feet longer than the Firth of Forth cantilever, then the longest in the world—and the total length, including approaches, was to be 3,240 feet. The plan called for a clearance of 150 feet above high water for a distance of 1,200 feet. After more than six years one of the cantilever arms was nearly complete. The collapse came on Thursday, August 29, 1907. Friday's newspapers said there had been no warning.

A very few of the workers and at least one of the engineers knew better. Some of them had died with their secret. Superintendent B. A. Yenser and foreman E. R. Kinloch had been uneasy for two or three days. Yenser may have been relieved to hear the whistle blow on Thursday afternoon. On Wednesday he had wanted the work stopped until there could be a careful inspection of the detail that had disturbed both him and Kinloch. But the engineers on the spot had reassured him and he had changed his mind. No one would ever know what Yenser was thinking when the whistle blew. Kinloch, when later he was asked, could tell only what he and Yenser had been discussing the day before.

And there was one engineer, too, who had not wholly reassured Yenser and Kinloch. This was the celebrated consulant, Theodore Cooper, in New York. The fears of the men had been communicated to him the day before the wreck. On Thursday Cooper had sent a telegram ordering the work suspended. But the telegram had somehow miscarried.

When the papers came out with the story of the catastrophe, however, Cooper was not the only one who was troubled. In every office of every steel construction company all over the nation, engineers asked one another, "Why?" The Quebec Bridge had been built precisely according to the formula used on many successful American cantilevers. Under the auspices of the Dominion government only the most experienced bridge engineers of both Canada and the United States had been appointed to the job. The steel fabrication had been carried on by the famous Phoenix Bridge Company of Phoenixville, Pennsylvania. At every stage there had been rigid inspection of materials and checking of methods. There had been no hint of dangerous economizing, no economic or political scandal of any sort. If such things could happen, the whole American theory and practice of bridge building would be in doubt. It was a blow to the entire engineering profession.

2 In a Vermont village not far from the scene of the disaster, a young man who had the country's engineering reputation much at heart, was spending his vacation. As soon as he heard of the collapse, Charles Whiting Baker, editor of the *Engineering News,* and secretary of the Engineering News Publishing Company, knew what he must do. First he sent a telegram to his expert on structural work, Fred Schmitt, in the New York office asking Schmitt to join him in Quebec at the earliest possible moment. He then went himself to the scene of the bridge failure and asked the bridge administration to put every facility for inquiry at his disposal—something the officers in charge in their bewilderment and distress were only too anxious to do. They had, after all, nothing to conceal and if any light could be thrown from whatever source on the cause of the tragic bridge failure these men wanted it.

The *Engineering News* had in 1907 the highest standing on the top civil engineering level of any American technical paper. It was owned and published by George H. Frost and his associates. Another paper, the *Engineering Record,* published by the McGraw Publishing Company and edited by John M. Goodell, was not as yet a dangerous rival, because the *Record* was dedicated to a less theoretical phase of construction.

When Schmitt arrived at the bridge the two men made what may have been the most rapid and at the same time the most thorough analysis of a bridge failure ever up to that time concluded in the United States. How, in those days of a relatively slow tempo, they were able to assemble the material for the story published in their paper precisely a week later is a question we cannot help asking, as we read the article in the September 5 issue of *Engi-*

neering News. They must have been everywhere at once, asking questions, making calculations, directing the photographers, and climbing out on the wreck. We know that Schmitt repeatedly risked his life on what was left of the cantilever arm. That they were able to get back to New York, write the story, edit it, supervise the composition, and present it to the still dumfounded profession with scarcely a typographical error on the paper's regular publication day shows a degree of cooperation in the offices of the *News* that is worthy of the best publishers half a century later.

Schmitt's article told how by a process of elimination he had isolated the most probable cause. The failure had evidently not occurred in any of the tension members because their eyebars were found intact in the wreck. In the compression members, however, there was unmistakable evidence of buckling.

> At the time this is written [Schmitt wrote] at Quebec, on the fourth day after the wreck, *the initial cause of the wreck seems to be the failure of some compression member in the anchor arm of the cantilever.*[1]

The article tells how Schmitt arrived at his conclusion not only from an inspection of the wreck but from the account of the happening as survivors told it.

> The first warning was when the men felt the floor sinking beneath them . . . the slowness of the fall points to a compression member as the one to give way. The gradual fall could not possibly occur in the case of a sudden snapping of an eye-bar, or, rather, a panel of eye-bars.[2]

But Schmitt went further. He put his finger precisely on the ninth chord member of the left truss. Six months later, after all the testimony was in from all witnesses including the eleven injured survivors and after one of the most elaborate investigations ever conducted into an engineering failure, the Canadian Royal

[1] *Engineering News,* vol. 58, no. 10, p. 256, September 5, 1907.
[2] *Ibid.,* pp. 256, 257.

Frederick E. Schmitt

Commission came to the identical conclusion reached by the *News* four days after the collapse.

In the course of the commission's inquiry several other matters were revealed, some of which had an important bearing on the whole of engineering philosophy. Among others the inquisitors had grilled Kinloch. Why had he been so uneasy that even Mr. Cooper in faraway New York had heard about it? Why had the dead Yenser been troubled and why had he changed his mind? The commission had to be careful in weighing the testimony of workers because some of them or their families were certainly going to bring suit against the construction companies. But nothing could shake Kinloch's testimony.

It appeared that for several weeks there had been rumors. Well,

ENGINEERING NEWS Vol. 58. No. 10.

FIG. 2. VIEW OF QUEBEC BRIDGE ON AUG. 14, 1907, FIFTEEN DAYS BEFORE ITS FALL.

The south cantilever is complete and two panels of the suspended span have been erected. The small or top-chord traveler is in position to erect the third panel. The main traveler is on the ninth panel of the cantilever arm, and is being taken down for re-erection on the south side.

From "Engineering News" report on Quebec Bridge disaster, September 5, 1907.

there were always rumors on a big construction job. But this one persisted. Back in the storage yard where the pieces of the bridge were kept till they were needed, a certain chord member had been dropped by accident, bent slightly, and repaired. After it had been attached to the anchor arm, Kinloch and Yenser had watched it, day after day, and they had seen it begin to deviate from the normal. Finally when it had bent more than an inch, they realized that the deviation was progressing far too rapidly. It was then that Kinloch had communicated with New York. Yenser, meanwhile, had talked with the resident engineers who might be expected to know more about the situation than a consultant 600 miles away. The resident engineers had told Yenser his anxiety was unreasonable. They showed him their formulas. They told him the chord was of such dimensions and construction that it could endure a far heavier load than it could ever be subjected to. So Yenser, the night before his death, had had his first good sleep.

 It appeared from this evidence that the chord member these

men had worried about was the exact member Schmitt put his finger on immediately after the accident as having been the first to buckle and which, one week later, the *Engineering News* had designated as having caused, by its buckling, the wreck!

The *News* printed all the evidence as it came out. It was then that engineers, confident in their formulas, their mathematics, and the excellence of their design, began to realize that when the practical man, the worker whose life depends on the stability of his structure, utters as sharp a warning as Kinloch's it is well to listen, despite all theoretical "infallibility."

In the spring of 1908, after the Commission's report had been published, the *News* commented on this and gave an editorial opinion on the administrative cause behind the technical cause of the failure. The engineers working on the theoretical level had, all except one, refused to believe in the danger. The one exception was Theodore Cooper, the New York consultant. But when Cooper was interviewed he confessed he had acted on hearsay, for he had never been to Quebec while the bridge was under construction!

> It was [commented the *News*] an error of administration. . . . Real authority lay at New York, 600 miles away, with an engineer who had never seen the structure for which he was actually carrying the entire responsibility.[3]

3 It would be hard to find a more telling illustration of the value the technical press was coming to have for the engineering profession than this performance in the first decade of the twentieth century. Instead of having to wait half a year for the official report, engineers were given a precise factual account in their own professional language, an account written by experts, a single week after the event. Instead of having to go themselves to crowd the scene and make their own guesses, the hundreds of construction engineers who were so distressed by the failure were furnished with an immediate detailed 10,000-word story illustrated

[3] Vol. 59, no. 12, p. 318, March 19, 1908.

September 5, 1907. ENGINEERING NEWS

FIG. 4. WRECKAGE OF SOUTH ANCHOR ARM, QUEBEC BRIDGE, SEEN FROM THE BLUFF WEST OF THE APPROACH SPAN.

The continuous line of the top-chord eyebars, showing clearly in this view, makes it apparent that no tension failure in the top chord caused the wreck. The lower section of the fourth intermediate post (between panels 7 and 8) of the left truss lies across the wreckage in the distance, with the joint at midheight of the post lying near the right top-chord eyebars.

From "Engineering News," September 5, 1907.

by eighteen half tones of photographs, taken within four days, and four engineering drawings making the story's conclusions crystal clear.

At the same time the editors did not help their readers out of the bewildered sense of guilt the crash had brought them. The tragedy, the *News* candidly stated, was an indictment on the entire profession. In undertaking this colossal project, the engineers had relied on data that had proved successful only for smaller bridges.

With the disaster at Quebec facing the profession, it is well to confess that our knowledge of the actual limits of safe stress on long steel columns of exceptional size is by no means perfect.[4]

Beyond doubt the event had shown that

. . . in using experience on lesser structures for the design of greater there is always a chance that some element unimportant in the small work will became important in the larger.[5]

It was, in short, the sort of mysterious discrepancy between small and large that has recurred through the history of technology. In James Watt's experiments with steam engines his models worked perfectly; his difficulties began, he said, with "the practice of mechanics in great."[6] It was the same with Professor Langley's aerodrome—a precise enlargement of his successful airplane models. Even today chemical formulas that produce perfect results in the laboratory fail in large-scale production so that the pilot plant is coming into general use in development programs. There are, of course, quite different sets of factors in these various translations but the mystification of the technical planners is strikingly similar.

Actually, smaller compression members had always been tested by testing machines which had exerted pressure "to destruction," that is, until the steel collapsed. But there were no testing machines big enough for the Quebec columns. So the engineers had simply projected the dimensions by mathematical implementation.

Two weeks after the Quebec crash the *Scientific American* commented on

. . . our esteemed contemporary, *Engineering News,* whose candid admission of the serious bearing of the disaster upon the prestige of the profession cannot be too highly commended.[7]

[4] Vol. 58, no. 10, p. 256, September 5, 1907.

[5] *Ibid.,* p. 257.

[6] Samuel Smiles, *Lives of Boulton and Watt,* J. B. Lippincott Company, Philadelphia, 1865, p. 114.

[7] *Scientific American,* vol. 97, no. 12, p. 202, September 21, 1907.

Before the month was out the office of the *News* was flooded with letters from grateful engineers and, as we read them, we seem to hear a concerted gasp of relief that reasons were being found that would lead to better design. And many of the correspondents after thanking the editors went on to technical suggestions for future bridge design so that the paper became a forum for the exchange of ideas.

The Quebec Bridge failure, however, was only one, though the most far-reaching, of the engineering errors that the *News* analyzed.

> Your valued paper [wrote one bridge designer] has continually given space to the recordings of great and lamentable disasters in engineering structures. Much valuable criticism followed, and great advancement was made thereby in the knowledge of engineering design and structural materials.[8]

The writer of this letter then went on to state his position on eccentricities in steel columns, and the cogent comments by the editor complete an excellent example of what the technical press was able to do as moderator in these critical discussions.

4 In another chapter we saw the origin of *Engineering News* in a little sixteen-page paper called the *Engineer and Surveyor* which started in Chicago in 1874. At that time there was confusion in the American mind as to the difference, if any, between a surveyor and a civil engineer. George H. Frost, the publisher, had won a degree in civil engineering from McGill University but he was starting his career as land surveyor. The financially depressed year of 1874 was the worst possible one for launching a new paper, especially a paper whose title appealed to so limited a group. The word *surveyor* weakened the term *engineer* for men who had moved to realms beyond the transit and the level. Frost's courage, however, attracted a few friends of

[8] Letter from A. M. Meyers of Kansas City Structural Steel Company, in *Engineering News,* vol. 58, no. 15, p. 366, October 3, 1907.

standing in the profession and by the end of the following year the paper, its name changed to *Engineering News,* had already acquired something of a reputation through a serial article on the graphical analysis of roof trusses by Charles E. Greene, professor of engineering at the University of Michigan. From this point on the paper's rise through more than thirty years to its level at the time of the Quebec event continued steadily under the aegis of the publisher who started it.

This rise, however, was not easy. An editorial in the first issue after Frost moved his paper from Chicago to New York stated,

> Through five of the dreariest years in the financial history of the country we have worked away, using to the best of our ability such facilities as we could command.[9]

Frost had moved because, although Chicago was, according to his editorial, "the most enterprising city on this continent," it had no libraries, no engineering offices, no publishing facilities, no scientific periodicals, and "only rare opportunities of meeting with men prominent in the profession. . . ." Chicago, indeed, was growing too fast for the kind of reflection the *News* needed. What a contrast it must have presented to its present scene!

The word *engineer* was beginning in 1879 to include so many kinds of practice that an engineering journal was expected to cover a large area. It was several years before Frost's paper narrowed its focus to civil engineering. This was, of course, one of the oldest arts. How such immense works as the pyramids of Egypt and the aqueducts of Rome were designed with so little mathematical aid has formed a mysterious chapter in the history of civilization. As schoolboys know, Julius Caesar gives abundant details on the construction of military bridges, and we have learned a good deal about methods during and after the Renaissance. Many historical enterprises have proved the correctness of later mathematical formulas. It was with such formulas that Amer-

[9] *Engineering News,* vol. 6, no. 1, p. 1, January 4, 1879.

icans were beginning to work in the early years of *Engineering News* after executing such colossal projects as the Erie Canal and many city waterworks by a sort of rule of thumb.

There came, therefore, in this time of transition from trial-and-error practice into what was later called the *scientific method,* vast scope for the current printed word. Books could no longer do the job; things were moving too fast. In the twenty-eight years from 1879 to the fall of the Quebec Bridge we may trace the week-to-week progress toward scientific construction methods in the columns of *Engineering News,* and we can see from that disaster that even then the progress was not yet complete. But always the paper's sharpest focus was on a theoretical area and this continued until in 1911 the *News* was bought by John A. Hill.

5 In the meantime another paper was making a somewhat different approach to the same problems. This time the call for engineers came from the sickbed. Throughout the civilized world in the 1870s physicians were urging reforms in the crowded cities which would prevent many of the diseases they found it so hard to cure. Actually the decade marked the threshold of a revolution in medicine. The work of Lister and Pasteur was exciting interest and controversy among medical doctors everywhere. There was still confusion in professional minds about the germ theory. It was generally believed that such diseases as typhoid fever and diphtheria were transmitted by noxious gases from drains and sewers and it was generally accepted that dirt was unhealthy as well as unpleasant. The term *sanitation* was beginning to be used in connection with the disposal of waste.

The present late American passion for sanitation and cleanliness has made us reluctant to believe the appalling conditions that prevailed in our cities in most of the nineteenth century. In Chicago at mid-century, according to the state historian of Illinois, the streets were "reeking with every description of filth" which had been taken out of the houses and emptied into the gutters.

Michigan avenue was decorated with manure heaps while the contents of stables and pigsties were deposited upon the lake shore. . . . The rain washed this filth into the lake to be mixed with the drinking supply of the city.[10]

In Philadelphia as late as 1870, pig scavengers in the streets were a common sight and a part of the population drank water from the Delaware River

. . . into which the sewers threw thirteen million gallons of waste daily, which was carried by the tides to the induction pipes.[11]

The following year in New York an epidemic of smallpox killed more than 800 people and the same disease in the same year caused 2,000 deaths in Philadelphia.

The most casual investigation showed that a great part of the deaths were preventable by better housing and a few elementary measures of sanitation.[12]

Even in England, disease during the seventies was often blamed on bad sewerage, as in the case of the illness of the Prince of Wales from typhoid fever. Leaky drains in Marlborough House where the Prince lived were found to have turned the cellar into a cesspool.

It was not unnatural, then, that all the agitation over these conditions should have produced in New York in 1877 a business paper named *The Plumber and Sanitary Engineer.* The founder, Maj. Henry C. Meyer, seems to have established it for purposes of propaganda against a trend that was hurting his business. Meyer, a distinguished veteran of the Civil War who had received the Medal of Honor, was a manufacturer of brass pipe and fittings for plumbing fixtures. The trend he feared had been

[10] Arthur Charles Cole, *The Era of the Civil War, 1848–1870,* vol. 3 of *The Centennial History of Illinois,* Springfield, 1919, pp. 3, 4.

[11] Allan Nevins, *The Emergence of Modern America,* The Macmillan Company, New York, 1927, p. 321.

[12] *Ibid.*

The Plumber

AND

SANITARY ENGINEER.

WATER SUPPLY, DRAINAGE, HEATING AND LIGHTING.

Vol. 1. No. 1. | NEW YORK, DECEMBER, 1877. | Terms, $1.50 per Ye[ar] SINGLE COPIES, 15 [c]

THE PLUMBER AND Sanitary Engineer.

CHAS. F. WINGATE, EDITOR.

PUBLISHED MONTHLY, AT $1.50 PER YEAR, POSTAGE PAID.

Application for advertising and all communications should [b]e addressed to

The American Plumber Publishing Co.

JAMES BUNTING, MANAGER,

[B]ox 3037. No. 297 Pearl Street.

Liberal Terms to Clubs.

The reading columns and opinions of this paper [a]re POSITIVELY NOT FOR SALE. *Our advertising [r]ates are published, and advertisers are responsible [f]or any statements they may make in their cards, [b]ut no reading notices, editorial puffs, or other [s]imilar matter will be obtainable, and our canvas[s]ers are forbidden to promise such favors.*

TABLE OF CONTENTS.

[I]NTRODUCTION.

Th[illegible]-class journal devoted to the [in]terests of the bu[illegible] water supply, drain[a]ge, heating and [illegible] long been felt. To [fi]ll the existing vaca[illegible] object of this jour[n]al, as its name indicate[illegible] aims to make every [p]lumber a sanitary engine[illegible] the title [g]iven to members of this trade a[illegible] it well [d]escribes their province. There is ne[illegible] [st]andard of excellence among them. [illegible] [p]lumbers have no real practical capacity—[illegible] [m]ight well be called mere joint wipers. A tr[illegible]

plumber should be something more, and we shall strive to bring about this result by making public the best current information bearing upon this branch of industry. We shall endeavor to stimulate members of the trade to study and improve in their particular line of business, both as a matter of duty and of interest. An unjust odium has been cast upon plumbers, gas and steam fitters, owing to the lack of skill on the part of certain incapable workmen.

The public should know that there are as intelligent and as honorable men in this as in any other line of business, and that if they will only discriminate they can get first-class work at reasonable rates, and from intelligent parties.

THE PLUMBER will contain the fullest and latest information on all matters pertaining to the Plumbing, Gas and Steam Fitting Trade.

This will be supplemented by frank and impartial discussions of timely topics, such as practically effect the trade, including everything relating to the water supply, lighting, ventilation and sanitary regulation of buildings. The ablest contributors will be secured and no pains will be spared to make it a first-class periodical, such as will deserve and therefore receive the support not only of the trade, but of the community at large. Communications of every kind are invited. This journal represents and will cater to no personal or class interest, but will speak for the whole trade.

A CASE IN POINT.

If you had a child afflicted with a serious malady, would you start out to find some one who would agree to cure him for a certain sum and contract with whoever would propose to do it for the least money, assuming that the price was the only consideration that should influence you in making your selection?

If you had a valuable horse to shoe, would you employ a street paver to do it, because he might do it cheaper than a responsible horse shoer with a business reputation to sustain? You say these questions are absurd; we answer they fairly illustrate what intelligent people do every day in the matter of plumbing.

If any plumbing is to be done, no matter whether it is to put in a new faucet, repair a waste [p]ipe, remove a bad smell or drain a cellar, people [are t]oo apt to go out, in search of a man "who [wor]ks himself," supposing he will therefore do it [illegible] money.

Responsibility, experience, intelligence, [go] for nothing; the sole consideration is who [will do] it cheapest? That is the great point, an[d] through the lunacy of the house-holder, a[nd] ignorance of the botch who claims to be a [plum]ber, the lives and health of families are [im]peril. You say this is an exagerated p[icture;] let us therefor simply state a case tha[t came] under our notice within the past two week[s.]

In an elegant house on a prominent [street] there have for some time past been frequen[t com]plaints of bad smells arising from the ce[llar. A] so called "plumber" was sent for, who ca[me and] found the cement bottom of the cellar dan[p and] crumbling away. He prescribed more c[ement,] plastered it over, sent, and collected his bi[ll, and] soon was sent for again, and again prescri[bed the] same remedy. Finally some member of the [family] was taken ill, the stench coming out of the [hot air] registers becoming unbearable. Then, a[nd not] till then did the house-holder inquire wh[ere he] could get an intelligent plumber; one was [recom]mended, for they are to be found, and [in this] city too. He went into the cellar, wh[ere he] found a portable hot air furnace. The cella[r smelt] like a privy; he noticed the crumbling an[d damp] cement, and with his foot removed enough [to ex]pose the main waste pipe from the house[, which] came down inside the cellar wall and s[ank] within a few inches of an open brick dra[in;] all this less than twelve inches from the s[urface.] The contents of the waste pipes had thor[oughly] saturated this cellar bottom and the rear p[art of] this Madison Avenue cellar was nothing m[ore or] less than a cesspool; while the impure a[ir was] heated by the furnace and sent througho[ut the] house. The matter has at last been pr[operly] attended to, and we trust none of the occ[upants] will die from the effects of this stupid[ly done] plumbing in a first-class house. We believ[e there] are a multitude of similar cases in New [York] to-day. To do without plumbing in our [houses] won't avail and is out of the question. Disc[rimin]ation on the part of occupants of house[s and] ordinary common sense in the selection of [plumbers] to do such important work is the only rem[edy.]

PENNY WISE AND POUND FOOL[ISH.]

Frequently we see a man who wants to b[uild a] house; he gets an architect to draw his [plans] and write his specifications. The architect [is sup]posed to have had experience, and to unde[rstand] his business. The benefit of this experi[ence is] embodied in the specifications on which c[ontract]ors make their estimates, and in accordar[ce with] which they contract to do the work. O[ur man] thinks that now he has got from the archit[ect all he] knows, and that he is smart enough to pr started by frightened citizens who were advocating a return to privies in the cities!

The early issues of the paper are not impressive to a reader of the mid-twentieth century. The illustrations, however, and, especially, the advertisements are historically instructive in showing the origins of the great American achievements in sanitary engineering. One amusing editorial shows that the plumber in the seventies was even more the target of satire than he is today. The editor deplores this treatment of a lowly but dedicated lifesaver. The word *plumber,* however, presently disappeared from the paper's title and the change to the simple, dignified *Sanitary Engineer* marks the first stage in its climb.

Though Meyer may have been motivated in starting the journal by fears for his own business, he never used it for editorial exploitation of his products. He seems to have been an extremely high-minded person and as he became more and more immersed in journalism and less in manufacturing, he became a true crusader. Eventually he relinquished control of his business and devoted himself wholly to the various causes that attracted him. Thus through his editorial columns he secured the passage of important sanitation laws. As sanitation became an integral part of architecture and construction, he interested himself in tenements, schools, and public structures; and some valuable building legislation was the result. Gradually, then, as architects and civil engineers began to contribute to the paper, its character changed and the change was followed by new titles. It finally became *Engineering Record,* which it remained for nearly thirty years.

6 Considering its pedigree we should naturally expect a more down-to-earth character in the *Record* than that of the *News.* Both started, to be sure, with artisan readers, but even at the beginning the surveyor was on a more theoretical level than the plumber. All the way through the careers of the two papers, one had gone into the realms of mathematics, of formulae, of physi-

First issue of "The Plumber & Sanitary Engineer," 1877.

cal theory, while the other had concerned itself with natural things: pipes, ironwork, tiles, bricks, lumber, and concrete. In its first years as a McGraw publication, however, the *Record* tended to become more like the *News.* This, at least, was the complaint of Smith T. Henry who joined the *Record's* staff in 1904.

The editor then was John M. Goodell, a graduate civil engineer and, from Henry's memory of him, more interested in the science of engineering than in its practice. He seems to have been trying to lift the paper to his own educational level. Henry, on the other hand, wanted to find out "how people were doing things, rather than just how they designed them." In 1906 Goodell sent Henry on his first field assignment.

> Although [remembers Henry] it was an engineering assignment, I made a dirt-moving assignment out of it. That was the building of the Western Maryland from Norfolk, Virginia, to Deepwater in West Virginia. I rode the length of the line on horseback. I bought my own camera. Goodell wouldn't approve a camera. Then I . . . wrote the story out in long hand. I sent it in to Goodell. He wrote back immediately, "Where's the engineering?"
>
> I sent him the engineering drawings and said, "You figure out the engineering. *This* is a real dirt-moving story."
>
> He printed it but didn't like to. That was the beginning of our first field work in an editorial approach.[13]

After that McGraw saw what Henry was trying to do and backed him up. The field work became more and more concerned with practical aspects and thus the *Record* came back to some extent to the level of its early days. It never could become wholly engrossed in the practical side of engineering because, as the study advanced, theory penetrated even Henry's cherished "dirt-moving."

But this is a partial explanation of why *Engineering Record* gave a different treatment to the Quebec Bridge disaster in 1907

[13] Smith T. Henry, recorded interview, p. 5.

from that of the *News*. It gave the story plenty of space even in its issue of September 7. But the *Record's* account was pure reporting. It told all the factual details. It was precise as to the part of the bridge that collapsed, the time of the accident, the number of men on the bridge, and the background, that is, the history of the construction up to the moment of the disaster, the personalities involved, and the dimensions on the design. But there was no analysis. There was no assignment of cause. It was the sort of story that might be printed in any careful newspaper or magazine. Furthermore, it was not printed in the body of the magazine but in its "Current News Supplement," a department made up shortly before publication to assure the readers good reporting. But a John Goodell, reading it, might well have asked, "Where is the engineering?"

James McGraw may have envied the reputation the *News* got for its handling of the incident. Perhaps Schmitt's remarkable performance spurred him and his editors to new efforts with the *Record*. We know that in the next decade the rivalry became hot indeed, so that, as we look back on it, the end result seems inevitable.

CHAPTER ELEVEN

Below the Earth's Surface

In the year 1859 two events occurred which profoundly affected the American destiny. One was the discovery on Sun Mountain in the territory of Nevada of the rich gold and silver vein that was known as the Comstock Lode. This not only began deep mining of the precious metals by Americans; it started the eastward migration from California into the land that had been skipped in the frantic gold rush to the Pacific ten years before, thus uniting the northern nation. Perhaps, too, it affected the outcome of the Civil War by bringing California to the Union cause. The other event was the finding of "liquid gold" by a railroad conductor in Titusville, Pennsylvania: the petroleum that today is the world's dominant source of energy.

Gold had been found in North America in considerable quantities before 1859. But the gold in the valley of the Sacramento which had drawn such a huge migration to California had been placer gold, surface gold, laboriously extracted in little lots by men who rocked their pans in the water all day and often spent their day's accumulation at night in drinking and gambling. A few individuals amassed fortunes of a sort, but the national economy was not greatly enriched by the California placer gold. That it had played a vital part in the conquest of the continent was another matter.

Yet it had split off California from the national continuity. California had become an outpost. Many of the new settlers knew nothing of the vast space between it and their old homes because they had come by sea. Even those who had made the long, terrible trek by wagon knew only of desert and mountain, heat, alkali dust, wild beasts, and hostile Indians. But California, besides being El Dorado, was an almost self-sufficient paradise and, in the decade after 1849, the formation of an independent, Pacific republic was seriously advocated. Then California gold had begun to peter out, and high in the Sierras the wandering Canadian, Henry Comstock, had found a group of ignorant prospectors digging handfuls of nuggets in what he said was his claim. The great bonanza mines that resulted—Ophir and Chollar and Gould and Curry—sent capital to Eastern industries, helped promote transcontinental railroads, and united East and West in a way that prevented the splitting off of sections. In the meantime, however, the men with the nuggets in their hands had a lot to learn.

2 Although mining was one of the oldest of the industrial arts, the eager prospectors in California knew little about it. From the days of King Solomon to the Spanish exploitation of Peruvian gold an extensive lore and literature had grown up. During the American colonial period there had been large coal-mining operations in England. Iron and other minerals had been extensively mined in Sweden and all over Europe. But Americans had been content with iron found in bogs; coal had been ignored while the forests supplied charcoal; the dream of gold had expired after the East had yielded no hint of it and, in the first half century of the Republic, the only use for petroleum was as a medicine guaranteed to cure blindness, rheumatism, burns, coughs, colds, sprains, and baldness.[1] The great American preoccupation was agriculture and the agricultural yield was so rich that El Dorado seemed all about us.

In the cultural centers, however, there was teaching and literature about mines. By the 1850s not a little science had been used in the great Pennsylvania coal and iron deposits. Pure copper had been mined on the southern shore of Lake Superior and in Arizona and Montana. There were books on geology from which knowledge of ore deposits could be gained. It is said that the Grosch brothers, the men who discovered the silver secret of the Washoe country and whose tragic deaths kept the secret hidden, had read deeply in such books. Benjamin Silliman's *American Journal of Science and Arts,* now usually called *Silliman's Journal,* that prolific early source of technological information, had given much space to mining. There had even been sporadic attempts at American mining papers such as the *Mining Journal* of 1845 and the *Mining Magazine* in 1853. But educational institutions such as the Columbia School of Mines and the Colorado School of Mines lay in the future.

In Europe, however, there were advanced schools in which the scientific bases of all phases of mining and mineralogy were taught, and Americans were beginning to take advantage of the opportunities they offered. Thus, at the very moment when the ignorant Sierra prospectors were jumping one another's claims and engaging in all the shooting and drinking and wasted energy that accompanies a gold rush, two of the men who were about to become important to our story were studying seriously in

[1] R. E. Sherrill, "Oil Industry," in *Dictionary of American History,* Charles Scribner's Sons, New York, 1940, vol. 4, p. 165.

Europe. For the next thirty years these men would be in the van of those who would bring the power of print to bear on mineral exploitation in the United States and give perhaps the strongest proof of the value to American industry of the American industrial press.

Rossiter Worthington Raymond was a boy of eighteen when he graduated at the head of his class from the Polytechnic Institute of Brooklyn. His background had been intellectual and cultural; his father had been a newspaper editor and later a teacher of English. Immediately after his graduation young Raymond went to Germany to study. For three years he studied at Heidelberg, Munich, and Freiberg. From the Royal Mining Academy at Freiberg he came home in 1861 to serve on the staff of Major General Frémont in the Civil War. After three years in the army he began practice as a consulting mining engineer in New York.

Richard Pennefather Rothwell was a Canadian of Scotch-Irish descent who came as a boy to Troy, New York, and graduated from Rensselaer Polytechnic Institute there in 1858 with a civil engineer's degree. He then spent two and a half years in Paris and earned a degree as mining engineer from the École Centrale des Mines. He followed this with postgraduate courses at Freiberg. In his first years in industry he seems to have acted as a mechanical as well as a civil and mining engineer: a fact which probably had a bearing on his later editorial interests. When, in 1866, after experience in England and in Canada, he settled in Wilkes-Barre, Pennsylvania, he turned his attention to the mining of anthracite coal.

3 The year after the end of the Civil War a magazine started in New York which was to continue an uninterrupted growth for more than ninety years and which will see its hundredth birthday in the near future. It was founded in the midst of the gold and silver fever that centered around Virginia City in the Washoe country. The mining of the Comstock Lode had been in progress little more than five years and the tales of bonanzas were thrilling the nation. In New York gold was becoming the substance in which many speculators were primarily interested. The first transcontinental railroad was building fast and would soon provide a means of migration into the immense empty spaces that had been skipped in the first rush to the Pacific.

A young man, appropriately named Western, provided the inspiration for the *American Journal of Mining,* first published on March 3, 1866, by him and his brother. Charles Callis Western had been through the mill in California. Born in New York in 1842, he had gone west when he was sixteen and had worked in the gold diggings with pick and shovel and had almost died of the hardships he had endured. Turning from gold to journalism when the gold began to peter out, he had started a paper in San Francisco, sunk all his profits in it, and had returned, sick and poor, to New York three years after he had left. Because he was too weak to return west, Charles interested his brother Benjamin in starting the *Journal.*

We caught a glimpse earlier of the *Journal of Mining* in its first struggling year when it succumbed to the prevalent custom of the times of printing the advertisements of dubious patent medicines. Its first editor was George Dawson, of whom we know very little. The early issues reflect its struggle. Yet even then it managed to get into its sixteen pages a lot of news from all the important mining centers. The editorial page of the very first issue reflects the immense potential beneath the American earth's surface.

> The gold and silver mines of Nevada, Montana, Idaho, Colorado, Arizona, Oregon, and New Mexico never yielded larger returns. . . . The copper product of the great copper region bordering Lake Superior exhibits no decrease; and the coal, iron, and lead mines of Pennsylvania, Wisconsin, Illinois, and other states certainly hold their own. . . . The petroleum product, in spite of the heavy tax imposed upon "crude," is growing, and when Congress shall have lifted the galling burthen from the producers' shoulders, it must become a highly remunerative branch of the mineral industry.

An early issue of the "American Journal of Mining."

AMERICAN
Journal of Mining,
Milling, Oil-Boring, Geology, Mineralogy, Metallurgy, etc.

I.
3.

NEW YORK, APRIL 14, 1866.

$4 A Year in Advance
Single Copies Ten Cents

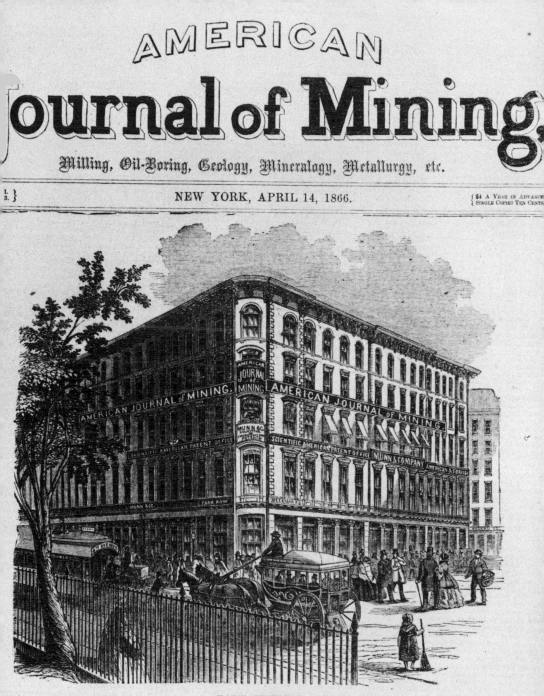

PARK BUILDING.

y our location, we present the accompanyng of this well-known edifice, which has ny years one of the landmarks and ornae city of New York. Its beautiful situa- Park, imparts an air of sylvan cheerful- its close contiguity to all the great tres of the city renders it a most desirable Here, for many years, has been established own *Scientific American*, whose reputation ned to the American continent, but has ough every country in Europe. Imme- the *Scientific American* is the office of the

rican Journal of Mining,

stined to become as widely known, and as eciated, not only in the United States, but country in the world

so, from the manner in which it is received by the community. One department of the office will be set apart for the reception of specimens of all minerals and metals; and contributions of rare and valuable ores are most respectfully solicited from every part of the world. It is the object of the JOURNAL to present the vast and varied mineral metallic resources of the continent, and nothing can more directly further that object than a complete collection of specimens, placed in such a public and conspicuous place. Great attention will be paid to the assaying and analyzing of minerals for miners and others, and prompt returns made. Engraving and Lithography will be executed in the highest style of the art—while Job Printing of every description can always

The Land of Legendary Wealth.

Has it never occurred to the hardy and advent ous men who make up our pioneer community, t they are dwelling on the confines of a region t for centuries past has been the supposed seat of i mense mineral riches? Do they know that they hovering on the borders of a land, in the unexplo depths of which, the generations of the past pla the fabled El Dorado, with its lodes of metallic silv and mountains of gold? And yet, such is the ca In the awful wilderness that stretches away on t southeast to the Rio Colorado, embracing in desolate wastes the Valley of Death, encircled by t Amargosa—river of bitter waters—lie those gold

More significant still, in view of later developments, was the department entitled "The Market Review." Here we find lists of mining stocks and current prices of the products of the mines. In it we cannot fail to see a remote ancestor of one of the most notable of the McGraw-Hill enterprises, *Engineering and Mining Journal Metal and Mineral Markets,* born sixty-four years later.

Somehow the little paper attracted the attention of Rossiter Raymond and from that moment on its fortunes changed. He was then, early in 1867, a partner in the firm of Adelberg and Raymond, consulting mining engineers. An important book on geology had just appeared in Germany. Adelberg suggested to Raymond that he translate parts of the book and submit the translations to the *Journal* with the by-line, "Translated for the *American Journal of Mining* by Adelberg and Raymond."

I made the translation . . . [Raymond remembered nearly forty years later] and gave it to the Journal partly to help that enterprise and partly (perhaps chiefly) to advertise our firm.[2]

The translations ran through seven issues from April to June, 1867, and in September appeared the first original article signed by Raymond. From then on he was a regular contributor. Before the year was out he had accepted the Westerns' invitation to become editor, though he did not work actively in that post until the following year. Raymond's articles and editorial direction raised the little paper to the level of scientific authority that it has occupied ever since. Also, its educational function began in those early days when miners were becoming engineers and needed all the knowledge they could get. During the next ten years, the *Journal* would see the beginnings of that kind of instruction in the United States that would eventually make it unnecessary for prospective American mining engineers to go abroad to study.

In 1869 the words *engineer* and *engineering* were being used

[2] R. W. Raymond, "Editorial Reminiscences," *Engineering and Mining Journal,* vol. 81, no. 13, p. 611, March 31, 1906.

in connection with nearly every branch of technology. Developments of all kinds were coming along so thick and fast that editors of the technical press felt that they must keep up with them all, whatever phase a particular journal might be dedicated to. Thus, in July of that fateful year, the *American Journal of Mining* became the *Engineering and Mining Journal* and an editorial explained:

. . . we have decided to offer to the reading public a paper devoted to the engineering and mining interests combined. These two branches of the industrial arts are so nearly related to each other, that, in giving them an equal representation upon the title-page, it seems to us that we only arrive at a symmetrical arrangement as regards the scope of the paper.[3]

Carrying out the plan, the issue contained pieces on a French arch bridge, a submarine steamship, the roads of New York's Central Park, a new form of spectrum telescope, "interesting" submarine operations, a method for increasing the flow of wells, and Roebling's projected East River (Brooklyn) Bridge, as well as several strictly mining articles. An advertisement announced that the reborn magazine would cover civil engineering, mechanical engineering, agricultural engineering, mining, the coal trade, the metal trade, and market reports. A large order, indeed! But in those days there had been so little valuable printed matter on all these subjects that the wide canvas seemed possible for a single paper.

To a student of the technical press the alternate expansion and contraction of such a paper, as its background altered, is fascinating indeed. Today the thought that any paper could cover this field would seem absurd to anyone who understands the needs of professional readers and specialist advertisers. Over the years as other papers sprang up to dedicate themselves to each of these branches, the *Engineering and Mining Journal* tended more and more to concentrate on its first purpose.

[3] *Ibid.*, vol. 8, no. 1, p. 9, July 6, 1869.

4 Readers of today's highly specialized and news-packed oil-industry papers, *National Petroleum News* and *Petroleum Week*, should be interested to know that *Engineering and Mining Journal* led the way in this new, exciting field. Less than ten years after the discovery of Drake's celebrated Titusville well, the *Journal* was printing a piece in nearly every issue about new uses for the fabulous petroleum, new methods of extracting, transporting, and refining it, and its marketing. An editorial in the July 6, 1867, issue told of experiments in which petroleum had been successful as a fuel for marine engines. The paper could not, of course, foresee the use of gasoline in internal combustion engines, but it forecast a wide employment of crude petroleum as a substitute for coal in steam prime movers. Another article told what petroleum was: its origin in remote millennia by plant and animal accumulations in the successive layers beneath the earth's surface. In the early issues, statistics of production, distribution, and prices of petroleum were included in the market reviews.

Coal was one of the *Journal's* preoccupations from the start. It was the means of introducing Richard Rothwell to the paper. In the late sixties Rothwell was becoming a hero among many Pennsylvania coal miners. He had taken a personal part in preventing firedamp explosions and in rescue operations that had saved the lives of trapped men. His European studies had taught him how to make split-second decisions that made the difference between life and death to scores of men. To put his knowledge of ventilation and firedamp behavior into effect, he never hesitated to go himself into the most dangerous parts of the mine, and he never ordered men to go where he dared not. His first contribution to the *Journal*, published March 2, 1867, described an explosion in one of the Wilkes-Barre collieries and shortly afterward he became a regular contributor with articles on the prevention of such accidents and on new methods of ventilation. In 1874 Raymond who was working for the government and, as he said, editing the *Journal* "with my left hand," induced Rothwell to come on the staff. From that time on, Rothwell became the *de facto* editor and from 1875 to his death in 1901 was the principal owner of the paper.

Meanwhile the Western brothers had sold the *Journal.* In spite of its growing prestige it was far from a financial success. The Scientific Publishing Company which bought it carried it with difficulty through the depressed years of the 1870s. Publishers of periodicals in those days had not come to realize that a magazine cannot properly be supported by its readers alone. Also the kind of advertising that today gives a magazine to its reader for $2 a year though it costs $15 per year to produce had not yet come into being. The result was that during the first fifteen years of its existence the *Engineering and Mining Journal* was almost wholly a labor of love. Raymond once said the paper had cost him personally $30,000: money he earned outside while he edited "with his left hand."

In the Scientific Publishing Company that took over the *Journal* we see the beginnings of the book publishing that has formed so important a part of the McGraw-Hill enterprise. There had been sale of technical books in connection with the *Journal* since 1869, but actual publishing came a decade later. The large sale of Rothwell's *Statistics of Coal* and F. B. Stone's *Magnetic Variation in the United States* helped the rise in prosperity of the company which had already begun. Meanwhile the paper had jumped into the midst of the Leadville boom by establishing an office in Denver.

Whether John Hill, a boy of nineteen who had caught the Leadville fever and was prospecting there before the beginning of his railroad career, read the *Journal* in 1877 is not known. From what we know of his reading proclivities, it is difficult to see how he could have escaped it, and the memory of it as a miners' guidepost may have stayed with him. By this time the paper's prestige had been stepped up by the editorial work of John Adams Church and Benjamin R. Weston and by the educational course of lectures by Warrington Smyth, professor of mining in London's Royal School of Mines. By absorbing the *Polytechnic Review* in 1879, the *Journal* added its editor William Wahl to its staff; and Wahl instituted a department of background news with the all-inclusive title, "Progress in Science and Art."

Through the eighties the *Journal* added half tones to its woodcuts and engravings. By modern standards they were foggy enough and, as we look back today over the old issues, the cuts made from drawings are far more pleasing. These pictures, some of which, like the full-page sketch of Bolivian natives guiding their precarious craft through the Cañon of the Tipuani, are exciting and do much to relieve the forbidding text packed with its eye-straining type. If we can bring ourselves to read some of the text, however, we shall discover a good deal of engaging material. There were withering editorials, for example, attacking the fraudulent practices so widespread in that age of overnight fortunes. As we read of salted mines, of the sale of blue-sky stock, of the corruption with which much of the mining industry was honeycombed in that decade of low morality, we marvel at the apparent cynicism of the times. In other papers we read of the wars between the organs of the technical press. At one time, for instance, the *Journal* carried on an angry battle with its excellent contemporary *Iron Age,* which it accused of jealousy of the *Journal's* warm relations with the Institute of Mining Engineers. The discretion with which today's rival papers deal with one another did not exist in the eighties. *Iron Age* and the *Journal* never hesitated to name names, and we can feel the pleasure the editors must have taken in their elaborate and, to us, often elephantine sarcasm.

5 One of the *Journal's* distinguishing features from the very start was its careful attention to statistics. Nothing, of course, is more valuable in this field than the publication of accurate figures as part of the weekly news—figures on prices, stock quotations, production, and capital in the metal and mineral industries. The *Journal* was fortunate in having two such dedicated statisticians as Raymond and Rothwell on its staff. Sometimes in

Sketch of the Cañon of the Tipuani. (From "The Engineering and Mining Journal.")

addition to the weekly reports these editors would bring out a special statistical number. In 1893, Rothwell, exasperated by the government's delay in publishing the statistics of the United States Geological Survey, established an annual volume which he called *The Mineral Industry,* adding as a subtitle "Its Statistics, Technology and Trade." This periodical jumped the gun on the government publications.

Before the end of the decade, *The Mineral Industry* came to contain some 900 pages of text and more than 50 of advertising. It sold for the almost incredibly low price of $5! It contained statistical articles on almost sixty metals and minerals, many of them illustrated, and dealt also with tunnels, ore dressing, and mine accidents. It had articles and tables on mineral and metallurgical production, and on exports and imports in twenty foreign countries. Some forty writers, all experts in their fields, contributed the various articles.

It is amusing to thumb over some of the early volumes of *The Mineral Industry* and to reflect on some of the changes that have come in the industry as a result of scientific discovery. In the 1898 issue, for example, the two-and-a-half-page article on uranium explains that far more of the ore had been mined than there was any market for and that "an accumulation of about 15 tons" extracted since 1871 "was allowed to lie at the smelting works at Argo until last year, when it was purchased by the agent of a French metallurgical works for shipment to France."

Editors of the *Journal* and of *The Mineral Industry* in the nineties included Walter Renton Ingalls, William Philips, and Frederick Hobart. It is interesting that in this late Victorian period, the treasurer of the Scientific Publishing Company and business manager of the *Journal* was a woman, Mrs. Sophia Braeunlich. The foreword of *The Mineral Industry* for 1898 states:

> To her remarkable business ability is due in no small degree the success which has crowned this undertaking.[4]

With the absorption of the magazine *Coal* in the mid-eighties, the *Journal* was covering so much below the earth's surface that there was little room for the other phases of engineering. By this time, too, there were, as we have seen, excellent papers for the civil and mechanical engineers.

By the end of the century the *Engineering and Mining Journal* had given news of some of the greatest events in American mineral history. The development of Anaconda copper, the vast exploitation of the iron deposits in the Menominee and Mesabi Ranges, and the Klondike gold rush were only a few of them. The whole growth of large-scale steel production in the United

[4] P. 653.

States through the bessemer and open-hearth processes had taken place in its lifetime to 1900. It had watched the progress of electrolytic reduction of aluminum, the inventions of high-speed steel and many steel alloys, and the mining of such alloy metals as nickel, vanadium, and chromium. At the turn of the century it saw the immense consolidation that resulted in U.S. Steel.

6 The *Engineering and Mining Journal* then passed through a curious sequence of owners involving most of the men who have thus far dominated this history. Richard Rothwell died early in the summer of 1901. His whole career had been honorable and constructive and high tribute was paid him in the memorials that followed his death. He had been a leader in the Institute of Mining Engineers and his technical work and brilliant inventions had advanced the practice of American mining by long strides. When he died, the paper that he owned and to which he had dedicated much of his life drifted for a time on stormy seas.

His executors apparently were only too anxious to be relieved of the responsibility of publishing the paper. They sold it, therefore; the best bid not merely in money but especially in prestige seemed to come from James H. McGraw. Most publishers of business papers in this transition age were occasionally tempted into speculation. It is doubtful if McGraw even seriously intended to add *Engineering and Mining Journal* to his already prospering chain. But he was able to buy it cheap—reputedly for $183,000—and with the accumulated McGraw prestige, sold it to our old acquaintance William J. Johnston, who had done so much to build *Electrical World,* for a $100,000 profit. According to the indignant story of Thomas A. Rickard, McGraw had trusted Johnston too far and Johnston's cash failed. Rickard was an extremely able mining engineer but a cantankerous writer. His withering account of the transaction in *Mining and Scientific Press* attacks all the principals in the various deals. He seems to have moved about among the various temporary owners of the *Journal,* occasionally accepting editorial jobs. He went into partnership with

John A. Hill, at the Board of Directors' meeting of the "Engineering and Mining Journal" in 1904, at which he declared that the preferred stockholders were a nuisance. Hill is at far left; Richard at far right.

Johnston, whom he criticizes for his "vague business sense," and apparently helped finance the *Journal* in its dubious days, and the chances are that McGraw did not suffer in the long run. But the various controversies are not part of our story and anyone who is interested in these dull and complex matters can read for himself Rickard's detailed diatribe.[5]

Horace M. Swetland comes back into our picture when he bought the *Journal* from Johnston in 1904. His ownership was brief, however, and obviously speculative. During his proprietorship, Rickard was editor and "for the first time was able to attend to my editorial duties without fussing with the business administration."[6] It is a tribute, perhaps, to Swetland that he and

[5] "A Chapter in Journalism," *Mining and Scientific Press,* vol. 120, no. 21, pp. 745–757, May 22, 1920.

[6] *Ibid.,* p. 750.

Rickard "worked together in complete harmony."[7] By 1906 the *Journal* had found a safe haven in the house of John A. Hill where it remained as long as that house endured. Swetland had realized $105,000 profit on the exchange. But there was nothing speculative about Hill's attitude toward the paper. To him it was one of his valuable properties and one in which he was deeply interested.

Hill, in Rickard's opinion, was "rough and overbearing."[8] It soon became evident that the two could not work together. Rickard paints a sharp picture of his new chief: one which is so at variance with other accounts that our story would not be wholly complete without it.

> At the meeting of our directors, Mr. Hill took the upper hand unmistakably and bluntly; if . . . I had anything to say, he would lay down the law roughly. "What are you going to do about it?" was his retort. He was the boss; he looked upon the stockholders as a nuisance. . . . In short we were mutually antagonistic; he regarded editors as necessary evils; I regarded speculative publishers in the same light.[9]

We see here the first moment at which James H. McGraw and John A. Hill came briefly upon the same scene. From now on destiny will draw them into the same net. They were wholly different in temperament and in their relations with men, but their agreement on publishing principles, on business integrity, and on their obligations to their readers dominated every moment when they appeared together on the stage of the industrial press. If John Hill's spirit is uneasy at the thought that his memory as well as his portrait are contiguous today in the Big Green Building with those of James McGraw, it is certain that the aims, the preaching, and the practice of the two men are all in the cornerstone of the business.

[7] *Ibid.,* p. 749.
[8] *Ibid.*
[9] *Ibid.,* p. 750.

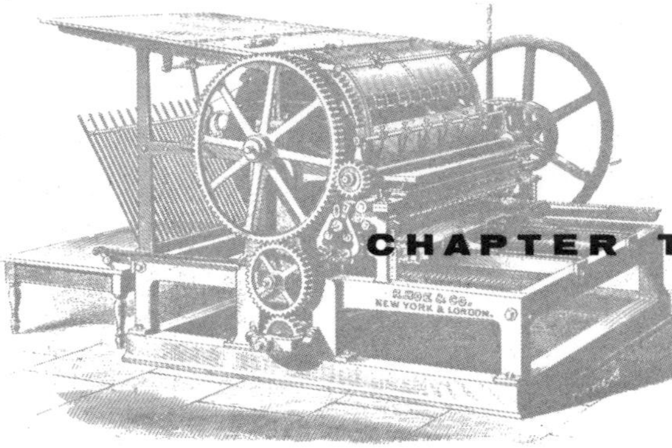

CHAPTER TWELVE

ABP and ABC

Perhaps never has there been a greater contrast between two men whose names are permanently linked in a business enterprise than that between James Herbert McGraw and John Alexander Hill. McGraw, the pedagogue, the intellectual, the builder of men and organizations, to whom an intense business preoccupation brought austerity was the total reverse of the practical Hill. Warm, charming, both in his person and in his writing, a quick journalist who dealt always with action rather than reflection, fascinated and adept with machinery, accustomed to meeting men on their own level, Hill's character was essentially down to earth. Both men were dictators of a sort—and in their day successful businessmen were usually dictators—but with this difference:

Hill's business was a one-man show with all its actors almost worshipfully loyal to their boss and wholly dependent on him; McGraw's operation involved the careful molding of every employee into his own image. The result was that when, after Hill's death, the two organizations merged, there were in the McGraw company dozens of such McGraw men, and in the House of Hill only a nostalgia for the unique, lost John Hill.

Everyone who remembers the separate companies in their heyday agrees that there could never have been a true partnership between these two individuals. Both were too dynamic, too independent, too insistent upon personal control to have worked in harmony on the same level. Yet on the basic techniques of business-paper journalism and publishing both, in their separate orbits, maintained the same standards; and together they helped to lift the whole enterprise out of the haphazard, amateurish, and often unscrupulous ambience in which they found it into the realm of legitimate publishing.

To both men early in the game came the conviction that the publisher of a periodical must hold himself responsible primarily to its readers. This, they thought, was not only sound morals but sound business. An advertiser's ultimate respect must go to the paper that kept its readers satisfied. No publisher whose first aim was to please his advertisers directly could keep those advertisers long. Sooner or later there would be suspicion of discrimination, of favoring one above another. But the publisher who pleased his advertisers *because* he pleased his readers was in a better position for long-run publishing. He had an independent standard that put and kept all the advertisers on the same level.

Those who reflect on the philosophy of periodical publishing are usually fascinated by the apparent paradox it presents. Its origin is historical. When production costs rose above a certain point, it became evident that readers could no longer pay the expenses of a periodical unless the subscription price were prohibitively raised. Thus with every jump in circulation, the publisher was plunged deeper into the red. The difference between cost and price, therefore, had to be made up either by institutional subsidy or by the sale of advertising space.

There are, and always were, a few periodicals for which the reader pays all the costs. A conspicuous modern example of this is *American Heritage* which sells at $2.95 a copy. But the sale of such a magazine is necessarily limited. Another twentieth-century phenomenon is *The Reader's Digest* whose editorial and production costs were low enough to be covered during most of its career by a modest subscription price. But the majority of papers are either endowed—as are the society or propaganda publications—or they depend for their support on advertising.

The seeming paradox arrived when men with the convictions of McGraw and Hill said, in effect, to their advertisers: "We welcome your support. It is true that we could not continue without you. But we can give you nothing in return for your support except the opportunity to display your wares to those readers to whom our periodical is dedicated. In other words, you are supporting something in the management and direction of which you have nothing whatever to do. A kind of theater has been created in which a show will be presented to an audience; you, the advertiser are asked to pay most of the expenses of that theater and in return you are permitted to present your story incident to a show which we have designed for an audience that only pays a small part of that show's cost!"

Behind the fight that publishers and editors waged for many years to make the paradox a valid publishing principle was, of course, that great American ideal: freedom of the press. It is obvious to us today that no press can ever be free whose editorial policies are for sale to private commercial interests. Yet it took all the courage and perseverance the champions of this doctrine could muster to convince those interests that their policy was essential to freedom. Even in the first decades of this century certain sellers, for example, of proprietary medicines, were using bribes and threats to induce newspapers and magazines to print testimonials in their news columns and editorials opposing the pending drug legislation.

A second conviction of these leaders of the business press was that advertising rates must be uniform. In the early years of both McGraw's and Hill's publishing careers, rate decisions were in the hands of "solicitors." These men—now called salesmen—had one asking rate and another for which they settled. It was also customary for solicitors to accept various objects in place of money. The effort to establish and maintain fixed rates uniformly paid was difficult in the lean years. It was not easy in the times when standards of all kinds were few and elastic, in the high, wide, and handsome days of *caveat emptor,* in the years when most business was conducted on a haggling basis, and in the era when cutthroat competition was unbridled by business ethics.

A third belief held in common by these pioneers was that advertising rates should be based on honest circulation statements. It must be remembered that in the early part of the business careers of McGraw and Hill there was no machinery for determining the truth of a publisher's circulation claims. "Buyer beware" was the watchword of the advertiser. When he asked a salesman for figures on his paper's readers he was always prepared to cut the answer in half or more, depending on his judgment of the salesman's probity. In the 1880s one or two papers had tried to curb their salesmen's damaging exuberance by publishing the true figures of the number of each issue printed; and these figures appeared so conservative that advertisers came to accept them.

A fourth policy at variance with the custom of the time was to refuse untrue or misleading advertisements. Refusal of deceptive advertising copy was one of the early indications of a new dawn of business conscience. It marked the beginning of the end of the *caveat emptor* era. Sensational demonstrations of the changing practice came in the first decade of the twentieth century with the courageous stand taken by *Collier's Weekly* and the *Ladies' Home Journal* against the fraudulent advertising of quack doctors and proprietary medicines. But by this time a few business papers had led the way.

In the beginning the occasional business journal which adopted these principles was in a difficult position. Many advertisers preferred the old, haphazard way of doing business. The men who were promoting the advanced standards, therefore, were anxious to have them universally accepted, to set up some form of control that would assure a uniformity of practice throughout the business press.

2 Although James McGraw and John Hill were both strong advocates of these novel measures, they were not entirely alone in their views. Some of the journals we have seen in their early years were managed according to one or more of these principles. Such publishers as Bailey and Miller of *American Ma-*

Henry G. Lord. Photograph taken at about the time of the founding of the Trade Press Associations at Niagara Falls.

chinist, Frost of *Engineering News*, and Johnston of *Electrical World* had been strict in separating the advertising and editorial provinces and told the truth about circulation. But the most dynamic fighter for total revolution in the practices of the business press was a Yankee genius who had entered the publishing business as a boy of eighteen and is still active in it at the age of ninety-three.

Descended from a line of shipbuilders and others who had gone down to the sea in ships, Henry Gardner Lord inherited the most vital and rugged of New England's traditions. His father had bridged the gap between seafaring and business with a career as supercargo in the China trade.

> Supercargo [Henry Lord explains] was the businessman who went along on trips. . . . The supercargo was the one who sold the cargo to the best advantage wherever the port might be, and who bought the return cargo. He had to use his judgment. As a training, it was some of the best business training that I can conceive of, and was the basis for many of the great, prominent Boston families . . . who started in the shipping industry.[1]

As a boy Henry Lord entered the basic Massachusetts wool business through a brokerage house. This house published a small paper on textiles, *Fibre and Fabric*, and at eighteen Lord had become half-owner of the journal. At twenty-three he started a paper called *Textile World*, a publication that has grown in importance and in value to the industry through more than seventy years.

During his first publishing years, he entered our story through his acquaintance with Horace Swetland and James McGraw while they were engaged in some of their early Boston operations. From their first meeting he had looked up to McGraw as a leader of the business press and one who had much to teach him.

> Most of all [Lord remembers] I agreed with him in his very definite policy that the editorial aspect of this business is the most important

[1] Henry G. Lord, recorded interview, pp. 2, 3.

CIRCULATION 10,000 OR MORE COPIES EACH ISSUE. See Sworn Certificates on third page.

TEXTILE MANUFACTURING WORLD.

VOL. I. BOSTON, MASS., U.S.A., JANUARY, 1888.

Textile Man'f'g World.
PUBLISHED MONTHLY AT
92 WATER STREET, BOSTON, MASS.
GUILD & LORD, Publishers,
W. S. KELLEY, Editor.
YEARLY SUBSCRIPTION RATES.
YEARLY ADVERTISING RATES.

FEATURES IN THIS NUMBER

INTRODUCTORY.

With this its first issue, the Textile Manufacturing World is introduced to the public, and beyond a word now as to its purposes and aims, the paper will be left to speak for itself.

Some will undoubtedly say that there is no room for another textile publication. Having carefully considered this subject, we think otherwise: our measure of success must prove the correctness of our position. What, with ordinary trade-paper methods would be an unprofitable field, we propose, by the application of more systematic and business-like principles to develop into an unusually desirable property.

Having definite objects in view, — without which its publication would certainly not be warranted, — we shall strive to employ methods so generally acceptable as to insure a liberal share of patronage. We shall endeavor to merit the cordial support of all engaged in the various branches of textile manufacturing and allied interests.

We propose to make the paper eminently practical: to present to our readers, in as concise and clear a form as possible, that which is instructive and of interest to all intelligent workmen, anxious to better fit themselves for a step forward when the opportunity offers; to discuss the principles and present the salient points in the various processes of textile manufacture, as well as to present clearly the merits of current public questions bearing upon this interest.

We shall endeavor to interest bright, intelligent, thinking men in all departments, not in filling our columns with personalities, I-know-it-and-you-don't controversies, interesting only to the writers, for this will be strictly ruled out; but in favoring us with short, crisp, correspondence upon topics and points of interest, which come up from time to time in their work, about which they are seeking information, or which is likely to prove interesting and instructive to others. All such correspondence we cordially invite, and shall strive to make it well worth the while of those favoring us in this way.

Men who work ten hours a day for six days in the week, haven't time to read a column for what a paragraph should contain; neither has the superintendent nor agent nor the business man, with many and varied calls upon his time. Recognizing this fact, we shall make it a point to present all matter in as condensed a form as possible, consistent with clearness; furthermore, it will be our aim to make the paper in all departments thoroughly reliable, by carefully verifying all statements of fact.

One in a position to know recently remarked, "The paper that reaches the greatest number of men inside the mills, is the one that pays the best to advertise in; for the ones who have the responsibility of its management, generally have a deciding voice in selecting the machinery; and this holds equally good concerning supplies."

Being thoroughly convinced of the correctness of this position, — that the best-read paper is the most valuable to advertisers, — we shall strive to make the Textile Manufacturing World so bright, interesting, and instructive that it will be indispensable to practical men everywhere throughout our factories; and we believe that success along the lines outlined above will accomplish this.

An important factor in this result is the remarkably low subscription price, which places it within the means of all.

OUR PLATFORM.

Whatever influence this paper may exert will be thrown in favor of the further development and building up of textile manufacturing and allied interests in the United States, so far as we are able to understand and appreciate their necessities.

The business man and the manufacturer, with capital invested and large interests at stake, will want to know, and those who have favored us with such liberal patronage have a right to ask, how we regard these interests, and what stand we shall take upon the various questions of public and private policy, the proper treatment of which is so vital to their prosperity. Will the "Textile Manufacturing World" advocate protection or free-trade? What will be its position upon the so-called labor question? will it pursue a settled policy, or try to throw sops to all sides? What are its politics? Is it the organ of any class or clique? Is it mortgaged to any business interest?

Will it cater to class popularity, or has it brain and backbone enough to pursue a straightforward independent course, and do justice to all? The latter, in a nutshell, is the course we propose; and our utterances from month to month must show how near we come to the mark. Briefly, then, the principles upon which the conduct of this paper will be based, are as follows: —

We do not believe in prohibitive duties, but in such a measure of protection to home industries as will enable our manufacturers to pay good wages to their workmen, and successfully compete with all comers. Believing it desirable to cultivate foreign markets for the disposal of our surplus products, also that the prestige of a nation abroad depends largely upon the ships that fly its flag in foreign ports, and that commerce follows the flag; therefore, to develop commerce abroad, and build up a profitable foreign trade, we favor a liberal policy on the part of the General Government in providing for the carriage of mails in American bottoms, and otherwise encouraging American shipping.

Party politics will have no place: a trade paper may, aye, should have, principles, but not politics. We have only condemnation for any so little in sympathy with American institutions, and so little able to appreciate that liberty of speech and action which the citizens of few countries enjoy, as to attempt or even counsel the overthrow of our social structure, whether they call themselves Communists, Socialists, or Anarchists.

We have no sympathy with disturbers in any relation, — whether social, economic, or industrial, — particularly with those who maliciously, or otherwise, attempt to antagonize labor and capital by raising false issues and blinding labor to its own best interests.

There can be no real antagonism between capital and labor: each is essential to the prosperity of the other, — as one prospers, so does the other; as one is disturbed, nervous, demoralized, so is the other.

We believe in equal rights and opportunities to the individual, the firm, or the corporation, to manage their business in their own way, subject to the laws of the land, without dictation, or coercion from outside.

We believe that labor throughout the country is entitled to, and should demand, — in a manner that cannot be misunderstood, — protection from unrestricted immigration: the workmen throughout our mills and workshops have as much right to be protected from the competition of

(Continued on third page.)

one. . . . He always threw the weight of his thinking toward the editorial end.[2]

But Lord, too, had been one of the first to print his circulation figures. He did this in *Textile World* on its masthead.

Between 1888 and 1905 Lord had become a successful business-paper publisher in more than one field. In the early years he had had a brush with Swetland. He had acquired a paper called *Power and Machinery* at the same time that Swetland was publishing *Power*. He remembers that Swetland told Lord his title was "cutting it close." So he changed to *Lord's Power and Machinery Magazine* and the advertisers asked the salesmen if it was a religious paper dealing with the power of prayer!

Lord absorbed several other textile magazines and built them into *Textile World*. By 1905 he had become an important figure in business publishing. By this time there were several so-called trade-paper associations, local institutions that met at intervals to discuss local conditions. There was one in New York and another in Chicago. Lord was president of the New England group. Then in 1905 something happened that brought them all together, and for the first time there was a national gathering of trade-journal publishers. It was the opportunity for which the leaders had been waiting.

3 There was nothing particularly impressive about the event that brought them all together. There was not even an intent to form an organization, protective or progressive. Some of those who were there had thought very little about codes of publishing ethics or practice. They went to Niagara Falls in the autumn of 1905 to protect their own interests, because the United States government had stepped on their toes.

In Washington a bill was pending which, if passed, would raise the rate for second-class-mail matter from its time-honored level of a penny a pound. The bill, indeed, proposed to double

[2] *Ibid.*, p. 23.

First issue of "Textile Manufacturing World," January, 1888.

the rate! Like other publishers, the men of the business press were quick to meet to protest. As their business was quite apart from the rest of the publishing world, and as the publishers of general magazines were inclined to look down their noses at it, these people held a meeting of their own.

It must have been a diverse gathering. There were publishers of papers representing grocers, shoemakers, dry-goods merchants, railroad men, jewelers, plumbers—some successful, some struggling, some hardly able to scrape up the fare to Niagara. For the most part they had but one motive—to defeat the Post Office bill—but it was the first national meeting of these publishers, and other matters were sure to come up.

One of these was of lasting consequence. At the meeting men from all over the nation met for the first time. This sense of unity and the acquaintanceships that grew in the few days into friendships had the result that many such first meetings have: when it was over there was a chorus: "Let's do it again." In this way was formed an organization that developed great power and established a set of standards that has endured for half a century.

The first officers were regionally chosen. John Hill of New York was made president; John Newton Nind of Chicago, vice president, and Henry G. Lord of Boston, secretary-treasurer. Of precisely what they discussed there is no record. All these men were the heads of their local associations. The group met every year and discussed every phase of trade-paper publishing. It was, Lord remembers, mainly a "debating society," but gradually the members all became convinced that the organization must be powerful enough to enforce certain standards both for themselves and for those who would buy the advertising space they offered.

During this time there came about a perennially increasing distaste in the higher echelons of the publishers for the term *trade paper*. To the outsider it seems like good enough nomenclature. Perhaps today the word *trade* has come to have a broader meaning (as indeed it had in older times) than it had in the early twentieth century. About 1912 it came to be looked upon as carrying

Officers and delegates, Federation of Trade Press Associates Convention, Washington, October 10, 1907. Third and fourth from left in front row are John A. Hill and Henry G. Lord.

a sort of service-entrance implication that seemed far below the dignity of industrial publishing. On the other hand, the word *business* was acquiring great prestige and all-embracing definition. To the detached observer of these philological subtleties, it is surprising that such emphasis should have been placed on them by businessmen. Seen against the historical background, however, it becomes evident that they reflect the changing times.

The abstract idea of "business" had come to dominate the American scene. Local business units had given way to huge national organizations. The men at the head of them were of a wholly different caliber from the traditional owner-manager of the nineteenth century—the man who was proud to say he "did his bookkeeping in his head." The new giants lifted the smaller aspirants to a higher level. "Business" now permeated all industry. Engineers or technical men were beginning to move into management. Lawyers were becoming partners in business enterprise. Associations were forming everywhere which included firms or corporations that formerly had been cutting each other's throats in wasteful competition. "Business," in short, had acquired a new dignity; "trade" was a sort of throwback into what business had once been.

Conscious of themselves as an increasingly activating force in every phase of this activity, the industrial, technical, trade or "class" press decided to call itself the *business press* and its members *business papers,* whether they dealt with architecture, engineering, manufacturing, or merchandising. Thus, the Federation of Trade Press Associations became Associated Business Publications, Inc.,—or ABP; and, some ten years after the first national gathering, it was a permanent institution with a headquarters and the promise of prosperity. It had, too, a code that it could enforce.

4 In the meantime advertisers were also riding a wave of reform. Turned, with the turn of the century, from amateurs to professionals, they, too, had formed associations, exchanged common experience, discussed common problems, and tried to formulate codes that could be enforced. At about the time of the exposures of medical fraud by *Collier's* and the *Ladies' Home Journal,* the Associated Advertising Clubs of the World started the celebrated truth-in-advertising movement and fought for a decade or more a bitter battle for integrity. During these years, assisted by other associations, one of the objectives was to persuade the publishers of their media to tell the truth about themselves. Aware that advertising was changing from a hit-or-miss game into a combined art and science, they felt that publishing was still largely in the amateur stage. Working with careful analysis of media to obtain the best estimate of sales result per dollar expended, they were stymied by the difficulty of getting authentic circulation figures. They could rely on the statements of the more scrupulous publishers; with the others they were shooting in the dark.

The great difficulty was that definitions of circulation did not agree. There was no standard. In other business there was usually an inflexible criterion, such as a universally accepted unit of weight or measure. A pound was a pound whether in the butcher shop or on the housewife's kitchen scales; you could check on the yard of cloth you bought and be sure of your money's worth. But what was the "circulation" of a paper or magazine? Was the unit a payment or the word of a reader? Was it a copy bought or a copy printed? As William Boyenton of the Rutgers School of Journalism states in his excellent history of this problem:

> To the strict constructionist, circulation was copies sold at the regular price; to the liberal constructionist, circulation might be press run, including copies given away, copies sold at large discounts and even copies never placed in readers' hands. Furthermore, the total circulations reported by publishers included all subscriptions and single copy sales regardless of channels, prices and methods of payment.[3]

The publisher often believed he had a right to distribute his publication as he pleased. And might not a reader be as much impressed by an advertisement in a paper he had received free as by one in a paper he had bought? He did not pay, after all, to look at a billboard. Advertisers, on the other hand, were coming to believe in a certain differential among the media: that a reader valued more highly a paper for which he paid than one he received gratis, and that, therefore, an advertisement had greater value therein. But even if he admitted that the matter was debatable, the advertiser wanted to know. He wanted to be able to choose for himself on the basis of an authentic and indubitable presentation of the facts. He wanted publishers to submit their publications to an impartial auditor who would break down the figures: so many paid subscribers, so many newsstand sales, so much free distribution, so many copies sold at a discount, so many

[3] William H. Boyenton, *Audit Bureau of Circulations,* Chicago, 1952, pp. 3, 4.

with a premium. In this way he would have a yardstick, a precise standardized measure which could show him what to pay to get the maximum money's worth.

The period in which these things were fought for was the period of gestation for the Audit Bureau of Circulations. Perhaps in the history of periodical publishing there has been no greater boon to publishers and advertisers alike than the work of this agency.

The ABC, as it is now universally known, came into being in Chicago on May 20–21, 1914, through the merging of two experimental organizations, the Advertising Audit Association and the Bureau of Verified Circulations. The first board of directors consisted of eleven advertisers, two advertising agents, two newspaper publishers, two magazine publishers, two farm-publication publishers, and two business-paper publishers. It is obvious from this proportion that the publishers had been won over. As Mr. Boyenton says:

> The willingness of the publishers to allow this provision for buyer control through majority representation on the board is evidence of a desire on their part to put an end to old abuses and establish standards for sound circulation practices.[4]

Through the years the Bureau enlarged the scope of its audits, breaking down, in the case of many specialized journals, the circulation figures by professional or business connections of readers. It has become as indispensable today to both advertisers and publishers as a slide rule is to the engineer. In 1938, speaking at the Bureau's annual meeting, Senator Arthur Capper said:

> So far as I can call to mind, the Audit Bureau of Circulations is the only institution in America in which the producer and consumer, the manufacturer and the customer, the seller and the buyer, have voluntarily sat down together and for twenty-four years have cooperated, harmoniously and with good feeling, in establishing standards of practice. . . . The Bureau came into being, not upon compulsion, not through governmental edict, but through the voluntary action of men

[4] *Ibid.*, p. 11.

of integrity who saw that decency and fairness and honorable dealing are the prime essentials of business.[5]

ABP and ABC

5 Leading the way among "men of decency and fairness" toward a standard circulation audit were Henry Lord, John Hill, and James McGraw. To them the formation of a sound publisher's association, such as Associated Business Publications, was dependent upon the establishment of an audit bureau. The ABC was to them the first step toward any establishment of a standard code of publishing practice. From the first suggestion of a bureau, the members of the Federation of Trade Press Associations promoted it with all the force at their command. To the convention that established the ABC in May, 1914, the Federation sent a committee to represent them. These men of the business press foresaw that in certain ways the ABC would have more importance for their papers than for any others. Certainly it has worked out that way, for today's advertiser demands a peculiarly close analysis of a business paper's circulation.

With part of its problem taken care of, the emerging Associated Business Publications was able to carry out its other purposes. It issued a Code of Ethics in which were included the obligation to consider the reader first, to publish nothing of an advertising nature in news or editorial columns, to reject misleading advertising, to publish their advertising rates and apply them without discrimination, and to publish verified circulation statements.

Thus out of a simple desire to prevent a rise in postal rates—which was, incidentally, forestalled—came a powerful organization for the promotion of standards. In the course of its formation and the formation of its fellow, the Audit Bureau, John Hill and James McGraw came often together. Before the formations were complete the two had found a way to merge a part of their interests without merging their personalities. As we look back on the event, it seems a portent of things to come.

[5] *Ibid.*, p. 13.

CHAPTER THIRTEEN

The Marriage of the Books

Some of the most momentous projects in business history have been hatched over a restaurant table. Away from the noise and interruptions of an office, in intimate privacy, in a place where the sole possible eavesdropper on confidential exchanges is an indifferent waiter, a lunch table stimulates creative impulses. In the New York of 1909 where only an occasional automobile horn punctuated the long sequence of hoofbeats and streetcar bells, lunch was a quiet and leisurely affair. In such an atmosphere in the spring of that year, two ardent business rivals sat on comfortable, leather upholstered chairs in the gilded rococo dining room of a Park Row restaurant known as Haan's and made plans to end their rivalry.

Both were book men—heads of departments in publishing houses. Edward Caldwell of the McGraw Publishing Company and Martin Foss of the House of Hill were not, at the moment, concerned with the main business of those organizations—the publication of technical or business periodicals. Their work was with accumulations of important technical and educational material that had first appeared in magazines and had then been given permanent form between book covers. More and more such material had been printed as the journals had grown and their reputations had spread. Engineers and technicians had repeatedly asked that a series of articles by some final authority on mining, building, tool designing, or the generation of power be expanded and made into a book that could be kept on the reference shelf. There were, to be sure, such publishers as John Wiley and D. Van Nostrand who specialized in technical books, but both McGraw and Hill were in a particularly fortunate position for this sort of publishing because they had their own magazines as feeders.

In some cases, books had been published as by-products of technical papers before those papers became McGraw or Hill properties. The Scientific Publishing Company, for instance, brought out some successful geological books that had first seen print as articles in the *Engineering and Mining Journal.* It had been Hill's practice, however, to turn such book material over to Wiley. In 1906 it occurred to him that he was letting slip in this way what might be a profitable business for himself. So he established a book department and in 1907 called in Martin Foss to head it. McGraw's ventures in this direction had a much older history, going back, indeed, to the early days of his electrical papers. Because Edward Caldwell had worked for some eighteen years with these papers, he had come more and more into touch with book authors and book buyers, and was now, in 1909, in charge of McGraw's book-publishing department.

The difference between these two men, Caldwell and Foss, was almost as great as between their employers. Both reflected to some extent the traits of their respective bosses, or at least the characteristics of the houses in which they worked. Caldwell was inclined to be austere, completely dedicated to his career, an indefatigable worker with scarcely a thought outside the orbit of his tasks. Foss was warm, genial, a good mixer, a man about town, with many interests away from the office, and enjoying life to the full. The two were characterized in the reminiscences of one who worked with them:

> Mr. Caldwell . . . seemed too severe and too unbending. He didn't smoke. He didn't joke. He could laugh if someone else told him a joke, but life was very severe and hard. Foss, on the other hand, was dynamic, handsome, a good talker and story-teller, gregarious, an extrovert. He belonged to clubs and had a good sense of humor. . . . He was full of new ideas. . . .[1]

[1] James Stacy Thompson, recorded interview (edited), pp. 24, 25.

Edward Caldwell, about 1927.

Caldwell, however, was greatly admired and respected, even by those from whom he required the hardest work. Like McGraw he was a relentless driver but

> . . . a man of high principles, quiet and restrained in speech, modest, meticulous about details. His standards reflected his arts education at Knox and engineering at Cornell. His hobby was rare books and Americana. He loved good printing and fine bindings. He collected a great library on the Mississippi Valley and gave this to Knox as a memorial to his wife who also graduated from Knox.[2]

Yet the men were good friends from their first meeting, and when Martin Foss laid his plan on the lunch table in Haan's restaurant, Caldwell's response was immediate and enthusiastic. He may have been less exuberant than Foss but he brought to their conversation a good deal of sound business sense.

2 The plan was the first McGraw-Hill merger. There was no thought in the mind of either of these men of combining the magazine-publishing companies. Rather they proposed to take the book departments away from both companies and join them in a separate organization whose sole business should be books. This new house would, of course, be jointly owned by McGraw and Hill and would be fed by the McGraw and Hill papers, but it would also go out into new fields and acquire new properties. Neither James McGraw nor John Hill need be bothered with the management of the McGraw-Hill Book Company; the whole affair would be in the hands of Foss and Caldwell, relieving the senior partners of their book worries.

The two men then prepared briefs to be shown to their respective bosses. After all, McGraw and Hill were the only leading publishers both having offices in New York who published both business papers and technical books. The books they published were much alike, dealing mainly with engineering subjects and largely derived from papers such as *Engineering and Mining Journal, American Machinist, Engineering Record, Power,* and

[2] *Ibid.,* p. 26.

Electrical World. If the book departments should merge, economies would be effected. The new company could draw on all the McGraw and Hill magazines. It could develop a college list and the machinery to promote adoptions of texts which the two separate companies could not afford to do. There would be savings on salaries, advertising, catalogues, and selling costs. The increased size of the new company and the more diversified list that would become possible would attract more authors and command a wider market.

Next, Foss and Caldwell examined the figures representing the business the two companies had done in books during 1908, the year just past. In comparison with later operations they seem ludicrously small. Gross receipts from sales on the books they published came to about $64,000 for McGraw and $61,000 for Hill. In addition they had done a retail business in the books of other publishers that came to some $40,000 for McGraw and less than half of that for Hill. Net profit had been only $14,000 for McGraw and $11,000 for Hill. Hill's expenses had been uniformly higher than McGraw's; his advertising and promotion had cost him more than three times as much and he had paid considerably more in royalties. This breakdown revealed a situation that left a lot to be desired on both sides and it implemented the other arguments.

When the two men had prepared and written out their stories, they presented them to their bosses. There seems to have been immediate opposition. There are few records of the discussions and we must rely on the memories of men who were in the confidence of the principal actors in this first McGraw-Hill drama. Those close to James McGraw knew that he would have been certain to bring every possible argument against such a project—merely to draw out its promoters. This was his habitual way: even when he favored a new proposal he would appear to fight it until every pro and con had been thrashed out before him. But perhaps, too, in this case he was not yet prepared to join forces with a man he knew was his closest competitor. James McGraw loved competition. He believed its pressure was good for his business. It was essential, he thought, to the morale of his employees.

Hill may have fought the merger because it suggested a loss of control. But these speculations are digressions from the theme of our story. Both principals were finally convinced. They were both far more interested in their papers than in their books. With the book publishing adequately handled by men wholly dedicated to the project, they would be able to focus their attention more sharply on their main interest. In the meantime the new book company would be almost certain to increase their profits. Probably neither principal could foresee the rich future that would evolve from the work of the two young men; nor did they fully realize the power inherent in the McGraw-Hill name.

3 The story has often been told of how James McGraw and John Hill finally met and flipped a coin to determine the name of the new company. The winner of the toss was to have his name first in the title. The loser was to be president. McGraw won and Hill became president of the McGraw-Hill Book Company. The merger was completed in July, 1909, some three months after the luncheon at Haan's. The new company established its offices in the McGraw Publishing Company's building at 239 West 39th Street.

First offices of the McGraw-Hill Book Company.

Different as they were in temperament and interests, Foss and Caldwell complemented each other as business partners. Foss gave his whole attention to the editorial side. Planning publishing schedules, getting new authors, organizing staffs of outside editorial experts, building machinery for the adoption of college texts, and establishing relationships with college and university professors—these activities made Martin Foss's life, and he was content to leave all the business details to Caldwell. Foss, in short, was concerned with manuscripts.

Caldwell's job was to convert these manuscripts into books. He had charge of production. Of course they would confer on the format, but once a manuscript was in the works, Caldwell took charge of it entirely. He also supervised the office. All the techniques of billing, accounting, credit, and management of the shipping and stock rooms—that was Caldwell's job. He handled the mechanics of the process.[3]

Caldwell was the anchor, holding the business to a solid rock bottom. Confident of its stability, Foss could go his brilliant way establishing warm friendships, building loyalties, inventing, creating, reaching out for new extension in every direction. Foss knew his way around, not only in the world of journalism and literature but in the academic world as well. He had put himself through Harvard by newspaper work; even as an undergraduate he had been a correspondent for no less than thirteen papers. This activity, he later confessed "had one main defect—it helped me to avoid an education." [4] He was, of course, getting a far more important training for his later life than if he had stuck to his academic studies. At the same time he made friends among the faculty and became familiar with the patterns of college curricula.

He had intended to become a writer. Like all incipient writers, he had need of a job to support him, so he had signed up with the then celebrated firm, Baker & Taylor, who at that time were

[3] *Ibid.*, p. 24.

[4] "Technical Books as Valued Wartime Tools," by Robert von Gelder: an interview with Martin Foss, etc., in *New York Times*, Book Review, February 22, 1942, pp. 2, 23.

publishers as well as booksellers. Foss wrote stories on the side. But the job was uncongenial; he disliked his boss and when a telephone talk with John Hill had brought the offer of $1,000 more than he was earning, he had thrown his writing career out the window and given his full time to study of the technical-book business.

As soon as the merger was complete, he started to carry out his large, bold plan. He knew the prospects were good but he had no idea of their extent—of the urgent potential demand for certain types of technical books. The need came less from top men in management or graduate engineers than from men down the line: machinists, technicians, patternmakers, foundrymen, draftsmen—skilled workers whose grandfathers in similar occupations had scarcely opened a book in the course of their careers. But the world had moved beyond the stage where an apprentice could learn from his master all he needed to know. Techniques had multiplied; simple things had become complex; methods, following the teachings of Taylor, Gilbreth, Gantt, and the other pioneers of scientific management had become standardized as a result of careful time and motion study. Now that the old mysterious father-and-son magic, giving each artisan an individual and different skill, was proving inadequate for those who must work in organized production on a time schedule with semi-automatic machines, with jigs and fixtures that had taken the skills from the craftsman's hands, with tools of high-speed steel that needed special maintenance, and with foremen who must follow rather than invent rules, men must learn from books the universal optimum operations that had evolved from the study of highly and specially educated planners. Print had crystallized the techniques as no group of oral teachers could ever do.

It was true that many men on the operating level had been studying the magazines. The correspondence columns of *American Machinist,* for example, had from the start printed "Letters from Practical Men" which other practical men had read with profit. That these readers would buy books had seemed doubtful to Martin Foss when he first worked with Hill in 1908. He later told the story of the surprise he got from one of his early ventures. This was a book compiled by an editor of *American Machinist,* Fred H. Colvin, and a Western shop expert, Frank A. Stanley. It was called the *American Machinists' Handbook* and was a full compendium of shop methods in metalworking. There was much material in it that had appeared in the paper over a period of years plus a great deal of new substance, but all arranged for quick and handy reference by men who had one eye on a machine while the other was in the book. It was a book for thumbing by grimy fingers, as much a tool as any that fitted in a lathe or miller.

Foss opposed it. There was already a good handbook in the field published by John Wiley. After a considerable fight he agreed to print it, but with a cautious provision as to royalties. It was the custom in publishing houses to promise a big royalty to an author only after his book had sold a large number of copies. This is known as the sliding scale: for example, an author would get 10 per cent on the list price up to 5,000 copies, 12½ per cent to 10,000, 15 per cent on copies over 10,000, and so on. On the contract for the Colvin and Stanley book:

> I named a figure (Foss remembered) that I was perfectly certain would not be reached.[5]

By the time the merged company was well under way, the impossible figure had been passed. In ten years from publication in 1908, the hundred-thousand mark had been reached. By the time Foss told the story in 1942 the handbook had sold, in its thirty-four-year career, more than 400,000 copies. It was greatly in demand in World War I; then, in 1941, its thirty-third year, it had sold 40,000 copies.

4 After the merger, Foss spent much time traveling, calling on professors who had or might have manuscripts to sell. The

[5] *Ibid.*

company was still small and careful when, as Foss tells it, "the first big break came."

. . . I was doing one-night stands through the Middle Western colleges, talking up our books to professors and wearing dark gray shirts because of the laundry problem. Late one afternoon after about six weeks on the road I had an appointment with a Professor of Mechanical Drawing—Thomas E. French, Ohio State. He had a book he wanted me to look at—a new method—I'd been warned about that—warned that all the mechanical drawings always had new methods and manuscripts but this looked good. We published it, it has been revised five times, and it is still the standard work for colleges.[6]

There have been three more editions of *A Manual of Engineering Drawing* since Foss told the story. The eighth was published in 1953. In its long career since 1911, the book has sold more than 1,500,000 copies. There was scarcely a course in any engineering school that was not based on it; and the Reinhardt system of lettering which it introduced has become almost as universal in its use among engineers as the slide rule. Foss's meeting

[6] *Ibid.*

Martin Foss's notes on his meeting with Professor French, February 9, 1910.

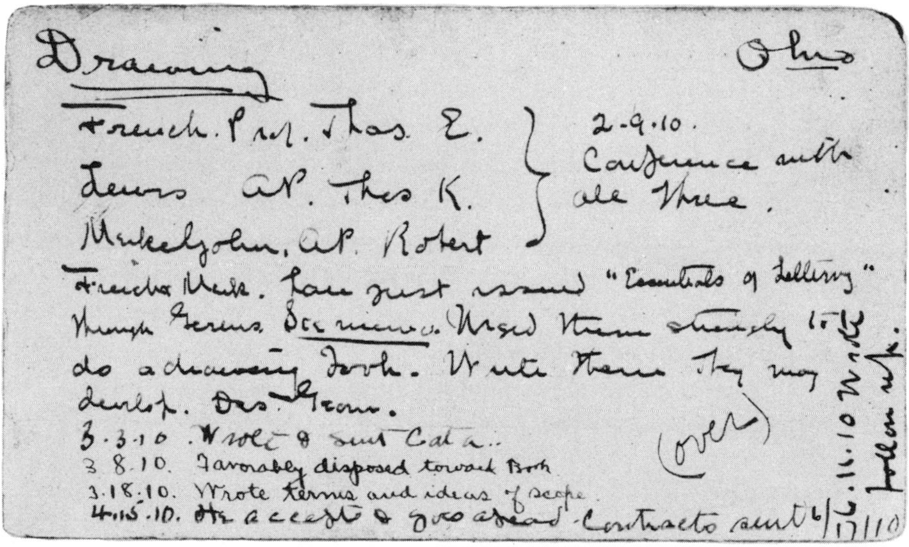
Drawing Ohio
French. Prof. Thos. E.
Lewis A.P. Thos. K.
Meiklejohn, A.P. Robert
2-9-10. Conference with all three.
French [illegible] have just issued "Essentials of Lettering" through [illegible]. Urged them strongly to do a drawing book. Write them they may develop. [illegible]
3-3-10. Wrote & sent Cat a..
3.8.10. Favorably disposed toward Book
3.18.10. Wrote terms and ideas of scope.
4.15.10. He accepts & goes ahead. Contracts sent 6/17/10
(over)
6.11.10 Wrote follow up.

Thomas E. French.

with French at the end of a long, weary day was a break indeed—one of those exciting accidents that punctuate the more dramatic chapters of publishing history.

Other landmarks of the first years were *Engineering Mathematics* by the genius of General Electric, Charles Steinmetz, in 1911, and Dexter Kimball's bible, *Principles of Industrial Organization,* in 1913, a book so clear and simple in its definitions and explanations that it has fascinated many laymen with inquiring minds as well as industrialists. These books all have a finality that defies the obsolescence so common in technological literature. The Steinmetz after more than forty years has had such continuing success that it has been reissued in revised form and the Kimball is in its sixth edition.

Besides these monumental volumes, Foss built up a rounded
 list. At the start the McGraw-Hill books were nearly all con-

Charles Steinmetz.

cerned with some phase of engineering. But Foss soon reached out into the fields of chemistry, physics, mathematics, agriculture, business administration, and economics. He created a college department to supply textbooks for engineering and science students that even included manuals on English. Foss always maintained that he knew nothing, himself, of technology. He is supposed to have told one author, "We can't publish your book because I can understand it. We only publish books that are entirely beyond my comprehension." We may doubt the accuracy of some of Foss's claims, but we know that he understood how to get people who *did* know every field to read and criticize the manuscripts.

The first editorial assistant he attached was James Stacy Thompson to whom we are indebted for many of the memories of the early days. Like Foss, Thompson was a nontechnical man with journalistic training, having started on a country newspaper for which he had written, set the type, and worked the press. But Thompson, too, had a nose for the kind of author and manuscript the company needed. He became adept at interviewing professors and in initiating series of books for which he would appoint an especially learned professor as consulting editor.

In the first ten years a very considerable staff of outside editors was developed who supplied all the technical knowledge in which Foss and Thompson were deficient. Among them were professors of chemistry, agrostology, electrical engineering, applied mathematics, metallurgy, and marine engineering, as well as advertising, business administration, and industrial management. The list included such distinguished educators as Harry E. Clifford and Lionel S. Marks of Harvard, Henry P. Talbot of M.I.T., Charles Sumner Slichter and George Albert Hool of the University of Wisconsin, and Edward Burke McCormick of Kansas State Agricultural College.

In this period the dreams of Caldwell and Foss had come true to an extent that surprised them both. From the 250 books with which they started, the list had grown to nearly 1,000 titles. To the two who were holding down the office when Thompson arrived and was surprised to see them opening their own mail, seven executives had been added, including Frank L. Egner who had instituted a thriving mail-order department.

5 To the austerity of scientific- and technical-book publishing, Martin Foss must have brought a genial warmth. In the midst of their profound concerns he made men laugh. There were never any disputes or known disagreements between the two partners. Each respected the other's talents and was tolerant of whatever faults there may have been.

When the business day was over Foss would put away his papers and leave. He liked to play as well as work. He was a bridge addict. He enjoyed conversations in his clubs. He was an adroit raconteur and his many friends thought him a wit. But when Foss left the office Caldwell would stay on, often working until late into the night.

Foss's favorite clubs were the Engineers and the Players. He used to say that the members of the Engineers Club regarded him as an amateur of the arts and a patron of the theater while habitués of the Players thought him a walking encyclopedia of technical knowledge. Having neither of these assets, he used to enjoy the alternating reputation.

Looking back on this early merger, it appears as a forecast of events to come. Through it the names McGraw and Hill were for the first time joined by a hyphen. Thus a symbol was established in the industrial world and this fact made the second, total merger almost inevitable.

CHAPTER FOURTEEN

The Two Giants

As the century moved into its second decade a sense of security and peace pervaded most of the Western world. The *Pax Britannica* which had endured through the reign of Victoria had continued into the Edwardian years and there was a general belief that the balance of power could be maintained by the simple device of sending a British gunboat to any trouble spot that might appear. If war should break out it could be localized, as the Russo-Japanese affair had been and as the Balkan controversies were about to be. In the United States it seemed as though war had become outlawed among "civilized" peoples and a long vista of undisturbed prosperity stretched ahead. Thus, as Edward VII died in England, as Wilhelm II consolidated his control over the

German Empire Bismark had made for him, and as William Howard Taft reached the mid-point of his term in Washington, the rumblings beneath the surface of international society were well muffled.

By 1910 American wealth and American industrial production had in several departments moved into world leadership. Our national income came to a total three times as large as that of our nearest competitor and our per capita income was some $70 more than that of Canada, second on the list. In the production of pig iron, steel, copper, coal, and petroleum, we had swung far into the lead, and Henry Ford's quantity manufacture of cheap cars put us in the van of the world's automotive industry. By 1914 the United States had nearly twice as many motor vehicles of all kinds as all the nations of Europe combined.

In other enterprise, however, we lagged behind. Despite the initiative given by the Wright brothers, Europe was ahead of us in aircraft production, and we were a weak competitor of Germany in chemical and optical manufacture. In the making of firearms we had lost the lead we once had: a factor which would presently become significant. As our merchant marine had largely disappeared, our shipbuilding was far behind England's.

For the civil engineer one American project seemed to dwarf every other, wherever it might be. This was the great Panama Canal, started under United States auspices in 1904 and opened for commerce in 1914. Its problems of construction gave abundant material to the engineering press all over the world. The two papers of our story had taken an active interest in the project before construction had begun. The *News* had entered the discussion of routes and the celebrated lock–sea-level controversy as far back as 1896. The *Record* caught up in 1901 and from then on did an even more prolific job on it than the *News*. When the work was in mid-career, visits were paid to the canal by Editor Baker of the *News* and by Editor Goodell and Publisher James H. McGraw of the *Record*.

The electrical industry, McGraw's favorite, had increased production to what seems to us a fabulous extent since his interest had first focused upon it. From a total of $19,000,000 in 1889 the value of electrical machinery and supplies manufactured in the United States had risen by 1914 to the colossal figure of $335,000,000. From 1899 when the McGraw Publishing Company started to 1914, the value of American-made dynamos alone increased from 11 to 23 million dollars. Yet electric power was in relatively small use in manufacturing and John Hill's *Power* was still known as "the steam paper."

The picture in both publishing houses between 1910 and America's entrance into World War I was a fast-moving one. Hill, who had astonished the business-paper world in 1902 by paying $400,000 to Horace Swetland for *Power,* paid close to a million in 1911 for *Engineering News.* Though earnings during the first three months' operation of the *News* under the new ownership were very poor, the treasurer of the company in his annual report for 1911 was optimistic.

Engineering News [the report read] is the oldest and best paper in the largest and most active field of engineering, and I have great hopes that it will be one of our best earners. . . .

In paying for the *Engineering News,* we used up our reserve fund, and have already paid on the property $500,000, and as we have all kinds of time to pay the rest, it will never embarrass us. . . .

The adding of the *News* to our assets has made it necessary to increase this amount, and the good will, franchise, etc. now stands on our books as $3,500,000. . . .[1]

That there may have been too much optimism is suggested in Hill's report for the next year, 1912, which began:

In presenting to you the following figures for the past year's operation, I must appear as a false prophet—I predicted a $400,000 year, and we have fallen away below that.

[1] Treasurer's Annual Report, Hill Publishing Co., 1911, in McGraw-Hill Archives. Net profit on *Engineering News* from date of acquisition, Sept. 1, 1911, to end of calendar year 1912: $109,677.19.

And he concluded the report:

I shall make no statements for 1913, lest I fall down again and you elect me to the Ananias Club.[2]

In the meantime, nevertheless, Hill had bought a large piece of real estate on Tenth Ave at 36th Street and was making plans for a building that would be

. . . the best in the world from a sanitary and physical comfort point of view, as well as adaptation to our own business. It is hoped to have it finished in about a year.[3]

The plans for the building, many of which were inspired by Hill himself, show some novelties in business-building design that were considerably ahead of the time. Hill's personal interest in the mechanics of printing which had persisted since his boyhood years had led him to project an ideal printing plant as the focus of the building's specifications. The heavy presses required special materials and methods. But the most novel feature was a system of air conditioning with the primary purpose of keeping dust away from composing and pressrooms. The plate-glass windows in their steel frames were designed to be kept closed and an elaborate ventilating system was to pump "washed" air into the building. Some stories told by the men and women who later worked there imply that the operation of the scheme never quite lived up to the plans—at least from the "sanitary and physical comfort" point of view.

One difficulty seems to have been psychological. Some of those who worked in the new offices were convinced that they would suffocate if the windows were never opened. One executive remembers that one hot day ten girls fainted because they "couldn't get air." Hill was on the spot at once and understood the trouble. He sent out to a nearby five-and-ten and got some ribbons. He tacked these up near the ventilator openings, and as soon as the

[2] *Ibid.*, 1912.
[3] *Ibid.*

The Hill Building at Tenth Avenue and 36 Street.

girls saw them streaming in the drafts of air, there was no more trouble. Most of those who recall the system, however, remember certain summer days when an open window would have been welcome indeed, but they give John Hill credit for prophetic experiment. Air conditioning as we know it was scarcely dreamed of in 1914. The plants in the Hill Building were among the earliest installations of such facilities.

A feature that especially delighted Hill was a sort of roof garden, spacious enough for all the employees of the company to assemble on at once. He loved meetings at which he could talk to his entire force, including stenographers and office boys.

The building so fascinated Hill that during its construction he
 forgot about his business for days at a time and there is little

The Hill Publishing Company personnel assembled on the roof of the new building, 1914.

doubt that climbing ladders and walking along girders 200 feet up aggravated the heart trouble that ended his life at an age when most men are still near their prime.

In the years between the completion of the building and 1916, the Hill company rose to its all-time peak. By 1916 it had five papers: *American Machinist, Power, Engineering News, Engineering and Mining Journal,* and a paper this last had spawned—*Coal Age.*

2 A few blocks northeast of the new Hill building stood the older structure that contained the McGraw enterprise. Here, too, was a printing plant under the direction of a separate corporation. Like the House of Hill, the McGraw building had been

The McGraw Building at 239 West 39 Street.

especially constructed for its purpose, but it had none of the sensational features that Hill had inspired. It was, indeed, for James McGraw, merely a means of housing his business and not a three-ring circus in itself. It had some conspicuous advantages: one was a copious ground floor designed for occupancy by the district Post Office so that all the McGraw mail could be handled right in the building; another was that its solid reinforced concrete absorbed the vibration of the presses. In this building, 239 West 39th Street, about a year after its completion, Foss and Caldwell's McGraw-Hill Book Company began its career.

First on the McGraw publishing list—at least in James McGraw's view—stood *Electrical World* and the old horsecar paper now grown to full maturity as the *Electric Railway Journal.* Next

The McGraw Publishing Company staff in front of the McGraw Building, 1907. Curtis E. Whittlesey and James H. McGraw are fourth and fifth from the left in the front row. Second from the right is Edward Caldwell.

came *Engineering Record,* whose editors and managers by 1911 were spurred to new speed by the fear that Hill's *News* had passed them in the race. The *News* and the *Record,* however, were the only real rivals in the two houses.

Occasionally *Power* and *Electrical World* seemed to come near stepping on each other's toes but for the most part they moved in separate spheres. Both were concerned to some extent with the generation of electricity. But *Power* was primarily interested in private power plants that ran their dynamos by steam; it dwelt on turbines, boilers, and fuel rather than on generators and transmission. *Electrical World* specialized in the growing utilities: central stations, hydroelectric generation, long-range transmission, and the sale of "juice." There were certain similarities in the editorial patterns of the two papers. Both ran question-and-answer departments, columns of instructive letters from practical men, and catechisms. But outside the field of electric power the journals moved wide apart. *Electrical World* had no interest in gas engines or in the shafting and belting that in those days made factories so noisy and dangerous; *Power* let communications and electrochemistry strictly alone.

At this very time, however, James McGraw held a controlling interest in a magazine called *Electrochemical Industry* whose wide circulation was evidence that a new class of engineers was rapidly growing: men who were dedicating their lives to the engineering side of chemistry. In 1913 this paper, its name significantly changed to *Metallurgical and Chemical Engineering,* came officially into the orbit of the McGraw Publishing Company.

Meanwhile the comparisons between the *News* and the *Record* naturally kept coming up in the conferences of the McGraw company. The *Engineering Record* in those days had a large format and a cover of a garish orange color. The *News,* since Hill had made it smaller in size, had a quiet, dignified look; its typography and layout had a symmetry that showed an interest in aesthetic values unusual in the American business press of the day. It looked, the McGraw people used to say, like an English paper. Its subject matter, too, had become by 1911 more concerned with the technical or scientific rather than the practical aspects of civil engineering. But an important difference between the two papers from the sales point of view was that of cost: the *News* was $5 a year; the *Record* only $3.

Apparently, young, low-salaried engineers took the *Record* because it was cheaper, but one wayward fellow scared a *Record* man by saying that if the *News* was $3 he would buy it in preference to the *Record.* Of the *Record's* startling cover:

> One engineer's wife (and her husband joined her in the argument) said it harmonized with absolutely nothing in her house, and baby dresses were often ruined by the running qualities of the coloring matter. The

chief engineer of one of our railroads who takes three copies says "it's a bully good paper, but the color comes off on my coat when it rains."[4]

On the other hand, the *Record* was often complimented on its arrangement. The table of contents was where busy men could find it quickly. The editorials and notes were "headed or sufficiently explanatory in the first line so that one knows the subject matter at a glance." The *News* buried its masthead, contents, and editorials in the body of the paper. And so on. . . .

Evidently older engineers made up for the appeal of the price differential to their juniors, for the *News* circulation ran consistently a little higher than that of the *Record*. In 1911, too, the *News* carried about 2,000 square inches more advertising than the *Record*.

3 No one can look at all the papers of the two companies in the successful years without recognizing certain fundamental standards that applied to every one. These had nothing to do with format, layout, arrangement of contents, reader level, circulation figures, or quantity of advertising space. Whether articles were staff-written or contributed, whether they were long or short, theoretical or practical, purely technical or with economic, administrative, managerial, or political qualification—all those questions that so disturbed the men who sat in the executive chairs at the time—need have no weight with us, looking down the long corridors of history at the basic elements that combined into McGraw-Hill. What was there, after all, in those materials that gave a particular color to the publishing enterprise in which we are interested?

First of all, perhaps, came integrity. It is easy to sentimentalize integrity. But the picture of Diogenes searching with his lantern for an honest man is not altogether applicable to business history. The suggestion there is that to be honest a man must sacrifice success or enjoyment. But as organization has tightened, as

[4] Report of Annual Conference of the Staff, McGraw Publishing Company, Feb. 1–4, 1911, p. 248.

cooperation has replaced the old mayhem of cutthroat competition, as the cult of secrecy has dissolved, unscrupulousness in business has become unprofitable. Deceit, fraud, bribery, conspiracy are not only unprofitable but often impossible in the high visibility of modern commercial operation. The result is that the honest businessman is no longer a lonely figure deserving of tearful praise.

Neither James McGraw nor John Hill was a saint. But they were both fearless men who saw farther into a future world than most of their competitors, and they were willing to fight toward the realization of that future. There were times when the conflict was strenuous but there were few losing battles.

Both men started in an era when integrity was not regarded as an asset in the press, especially in the business press. Even as late as the second decade of the twentieth century, business managers of McGraw and Hill publications were told by their advertising solicitors that their papers were losing in the race with papers that ran puffs for pay or papers that made rate concessions to favorites or with papers that yielded in some manner to the bribes and threats of advertisers. Again and again in the recorded reminiscences of men who worked for these bosses, we find stories of advertisers who angrily withdrew their advertising because of some refusal. But McGraw and Hill would always say, "Let them go. They'll come back." And almost always, after they had thought it over, they did. Perhaps it was the very fact that these men were so willing to let the advertisers go rather than compromise their code that convinced the space buyers that the McGraw and Hill principle of equality of treatment for all was sound.

Another attribute that made both these publishing houses distinctive was a certainty who the readers of each paper were. Editors who are forever guessing at what will interest their readers are unlikely to make an enduring success. The periodical graveyard is full of corpses of magazines that tried first one thing, then another, in vague attempts to please everyone. Actually some of the ancestors of McGraw and Hill papers were dangerously near the abyss before they came into the hands of these publishers. But the emphasis in both these houses was on editorial field work: constant movement among readers and potential readers, analysis of the categories within each industry, and then sure aim at only the precise targets the exploration had determined. This paper was for contractors, that for operating engineers; this one was for practical electricians, that one for managers of a utility plant. There was always, to be sure, a fringe of readership: readers who wanted to acquire *on the side* what for someone else was a central need. Experienced men who wanted what might be called refresher courses in things they had forgotten would read a practical paper; men farther down the ladder would look for a lesson in higher education to help them up. But for each paper there was a main focus and the editors kept their eyes on it.

Once there were reader reference points, the aim at advertisers became easy. Both McGraw and Hill soon realized that in a business paper, the advertiser's effort must not be wasted. Circulations were small and there could be no wide hit-or-miss attack by the advertiser on his market. The publishers' advertising managers, therefore, made careful surveys which the salesmen could present to the advertisers showing the precise potential market of each paper. They then instituted service staffs who would write the copy for the advertisers—copy based on their inside knowledge of who the readers were.

Finally, there was the aim of both publishers to make of their houses something more than business concerns, something with an institutional quality. That McGraw, with his pedagogical background, should have felt this ambition is not surprising. That John Hill should have shared it seems less logical. Yet to the readers of *Power, American Machinist, Engineering News, Engineering and Mining Journal,* and *Coal Age* these papers had become a sort of university.

A useful feature of *Power,* for example, in these late years of the Hill Company was the "Engineers' Study Course." This gave regular lessons in boiler efficiency, heat balance, feed-water treatment, and lubrication. From November, 1913, to February, 1914, a course of eleven lessons in trigonometry began at the beginning with definitions and explanations in the simplest language and followed through the subject exactly as a school course would have done. There were problems in each lesson, the answers to which appeared the following week. This was followed by a series of three lessons on the slide rule. That many a young engineer got his start in this inexpensive school is evident from the letters that came into the editor's office. This sort of thing has always been a part of *Power*. The methods of instruction have improved with the years as the thirty-six-page study of corrosion in the December, 1956, issue shows. Here the simplified colored diagrams complement the direct language of the text, giving the student a quickness of understanding in tune with the rapid tempo of the times.

McGraw's *Electrical World* went so far in this educational direction that a business manager complained in 1911 that the paper had been "put on a pedestal."

Most of our subscribers [he told a conference] do not expect a technical journal to be a text book.[5]

Yet to some extent all the McGraw papers seem to have been just that plus many other things. Besides being institutional in the way of instruction, they provided forums in which ideas might be presented and problems discussed.

It was in these directions that by 1916 the houses of McGraw and Hill appeared to be leading the world of business publications. This does not mean that none of the qualities these publishers possessed existed elsewhere. Such men as Henry Lord, Horace Swetland, and Andrew Haire conducted their papers on the highest level of integrity. Journals of the caliber of *Iron Age, Dry Goods Economist,* and *Textile World* held top places in their respective fields. It simply means that there was a similar combination of similar attributes in the McGraw and Hill establishments which made, as we think back on it, a coincidence of signal portent.

[5] *Ibid.,* Feb 4–5, 1911, p. 11.

2 · GROWTH

CHAPTER FIFTEEN

McGraw-Hill

John Hill died on his way to his office on January 24, 1916. For a year or more he had known of his heart trouble and he feared the sudden death he expected among the indifferent public of a train. That was why he chose to be driven to work from his home in East Orange in his own car by a chauffeur who understood his condition. With him, as a rule, went a neighbor, Otis Davey, who acted on these trips as a confidential secretary. Davey was in the car when Hill died. A sympathetic obituary told the simple story:

> For several minutes Mr. Hill chatted with Mr. Davey, but just as the machine reached Branch Brook Park he suddenly exclaimed, "My head

aches me and I feel as though I was going blind." Immediately afterward his body relaxed and his head fell on Mr. Davey's shoulder.[1]

The chauffeur turned and quickly drove them home, but it was too late.

It was a good death for John Hill, still vigorous in mind and will, still working at top speed and effectiveness in the career he loved, and surrounded by a devoted crew. But John Hill's death shook his company to its foundations. He had hidden his infirmity from most of the men and women in his force. The unexpected news came in the midst of plans and hopes of large proportions. It seemed to halt the whole rhythmic movement toward total success. He was, after all, not quite fifty-eight. He had looked as robust as ever and the general belief was that he would carry on for many years in full control.

It immediately appeared that there was no one to take his place. It is probable that Hill had begun to realize this lack. In his report to the stockholders for the past year, he stated:

> The Hill Publishing Company as a whole is carried on practically by four men and one woman, all of the other officers are concerned with a single department or paper. If one of these five persons dropped out for any cause, we have no men in the business department in training for these jobs. . . . I think it wise and to the best interests of the concern that their places on the Board be taken by young men . . . we do need the youth, the vigor and enthusiasm of four active men.[2]

Hill died before the report could be delivered. No one knew quite what was in his mind. But those who remember the crisis doubt that the situation would have differed much had Hill lived out his rightful span. He had become too much the central focus, the final arbiter, the master mind that knew all and directed all. No one in the company had learned to shoulder over-all responsibility because none had ever had to. The editors of the individual papers had a high degree of independence; their staffs were more autonomous, perhaps, than those in the house of McGraw. But their re-

[1] Newark *Eagle,* Jan. 25, 1916, p. 10, col. 3.

[2] Report to the Stockholders of the Hill Publishing Company, January, 1916.

John A. Hill, about 1915.

sponsibilities did not extend beyond a particular paper's scope. When a problem involved the company as a whole, it was laid in John Hill's lap. He had left his office door always open for the purpose. His was the only office with a door in the entire building—other men and women worked out in the open or in alcoves—and his orders were that the door should not be closed.

Now that John Hill was dead, who would occupy that office? Whose lap now was ample enough for all the perplexing questions? The will took care of the family—Mrs. Hill and a daughter—and left money to some of the employees, but it appointed no successor to the head. It did, however, appoint a trustee.

2 Arthur Baldwin was John Hill's attorney. He was a brilliant lawyer with wide interests and a large acquaintance. He was criticized in some quarters for his part as legal adviser to New York City Democratic politicians who were open to criticism, but John Hill was not concerned with who Baldwin's other clients might be. Hill and his family were devoted to him both as a friend and as a lawyer and he seems to have served their interests in a way that justified their faith.

Those who knew Arthur Baldwin, whether or not they approved of him, were charmed by him. Like McGraw he had grown up on a farm in upstate New York. He had graduated from Cornell in 1892. He was a constant reader of broad tastes and an amateur poet and writer. He was sentimental and generous—it was said of him that any well-told sob story would bring forth help from his well-filled pockets. He had a gay, Irish humor and could tell the kind of yarn that made him a popular after-dinner companion.

His family life was singular. For many years he and his family had shared a house with his brother Leonard. The Leonard Baldwins took an equal share in the housekeeping. They even had a joint bank account. Mrs. Arthur would run the house for a month; then Mrs. Leonard would take over, and so it would go year after year.

When John Hill died, Arthur Baldwin was instantly on the spot to take care of the Hill family interests in the business and, as he had a good understanding of its financial side, it seemed logical after a time for him to become the company's president. There may have been a sigh of relief from the employees that an outsider who was so obviously dedicated to the Hill interests should take over at this point and obviate the possibility of jealousy or injustice among men who were so nearly equal in standing. If they had known what he was going to do they might have been less eager. But it is probable that he did not himself know until he had tried to be a publisher for a time and had come to the conclusion that his talents lay in other directions.

The House of McGraw was generally regarded in the House

of Hill with the sort of suspicion that hotly contesting rivals are bound to feel for each other. James McGraw himself was an unknown figure to most of the Hill crew. Apparently he had never been seen in the Hill building, although it was known that he and Hill met regularly at the board meetings of the McGraw-Hill Book Company. There were rumors of his austerity. In contrast to the lush interiors of the Hill offices with their Oriental rugs, it was said that the McGraw building was bare as a barn. There was talk of McGraw's ruthlessness toward his employees, and any suggestion of a merger would have put fear in the hearts of the men and women who had lived so happily under the Old Man as Hill loved to be called.

3 An old-timer in the House of McGraw recalls an incident which convinced him that consolidation was in the back of James McGraw's mind at least a year before the merger took place. On the day Hill died, McGraw was late to the office. When he arrived and was told the news,

> . . . he never said a word—not a word! It was one of the most peculiar reactions I ever saw. . . . I think he sat there for fifteen minutes before he said a word. Then he said, "Henry, that's too bad. What are we going to do about it? We've got a responsibility now. . . ."
>
> That was the beginning of the merger right there.[3]

No one knows whether or not the same thought of consolidation entered Arthur Baldwin's mind as he picked up the reins. No one, curiously enough, knows much about the preliminaries to the merger. And there are so few records extant that there seems to have been an astonishing informality in this most important act of our drama. The principals seem to have trusted each other implicitly. Both McGraw and Baldwin were accustomed to intuitive thinking. The astute lawyer would have been certain to detect any possible trap in the negotiations and would have insisted on stenographic reports and elaborate records of every de-

[3] Smith T. Henry, recorded interview in McGraw-Hill Archives, p. 50.

Hill's office in the Hill Building, 1914.

tail. That there was much talk seems certain from the reminiscences of those who watched from the wings.

There is, for example, the story of a midnight conversation on the top of the Blue Ridge Mountains. McGraw, Baldwin, Horace Swetland, Henry, and a few others had gone to North Carolina to explore the possibility of acquiring a paper mill for the joint use of several business-paper publishers. For this purpose the president of the Clinchfield Railroad had put a private car at their disposal. One night on the way back after dinner McGraw said to Henry, "Let's talk with Baldwin" and asked Henry to sit in.

Well, the talk went on all night in this private car up on the top of the Blue Ridge. That's where the fundamentals of the consolidation were worked up. . . . Now that didn't mean how many shares of stock in the new company the Hill interests would get. It did mean, though, such things as that McGraw would definitely be the head of the new business . . . and that the Hill interests would have nothing to say about how the business was operated. That was the first fundamental

McGraw's office in the McGraw Building, 1908.

we clashed on. Arthur said, "Well, what protection have the Hill interests got?"

McGraw said, "They've got James H. McGraw!"

I'll never forget that. I can hear it yet: "They've got James H. McGraw!"

To him, that was all the security that was necessary. . . . He didn't mean that they had him as an individual. He meant that they had what he had built as the company: the policy, the business, the assets.[4]

One may hear all kinds of stories in the Big Green Building and, whether or not they are apocryphal, most of them tend to confirm the informality of the proceedings. There is a story, for example, that McGraw and Baldwin stood in a room with their backs to each other for a while until McGraw wrote something in pencil on a slip of paper; when he turned and handed it to Baldwin, Baldwin simply wrote "O.K." and initialed it. On the

[4] *Ibid.*, pp. 52, 53.

paper was the figure McGraw was willing to pay for the Hill business!

A more probable story was of the announcement to the Hill employees after the deal was consummated. McGraw came to the Hill building and when all the men and women were assembled he stood on the top of a desk so that everyone could see him and Baldwin stood on top of another. Baldwin then explained that this deal was not a "sell-out" as the rumor ran, that it was a marriage, that McGraw was the bride and Baldwin the groom. After this gay, informal speech, the Hill people were supposed to have felt better about the merger.

They were not, however, too happy. Obviously some of them would have to drop out—otherwise where was the economy in the merger? But in addition to the loss of jobs, the Hill people felt that there would be a loss of something less ponderable, more sentimental, perhaps. It was impossible for people as dedicated as most of the Hill workers were, both to a man and an institution, not to experience a severe wrench as the old gods faded out and strange new ones took their places. But as time went on, those who were able to adjust to the different ways of the new boss found new successes. The more perceptive of them discovered, too, the basic samenesses—especially the same sense of justice—in the two men. If an employee was in the right, McGraw would back him to the limit, as Hill had done, no matter who was present and regardless of any embarrassment the employee might have caused. In the files of McGraw's correspondence as well as in Hill's, angry letters from powerful captains of industry whose demands had been refused by an advertising salesman were answered by a brusque defense of the young man and with a stated disregard of consequences.

Those who stayed discovered certain new advantages. McGraw, they found, believed in high salaries for good men. He not only raised the pay of many Hill men well over what Hill had paid, but he encouraged them to buy stock and lent them money to buy it with. At the same time he did drop the men who he felt were not equal to his rigorous demands. And there were at times high casualty lists in the McGraw-Hill organization. According to some who criticized his ruthlessness, men, in the McGraw-Hill Company, were expendable.

4 Coincident with the merger came the uniting of the two great civil-engineering papers into the *Engineering News-Record.* On both sides there were objections to that marriage in the editorial staffs. This was natural, for a magazine has a personality. In the rivalry this sense of personality had become keener to the editors. They had looked with contempt on the face and figure of the competing person. The *Record* was ugly, aggressive, vulgar. The *News* was stodgy, abstruse, holier-than-thou. In the Blue Ridge talks Henry remembers that he fought

View from the mezzanine floor of the Hill Building.

hard for his *Record's* independence. But McGraw wanted alliance with the *News* because of its standing in the higher echelons of the profession; he knew that the *Record* needed some of that very conservative, erudite, theoretical quality that rubbed the more practical *Record* men the wrong way.

The first issue of the combination appeared on April 5, 1917. It opened with an editorial by James H. McGraw stressing the familiar theme.

In sum, [this concluded] the paper must be above personalities, above editors and publishers—it must be an institution. Its principles must be so grounded in truth that they cannot be changed, its policies so well crystallized that they appear unconsciously in every issue. . . .

In the letters that poured in during the following week, this theme was echoed again and again by devoted long-time readers of both papers. Professors likened the *News* and the *Record* to their own universities, and an educator at Harvard compared the merger to the cooperation between Harvard and the Massachusetts Institute of Technology.

The *News-Record* appeared at what was, for Americans, a psychological moment. The day after the first issue came out, the U.S. Congress declared that a state of war existed with the German Empire. From then on engineering would have top priority among the civilian professions. The cooperation of civil and military engineering in the United States for the war effort would introduce a variety of new themes for the new paper and give it an opportunity of leadership, not only in normal industry and business but in the supreme, all-encompassing drive toward victory.

5 The McGraw-Hill Publishing Company occupied the Hill building. This may have been something of a comfort to the Hill employees. There, using the presses that had meant so much to John Hill and which he had tenderly covered with coats of white enamel so that they looked like no other presses in the world, the ten papers of the two companies appeared without a

Hill's white-enameled printing presses.

break under the new imprint. The number—ten—was completed in 1916 by the purchase of a new paper by James McGraw.

This was designed to take part of the overflow from *Electrical World.* Electricity in the twentieth century had come to invade the great Elysian fields of American gadgetry. Flashlights had long been commonplace; vacuum cleaners and washing machines of a sort had been produced; electric ranges, though they were rare, were on the market; an electric refrigerator had already arrived; and there were numbers of small devices such as toasters, waffle irons, curling irons, and percolators. Radio telephony was about to enter the ham stage and, though there would be no broadcasting for another half-dozen years, there would be a considerable market, meanwhile, for the components of amateur receiving sets.

It was evident to McGraw and to the editors of the *Electrical World* in 1916 that here was a field that would one day be enor-

Engineering News-Record

A Consolidation of Engineering News and Engineering Record
McGRAW HILL PUB[illegible] COMPANY, Inc.
[illegible] 1917

Two More Cantonment Articles in This Issue!

One tells about the rush work at Camp Grant, Rockford, Ill. The other describes operations at Camp Taylor, Louisville, Ky., where topographical conditions offered opportunities for city planning. The pictures above are from The Louisville C[illegible] mous in extent and one that *Electrical World* could not possibly cover. So far the merchandising of the gadgets had been a function of the utilities and thus belonged more or less in *Electrical World's* province. But now it appeared that most of this business would be taken over by appliance stores, hardware stores, department stores, and mail-order houses. For this there must be a new business paper. Actually there was already a paper that had reached out into this field but its very title, *Electrical-Merchandise and Selling Electricity*, confused the issue. Under this top-heavy name it evidently meant to give service to the utilities in the new selling endeavors.

McGraw bought this as it was falling between its two stools and changed its name to *Electrical Merchandising*. He acquired it at a time that was unfortunate in some ways, because the nation was then so near the threshold of exclusive war production; but the paper survived and became one of the most successful and dynamic on the McGraw-Hill list.

In the same year he acquired a journal called *The Contractor* which in 1918 he built into the new *Engineering News-Record*. This would have made a total of eleven papers for the new company but for the fact that the *Engineering News-Record* had turned two papers into one. In the spring of 1917, then, the McGraw-Hill Publishing Company was issuing: *American Machinist, Coal Age, The Contractor, Electric Railway Journal, Electrical Merchandising, Electrical World, Engineering and Mining Journal, Engineering News-Record, Metallurgical and Chemical Engineering*, and *Power*. It was a list that, as James McGraw proudly explained, covered the entire field of engineering and most industry as well. With the Book Company greatly enlarged since its founding eight years before, McGraw-Hill became in 1917 the largest technical publisher in the world. It was a good time for such a publisher to be at hand. Unlike other American wars before it, this one could not be fought without the power of the printed word.

An early issue of "Engineering News-Record."

CHAPTER SIXTEEN

A New Kind of War

It took the American people at least two years to realize that World War I was different from every other war in history. It took the proverbially conservative U.S. Army even longer. At the officers' training camps in the spring and summer of 1917, the men were taught Civil War tactics culled from textbooks half a century old. It is not surprising, then, that several book publishers, McGraw-Hill among them, missed the boat in the confused years before America entered the conflict.

In 1915 the McGraw-Hill Book Company, feeling certain that the United States would soon be drawn into the conflict, planned numerous books on every phase of military and naval tactics. By

April, 1917, not a single one of these plans had matured. The editors had found that the new war effort no longer demanded manuals on scouts, flank patrols, cavalry screens, or the care and feeding of horses. Instead it called for a huge number of highly specialized engineering books in fields that were new even to technical publishers. Radio communication, aviation, and the manufacture and maintenance of aircraft, chemical warfare, the construction of trenches, automotive transportation, and aerial photography were only a few of these areas. And there was a host of new naval techniques, not the least of which was a means of defense against submarine attack.

A New Kind of War

One of the discoveries made by book publishers was that books intended for peacetime use could be converted just as factories were being converted from the manufacture, say, of bedsprings, to that of munitions. Thus, as the McGraw-Hill book editors were groping about for new ideas for war books, a flood of orders began coming in for the *American Machinists' Handbook*—first published nearly ten years before. This, in a somewhat revised form became, as was told in a later historical review:

> . . . the great war book of the First World War. Because lathes are lathes and metal is metal in war or peace, tens of thousands of copies were sold to help the Allies swamp the enemy by the sheer tonnage of munitions.[1]

The special value of the handbook came from its ability to teach inexperienced men how to use machine tools. It was written in such a way as to replace the old apprentice system with simple, uniform sets of instructions. All over the country every available tool was being put to use and hundreds of thousands of new ones were being built. Some of them, of course, were special-purpose machines, but the old basic tools—lathes, millers, drills, and planers—were needed in every shop; and the army of men who were to use them was larger than the army that would

[1] *The Story of Forty Years of Growth*, brochure issued by the McGraw-Hill Book Company, Inc., 1949.

use their products. And those men had to be trained almost overnight.

But books were needed at every stage from the small shop to the plant drafting room or the advanced technical school. Often a top civil engineer, finding himself in the field, would need some elementary manual for himself or his men. Refresher books, mathematical texts, books, on mechanical or topographical drawing had sales figures of the sort we usually associate with popular novels. Everyone was going to school. However experienced a man might be there was something new for him to learn. Engineers, artisans, lawyers, surgeons, and clergymen—all were learning to adapt their professions to wartime uses.

Under special contracts with the Navy Department, McGraw-Hill edited and produced some twenty texts for the aviation and submarine sections of the Navy. Outstanding among the books of 1917 was one by the editorial staff of the *American Machinist:* a book entitled *Manufacture of Artillery Ammunition.* Another was *Topographical Drawing* by Col. Edwin R. Stuart, a West Point professor. There were also special texts on aviation, aircraft mechanics, radio work, shipbuilding, and several branches of military field engineering, many of which were officially adopted and therefore became best sellers.

One of the Book Company's wartime feats was the shipping of 150,000 technical books to the Army Educational Commission of the American Expeditionary Force in France. These books were "practically all printed, bound and specially packed" in 1,500 packing cases for overseas shipment in 10 working days! "So far as we know," the company's boast continues, "this was the largest single order for technical books ever placed with any publisher." [2]

All in all, World War I gave the most vivid possible demonstration of how the old order had changed: the breakdown of rules of thumb, of special craftsmanship, of the ancient word-of-mouth apprentice pattern; in their place were the necessity for

[2] *Ten Years,* brochure issued by the McGraw-Hill Book Company, Inc., 1919.

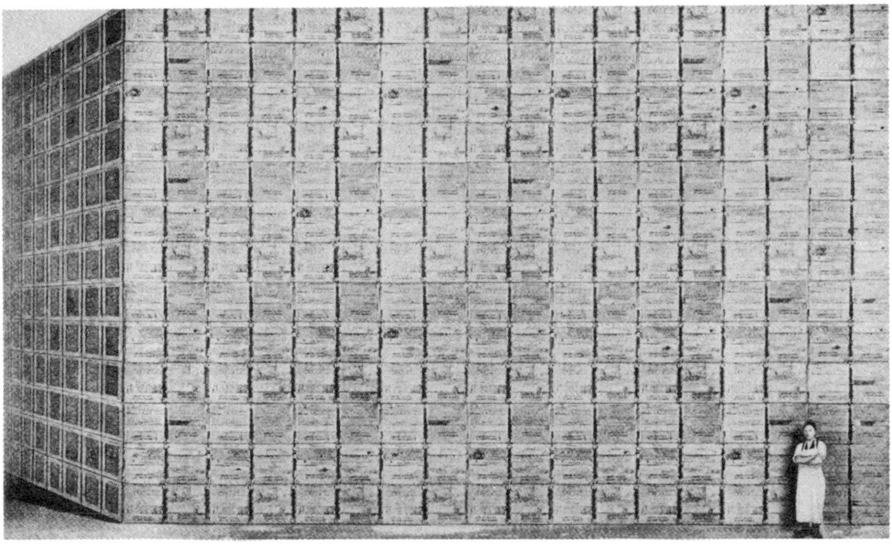

1,500 packing cases full of McGraw-Hill books for the Army Educational Commission. (Of course, these cases were never piled up this way, except by the photographer.)

standardization and mass production—needs that would totally transform the postwar world of industry. In that world there could be no substitute for books.

2 As far as the day-to-day progress of the war was concerned, however, there could be no substitute for the periodical contribution. Only the periodical could keep up with the fast sequence of total innovations dating from the first outbreak in 1914—innovations, not only in war techniques but in moral behavior as well. We think today of World War II as having initiated more practices than any before it, but for the most part these were improvements or amplifications; the total novelties came in World War I. The air-raid terror, the gas attacks, the sinking of civilian ships, the tanks, radio communication, depth bombs, and such propaganda techniques as the dropping of leaflets: these things

came in such breathtaking succession that books were too slow. At the same time the handicaps of inaccurate information and stern censorship limited the papers in their wartime reporting.

In these matters the technical press was in a better position than its other colleagues in the fourth estate. Contacts with industry were close; editors were well integrated with the industries they represented and were able to get accurate facts about progress. Furthermore, the government usually welcomed the contributions to both technology and morale made by the best of the industrial papers. As most of the papers were mainly concerned with engineering problems on the home front, they avoided the distortion by rumor and the interruption by censorship of the news from the field.

As orders for war materiel began, as early as the autumn of 1914, to pour into American shops, the *American Machinist* was interested from the beginning and, as a wartime editor remembers,

> . . . devoted much space to the description of the manufacturing methods—many of which had been improvised almost overnight in order to meet sudden emergencies—that were being employed in the various shops that had foreign contracts. The articles served the purpose of instructing plant owners and superintendents in the kind of work being done and thus helped prepare the shops for work of this sort in the event that the United States should be drawn into the war.[3]

By 1916 this event seemed inevitable. Obviously one of the first needs would be an unprecedented quantity of rifles. The standard infantry arm was the Springfield. Detailed information about the manufacture of this piece should, therefore, be made available to all potential manufacturers as soon as possible. The general to whom the War Department assigned the task of gathering and distributing this information decided that the ideal person for the work would be an editor of some periodical dedicated to machine tools. Thus it came about that in August, 1916, Fred

[3] Fred H. Colvin, *60 Years with Men and Machines,* McGraw-Hill Book Company, Inc., New York, 1947, pp. 181–182. Actually, by the time America entered, *American Machinist* had published some 800 pages on munitions manufacture.

Colvin of the *American Machinist's* staff was installed in the armory at Springfield and given the large job of research necessary to the compilation of all the data. He was able to complete this work in about four months.

Beginning with the barrel, we studied the rifle piece by piece and meticulously followed the operations being performed. We reported on the kinds of material used, the tools and cutters, feeds and operating speeds, cutting lubricant, heat treatment, and the time required for each separate operation. This detailed information then appeared in the *American Machinist,* first in successive issues, then in a special edition, and finally came out in book form.[4]

Colvin discovered some glaring inefficiencies in the national armory's methods and equipment. They were slow and antiquated. In the long peace—the Spanish skirmish of 1898 scarcely counted as a war—the national armorers had forgotten the great days of firearms manufacture when the interchangeable-parts pattern first devised by Eli Whitney was known as the "American system." After publishing several historical articles on that system in the *American Machinist,* Colvin was naturally shocked to find that "not a single dimension of the Springfield rifle showed a tolerance on any drawing then in use."[5]

Colvin, after getting no satisfaction from the officers in the War Department, took his findings directly to Newton D. Baker, Secretary of War. He reports the following dialogue:

It may be [Baker admitted] that you are entirely right about some of these points. But it will require a little more investigation before we can come to any definite decision or make any extensive changes in our present methods and machinery. . . . Moreover, if these West Point officers, who use the rifles and train other men how to use them, do not know how to make rifles, who in the name of reason does?

[4] *Ibid.,* p. 184. The book is entitled *United States Rifles and Machine Guns,* McGraw-Hill Book Company, Inc., New York, 1917. Colvin's collaborator was Ethan Viall.

[5] *Ibid.,* p. 192.

To this Editor Colvin replied:

Mr. Secretary—Anna Held, the current toast of Broadway, uses perhaps a box of face powder a day—but Colgate hasn't made her its factory superintendent on that account.[6]

War came to America eight months after Colvin began his research. Meanwhile he had experienced frustrations enough. The officer in charge of his work had issued an order branding him as *persona non grata* because of his criticisms and Secretary Baker had personally reinstated him. Four months after the declaration of war, Colvin had visited a key arms plant to discover what was being done to produce rifles. He found inaction, pending decisions by the War Department, so he caused a scathing editorial to be printed in the *Machinist,* headed "How Can Our Boys Fight Without Guns?"

This editorial [the righteously indignant diatribe reads] is not an attack on any individual, but on a system. . . .

Scores of skilled rifle makers in one of our best-known American plants have been for weeks and are today retained on the payroll, killing time with checkers and cards during working hours, simply because certain officials have been unable to arrive at a decision regarding details. . . .

Months after war has been declared . . . it is a crime against our boys who will bear rifles at the front to permit American rifle makers at home to pass week after week . . . waiting for something to do.[7]

Washington got wind of the editorial and the officials made strenuous efforts to get it suppressed, but "freedom of speech triumphed in the end and the editorial came out on schedule."[8] To forestall any official denial, Colvin had taken several photographs of the checker players and although these were not published, a notice in the *Machinist* stated that they were in the editor's possession and could be produced if proof were necessary.

[6] *Ibid.,* p. 185.

[7] *Ibid.,* pp. 188, 189. Reprinted in Colvin's book from *American Machinist,* August 16, 1917.

[8] Colvin, *op. cit.,* p. 188.

The *Machinist's* editor in chief, John H. Van Deventer, was soon aware, from the storm of censure from official sources, that the editorial had been effective indeed. Colvin had become "about as popular with the Ordnance Department as the proverbial skunk at a garden party." [9] It was obvious to both men that this was the sort of thing the technical press should do in wartime. More than any others, its editors could be sure of their facts. So Colvin continued to investigate—in spite of the obstacles thrown in his way by the military—and Van Deventer followed his first blast with a double-page spread a month later headed "Wanted—a Master Hand" dealing with the waste resulting from duplication of work, competition between the services, lack of centralization, red tape, seniority, and precedent.

We are all stockholders [read this second attack] in this great corporation known as the United States of America. Let us insist on applying at least as good methods as we demand in our own business, which becomes insignificant in comparison.[10]

To what extent the bold stand taken by the *American Machinist* contributed to the demand for the later investigation of wartime delinquencies is difficult to estimate. There were many factors here. Unhappily the full investigation came too late to be of much use in World War I; the record, however, was extremely useful a quarter century later when the nation was again involved. And while the *Machinist* in 1917 and 1918 reached far fewer Americans than the large-circulation magazines and newspapers, it did bring conditions home to men at the center of the industrial complex; and as technical record its articles are still invaluable.

3 From the moment of the declaration, *Power* was especially eloquent. We may smile today at some of the angry expressions in its editorials but they reflect the color of American patriotism of 1917. It was treason in those days to think of any-

[9] *Ibid.*, p. 190.
[10] *American Machinist,* vol. 47, no. 12, p. 519, September 20, 1917; Colvin, *op. cit.*, pp. 193, 194.

thing less than hanging as a proper fate for the German Kaiser. While our "brave boys" were marching into war, presumably with bands playing and flags flying, doubts about the draft were entertained only by traitors. Thus a *Power* editorial whose alliterative writer withered "piping pacifists" and "skulking slackers" was in tune with the rhetoric of the time. So were the battle hymns by Berton Braley which also appeared in that presumably technical paper.

But *Power* also echoed the new war cry: the call to industry to play its vital part in the effort. For perhaps the first time in history, the factory worker was put on the same level as the combat soldier; the propaganda emphasized the close teamwork that was necessary between plant production and field fighting. Cartoons showed the uniformed doughboy with his rifle and the overalled mechanic with his wrench marching side by side into battle.

This is a war of industry [proclaimed a *Power* editorial just after the declaration]. The side that can get the most material into shape to be used and into the places where it is most needed will be the victor; and to do this requires power.

The power plants of America have got to win the war. The gun may throw the shells, but the power plants make both guns and shells and the steel that they are made of and the explosives with which they are filled and the railroads and ships that carry them and we must have more steel, more rails, more guns, more powder, more shells, more ships.[11]

The newborn *Engineering News-Record* began life with a call for military engineers—men qualified for road building, railroad construction, quarrying, and bridge building. This was, to be sure, a carry-over from the *Record's* efforts in 1916 when National Defense was the byword. A series of articles on military preparedness by Maj. P. S. Bond of the Engineer Corps had run through March

[11] *Power*, vol. 45, no. 16, p. 531, April 17, 1917.

and April of that year, designed to wake the engineering "profession to a realization of its military obligations."[12] The *News-Record* on December 6, 1917, ran thirty pages of advertising entitled "Quarry-men—You're Wanted—Over There" calling for enlistment in the 28th Regiment of Engineers. These were donated by advertisers. This is a landmark: it demonstrates the willingness of the country's industrial leaders not only to increase production, for which they were paid, but also to contribute to the recruiting effort, for which they received nothing. To the Army's predraft recruiting service this was a boon indeed, as its advertising funds were quite inadequate to the purpose. The resulting rapid increase in engineer man power was evidence of the effectiveness of this collaboration of industry with the industrial press in speeding the war effort.

Editorially the *News-Record* was as energetic, if not as flamboyant, as its colleague *Power*. In November, 1917, in a blast entitled "And They Are Fighting in France" it attacked the sacred ASCE (American Society of Civil Engineers).

> With the exception of three war addresses, equally peaceful topics have occupied the meetings [of the Society] since last April. The fall program, so far as announced, contains no papers bearing on the tremendous industrial and engineering problems which the winning of the war demands that we solve. This is an engineering war yet this society seems not to recognize its opportunity.[13]

Another editorial in this same issue, entitled "Profiteering and the Industrial Unrest" showed the editors' awareness of early subversive activity on the American home front and said that the doctrine of *caveat emptor* should be reversed "to make the seller beware."[14]

The following month the paper sent its managing editor,

[12] *Engineering Record,* vol. 73, no. 18, p. 566, April 29, 1916.
[13] *Engineering News-Record,* vol. 79, no. 21, p. 951, November 22, 1917.
[14] *Ibid.,* p. 953.

Illustration from Tomlin's article on the construction of light railways in France, "Engineering News-Record," June 13, 1918.

Robert K. Tomlin, Jr., to France as war correspondent. He wrote a series of illustrated articles that kept engineers at home abreast of the work of road building, light railways, water supply, docks, and many other needs behind the front as well as problems of map making and motor transportation in the field. One piece on "The Light Railway along the British Front at Close Range" that Tomlin wrote in February, 1918, was turned over to the British censors just before the devastating mid-March German attack and apparently disappeared.

Nothing was heard of it for weeks [stated the *News-Record* when, finally it was printed] and it appeared that if the article was published at all it would be in the German technical journals. But the Boches did not capture it, and it has lately returned from the hands of the British censors.[15]

[15] *Engineering News-Record,* vol. 80, no. 24, p. 1119, June 13, 1918.

The piece, illustrated with photographs, was a revelation of the means by which a narrow-gauge rail system had revolutionized salvage operations.

4 These examples of war work done by McGraw-Hill publications are only a few illustrations out of a large number of contributions. The *Engineering and Mining Journal, Electrical World,* and *Metallurgical and Chemical Engineering* all played their part, though this last paper developed its greatest potential in the postwar period when leadership in the chemical field passed to the United States as a result of the German defeat.

But the American technical press in general, not merely the McGraw-Hill papers, acquired international prestige during the war, as was evident from the fact that the British Ministry of Information invited the representatives of the best American industrial and business papers to a conference in London at the war's end at which they were royally entertained and taken on a tour of the British front in France. Here our old friend Horace Swetland, James McGraw's first business associate, represented a large publishing company in which he had built some of the nation's most notable journals. The adventures of this group have been published in a book by Swetland. Some of them, while not vital, perhaps, to the McGraw-Hill story, do bring back the atmosphere of the period at which this company began its career.

CHAPTER SEVENTEEN

Fruits of Victory

For reasons which have not been disclosed, Arthur Baldwin rather than James H. McGraw was chosen to represent the McGraw-Hill organization at the London conference. Perhaps the chief was too busy. He had, after all, a large task ahead of him. A big and still unwieldy, not wholly coordinated business had fallen into his lap. The Hill people were distrustful and, in some cases, frightened. The best of them McGraw wanted to keep and mold to his own pattern. He had no intention of conceding any more than was necessary to the Hill traditions—certainly not to any of the Hill ways that were at variance with his own. In this time he probably did not wish to relinquish his personal control even for a few weeks. On the other hand, the absence of a man presumably wholly dedicated to the Hill interests would not be a hardship.

Furthermore, for the job, Arthur Baldwin was an ideal front man. He was extremely presentable. Handsome, witty, a celebrated raconteur, a born politician, friendly to everyone, and with a talent for facile if somewhat ornate speechmaking, he could be counted on to please the British. He fitted their preconceived picture of the typical American. The fact that he knew relatively little about the organization he represented and even less about the publishing business in general was no handicap. The after-dinner addresses that he was expected to deliver, coming as they did between toasts to the King and toasts to victory, filled the bill if they were sufficiently patriotic. If the term had been invented in 1918 he could have been called a public relations man par excellence.

Fruits of Victory

Horace Swetland was the leader of the group. Since his association with McGraw, he had built an organization called United Publishers Corporation which by 1918 had become McGraw-Hill's nearest competitor in size and importance as a business-paper house. It had acquired *Iron Age, Dry Goods Economist, Boot and Shoe Recorder, Automotive Industries,* and other leading magazines in their fields.

> The purpose [Swetland wrote in his book[1]] of inviting American industrial journalists to visit England and France as guests of the British Government, was to promote a better understanding between the people of Great Britain and the United States.[2]

This is an old and somewhat vague aim which has been pursued by both countries for many years with varying success. The time, however, was exceedingly propitious: some two million Americans had crossed the ocean in the late drive toward victory and Englishmen were, for the moment, happy about it. But more permanently valuable to understanding was the close international association of industry, applied science, and engineering which had grown out of the common purpose. The Ministry of Informa-

[1] H. M. Swetland, *American Journalists in Europe,* United Publishers Corporation, New York, 1919.

[2] *Ibid.,* p. 5.

tion could not have made a happier move than to include the industrial press of America in their invitation.

This section of the press was still far from its maturity in 1918. But the British business press also had much to learn and Englishmen were inclined to think that, whatever might be the case in other realms, Americans had something to teach them of business. In any case, the Ministry rolled out the red carpet for their visitors.

Prominent in the group was Henry G. Lord. This pioneer represented the firm of Bragdon, Lord, and Nagle which proudly published *Textile World,* the journal that Lord had nursed through its infancy. He had not at that time the least premonition that a decade later he would become one of McGraw-Hill's chief executives and that his paper would become part of the McGraw-Hill family. "Uncle Henry," as he is affectionately called in the Green Building, remembers the expedition as one of the happy experiences of his life.

The party left on October 26, 1918. A thirteen-day zigzag crossing with a still-camouflaged convoy brought them to England during the war's last days. The group's first party was at Sutton Place in Surrey where they were guests of the Duke and Duchess of Sutherland in a palace four hundred years old, once occupied by Henry VIII. This was on November 10. The next day the Savoy luncheon given by the M.O.I. was a scene of jubilation over the Armistice news. From then on, the succession of gala events was free from the shadow of war.

There was, however, one cloud of tragedy. On his arrival Arthur Baldwin was told of the death of his son on a Belgian battlefield. He crossed to the Continent for a few days for the last offices to the dead boy, then returned and went through the conference with high courage.

Visits to factories everywhere kept the group busy. It is probable that many were surprised at the industrial growth the war had brought to Great Britain. David Beecroft, directing editor of several of the motor magazines in Swetland's company, gave voice to the amazement that all members of the party felt not only at the efficiency, the cleanliness, and good lighting of the British plants, but especially at the attitude of the industrial employers toward the employees—something they had not expected in a land where a caste system was popularly supposed to operate.

The most amazing thing we have observed . . . is the great attention you have given to the workers. . . . A great many of your factories are object lessons to the world.[3]

At a luncheon given by Lord Northcliffe to the members of the American "trade press," Dr. Howard C. Parmelee of McGraw-Hill's *Chemical and Metallurgical Engineering* sounded a note which had much bearing on the future view of the chemical industry. Curiously, he said:

. . . we had come to think of the German people in terms of chemistry, and attributed to them knowledge and ability which they did not possess in greater measure than the rest of us. You will search the history of chemistry in vain for a single instance in which a German has initiated fundamental laws of chemistry or produced any of the epoch making discoveries in that science . . . but the German people put the ideas [of English and French scientists] into practice and built great industries upon them. They have established the closest cooperation between industry and the university and have set an example which we could well follow.[4]

Dr. Parmelee could not yet know the magnitude of the revolution in American chemical industry that would result from Germany's defeat. But he knew of the methods by which the Germans had maintained the legend of their knowledge and ability in the chemical field. And before many months should pass he would see the collapse of their near-monopoly of the industry.

2 The journal that Dr. Parmelee edited reflected, in its changes of title, the spectacular changes in the background of applied chemistry that had taken place in the short span of the paper's

[3] *Ibid.*, p. 42.
[4] *Ibid.*, p. 43.

existence. Perhaps nowhere in the technical press has the precise state of the climate of knowledge been more closely indicated than in the successive names of what in 1919 was *Chemical and Metallurgical Engineering*. To the outsider, when he first encounters it, the sequence seems the height of absurdity, the product of restless and whimsical minds. But once he comes to view it against the background of the fast-changing technology it represents, he sees how sensitive the publisher has been to the new trends.

In 1902 after the new quantities of power had become available through hydroelectric developments, it seemed as if the electrochemical possibilities were unlimited. A group of experts in this field felt the immediate need of a magazine to spread information and provide leadership. They soon found a publisher. With his flair for smelling every new electrical wind, James McGraw welcomed the chance to issue what would be a sister magazine to *Electrical World*. Thus *Electrochemical Industry* was born and the German-born Eugene Franz Roeber brought his education at Jena, Halle, and Berlin to its editorial chair.

Roeber has been described as

> . . . a little, round man with a round chin, round spectacles and a big round hat designed for a Texas sombrero, but which on his head straightway become *ein Professorenhut.*[5]

He seems to have been a kindly, sensitive person, friendly to everyone and with a powerful command of his subject. He never quite mastered spoken English but with Teutonic thoroughness he perfected his reading and writing to a faultless point.

Only three years after the launching of *Electrochemical Industry,* Roeber thought it necessary

> . . . to take account of new chemical and metallurgical developments with which electrochemical products may have to compete or which may react in some essential way on that industry.[6]

[5] *Metallurgical and Chemical Engineering,* vol. 17, p. 511, November 1, 1917.
[6] *Electrochemical and Metallurgical Industry,* vol. 3, p. 2, January, 1905.

Dr. Eugene Franz Roeber.

So, in January, 1905, the title was changed to *Electrochemical and Metallurgical Industry*. Five years later it was noted that this industry, like all others in 1910, was revolving round the engineer; he and not the chemist was its axis or its focal point. So, until the war changed all things, Dr. Roeber's paper became *Metallurgical and Chemical Engineering*.

Roeber was as truly a war casualty as any man who died in the field. He had applied for American naturalization papers and had become a staunchly patriotic American. Then the split in April, 1917, separated him from all that he had loved and cherished in his youth. To him the Germany he had known seemed suddenly and forever lost. In addition, the prevailing cruelty of that feverish spring when everyone who spoke broken English was suspect gave a body blow to his sensitive nature. He never recovered. In the fall of the year he died, quite definitely of a broken heart. Howard Parmelee succeeded him.

More than any conflict before it, World War I was predominantly chemical. There had always been a chemical factor since explosives were first used. But now there was poison gas: chlorine, phosgene, dichlordiethyl sulfide, or mustard gas, and the tear gases. As with explosives, the manufacture of certain gases was related to that of synthetic dyes and fertilizers. The use of natural substances in these manufactures was giving way to synthesis of the materials. In this the enemy had the advantage, for the Germans had worked for years to sequester and monopolize the applications of organic chemistry.

The stimulus to American chemical industries was therefore strong. We had to find out ways to make our own high explosives and poison gas. We were able to draw on the Chilean resources of the material guano for fixed nitrogen—denied by the blockade to Germans. But the Germans, driven to near despair by this loss, invented the extraordinary Haber-Bosch process for extracting nitrogen from the air and Americans were soon eager to imitate this. Thus the chemical industries on both sides advanced by giant strides, liberated as they now were from commercial limitations when cost was no longer an object.

As *chemical engineering* became the common term for the activity all this involved, metallurgy lost its earlier significance as a separate science; it was evident that it was now a province of the great chemical territory. This "led the publishers to rearrange the name of the magazine," giving metallurgy its subordinate place. Thus the change which at first blush seems whimsical made the paper's masthead a true barometer of an altering climate. *Metallurgical and Chemical Engineering* became *Chemical and Metallurgical Engineering*—more rhythmic perhaps, as well as more accurate, and surely less a tongue twister—in the last summer of the war.

This was not the end of the sequence, but *Chem and Met,* as the paper was nicknamed in the office, lasted a long time. Indeed, even in this late day when *metallurgy* has finally faded out forever from the cover, old-timers cling to the affectionate brevity.

So it was *Chem and Met* that Dr. Parmelee represented in England and in France. And in the long spring of the peace when he was back in the McGraw-Hill office, he was able with eager eyes to watch the birth of one of the greatest of all American industries. The basis came to us in that and the immediately succeeding years of the thousand and one new things that today have become commonplaces of our lives: plastics, rayon, nylon, silicones. . . .

3 Since organic chemistry first began to have industrial applications, Germans had sought to establish a monopoly in the field. They had done this by taking out patents in foreign countries on the various processes that had been developed in Germany—patents which they neither exploited nor licensed. Some of the most important of these patents had been taken out in the United States; they covered, among other things, many dyes, drugs, stainless steel, synthetic ammonia, and methanol, and much apparatus for the production of these things. The effect of the patents was preventive; as long as licenses were refused, the building of an organic-chemical industry in the United States was impossible.

As the war drew to a close, it became evident to chemically minded Americans that our future security would be endangered if the monopoly continued. The armistice, when it came, was, after all, merely an armistice. What if hostilities should be resumed? Thus, in February, 1919, when the German patents, like all other German property in the United States, were in the hands of the Alien Property Custodian, President Wilson gave an executive order that an organization be formed to acquire the patents for American benefit. The result was the Chemical Foundation.

The Foundation was empowered to buy more than 4,500 German patents for some $250,000 and make available under them nonexclusive licenses to all Americans desiring to manufacture the products the patents covered. The terms were to be fair and equal. The Germans protested about what they called the pittance they were paid. But even when the United States Justice Department later intervened, the highest courts in the land held that, in view of the history, the patent seizure was fully justified.

Perhaps never in the history of war have reparations been of such benefit to the advance of an industry. Not only was the liberation from monopolistic control a powerful stimulus to research and development in a climate of competitive private enterprise, but the educational work done by the Foundation prepared the public for the flood of new products.[7] From parachutes to stockings, from paints and lacquers to cellophane, the total revolution in materials has changed the whole aspect of American life.

But as the vast, growing industry was aided by the technical press, so, too, the industry helped the growth of the best chemical engineering papers. As the new products came thick and fast into use, the material grew for editorial content. So also the advertising acquired enormous volume.

4 Like the other McGraw-Hill papers, *Chemical and Metallurgical Engineering* listed education among its ideals. This had become one of the great functions of the technical press. All over the country boys were growing up with ambitions to take part in the great march toward the new green pastures of science. In the postwar years new opportunities seemed to open daily for young men who had a technological education. But those who could afford formal schooling in engineering were few. Men who came out of the Army with the handicaps of lost time and interrupted earning power simply could not spend still more years studying technics without pay. It was here that the technical press did its compensatory work. We have no way of guessing what would have become of these ambitious boys without the resources of technical books and magazines. We only know that story after

[7] For an account of the Chemical Foundation's genesis and activities, see *American Chemical Industry* (Williams Haynes, ed.), D. Van Nostrand Company, Inc., Princeton, N. J., 1949, vol. 6, p. 76 ff.

A phase in the development of moistureproof cellophane, about 1927.

story was told the editors in the field of men poring in after-work hours over the wealth of print that had come with the engineering advances—lifting themselves by their bootstraps, so to speak, into important places in the technical world.

As one of the editors for *Chem and Met* remembers:

Getting away from New York and the business offices and the universities, I found that men really lived with their technical magazines. They read every page. . . . Time and again I found fellows who were absolutely dependent upon McGraw-Hill magazines, not only in the chemical field, but particularly in the mining field. . . .[8]

On a trip to Seattle, for example, this editor met the head of a municipally owned power plant.

[8] Sidney D. Kirkpatrick, recorded interview in McGraw-Hill Archives, p. 5.

I sent in my card as assistant editor of a McGraw-Hill publication. The man came out and practically put his arms around me. . . . He said, "Do you know that I have never had a day's formal education in my life? The only things I know about the electrical industry have been what I have gotten out of the *Electrical World* and the McGraw-Hill magazines and books."

He gave me a little gift—an artificial gem of some kind which he had made experimenting with an electric furnace. He said "I want you to take that back to Mr. McGraw and tell him that it's from one of his great admirers." [9]

Appropriately, at this time the Book Company started a series of books that would meet the demands of the burgeoning chemical engineering profession. The Company has described the series in its instructive brochure, *Imprint on an Era,* as follows:

Our *Chemical Engineering Series* is one of the best illustrations of the way a series is built, book by book, to meet a prescribed plan. In 1925, a committee of chemical engineers was brought together by McGraw-Hill from industry and the universities to survey the needs for a permanent literature for this new and rapidly growing profession. Their report laid out detailed specifications for a correlated series of more than a dozen text and reference books: a chemical engineers' handbook; basic textbooks on the elements and principles of chemical engineering, on industrial applications of chemical reactions, on materials of construction, plant design, and chemical engineering economics. Also included were industrial and unit operations monographs on appropriate subjects, to be developed as need for them became apparent.

With the aid of the advisory committee (headed successively by McGraw-Hill editors H. C. Parmelee and S. D. Kirkpatrick), we began in 1926 a continuing search for authors and manuscripts. Since then we have published all but two of the committee's original textbook recommendations. The *Chemical Engineers' Handbook,* edited by the late John H. Perry (published in 1934) and now in its third edition, has become the world's standard reference book in this field. More than a dozen monographs have been added as chemical engineering has de-

[9] *Ibid.,* p. 6.

veloped over the last three decades. The entire series now totals 42 books; new ones will be added and old ones revised as time passes.[10]

5 While all this postwar expansion was going on, the schoolmaster-publisher was building his organization. It was in those years that he developed his noted "standards of dissatisfaction." Northing was ever quite good enough. Any word of praise was accompanied by an added "But you've got to do better." One editor who was particularly proud of his paper remembers being called again and again into the chief's office and asked, "What is the matter with *Electrical World?*" The Old Man would have a copy of this pet paper on his desk and as he leafed through it, he slapped his hand on page after page. "This must be better! It's still not right!" He had a way, another editor remembers, "when he was a little bit irritated of moving his jaw up and down so that his whiskers came out at you—almost like a porcupine."[11]

Many a man came out of the chief's office feeling beaten and depressed but the strongest of them were spurred—sometimes by anger—to new efforts. The more discerning men who worked for McGraw were aware of his total dedication to his business. Personalities meant little to him; he cared only for the substance of each man's contribution to the "institution." He loved to be opposed—provided his antagonist's arguments were sound. Often he would fight for hours until the man's views convinced him. There was one editor with whom he battled for weeks on end, even taking him on his vacation and carrying on the fight over a Georgia golf course. He once took a man on a field trip, made him share a train compartment, and talked all night.

He would see an employee he did not know in the elevator. "Who are you?" he would ask. "What do you do? Come to see me in my office." Then the person knew that he must go prepared

[10] *Imprint on an Era,* brochure published by McGraw-Hill Book Company, Inc., 1954, 1955, p. 9.

[11] S. D. Kirkpatrick, recorded interview, p. 9.

to be turned inside out with questions. He must defend any stand he might take with all the vigor at his command. If he withstood the browbeating and stuck to his guns he was likely to get the chief's backing in the end. Repeatedly an editor, for example, was let go his own way after the fight was over—even, sometimes, when James McGraw disapproved. Let the man try it. If it worked, the chief would be convinced and stand by the rugged editor with his blessing.

McGraw relentlessly enforced certain principles of publishing. He insisted that anyone who worked on a paper should know that paper's industry or business backward and forward. It was not enough that he have a facile pen or that he "sell himself" through his personal charm. Men must learn the business *from the inside.* As far as he was able without a formal technical education, he practiced what he preached. By attending conventions, by constant meetings with top executives, he was able at least to keep abreast of the march of the electrical industry—his chosen field.

James McGraw's work during the twenties in building an organization wore him out physically, though his mental power was to remain active for another score of years. Recurrent illness immobilized him for varying periods of time. Then he would hold meetings in his room and dictate from his bed—make McGraw-Hill come to him when he could not go to it. He wrote reams of letters in pencil on a yellow pad to his far-flung workers—west, south, overseas. The men in the office felt his presence and his pressure, even in his incapacity.

Perhaps if his sense of humor had had wider play his life might have been less strenuous. But James McGraw was deeply serious. He may have joked at times about outside things but never about the business. Anyone who spoke lightly about any phase of that was sharply reprimanded. Except for occasional golf McGraw allowed himself no recreation. For him the theater was out of bounds. Cards, genial drinking, the most innocent ribaldry were

James H. McGraw, early 1920s.

foreign to his nature. He rarely smiled or laughed, at least in business hours, and these were about twenty-four a day.

His writings, his speeches, his few personal reminiscences give little hint of greatness. Much of what has been printed of his words is—to an outsider at least—tedious, repetitive, and abounding in clichés and generalizations. It is difficult to find, among the formal records, any indication of the power that moves through the spoken memories of the men who knew him. We see it in the letters on yellow paper when he poured forth his warm "dissatisfactions" and, more rarely, praise, and a poignant yearning for friendship. It is these occasional glimpses, it is these echoes that one still hears in the Green Building that show the vitality of James McGraw's influence, the soundness of his constructive advice.

CHAPTER EIGHTEEN

The Autonomous Book Company

In the decade of the 1920s, the face of the industrial world underwent a change that seemed almost total. This was not only because of new technical factors in chemical, metallurgical, and power engineering, but more profoundly because of new economic, political, and social problems. These had come with the war. There had suddenly arrived, for instance, a new, close intimacy between industry and government. New questions had arisen of foreign trade and industrial relations with foreign governments. The tariff loomed large in the postwar years. The theories of Taylor, Gilbreth, Halsey, and Gantt had crystallized into new management practice. Management was being spelled with a capital M; it was becoming a science—what educators call a *discipline.*

As the industrial press had always reflected and often led industrial trends, it was evident that the papers could no longer confine themselves to purely technical matters. As Dr. Parmelee expressed it in 1921:

> The whole country was face to face with a brand new crop of problems and since industry had learned to follow its own technical papers in matters of science and technology, it naturally turned to the same source for leadership in these new conditions. The technical paper promptly sensed and accepted the situation. It became a magazine of opinion on labor problems, on the tariff, on wages, the cost of living, foreign trade, Government policies, the patent system, revenue legislation and finance and many other matters formerly regarded outside its editorial scope.[1]

There was, for example, in all industries, the necessity for considering waste, for instituting cost accounting, for taking safety measures in factories, for improved housing and sanitation, for deeper and more effective research. On the political side there was the burning question: How far should government go in its regulation of business? What new problems had been introduced by the Federal Trade Commission and the Interstate Commerce Commission?

Thus the scope of the technical papers became greatly enlarged and they became useful not merely to the engineer or technician but to the administrative executive and the various business managers as well. From this point on we shall see the independent magazines of the industrial press becoming more and more business rather than technical papers. In the meantime, the purely technical aspects could get more focal treatment from the subsidized organs of the great technical societies.

In the McGraw-Hill organization, however, there were adequate facilities for dealing with purely technical matters apart from the company's papers. These were perennially brought to the

[1] An address by H. C. Parmelee, editor of *Chemical and Metallurgical Engineering*, before the Chicago section of the American Chemical Society, Nov. 18, 1921, entitled "The Technical Paper and Its New Relation to Industry," *Chemical and Metallurgical Engineering*, vol. 26, no. 5, pp. 197–200, Feb. 1, 1922.

attention of the magazine readers, so that if a reader wanted to go into some specialty more deeply than his paper could take him, he would find the means near at hand.

2 In little more than a decade, the McGraw-Hill Book Company had moved into a position from which it was offering real competition to the older, long-established technical-book publishers. The whole American book business had, of course, hugely increased as a result of both the new technical revolution and the growth in number and strength of American educational institutions. It was natural, of course, for such older houses as Wiley and Van Nostrand to expand their lists in these burgeoning days. But that the ten-year-old McGraw-Hill book house had achieved, by war's end, such a foothold in the colleges, the technical and vocational schools, and in the engineering professions generally was due to the personal contributions of three men.

The anchor, Edward Caldwell, and the far-roving explorers, Martin Foss and James Thompson, made up the trio. Into the offices and laboratories of the professors on campuses from Boston to Los Angeles, from Maine to Oregon, Foss and Thompson brought a freshness, a sense of quick responsiveness to men who were tiring of routine publishing practice. Both were young, energetic, enthusiastic, and with that humility that goes with an ardent desire to learn that is so appealing to a teacher. Neither knew much about the subjects the professors talked and wrote of. Both had liberal arts, not technical, education: Foss at Harvard, Thompson at Wisconsin. Neither pretended acquaintance with the technologies. But they inspired confidence that they would get the manuscripts into the hands of experts for editorial handling and that they knew how to supervise the *business* of distributing the books.

Thompson confesses that he was a bit apprehensive when Foss first took him to Boston to meet the faculty people and left him to work on his own. He was really full of enthusiasm and eager to get going. A story he tells of his beginning gives a fairly ac-

McGraw-Hill Book Company 30th Anniversary Boat Ride, 1939. Left to right: James S. Thompson, Martin M. Foss, Henry G. Lord, Curtis W. McGraw.

curate picture of the pattern that developed in building the company's college textbook department from its very earliest days. Foss had left him in Boston and was on the Merchants Limited on his way back to the New York office.

I first called on Dr. H. P. Talbot, [Thompson remembers] a very kindly old gentleman who taught quantitative analysis in MIT, and who had two books in the hands of another publisher. He immediately said, "I don't like the way they handled these books, and I'm going to write a couple more. I think I'd like McGraw-Hill to handle them."

I was so excited. It was my first interview, and here, immediately, was the first manuscript. I rushed back to my hotel and wrote a note to Foss. . . . He immediately made Talbot the consulting editor for the International Chemical Series.[2]

[2] James Stacy Thompson, recorded interview, in McGraw-Hill Archives, p. 29.

The series has continued under different editors for nearly half a century with a total now in print of forty-one volumes. That was the system. If a prominent teacher, a recognized authority in his field, decided he would like to write a book for McGraw-Hill, they would say, "Why not a whole series? You be the editor. You help us plan a list of books needed in your field. Suggest names for the best authorship, and give us general advice on manuscripts and possible sales. That way we will establish not just one or two standard books but a series that will become an institution." It would, of course, grow with the changing times. The alert editor would be aware of every new facet in his discipline, so that he might teach it in his classroom; naturally he would seek out the best author for a textbook on the subject.

The International Chemical Series reflected, of course, the revolution that had replaced the old atomic theory with a wholly new concept. But in the period we have reviewed in which American chemical industry was profiting by the use of the German organic patents, the whole vista of new products and new processes called for equally new books. As the engineer came to the front of the chemical stage, astute editors knew that he must have books created especially for him and for the boys who were swarming toward this branch of the profession. But by 1925 when this movement came into full swing, McGraw-Hill had matured its methods of editorial planning. For the large diversity of the field, one outside expert editor was not enough to organize a series.

The search for authors and manuscripts for the new Chemical Engineering Series began in 1926. The series now runs to forty-two volumes. The innovation of using a committee that included professional engineers and scientists working in industry along with the professors to plan book series reflects the flow of science into industry, and the method has been used whenever appropriate ever since.

There were still many textbooks, however, that continued to cover the purely scientific material in such fields as botany, zoology, and physics, and the Book Company in the early days published mostly in the natural sciences and their uses in engineering. The occasional reachings out to touch the fringes of the behavioral sciences were few and tentative, and the large expansion on the plane of business administration was a development that came later.

3 The next step in which personality played a decisive part was in selling the books. A large share of the activities of Foss and Thompson was devoted to securing the adoption of textbooks. This was not the sort of high-pressure, drink-buying, cigar-distributing activity which in the old days played politics with state adoption boards for schoolbooks. The college level at which McGraw-Hill operated demanded a very different technique. Foss's charm and his selective intuition were backed by the confidence his books supplied. Nevertheless, when the company was new, the first entree into the professor's sanctum was always through what is known today as a low-pressure approach. Foss used to say that his pleas for adoption were clothed in "restrained enthusiasm."

But Foss did not confine himself to selling through adoption. There were plenty of books on the lists he had inherited which were not college books at all; they were books intended to assist the working engineer or technician—the man who had completed his formal education and was spending his days at his chosen trade. Now this person in the publishing legend of the time was hard to reach. Engineers were all supposed to be, figuratively speaking, from Missouri. Like the laboratory experimenters, they were accustomed to tangible proof. They had to be shown. They read the magazines avidly enough to be sure and accepted or discarded what they read. It cost them little to do this and a periodical, after all, was a more or less ephemeral thing to be superseded tomorrow by a new issue. But a book was something else again. Here was a solid thing that you bought for keeps, costing, relatively, a lot of money, so dignified and substantial in appearance that it deserved a place on a shelf with other precious books: dictionaries, infallible reference volumes, classics such as Charles Darwin's *On the Origin of Species,* or Adam Smith's *Wealth of Nations,* or Alfred Mahan's various works on sea power (though we may be giving excessive credit to the literary ambitions of American engineers in the 1920s). What if you did not accept what a book said, could you throw it in the scrap basket and spend another $4 or $5 for another book next month?

The outlets for technical books were the few stores that specialized in such matters or in mail orders in response to advertising. The special stores existed mainly in educational communities, not easily accessible to the busy engineer. The general bookseller could not afford to stock such books. Occasionally he would order one for a favored customer but this would take time. The advertisements for which McGraw-Hill had a happy vehicle in the

Sketch of Martin Foss by James Montgomery Flagg.

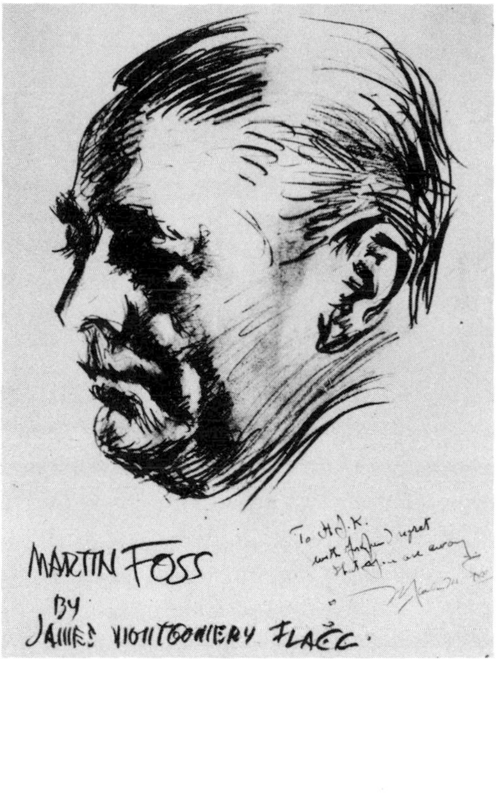

parent company's magazines brought orders, of course, but not enough. "Blurbs won't do it," said Foss, in effect. "These people have to be shown."

So Foss began a practice which is now so common that it seems curious to us that its effectiveness and safety could ever have been doubted. Yet even some of his close friends told Foss that it was too risky to try. Foss's idea was simply the send-no-money appeal that gave a man time to look at a book before he bought it. "You mean," his well-wishers asked him, "to hand a book to a man *free* and expect him to pay after he's read it?" "Yes," said the confident Foss, "after he's looked at it for ten days." And while the heads were still shaking the scheme went through, and several other publishers are said to have waited eagerly for the chance to say "I told you so."

But, actually, this was no pure act of trust on the part of Martin Foss. He knew the level on which he worked. He understood not only that technical men were probably reasonably scrupulous fellows but also that they did not handle the tools of their trade lightly, whether they were books or slide rules. And the kind of books he was letting these men see were, he believed, real tools that would not lose their edge through the years, books that a man would not read once but again and again, thumbing through for answers in times of doubt or crisis. Finally, through the parent company's journals, he was able to reach just those men with advertising at cost. So the cards were really stacked on Foss's side and his acumen was farseeing enough to know it.

But he not only advertised in the papers with a tear-off ten-day-approval coupon. He followed this advertising by borrowing from the magazines their subscription lists. To portions of these lists he sent letters and circulars. The results quickly justified his hopes. The percentage of sales went steadily up, the number of returned books went down, and the losses were negligible.

The stacked cards on Foss's side are germane to our story mainly because they furnish a rather sharp example of the beginnings of that interdependence of departments that characterizes the large shop today. In the 1920s the magazines were constant feeders for the Book Company. At the same time, the books, as they became more and more generally accepted, more standard, more widely acclaimed, brought new prestige to the papers. Together the books and papers built the McGraw-Hill name and increased that mysterious imponderable that accountants try so hard to put into columns of figures: the elusive but very real factor in any enterprise that is known as good will.

It was, for example, extremely convenient for a Book Company editor to call up some specialist on the editorial staff of a paper to check on some difficult technical question or to ask for a suggestion for an author in a particular field. At the same time there was autonomy on both sides. All through the twenties the Book Company did not even live in its parents' house but occupied a floor of the Penn Terminal Building several blocks away. The officers of the Publishing Company might advise on general policies and practices but they never advised on specific book projects. And Foss and Caldwell felt free to decline the advice. In the earliest days the books were largely repositories for the magazines' serials; it was not long before they drew from independent sources and the Book Company was never under any obligation to print serialized material in book form.

This curious combination of independence and interdependence that appears here in an early form became a permanent characteristic of the whole McGraw-Hill complex. This often appears paradoxical even to the persons in the Green Building. Yet if we oversimplify the view, it is not hard for outsiders to understand how it works. We may do this by comparing the organization with a federation of states. The divisions of the company are sovereign; so, too, is the company itself. Each paper, each department of the Book Company is a "state," sovereign in its field. The company supplies the federal connection. It gives services to all the "states" and at the same time maintains contacts with the outer world on finance and other broad matters.

Over the years certain functions have become centralized for the sake of economy in a tightly organized society. Printing, manufacture, the processing of advertising, and other matters can be most economically managed in central departments that can operate across the board.

All these developments have come gradually as a result of much trial and error. At times the federal aspect almost disappeared and the company would begin to look like a dictatorship, only to fall apart again into its more flexible pattern. Again, the connection between the parts would be so loose that there was wasteful duplication. But always there has been movement, change, as there must inevitably be in a live and complex American business organization in this incessantly changing business world.

The trend can be pinpointed, as the saying goes, in one of its first stages by this relationship of the Book and Publishing Companies in the decade of the 1920s.

4 One of the significant changes of that period which we have already noted was the breaking down of what had looked like a watertight compartment between the technical and management ends of industry. As more and more men with an engineer's training moved into executive positions in a company's business offices, and as the new economic pattern resulting from the experiments in "scientific management" began to impinge on a plant's operations, new books as well as a change of color in the magazines became necessary. Students of sociology were looking into such questions as human relations with workers, the integration of labor into a community, factors of fatigue, monotony of repetitive work, lighting, sanitation, aptitude, and a dozen other things that they believed affected production.

As the Book Company became aware of the trend, it was not necessary to change the character of their product but simply to add a new department or a new list of books in a new and related discipline. The purely technical books, the electrical and machinist handbooks, the practical engineers' manuals, and the textbooks still had and always would have a large, growing mar-

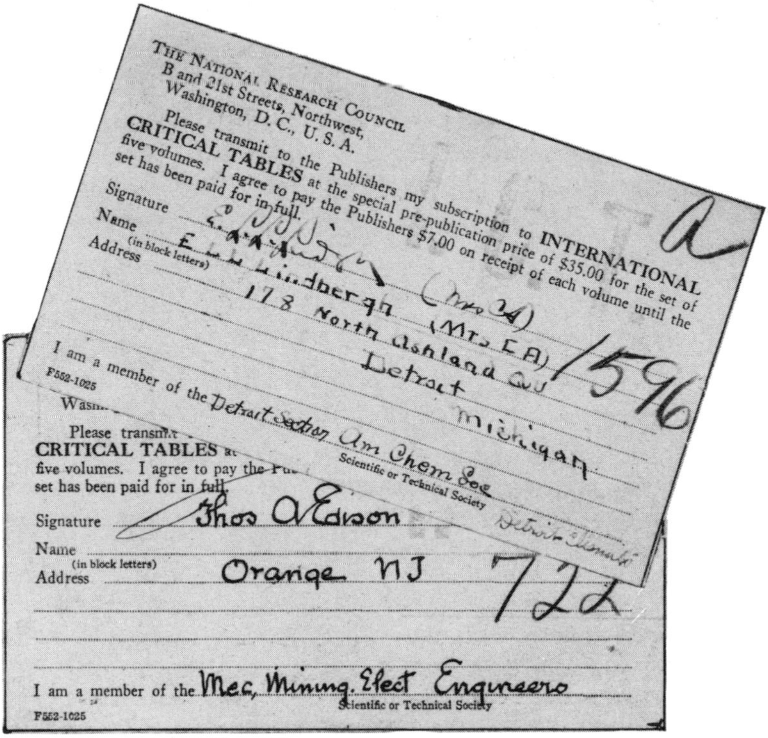
THE NATIONAL RESEARCH COUNCIL
B and 21st Streets, Northwest,
Washington, D. C., U. S. A.

Please transmit to the Publishers my subscription to INTERNATIONAL CRITICAL TABLES at the special pre-publication price of $35.00 for the set of five volumes. I agree to pay the Publishers $7.00 on receipt of each volume until the set has been paid for in full.

Signature E L L Lindbergh
Name (in block letters) E L L Lindbergh (Mrs C A)
Address 178 North Ashland Av Detroit Michigan 1596

I am a member of the Detroit Section Am Chem Soc
Scientific or Technical Society
F552-1025

Please transmit ... CRITICAL TABLES ... five volumes. I agree to pay the ... set has been paid for in full.

Signature Thos A Edison
Name (in block letters)
Address Orange NJ 722

I am a member of the Mec, Mining, Elect Engineers
Scientific or Technical Society
F552-1025

Among the mail orders for "International Critical Tables" were these two from Thomas A. Edison and Mrs. E. L. L. Lindbergh, the mother of the famous Charles A. Lindbergh.

ket. Certain reference books such as the *International Critical Tables (1926–1930)* had become as indispensable as dictionaries. Now the books on business administration and the social sciences could supplement these. The change, then, was simply an expansion.

One of the earliest ventures into this field was a little book called *The Human Factor in Works Management* by James Hartness, published in 1912, only three years after the Book Company began. This appeared soon after Harper's publication of Frederick W. Taylor's classic *The Principles of Scientific Management.* It was an early recognition by an engineer of the fact that production may be bettered by increased attention to the worker's welfare. In the twenties when this thesis had been tested, came Frank E. Weakly's *Applied Personnel Procedure* in which a chapter was devoted to early phases of the modern practices of "Interview, Selection, and Placement."

From this point on there was a steady broadening of the Book Company's scope. More and more books came every year: on the social sciences, economics, sociology, political science, psychology, and education, until in 1932 the company contracted to publish the report of the President's Research Committee on Social Trends in the United States. The two volumes of this plus the thirteen supporting monographs, appearing in 1933 as *Recent Social Trends in the United States,* were a far cry from the strictly technical books with which the company began. Here were discussed such matters of general interest as racial and ethnic groups, the family, social activities of women, child education, recreation, the arts, religion, crime, public welfare, and many other matters of importance to any studious observer of the American scene. The book was a symposium by many authorities in its various departments and remained a standard for many years.

Along with the expansion into business administration, ecoomics, and social sciences came new interest in the fields of botany, zoology, microbiology, agriculture, and forestry—all equally important in the college-textbook and reference-book field.

In the meantime the company had entered on a somewhat controversial experiment. There are still people in the Green Building who think the Book Company should have stuck to its last and published only works dealing with the natural and social sciences and the application thereof. But when the step was first taken, many inside and out of the company felt that to cultivate popular fields was beneath the dignity of so staid a house. If there were biographies and essays, the next step might be into fiction —perish the thought! Could the Old Man approve such a departure from the serious, studious tradition?

The Old Man, however, had from the start let the Book Company go its own way. Its activities were apart from his absorbing interests. He read the figures on the company's annual report with satisfaction. He attended the company's board meetings when he was in town but he usually sat through them in silence. That the Book Company was a profitable annex to his enlarging business, there was no doubt. He had total confidence in Caldwell, Foss, and Thompson, as, indeed, he often had in the men who managed activities outside his own personal orbit. He may have squirmed a little when the first un-McGraw-Hill book appeared and even more when in his late years a novel came off the presses, but he had disassociated himself from the source of such vagaries.

Furthermore, the title page of these volumes no longer bore the McGraw-Hill imprint. The name Whittlesey House was adopted for three reasons: to designate a new kind of McGraw-Hill list in the book trade; to attract and comfort authors and agents who would not want to publish trade books under an imprint known only for technical books; and to preserve the purity of the McGraw-Hill imprint in scientific and technical fields. These general books were called *trade books.* That word *trade* is publisher's jargon for literary commodities sold, in the main, through the general bookstore. So it appeared more convenient to have the selling details handled under another name. There was no corporate separation. Whittlesey House was not a different or subsidiary company. It was simply a new department having a separate editorial and sales staff, just as the college and educational-book departments had at that time. Eventually the name was dropped except for children's books.

The name had a pleasant connotation. It was the family name of Mildred, James McGraw's wife, and it was most intimately associated with McGraw's father-in-law who for many years was treasurer of the McGraw company before the merger. Curtis Whittlesey had played an exceedingly important part in building his son-in-law's business, and one of James McGraw's sons was named for him. This may have helped take the curse off the trade venture in McGraw's mind—if curse there was.

Whittlesey House did not begin with novels. It eased gradually into fiction. To follow that development at this point would carry us far beyond our story. But it did begin with books that were highly popular. The first of these was Walter B. Pitkin's *Life Begins at Forty,* which was published in 1932. Book Company people boast that this was a best seller though published in the depth of the depression. Actually it probably sold precisely *because* it came at that nadir and cheered its readers in a despairing interval. It had several reprints and has been published in a dozen foreign languages. For some years after the Pitkin success the company centered its list on popularized science, how-to books, and volumes on topical subjects. It was 1939 before Bellamy Partridge's *Country Lawyer* and other biographies in fictional form paved the way for true fiction.

The widest difference between trade and technical publishing is in the element of risk. Relatively few technical books are a gamble for the publisher. The public for each is carefully plotted beforehand and so may be accurately exploited afterward. The general publisher, on the other hand, takes a chance with at least half the books he publishes. A first novel by an unknown author must be thrown on the roulette wheel. A dozen imponderables affect its success or failure. The successful trade-book editor must have an uncanny intuition, unless he sticks to sure-fire subjects such as religion and self-help, and even there his selections must be judicious. He must build up his house's prestige through books that are financial failures but successes of esteem.

To enlarge the McGraw-Hill scope by establishing a trade department was to undertake an extremely difficult task and one for which the company had no experience. It required the building up of new editorial and sales staffs—from scratch. No doubt it was wise to begin with items of a highly promising, if not a sure-fire nature. Whether from the literary point of view it can meet the wide and strenuous competition from the army of old-line American trade-book publishers, it is perhaps too soon to say. It has reached at least one high peak with the celebrated Boswell books.

5 Whittlesey House began in a time of disaster. On the threshold of this disaster came several other ventures. In the later twenties as the clock moved nearer the moment of doom, there was industrial- and business-book expansion everywhere—too much, as Americans were destined to discover. The results of the crash when it came were, perhaps, more devastating than those of any event in our history except the Civil War. Yet, for all the over-production and distorted finance in the boom, many of the ventures of those years built a solid base for the future of American industry. In them came the immense growth of the automotive complex with the accompanying perfecting of the assembly-line techniques. In them came the foundations of synthetic manufacture. In them electric power from outside sources began to come into the factories to produce the flexibility of machine arrangement on which modern mass production is based. In them power transmission and distribution moved into smooth performance and, though certain utility pyramids suffered from fictional finance, the basis was laid for a sounder future structure for the sale and maintenance of kilowatts. In the twenties radio broadcasting acquired not only greatly improved technical performance but an economic pattern that has become part of American tradition. And with the reductions in power rates, the growing use of home appliances established an entire new business.

The magazine department of McGraw-Hill expanded in response to these growths. A periodical called *Radio Retailing* was started at the inception of regular broadcasting in 1925. Three years before that, from awareness that electric railway tracks might eventually be doomed by the internal combustion engine, a paper called *Bus Transportation* took its place beside James McGraw's pet, the *Electric Railway Journal.* Late in the decade *Construction Methods, Aviation,* and *Textile World* were added. Just before the storm broke McGraw-Hill took a step in the dark that resulted in one of the two most successful ventures in our story. A year later the other venture began with what, as we look back on it, seems an even more perilous step.

CHAPTER NINETEEN

Defying Disaster

Given clear enough hindsight, the mistakes made in the late twenties all through American business will not be made again. A book called *Oh Yeah?* by E. Angly, published after the first shocks, produced a good deal of grim laughter. The subject of our story was not immune. It looked at one time as if McGraw-Hill had stretched itself so far that the band must break. Those who remember the dark days say that its recovery was due to two things: the acumen and patience of a few leaders and the loyalty of the junior executives.

As a very minor example of a boom-year boner, the Book Company published a treatise on the stock market by an extremely authoritative professor of economics. He had already done a textbook on that general subject which had been very successful and is still in use. But this one undertook to prophesy. It analyzed the current situation, pointing out the developments that supported industry and investments. The terrible crises of the past when panic struck and depression followed were things that could never happen again. The book appeared on September 30, 1929, a month before the crash. It was titled, ironically, *New Levels in the Stock Market.*

The magazine *The Business Week,* was more cautious. In its first issue on September 7, 1929, an editorial stated:

> Security speculation has eaten nearly all of its credit cake. Stock prices are generally out of line with safe earnings expectations and the market is now almost wholly "psychological"—irregular, unsteady and properly apprehensive of the inevitable adjustment that draws near.

Adjustment seems a mild term for the holocaust that intervened before eight more issues could be printed, but the editorial sounded a note of warning that was rare in those days of mounting speculative fever. Yet immediately after the event, while men were jumping out their office windows, the magazine told its readers to keep cool, the crisis would pass, there was no reason for despair.

But what was this magazine that came into the world at that precarious moment? *The Business Week*—a title with a new sound for a McGraw-Hill paper! The others seemed dedicated to an industry or a technology. The engineering and mining papers, the electrical papers, and the *Machinist*—although they had all become more or less aware of the new science of management—were dominated by the mechanics or theories of their special subjects. The exception, treating the trading aspect, was *Electrical Merchandising,* but this, after all, covered only a limited area. Now apparently there was a weekly that promised to move horizontally all the way across the board, touching stock market, holding-company chains, the financing of utilities, wholesale and retail selling, and a hundred other matters as well as the executive offices of the steel mill or rubber factory.

THE McGRAW-HILL PUBLISHING COMPANY

ANNOUNCES THAT

THE MAGAZINE OF BUSINESS

WILL HEREAFTER BE PUBLISHED WEEKLY UNDER THE TITLE OF

THE BUSINESS WEEK

A Journal of Business News and Interpretation

BEGINNING WITH THE ISSUE OF

SEPTEMBER 7TH, 1929

There had been, to be sure, other journals that dealt vaguely with business, but their editors never seemed quite certain whether they were intended for the corner cigar store or the chambers of commerce. You saw copies of *Nation's Business,* for example, lying on the cutting tables of the local tailor as well as in Pullman lounge cars. There was something in each issue to appeal to both areas. You saw other, less successful ventures in the wastebaskets of busy executives. But except for such newspapers as the daily *Wall Street Journal* which, as its name implies, was largely concerned with finance, there was nothing that was truly essential to the upper levels of commercial activity, nothing that would keep the fast-thinking executive constantly abreast of affairs in the business world.

There was, however, a general magazine which was achieving in that era an immense popularity. This was *Time*—the Weekly Newsmagazine, as it called itself. *Time* had a way of digesting and presenting the stories of world events that was quite novel. It gave more background than the daily newspaper could; yet its style was journalistic enough to attract the reader who had little time for extended reading. It was a train magazine, a subway magazine, a lunch-hour magazine, a before-dinner magazine, a doctor's-waiting-room magazine. You could pick it up anywhere and lay it down at any time, but you were certain to learn something from it and be mildly entertained at the same time. Yet there seemed to be no one too high and mighty to read it, from cabinet officers to chauffeur-driven ladies on their shopping tours. Its success had been immediate and wide.

But *Time* could give only a column or so to business. Why not a magazine, not an imitation of *Time,* but a news weekly with the same directness of approach and compactness of digested material, devoted exclusively to business? This thought seems to have occurred to one or two McGraw-Hill men after a year or so of experiment with what is known as a "horizontal" business paper: one, that is, which would not confine itself to a particular industry. The result was one of the two most far-reaching events in Mc-

Announcement of the founding of "The Business Week," September, 1929.

Graw-Hill history and certainly one of its two brashest adventures in the face of the century's direst catastrophe.

2 It all began with James McGraw's purchase of the A. W. Shaw Company of Chicago in 1928. Shaw, like McGraw-Hill, published both periodicals and books. Unlike McGraw-Hill, however, Shaw's emphasis was on business rather than industry. He had, for instance, published the literary output of the Harvard Business School: its *Review*, its *Business Reports*, and its *Problem Books*. All this appealed to McGraw as complementary to his own enterprise. With his usual sensitivity to change, he had become conscious of the new management trends and he had begun to think "horizontally." He wanted a capstone paper: one that would join all the others on the management level. For this purpose the Shaw magazine *Factory* seemed to him most likely to fill the bill—or would, if McGraw-Hill editors revamped it.

Others in the organization saw a greater potential in Shaw's *Magazine of Business*. This was an offshoot of another Shaw enterprise called *System*, a magazine that reflected the efficiency-engineering epidemic in business offices following the Taylor revolution. *System* dealt with business machines, filing systems, and other techniques that were supposed to put new method into office operation. Some experienced and competent editors and business managers went out to Chicago to see what they could do with the *Magazine of Business*. They tried various experiments. But the more they played with it the more it looked like *Nation's Business*, the monthly published by the Chamber of Commerce in Washington. And the more it resembled *Nation's Business*, the more certain its experimenting doctors became that there was not room for two monthlies in the same field. For the emphasis in a monthly must always be on background rather than on quick-moving current events. Its articles must always take on the color of essays rather than that of news stories. It was from this conviction that these men turned to look, figuratively speaking, over Henry Luce's shoulder and decided that what was needed was a weekly news magazine of business. That was how what turned out to be the real capstone paper was born.

The Business Week did not, however, according to those who remember its beginning, make an immediate and total departure from everything before it. It seemed in its first year to have a sort of hangover from the monthly character. It continued to print essays—or what are now called think-pieces—and other matter that was too leisurely for the quickened tempo of a new era and too extended to compete with the immense volume of new articulation that was making such harassing inroads on the businessman's time.

Yet the statement of its concept and its intentions in the first issue seems to set a standard for *The Business Week's* conduct toward which in the three decades of its existence it has drawn constantly nearer. The statement insisted that as business could no longer be isolated from other world affairs, outside news must be given: news of the tariff, for instance, news of the postwar reparations settlements, news of crops, of taxes, of economic legislation, as well as the news of developments in management technique, of improved production processes, and of altered marketing methods.

> The whole story of the week [read the statement] is set forth in compact limits, a study in the fine art of saving the reader's time. Nothing irrelevant is included; nothing really important is omitted.
>
> There follows a digest of the significant statistics, the wheat sifted out of that overwhelming chaff-storm of figures that sweeps down upon the businessman from all points of the compass.
>
> Few facts have intrinsic interest. It is their meaning which concerns men; their relation to other facts. THE BUSINESS WEEK never will be content to be a mere chronicle of events. It aims always to interpret their significance.[1]

These were ideals. They constituted a beacon which would serve as a guiding light. As we look back at the early issues we may see how far they were from realizing these aims. Such irrelevant

[1] Publisher's statement, *The Business Week,* vol. 1, no. 1, September 7, 1929.

articles as "Taking the Fear out of Flying," "Jolly Wine Grapes Roll Eastward to Market," "It Could Only Happen Here"—an essay on Thomas A. Edison—and "A Golf Club is Pretty Select," and a good many others gave charm to some of the early issues, but they were not for the man who reads while he runs. Yet the streamlines had been set in that first statement and it was inevitable that the paper should eventually conform to them, for the men who laid them out were prophets of an era that had only just dawned.

In spite of the storm warning in the first issue's business weather report, it is clear that anxiety about what was to come was no more prevalent in the overextended McGraw-Hill organization than anywhere else. *The Business Week* project was on much the same scale as a hundred other blueprints of those grandiose days. The editorial staff was large. There was lavish expenditure on production. There was expensive color work on the covers. There were abundant illustrations: both line cuts and half tones. There was a full-page cartoon in every issue by some such famous caricaturist as Rollin Kirby, W. J. Enright, Oscar Cesare, Daniel Fitzpatrick, or Charles Kuhn. The stock was heavy and coated throughout. The type was set in the kind of runarounds that send up the composing-room bills. Everything about the paper suggested that the sky over McGraw-Hill was the limit.

On the staff there were, besides the managing editor, the European news director, the Washington and Chicago editors, and the art director, an economist, and experts in marketing and distribution, aviation, industrial production, finance and banking, transportation and utilities—in all some fifteen full-time editors. Looking back over the 1929 issues, we may see how hopeful were the times—even after the first shock.

And as the weeks moved on toward the day of doom, the "weather reports" on page 3 grew cheerier. Under the head "Generally Fair, Slightly Warmer" on October 12, came:

Cartoon by W. J. Enright from "The Business Week," September 14, 1929.

. . . there is so far no evidence, either in the statistical barometers or trade sentiment of any general or unnatural slump in business.

The following week—October 19—reported:

There is additional reassurance in the fact that, should business show any further signs of fatigue, the banking system is in a good position now to administer any needed credit tonic from its excellent supply.

And on November 2, following the crash, the reader was told:

The hysteria that accompanied the market upheaval will pass away in a few days. . . . Business will gradually and steadily recover as businessmen regain their perspective and go back to work.

Well, was that not what every organ of opinion was telling Americans in November, 1929, and was it not what most Americans believed? Were we not as reluctant then to accept the truth as we were on December 7, 1941, to credit the destruction of the Pacific Fleet at Pearl Harbor? But in the years that followed, *The Business Week* learned *not* to try to tell its readers merely what they wanted to hear. It learned that American businessmen for all their boasts of hardheadedness were often incorrigible romantics and that it could best help them by an objective realism, telling them the bare truth as they expertly saw it, whether it was pleasant or unpleasant, whether or not it accorded with prevailing prejudices. Through the difficult years of the recovery, the New Deal, and the rise of the labor movement, it maintained that attitude, "for if we are to give the business executive a realistic picture of the business scene . . . we must call the cards as they fall." [2]

3 When James McGraw bought the A. W. Shaw Company, he absorbed it gradually. At first, in 1927, he formed with it a merger, the McGraw-Shaw Company, which he announced was a subsidiary of both the Shaw company and the McGraw-Hill Company. Apparently Shaw wanted to sell out entirely and retire, but for the various reasons that motivate corporations when they merge, McGraw wanted the Shaw people to appear for a time at least on the mastheads of the papers for which they had become celebrated.

Prominent among these papers was *Factory,* a journal intended for manufacturing executives. To McGraw, as he looked over the Shaw properties, this seemed to him to have great horizontal or capstone possibilities. Conscious as always of new trends, he wanted to turn *Factory* into a paper that would stress the kind of scientific management that had come to have such a vogue during the past decade. As a first step he merged it with a magazine

[2] *The Business Week,* September 9, 1939, p. 37.

called *Industrial Management,* calling the result *Factory and Industrial Management.* The first issue appeared in January, 1928. It was dreary in outside appearance, though the layout and typography of the pages were sprightly enough. A month later the cover was spectacular. The background was a deep grass green with white lettering and a woodcut design also in white in the center.

Factory and Industrial Management opened with this explanation of its objective:

In charge of the manufacturing functions of the industrial organizations

Cover of the second issue of "Factory and Industrial Management," published in February, 1928.

of the United States are the executives who may rightly be called the "key men" of industrial production.

It is vital that these key men shall have a strong staff to lean upon, a virile, efficient, and constantly renewed source of inspiration and information. It is this conviction that has led to the consolidation of *Factory and Industrial Management.*

It will be remembered that at this period when so many changed factory methods—such as mass production on the Ford pattern—had become accomplished facts and had produced upheavals in organization, the beginnings of altered relations between management and labor were taking place. Here we see this magazine as a pioneer in presenting what was still an unpopular view. The editor felt, for example, that he had to explain a piece entitled "Why I Unionized My Plant" in the February, 1928, number:

Many a reader of *Factory and Industrial Management* will take violent exception to Mr. Mead's attitude toward labor unions. This question most employers deny is open to argument. . . . Because of its unusual viewpoint, it may help a good many industrial executives to see the other side of a subject generally regarded in management circles as having no other side.

The author began by stating: "nine years ago . . . we just saw red at the thought of having our plant unionized." Through four pages Mr. Mead tells of his experience. He does not argue. He just tells. At the end he writes:

For nine years now, our experiment with unions has been successful. It may not always be so. But so long as it is successful we shall, I imagine, continue to prefer dealing with unions to any alternative method.

We must put ourselves back in the period to see what a bold gesture the editor made in publishing the article. In the same issue were two other pieces by outside authors suggesting the new approach toward labor. These are examples of editorial observation of straws in the wind that characterized McGraw-Hill papers.

The acquisition of the Shaw Company and the launching of *The Business Week* were, however, only two cases of the expansion that was going on in the McGraw-Hill empire in the years before the depression. In March, 1929, *Aviation,* which boasted of being the oldest American periodical dedicated to aeronautics, joined the family. A double-page spread in the March 2 issue, with the inevitable portrait of James H. McGraw, tells of the purchase of the Aviation Publishing Corporation. It is probable that the chief had had his eye on the paper for some time. He seldom failed to notice the holes in his structure. Aviation had got to the point where its promise of changing the face of the world was pretty certain of fulfillment. This paper had been the pioneer in presenting that promise to a skeptical world. It had persisted in repeating it through the years when the United States was letting Europe get ahead of it in developing aircraft design and production. It had backed the prophecies of such enthusiasts as Glenn Martin and Gen. Billy Mitchell. From now on it would be recognized as on the winning side. So McGraw bought it, made an editor out of its former publisher, and kept most of the staff. The cover, format, and typography also remained the same.

But the most spectacular single stride to the brink of the gulf was still to come. It came, indeed, after the first panic.

4 Soon after Henry G. Lord joined the McGraw-Hill Publishing Company, bringing with him his *Textile World*—which, of course, increased the expansion—the question of a move came up. The company was scattered. The Shaw papers were still in Chicago. The Book Company was in one building in New York, the parent headquarters in another. Both Lord and James H. McGraw, Jr., known as Jay, believed all the activities should be under one roof, including the production department with its presses. Both presented their arguments at successive board meetings in 1928 and 1929. Eventually they carried conviction and several possible sites were considered. Then came the first crash in October, 1929, and the project was abandoned.

But those who remember the era know that in 1930 there was an upswing.[3] It was, of course, largely psychological. Economic America had always recovered from such crises in the past and several rising business barometers forecast fair weather after the storm. By summer this was reflected in the optimism of *The Business Week* which had reduced itself to some forty pages, including advertising, had scrapped its gay cover, its cartoons, and much of its editorial staff after the first crash.

> The business tide [it reported on July 2] reached its ebb during the last two weeks and is beginning to turn, very slowly and tentatively, in face of peevish, superficial and premature pessimism. . . . Then, in the same weeks when a year ago the downturn began, a decisive recovery will set in. . . . The rise of the business curve thereafter will be rapid. . . . By October it will be back to normal. . . .

Through the summer the paper kept up a virulent attack on the bears, quoting the best authorities as predicting quick recovery. On August 13 an editorial alliteratively referred to the "doleful diversions of the defeatists during the current depression"; on August 23 a headline announced "Business Recovering Courage"; on August 30 "Freshening of Business Breeze," and on September 6, "Business Has Rounded the Turn Say Nation's Utility Heads." But the actual business performance seemed to justify the claims. As F. L. Allen tells in his history of the times: "Prices leaped, the volume of trading became as heavy as in 1929, and a Little Bull Market was under way."[4]

In view of this wave of cheer and the fact that money was again becoming easy, McGraw-Hill resumed its building plans. Through a real-estate subsidiary it bought a plot of 47,000 square feet on 42d Street, New York, between Eighth and Ninth Avenues,

[3] There is a spirited account of this with abundant documentation in Frederick Lewis Allen's *Only Yesterday,* Harper & Brothers, New York, 1931, pp. 340 ff.

[4] Frederick L. Allen, *Since Yesterday,* Harper & Brothers, New York, 1940, p. 24.

and paid for it by the sale of its Tenth Avenue building. For the new building, it was able to negotiate a building loan with the Prudential Insurance Company through the Continental Mortgage and Guaranty Company for $3,800,000. The rest of the building cost was to be covered by other financial arrangements plus the company's own capital.

The architect chosen was Raymond Hood, celebrated for business-building design, and the builders Starrett Brothers and Eken. The ground was broken in August, 1930. The building was completed a year later and aroused much comment, good and bad, from the architecture-conscious folk it surprised.

Hood was extremely radical, for the times, in his concepts. Later he was looked upon as a pioneer. As a review of the period published in 1955 reported:

Many of the architects of the new office buildings . . . have followed the pioneering McGraw-Hill Building (1931) and discarded vertical emphasis for horizontal bands of windows. Sunlight in the office has won a battle. . . . Those buildings are an enormous improvement over the self-conscious Gothic turrets and spires of yesterday. There is, however, a depressing sameness about them. In the struggle against yesterday's rococo, individually has been lost.[5]

The McGraw-Hill Building, however, when it first appeared was individualistic in the extreme. There was nothing quite like it anywhere. Besides its unusual lines, it was remarkable for its color. As a contemporary article described it:

Color is of two kinds—the quick and the dead, depending largely on texture. In this case, the blue-green glazed surface of the terra cotta responds to the sky colors. Under a bright blue sky the color is correspondingly bright and blue. In the early dawn it picks up opalescent tints that change rapidly with the rising of the sun. . . . Equally interesting, perhaps, are its changing colors at sunset, passing into crepuscular shades until it becomes but a dimly outlined mass. In moonlight and fog and on gray days its changed aspect never dispels the realization of a great bulk, massive and dignified, impressing one with a

[5] "New York: 1935–1955," *Cue*, June 11, 1955.

feeling of solidity and security. The many aspects of color and texture contribute a living quality, rarely found in building. . . .

So much for the color. The article then echoes some of the contemporary doubts:

But is the McGraw-Hill Building architecture? That is the question for debate at this time. It does disregard every accepted principle of architecture in the most flagrant manner.[6]

The New Yorker deplored "the tendency to emphasize horizontal lines" which it maintains was borrowed from Germany by "the *avant-garde.*" Hood, it said, had completely reversed the "strongly vertical effect he achieved in the News Building" which, in *The New Yorker's* opinion, was the finest in New York.

. . . The fact remains that a tall building considered as a mass, goes up, not sidewise.[7]

In conclusion *The New Yorker* took a view diametrically opposed to that of Mr. North about the color, speaking of the "dispiriting gray-greenish tile."

A construction problem was presented by the need of housing a complete production plant—another large area of expansion which had developed over the years in the company. The seventh floor was dedicated to the composing room and the job press department. On the sixth were the twenty-five heavy rotary and cylinder presses. The bindery occupied the fifth. In the basement was the paper-stock storage. The knee-brace steel connections that took care of the load and the vibration from the big machinery[8] were so effective that McGraw-Hill employees used to boast that they could set a coin on edge on a desk or table and it would remain so. The interior arrangements in the building were so efficiently designed that for nearly thirty years of ex-

[6] Arthur T. North, "But Is It Architecture?" *American Architect,* January, 1932, pp. 30, 31.

[7] *The New Yorker,* July 25, 1931, p. 38.

[8] *American Printer,* June, 1931.

pansion they have served the company's purposes adequately enough.

Time and imitation have mellowed the shock of the building's first impressions. Hood's design may not have been beautiful by older standards and it may have missed the aesthetic values of the newer ones, but the McGraw-Hill people have come to love it, to be proud of it, and to appreciate its functional usefulness. One of the older executives who spends much of his extraoffice time at the University Club in 54th Street has trained the waiter in the club's dining room to seat him at a table near a window from which he can see the Big Green Building as he eats. "I want to be sure," he says, "that it stays there." When he gets in a cab he says "McGraw-Hill, please," to drivers who ask for the address. By now most of them know. Another old-timer tells the story of a taxi driver who said:

> You know, chief, what they do with that building whenever it gets dirty? It's all green tile. They don't have to paint it. They don't have to sandblast it. They just run over the whole thing with a damp cloth the way you would the inside of a bathroom.

The men and women who work there have most of them forgotten, if they ever knew, the griefs that accompanied the first two or three years of the building's life. As we can see in the history books, the hopeful days that *The Business Week* cheered on so loudly did not last. In 1931, the year the building was finished and occupied, there occurred a crash beside which the 1929 incident was small indeed. In 1932 the bottom of the economic world seemed to drop out entirely. But all that is another story and its impact on McGraw-Hill belongs in another chapter. Today all the misgivings have given way to the hindsight comment by the old-timers: "Wasn't it good we did what we did when we did!"

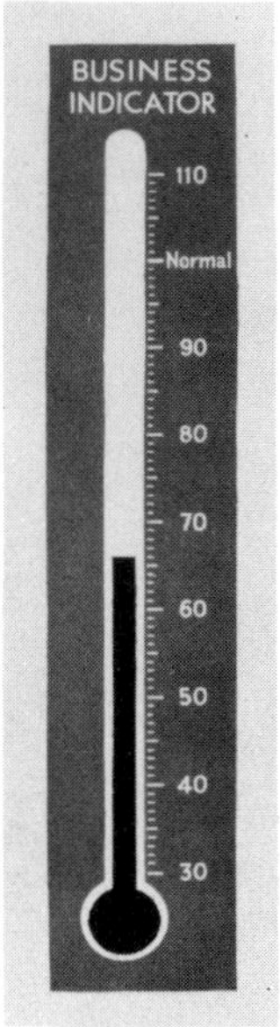

CHAPTER TWENTY

Weathering the Storm

In December, 1931, the "business indicator" which had become the most eye-catching feature of *The Business Week* showed a drop in its mercury to the all-time low of 65—35 degrees below the normal index of 100. Two months before, a shock that had been felt across the Western world had made its sharpest impact upon America. As Allen tells:

> . . . all over the United States banks were collapsing—banks which had invested heavily in bonds and mortgages and now found the prices of their foreign bonds cascading, the prices of their domestic bonds sliding down in the general rush of liquidation, and their mortgages frozen solid. In the month of September, 1931, a total of 305 American banks closed; in October a total of 522.[1]

[1] Frederick L. Allen, *Since Yesterday*, Harper & Brothers, New York, 1940, p. 51.

By this time salaries had been drastically cut and employees at every level throughout business and industry had reluctantly been laid off. At McGraw-Hill, now rattling round in its new thirty-three-story building in which many floors remained empty of tenants, some of the editorial and business staffs had been almost decimated. Yet there were men who refused to go; there were those who were so loyal that they were willing to work without salary. That demonstration is remembered with gratitude by some of the company's "elder statesmen" as one of the factors that held the organization together.

But the worst was yet to come. As Dixon Wecter tells:

> National income dwindled from eighty-one billion dollars in 1929 to less than sixty-eight in 1930, then cascaded to fifty-three in 1931 and hit bottom in 1932 with forty-one. Correspondingly, the country's estimated wealth over this span shrank from three hundred and sixty-five billion to two hundred and thirty-nine, a loss representing diminished values in real property, capital and commodities. . . . These three years took a toll of eighty-five thousand business failures with liabilities of four and a half billion dollars and the suspension of five thousand banks. Nine million savings accounts were wiped out, and wage losses upwards of twenty-six billion dollars sustained.[2]

In McGraw-Hill there were, nevertheless, compensations. One of the brightest spots in the darkness was the office of Henry Lord. When the merger of his New England company with McGraw-Hill had taken place, there had come with him a junior partner, the son of Joseph Bragdon from whom Lord had first bought *Textile World.* Lord's idea was to stay a year or two until young Bragdon was able to carry on alone with *Textile World* and then retire. But young Bragdon's premature death changed his mind. As it turned out, Lord was like the man who came for dinner. He never left McGraw-Hill, and at ninety-three he still comes to his office in the Green Building.

Almost immediately after his arrival Lord was made a director

[2] Dixon Wecter, *The Age of the Great Depression, 1929–1941,* copyright, 1948; reprinted by permission of The Macmillan Company, New York, p. 17.

"Business Week" covers, 1929 through 1958.

and was appointed Chairman of the Finance Committee, which included several of the responsible financial and operating executives of the company, and which probably was more directly responsible than any other single agency for bringing the overburdened company through the hazards of the depression.

Aside from the difficulties inherent in the regular operations of the company due to the shrinkage of its revenues was the heavy financial burden incident to the erection of the new building then under way. Another urgent aspect of the situation was that during the years before the crash, the company had sold stock to many of its employees.

It wasn't a case [explains Henry Lord] of trying to sell them the stock. It was a question of telling them how much they could buy. And most of them bought more than they could pay for, borrowed money from the banks and put up the stock for collateral.

Well, the stock went way down [after the crash] and these people took a terrible licking. The banks were calling on them to pay and they couldn't. Finally we managed to work out a plan by which they got all the stock they'd paid for and were released from further liability. None of them were sold out. I always considered that the best piece of work I ever did because there must have been about 100 such cases scat-

tered all around the banks, and I had to keep the banks happy and the men happy, too.[3]

Thus the Finance Committee was able not only to quiet anxiety in the financial institutions to which the company was in debt, but even obtained new support at a time when such backing was difficult to find. Quick action was achieved on the word of Mr. Lord and his committee. The support came quickly, before routine documentation of the company's security.

2 About *The Business Week* in these trying times, the Old Man is said to have had misgivings. It was, after all, not his own idea. As we have seen, the capstone paper he wanted was more on the order of *Factory and Industrial Management. The Business Week* was deep in the red all through the depression and for several years after recovery began. Between its start in 1929 and the end of 1935 it dropped about 1½ million dollars. It is not surprising that the chief was worried. The people on the other papers were worried, too, because it seemed to them that they were making sacrifices to keep a losing paper going, that it was draining their

[3] Henry G. Lord, recorded interview, pp. 45, 46.

resources. It is probable that they took some of their worries to McGraw. But a few foresighted men believed in the job *The Business Week* was doing and ahead of them they could see the way out of the woods.

Those who remember the red interval realize the value of their perseverance. The point was, they say, that the need for the paper has never been greater than in precisely that depressed period. Because it so adequately answered that need then, it established itself as essential. As a former publisher of *The Business Week* recalls:

> That was the time when business management wanted to read about business and what made business tick. The depression was a great force to broaden, shall we say, the scholarship of management. In other words, many men who had been running their business successfully for years by rule of thumb suddenly asked, "Now, what's the economics that's responsible for this? Where can I find out?" [4]

Business Week,[5] he believed, "just moved into that vacuum." Since its somewhat experimental start, its formula and philosophy had crystallized. It had been streamlined; the long leisurely think-pieces had been eliminated; articles were more closely geared to news, and everything that might waste a busy executive's time had been kept out. Nevertheless, its editors took pains to analyze the economic background. As the New Deal came into the forefront of all America's economic thought, there was plenty of news, news that had depth as well as breadth. NRA, for example, was arousing both conjecture and rebellion. It was viewed as an instrument of both immediate and long-run consequence. So were other drastic Roosevelt innovations. But *Business Week's* attitude here is interesting and sometimes tended to get it in trouble with the hotheads who relished opinion more than fact.

The paper stuck to its intention to present the situation realistically. It was the custom in those days when addressing businessmen to engage in diatribe against a government that was unpopu-

[4] Willard Chevalier, recorded interview, p. 111.

[5] As part of the streamlining, *The* was dropped from the title.

lar in the business world. But *Business Week* tried to show precisely what it believed businessmen were going to have to face whether they liked it or not. Perhaps the editors did not like it either, but they saw no value in butting their heads against a wall. Certain things were inevitable and wise folk should prepare to meet them. There was certain to be an increase in social security provisions, for example. Organized labor was sure to increase in strength. A more onerous tax structure would follow changing economic policies, both domestic and foreign. Isolationism was likely to break down. Finally there was not much probability, during the thirties at least, of a change of mood among the majority of voters.

It seemed more useful, therefore, to help readers to face conditions that the editors saw coming than to try to wish them into the dream world of their own choosing. Sensible people accepted this view and were glad of the realistic advice, but the extremists were up in arms and at times even accused the editors of being fellow travelers. These extravagances, symptomatic of the turbulent era during which business struggled back to its feet, did not, of course, persist, and *Business Week* readers who profited from its realism looked back to it afterward with gratitude. Thus the paper became deeply intrenched and once the corner was turned grew into one of the top money-makers on the list.

3 The effect of the depression that broadened "the scholarship of management" was sharply reflected in the publications of the Book Company which naturally went deeper into the background of the crisis than any periodical could do. The more thoughtful businessmen, who in the early thirties were likely to have enforced leisure in which to reflect, were deeply preoccupied with the questions: What caused the crisis? How shall we prevent it next time? The answers came, if at all, only after a good deal of probing into the elusive social science of economics. Until then most of the active executives had touched only the surface of their business: immediate supply and demand, quickly accessible markets, and the day-to-day fluctuations in the

A few of the Whittlesey House books published during the 1930s.

financial indices. Even the books could not give all the correct answers, produced, as they were, in the critical years; yet by going into the history of changes in the political economy, some of them set their readers thinking constructively.

One of the most impressive of these was a little book entitled *Business Adrift* by Wallace Brett Donham, Dean of the Harvard Business School. There was an introduction by one of the greatest of modern philosophers of economics, Alfred North Whitehead. This essay on "Foresight" reads as truly today as when it first appeared. Whitehead traces the successive periods of change affecting society from the time that a period was a million years long to the present day when it lasted less than a lifetime. He pointed to the rapid obsolescence of economic shibboleths in our time.

Such sharp-cut notions as "the economic man," "supply and demand," "competition," are now in process of dilution by a close study of the actual reactions of various populations to the stimuli which are relevant to modern commerce. . . .

The older political economy reigned supreme for about a hundred years from the time of Adam Smith, because in its main assumptions it did apply to the general circumstances of life as led, then and for innumerable centuries in the past. . . .

In the present age, the element of novelty . . . is too prominent to be omitted from our calculations. A deeper knowledge of the varieties of human nature is required to determine the reaction . . . to those elements of novelty which each decade of years introduces into social life. The possibility of this deeper knowledge constitutes the Foresight of which I am speaking.[6]

In other words the old reliable "laws" no longer worked. This may be obvious today but in 1931 it had to be said and repeated. Then Whitehead presented the opportunity to create a new era to rise from the ashes of the old.

Mankind is now in one of its rare moods of shifting its outlook. The mere compulsion of tradition has lost its force. It is the business of philosophers, students, and practical men to re-create and re-enact a vision of the world, conservative and radical, including those elements of reverence and order without which society lapses into riot, a vision penetrated through and through with unflinching rationality. . . . There is now no choice before us: either we must succeed in providing a rational coordination of impulses and thoughts, or for centuries civilization will sink into a mere welter of minor excitements. We must produce a great age, or see the collapse of the upward striving of our race.[7]

We may wonder, a quarter century later, if the signs of this great age have yet appeared. Certainly the words must have inspired the inquiring minds of 1931. In the body of Donham's book, there is an insistent argument for planning.

[6] Wallace Brett Donham, *Business Adrift,* McGraw-Hill Book Company, Inc., New York, 1931, p. xxii.

[7] *Ibid.,* p. xxviii.

The difficulties in which we find ourselves are, to a large extent, connected with this lack of a plan. An example is the way we have overbuilt our industries.

The lack of constructive leadership is clear to anyone who has read the recent New Year's outbursts on the present business depression. Inconsistent theories, advice, hopes, fears, and aspirations are laid before us all wholly uncoordinated to any general plan. . . .[8]

Dunham then outlines his own plan which, of course, cannot take into consideration the "novelties" of the next two decades: World War II, the cold war, the beginning of the atomic age, and the advances in communications, electronics, and nucleonics, which have all impinged on the world economy. But some of his provisions were adopted in the recovery program and even today the book is stimulating reading.

Another book that reflects the doubts and fears of the era is Prof. Isaac M. Wormser's presentation of the concentration of economic power in the United States which the author thinks was a contributing cause of the crisis.[9] Wormser was professor of law at Fordham University. His book is a surprising attack on big business which might today earn its author the epithet of "leftist" or, perhaps, "liberal," which is thought in some quarters to be as bad or worse.

When a handful of corporations, not over 200 in number, are earning 40 per cent of the nation's net income, thoughtful people are wondering how we are going to act toward these giants of undreamed-of size and uncontrolled power. Modern American society is a Frankenstein which has created these new and mighty monsters, which in turn have given rise to such momentous problems.[10]

And this must have made conservative readers shudder:

Corporate capitalists, if they would meet the serious situation which now confronts them, must regard themselves as "trustees." They must look to the welfare not only of themselves but of the general public.

[8] *Ibid.*, p. 36.

[9] Isaac Maurice Wormser, *Frankenstein Incorporated,* McGraw-Hill Book Company, Inc., New York, 1931.

[10] *Ibid.*, p. 229.

So far as they are unwilling to do so, their parent—the state—must compel such consideration. A socialized corporate capitalism is therefore inevitable—a capitalism which will preserve all the benefits and advantages of individual economic freedom, modified and tempered by an observance of and consideration for the social and economic welfare of the people at large.[11]

Ernest Minor Patterson had produced the first volume to appear with the Whittlesey House imprint, *The World's Economic Dilemma.* Coming in 1930 this book could not take into consideration the more devastating phenomena of the depression, but it emphasized, as both Donham and Wormser also did, the disregard by business of wide social needs. In the catalogue it was described as "a significant study of the acute dilemma now confronting the world which arises from the 'pull' of individual interests in opposition to the common interests of all mankind."

Perhaps the most ambitious Book Company enterprise of the period was the publication in 1929 of the two-volume report of the Committee on Recent Economic Changes, on the President's Conference on Unemployment. In a sense this furnishes the documentation for the thesis of Whitehead and Donham. It was a complete compendium with interpretations of the things that had altered the nation's economic complexion during the years that just preceded the crash. To the student of causes and remedies it was of great value and it is still useful to the historian. Herbert Hoover, an old McGraw-Hill friend, was chairman of the committee. Edward Eyre Hunt who edited the volumes of *Recent Economic Changes in the United States* also produced a supplementary volume, *An Audit of America.*

Other books helpful in the depression were Harper Leech's *Paradox of Plenty* and Laurence H. Sloan's *Everyman and his Common Stocks.* But the most sensational and financially successful of all was the inspirational volume with which Whittlesey House took its first long step away from business, economics, and sociology.

Life Begins at Forty by Walter B. Pitkin is 175 pages of pure

[11] *Ibid.,* p. 241.

rhapsody. It reads as if it were written at top speed. Even today, when many of its arguments are no longer convincing, it is a hard book to put down. And, although some of its exuberant promises have since been tragically blocked, it is easy to see what a lift it gave to depressed folk in the nadir of 1932.

> You who are crossing forty [the book begins] may not know it but you are the luckiest generation ever. The advantages you are about to enjoy will soon be recited, with a sincere undertone of envy. The whole world has been remodeled for your greater glory. Ancient philosophies and rituals are being demolished to clear the ground for whatever you choose to erect upon their sites. Every day brings forth some new thing that adds to the joy of life after forty. Work becomes easy and brief. Play grows richer and longer. Leisure lengthens. Life's afternoon is brighter, warmer, fuller of song; and long before the shadows stretch, every fruit grows ripe.[12]

It is easy to see how all this appealed to the man or woman who feared the approach of middle age—and they, incidentally, formed the principal book-buying brackets. In a chapter entitled "Youth in the Red" Pitkin tries to deprecate the importance given to youth in the popular concept. Young people, he writes, are ignorant, unreflective, and ineffective. He even goes so far as to lay the depression at the doors of those under forty!

> How little even our brightest college graduates know about anything in their late twenties and thirties. Pleasant, occasionally sparkling, they often spar around a subject . . . but never come to grips with it. And this, I feel sure, is one of the chief reasons for our shocking economic collapse. . . . Study the inside records of some of the most tragic bankruptcies and ruined fortunes; you will find a startling number of men under forty at the helm of the derelicts.[13]

It is evident to today's reader of these rhythmic arguments how far the professor has gone in letting his thesis ride him. But we have seen tragedy befall the depression's children; we have seen

[12] Walter B. Pitkin, *Life Begins at Forty,* Whittlesey House, McGraw-Hill Book Company, Inc., New York, 1932, p. 3.

[13] *Ibid.,* p. 21.

in war, hot and cold, the ironic working out of the thesis when life *had to* begin at forty after military duties had been fulfilled, and most of us have scarcely approached the Utopia Pitkin depicted for "life's afternoon." From the publishing point of view, however, the book precisely hit the mark and its enormous sale showed the possibilities in topical trade books.

4 One of the most revolutionary technics in the history of technology was coming, in 1930, to absorb the interest of industrialists, engineers, and businessmen alike. This was the vacuum tube, symbol of the application of the science of electronics.

Nearly two centuries before, Benjamin Franklin had referred to the "electrical fluid." After Franklin the notion that there could be anything in the nature of a fluid about electricity was discarded. Then in 1883 Thomas Edison, experimenting with his incandescent lamp, observed what seemed to be a "flow" of electricity between electrodes in a vacuum bulb. But Edison, who was extremely busy with other things and could see no useful application for his discovery, forgot about it. He recorded it, however, and it later became known as a scientific curiosity: the Edison effect.

The Edison effect particularly fascinated an Englishman, J. Ambrose Fleming, who at the time was acting as scientific adviser to a London Edison company. It was not until 1904, however, that Fleming found a use for it in connection with his investigations into wireless telegraphy. He then incorporated its principle in his celebrated invention, the Fleming valve, which he used to rectify oscillating currents from radio waves. This clever device let through currents moving in one direction while stopping those that moved in the other. The Fleming valve was later used to transform alternating into direct current. The next step came when the American, Lee De Forest, by introducing a grid between the electrodes, turned the Fleming device into an amplifier. In the hands of Henry Arnold, Irving Langmuir, Reginald

Fessenden, and many others the vacuum tube became a creative instrument of fabulous power. It was no longer merely a rectifier, a detector, or an amplifier; it was an actual generator of radio waves.

As such it completely revolutionized radiotelephony and its product broadcasting, which, by 1930, had become a *sine qua non* of American life. It had brought about the scrapping of enormously cumbersome and expensive generators. When the power of these little tubes was realized the industrial vista ahead seemed infinite.

Vacuum-tube development brought radio out of the amateur, home-building phase in which armies of boys aged from twelve to eighty had bought components and put them together so that they could hear signals through crystal detectors. From this phase the McGraw-Hill paper *Radio Retailing* had profited. But now with the setting up of broadcast networks and the frenzied public demand, the whole business had passed into an engineering phase. Neither *Radio Retailing* nor *Electrical Merchandising* could begin to cover even this field; and these combined with *Electrical World* could not hope to meet the demand for material on this vast new technological area. So these men who for years had been dealing with currents and circuits and generators and waves and signals got their heads together, talked with some communication engineers, and conceived a journal that they proposed to call *Electronics.*

The first issue of this venture appeared in April, 1930, six months after the Wall Street crash. It was for that time a model of layout and typography, printed on good substantial stock with an abundance of illustration, including colored charts. But its most impressive feature was a spread with messages from seven world-famous authorities demonstrating the need for the paper as herald of a new era: Thomas Edison, Lee De Forest, J. Ambrose Fleming, Prof. Robert A. Millikan, a pioneer experimenter, H. P. Davis of Westinghouse, Willis R. Whitney of General Electric, and Frank B. Jewett of the Bell Laboratories.

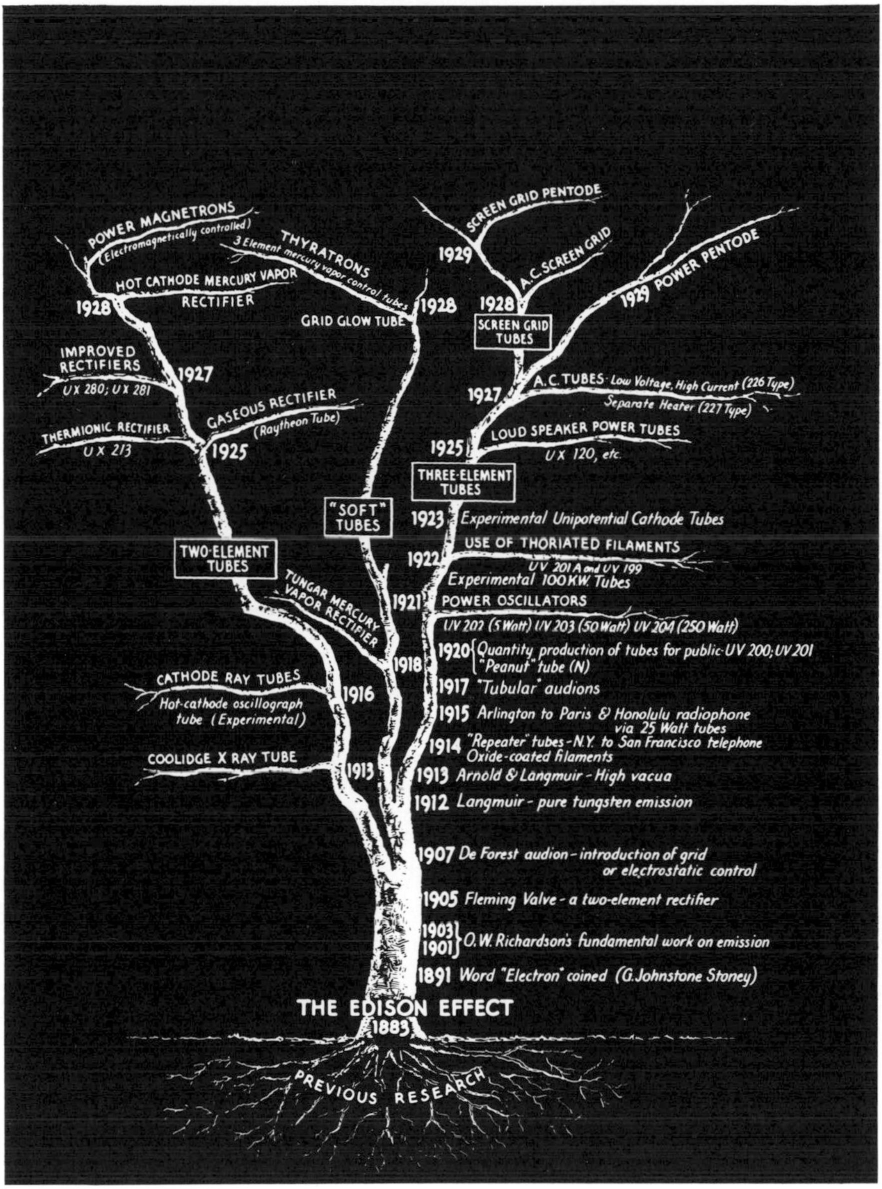

An illustration from "Electronics," May, 1930.

The significance of electronics was told in glowing terms.

No new physical appliance ever invented [wrote Millikan] has found such a multitude of enormously important practical applications in so short a time as has the vacuum tube amplifier.[14]

Of the tubes Edison wrote:

They open a field for research in physics, chemistry, electricity, heat and light, beyond imagination.[15]

And De Forest, noting that 100-kilowatt power tubes were already a commonplace, said:

. . . it requires no daring imagination to predict that in the field of power conversion and transmission the free electron in glass and copper will soon replace tons of electric generators.[16]

On a following page the editors listed the possible applications of electronics in motor control, factory equipment, power transmission, entertainment and cultural progress, medicine and therapeutics, navigation, aviation, measurement, lighting, mining, and metallurgy. All these pages must have been useful to wave in the face of the skeptics who saw no reason for the paper, especially in those depressed years.

Its way was far from smooth. It did have the advantage of being so far over the heads of other editors, managers, and the upper echelons of executives that no one interfered with its operations. But as one of the early editors said,

We did have to meet the annual rigamarole explaining why the company shouldn't throw *Electronics* out the window. There were no profits, no hope of any profits. . . .[17]

Yet, after the editors had demonstrated their faith, *Electronics* stayed in the shop. Everyone was touched, somehow, by the

[14] *Electronics,* vol. 1, no. 1, p. 8, April, 1930.
[15] *Ibid.*
[16] *Ibid.*
[17] Keith Henney, recorded interview, pp. 1, 2.

fringes of this mysterious new technological fabric that seemed destined to cover the whole world. So the decision of the company executives was: let them alone for a while longer and see what happens. There was, to be sure, a prestige connected with any paper that moved in so imponderable a realm that compensated for the lack of profits. And apparently there were no great losses—usually an even break each year. But then the depression was over and finally with World War II the technology took such an immense leap forward that huge new industrialization with the consequent advertising put the magazine well up in the lucrative brackets. It increased frequency of issue to three times a month in 1957 and became a weekly in 1958.

Today the *Electronics* people are proud of their history. The first issues, to be sure, look primitive today. With transistors replacing tubes and something else threatening to replace transistors, and with radar, television, computers, and automation all exploiting the technology, the field seems even larger than that envisioned by the pioneers.

As recovery came the complexion of the company began to change. With the Old Man increasingly absent from the scene, some of the executives were surprised to see how well the shop fared without him. It was then evident that he had left much of himself behind to move in the minds of those who were to carry on. Also it was quite obvious that the end of one-man business had arrived. From now on in a large, complex organization in which a variety of operations was carried on, there must be large delegation of authority plus semiautonomy in departments. After the depression there was truly a new era in business. In McGraw-Hill in the late thirties and forties, the internal trend was toward decentralization.

CHAPTER TWENTY-ONE

Recovery in a New World

One of the most revolutionary changes in the period following World War I was the replacement in many areas of the steam engine by the internal-combustion motor. This had repercussions in the McGraw-Hill organization. Its effect was felt, directly or indirectly, in the *Electric Railway Journal*, in *Bus Transportation*, in *Chemical and Metallurgical Engineering*, in *Coal Age*, in *American Machinist*, and even in *Engineering News-Record* and *Engineering and Mining Journal*. It was partially responsible for the formation of new papers from the twenties into the fifties, including the important lately acquired petroleum journals. It brought to the Book Company such enduring classics as James A. Moyer's *Gasoline Automobiles* and E. H. Hamilton's *Elementary Thermodynamics of Automobile Engines*.

The effects were visible everywhere in the United States. Even in the 1930s, diesel and diesel-electric locomotives were replacing the puffing steam giants that had played such an important role in American expansion. The last main-line steam locomotive constructed in the United States for domestic use was built in 1949. In the 1940s diesel-powered marine motors made swift progress. From 1930 on, truck transportation offered competition to the railroads in express and freight carriage. Buses for long-distance travel competed with railroad passenger traffic in addition to furnishing a means to journey to out-of-the-way communities not reached by the railroads or the interurban trolleys. These buses also made many branch rail lines or spurs obsolete.

The internal-combustion motor furnished a prime mover for construction machinery that was far lighter, more mobile, and more efficient than the cumbersome steam engine. Taking up little room but delivering great power, it could move derricks, cranes, excavators, and wrecking devices with new economy and ease of fuel handling. Watching the erection of a city building for example with its little motor in the street supplying most of the mechanical power, it is difficult for older people to remember the day when steam was the only power available for the major operations of digging and lifting, when human hod carriers used to climb the ladders that are replaced today by mechanical conveyors. The stationary internal-combustion motors were supplemented by a variety of mobile units from concrete mixers to bulldozers.

The rapid mechanization of operations in the 1920s that was already altering the whole face of the construction industry gave rise to a new McGraw-Hill enterprise. Until then every phase of design and construction had been covered by *Engineering News-Record.* But now the question arose as to whether it was reaching the large new class of contractors who were buying the new mechanical equipment. Engineers would always read it, yes; but should not those constructors whose interest was less scientific and more immediately practical have a paper dealing with actual construction methods rather than with design and theory, a paper with less text and more illustrative material, one that would carry the advertising of the equipment manufacturers more directly to those who were in the market to buy it?

This was an example of a prevailing McGraw-Hill practice: not of answering some crying need, but rather of anticipating a need. Here the fulfillment was provided even before the desire was articulated in the field.

The management of the *News-Record* envisioned a monthly magazine

> . . . devoted to the techniques of construction, *how* this dam was built, *how* this bridge was erected, *how* these piles were sunk, and new gadgets and tricks that are developed by the construction man in putting together the individual structure.[1]

Essentially it was to be a field man's paper. For many years the *News-Record* had, as we have seen, covered the dirt moving and steel handling as well as the design phases of civil engineering, but now in 1925 with all these new developments, its coverage needed to be extended.

It was a McGraw-Hill development policy not to start a new paper from scratch if an existing paper could be bought and converted to the McGraw-Hill objective. There was, at the time, a sort of cooperative house organ called *Successful Methods* which had been founded in 1919 by the Manufacturers' Publicity Bureau of Chicago representing a group of noncompeting manufacturers of construction and material-handling equipment. It was proposed that McGraw-Hill purchase this and turn it into such a supplemental magazine.

There was immediate opposition within the company. The new paper would compete, its opponents said, with *News-Record.* It would take away pages of its advertising at a time when the advertising of new equipment in *News-Record* was increasing. But the chief got the point. McGraw was quick to see that this could

[1] Willard Chevalier, recorded interview, p. 44.

not happen. *News-Record,* the weekly, with its long-established and world-wide reputation and following would continue to be needed by the advertiser, and the new paper would simply give him an additional coverage medium in a rapidly expanding market. This was shrewd, practical thinking against the background of hugely expanding technologies. And perhaps the clinching argument was the old one—heard almost from the beginning of the McGraw and the Hill businesses: "If we don't do it, someone else will."

In 1926, then, *Construction Methods* began publication as a paper for contractors and other construction men. It suffered heavily during the depression when construction almost came to a halt. It was looked at askance by the headshakers for several years. They waited anxiously for the fulfillment of their prophecy about its draining the life blood from the *News-Record;* but they waited in vain. In the thirties, *Construction Methods* began to make money; and it marched proudly side by side with its parent. The two papers have prospered and helped each other.

2 With the advent of certain special papers such as *Construction Methods* and *Electronics* came the beginnings of that decentralization and delegation of authority which distinguishes the McGraw-Hill Publishing Company today. Today each paper or group of related papers has a publisher. In all, there are twenty publishers and five associate publishers. In McGraw's heyday there was only one publisher and that was James H. McGraw. But it was no longer possible for one man to hold the reins as the chief had done. The organization had become too big and too diverse. The papers had become too numerous and too technically specialized. The staffs of the various papers needed more freedom in dealing with their chosen fields. Bit by bit the various publications had won a new autonomy. Editors and business managers were no longer accountable directly to the president of the company; they reported to and took orders from their publisher.

Direct, personal control over every paper eluded the president's grasp when these highly specialized journals arrived, each sponsored by an individual and his staff who alone completely understood its field and its mission. Both *Construction Methods* and *Electronics* were the "babies" of such individuals. They had to be nursed along by their progenitors; no one else could do it. The top brass of the rapidly expanding company no longer could know enough even to advise about the care and feeding of these uncommon babies.

But although these progenitors and one or two others, such as the general manager of the *American Machinist* who had an inherited autonomy from the Hill company, *were,* in fact, publishers, that title was not given them. First they were called general managers, then publishing directors. As one of them recalls:

> All this was for the purpose of avoiding the use of the word "publisher." Why? Well, the context was understood by everyone around here. There was only one publisher and that was Mr. McGraw. You could give the rest of us any titles you wanted, except that of publisher because Mr. McGraw was THE publisher. . . . We were slipping away from the idea of one-man publishing domination, if you please, but we were still maintaining a tabu on the general use of the title "publisher." [2]

This sort of beating about the bush to protect the appearance of a control that had, in fact, lapsed was by no means peculiar in those days to McGraw-Hill. The same thing was happening, for instance, on a far larger scale in the Ford Motor Company—that classic example of a one-man dictatorship. As we study the personal life of the great Henry we see, beginning about 1926 when the Model-T died, the controls slipping, one by one, from his grasp—a poignant sequence. But everywhere, though in many cases—as with the Du Ponts—the dynastic appearance was maintained, group complexes were replacing individuals, and functions split off from the central stem.

[2] *Ibid.,* p. 71.

There can be little doubt that McGraw senior was fully aware of what was happening in what had become the largest business and technical publishing house in the world. He had, however, kept his hand firmly on his own special "babies": the papers that were concerned with the electrical industries. In particular he kept it on the *Electric Railway Journal,* his old pet that he believed he had lifted out of the horsecar stage and then had built into the best of its category. When the sky darkened over that, there came a sad time for James H. McGraw. But that story takes us back to the new explosive motor with which this chapter began.

3 The first threat to the electric-railway industry came in 1914 about simultaneously with the introduction of the moving assembly line in the Ford plant at Highland Park, Detroit. This was the jitney, appearing on the streets of Los Angeles. The jitney was usually a Model-T Ford. It offered to transport passengers over certain routes for five cents. These routes were, for the most part, those on which the trolleys operated. The little cars would drive to the places where crowds were assembled waiting for trolleys and pick up the impatient. Then, being unhindered by tracks, the jitneys would make better speed through the traffic than the electric cars. They were uncomfortable and often dangerous. Passengers not fortunate enough to get inside had to cling to the running board. But in those days when automotive mass production was just beginning, there was a thrill to a ride in an automobile that compensated for much discomfort.

In his excellent history of local transit, John Anderson Miller tells of the effect of the jitney's competition on the electric-railway industry as it became epidemic in cities all over the country.

According to an estimate made by Edwin L. Lewis superintendent of the Los Angeles Railway, the loss of revenue in that city was more than three million dollars a year at the height of the jitney craze. . . . R. E. Danforth, general manager of the Public Service Railway of New

Jersey, estimated that the jitneys operating in the territory served by his company were costing it about four million dollars a year.[3]

When the jitney operators—mostly young men out of jobs or working the cars in their spare time—found that they could not sustain their profits at the nickel rate, the craze died down, but it had left writing on the wall that could never be erased. As street traffic increased, it was obvious that a vehicle confined to tracks was at a disadvantage. Furthermore, one that carried its own self-sufficient power plant was independent of the power failures that caused long blocks of trolley cars. Finally in the years immediately after World War I, the public was becoming more and more automobile-minded.

By 1911 the horses that had drawn omnibus stages in the great cities of London and New York had all disappeared. The stages were replaced by boxlike bodies mounted on truck chassis. Following this, a few forward-looking American electric-railway companies had bought some of these makeshift motor buses to supplement their trolley service. In 1920 the first bus "designed from the ground up" for its purpose was built in Oakland, California.[4] It was hardly a mere coincidence, then, that a McGraw-Hill publication called *Bus Transportation* started in 1922.

But at this point there came one of the rare instances of wrong guessing by the Old Man. He was perfectly willing to admit the advent of the bus as a public carrier. He even antagonized some of his friends in the electric-railway industry by having his paper urge them to buy buses to supplement their electric service. He believed that the development of the bus could be guided in this direction by the trolley companies and that competition could thus be avoided. As Miller observes:

> This idea seemed to appeal to the street-railway companies. All over the country they began buying buses. . . . At the end of 1922 there were about fifty street-railways operating 400 buses. . . . By January 1,

[3] *Fares, Please! From Horse-Cars to Streamliners,* copyright, 1941, by Appleton-Century-Crofts, Inc., New York, p. 150. Mr. Miller was formerly editor of the *Electric Railway Journal.*

[4] *Ibid.,* p. 154.

A bus of the early 1920s.

1925, there were 220 companies operating about 7,000 buses. Five years later some 390 street-railways were operating more than 13,000 buses.[5]

But this increase in bus service only increased the public conviction that tracks were on the way out. Also certain companies were finding that the supplementary idea was costly. To operate buses and at the same time pay for track maintenance seemed to them unnecessary expense. So they began to sell the tracks for scrap and do the whole job by bus. By this time buses were well designed and built; they had not only become comfortable but, in some cases, luxurious.

But even in the face of these changes James McGraw refused to be convinced. Whether from sentimental attachment to the industry he had helped build or because of his own personal lack of interest in motor cars—a fact which one of his mechanically minded sons remembers with amusement—he remained blind to the handwriting on the wall, however luminous it became. For the decline in the 1920s of electric railways, he blamed company

[5] *Ibid.*, p. 156.

management for not sufficiently modernizing their cars and equipment. In some of the jottings he was always making of ideas for speeches and editorials we find these notes:

> It is a difficult task to make the public believe that the electric railways are not in the process of dying out, while obsolete equipment is being paraded before their eyes every day.
>
> The man in the street is predisposed to severely criticize the slightest operating difficulty, and his mind is in excellent condition to receive the suggestion of the misguided local newspaper editor who suddenly comes to the conclusion that electric railways are headed for the scrap heap.
>
> Bus manufacturers are applying intensive sales methods of the automotive industry in the sale of their products.
>
> Although the bus has an important place in the transportation industry its functions are distinctive in itself. . . .
>
> It is a mistake to introduce the bus in a way that will cause it to become associated in the public mind exclusively with street car service and street car fares. . . .
>
> We hold no brief for the bus beyond its proper sphere of usefulness. We believe that when properly applied it is a valuable addition to present transportation facilities.
>
> It is not a substitute for them.[6]

This informal record shows the troubled state of the chief's mind better than any printed address or editorial could do. Precisely what he supposed the bus's distinctive function and "proper sphere of usefulness" to be is not clear. He did write in one of his notes: "We look on this new vehicle as a means of attracting to public transportation agencies many of the passenger miles now carried in private vehicles." But he could not bring himself to see the duplication in street and interurban transit that had come with the increase in size and efficiency of the bus. To him any gasoline-driven affair would always remain a puny thing compared with the majestic electric car operating over a vast system and powered by a far-off giant generator.

[6] Speeches and writings of James H. McGraw, in McGraw-Hill Archives.

Thus it was a sad day for McGraw in 1932 when his associates persuaded him to change the title of his beloved paper from *Electric Railway Journal* to *Transit Journal,* and an even sadder one ten years later when even that had become obsolete and the company discontinued it to save the red ink engendered by the publication of a paper that was no longer profitable. But by 1942 the chief had become an octogenarian and had long relinquished his control to younger men.

4 The other electrical papers did not, however, suffer from any technological obsolescence. Apart from the sort of transportation the *Railway Journal* had been concerned with, electricity came into its own in the postdepression period as it had never done before. Not only was there the progress we have noted through electronics in communications; there was large electrification of railroads. There was the rapidly increasing electrification of factories. Most popular of all, as far as the general public was concerned, was the electrification of the household.

In January, 1936, *Electrical Merchandising* reported that the depression in the appliance business had ended three years before and that 1935 figures were higher than even those of the boom year of 1929. There were, to be sure, some new gadgets and great improvements had been made in the old ones in the interval. Food mixers, glass percolators, automobile radio sets, roasters, coal stokers, and water heaters had been added to the list. Refrigerators in 1935 more than doubled the 1929 figure on unit sales. These along with dishwashers and washing machines were of much higher quality. With increased conversion of heating units from coal to oil, electrically ignited oil burners had doubled their sales. Sales figures for electric ranges reached a new high in 1935. According to an article in the January, 1936, issue of *Merchandising,* the prospects ahead were bright. As a result of the President's order establishing the Rural Electrification Administration the paper estimated that $250 million in potential business—wiring and appliances—had been created.

As we look at the pictures of all these devices in the magazine's advertising pages, they look primitive enough compared with today's commonplaces. The barrel-type washing machines with wringers attached were a far cry from the new fully automatic affairs that do the entire laundry while the housewife does her shopping. Toasters only toasted one side of the slice at a time and had not learned to pop it out. Driers and deep freezers were dreams of the future. But when we remember that the domestic servant had virtually disappeared from the American scene, we see the value of these crude archetypes of our present push-button home life.

During the next few years *Electrical World* reported the increase in the sale of "juice" and new distribution figures that ran parallel to the progress in appliance development. In the year 1939 there were 900,000 new customers reported by the utilities. Farm electrification accounted for 40 per cent of these. Two thirds of the farms wired were on lines of the Rural Electrification Administration, a fact showing the effect of the President's order in 1935. All these figures and many others demonstrating fast-rising revenues, reduction in operating expenses, new budgets, and financial operations were presented in compact form with charts, tables, and graphs in the annual statistical number of *Electrical World,* published January 13, 1940. This was one of the most impressive issues of that magazine ever printed up to that time; and it is of considerable historical value as showing the American electrical scene in the transitional years between the depression and World War II.

But in the eyes of the electrical enthusiasts at McGraw-Hill—of whom, of course, the senior McGraw himself was the most ardent—even the combination of these two papers was insufficient to cover the vast field that had appeared, even back in the late twenties, to stretch into infinity. In 1928 McGraw bought a Chicago company which published *Jobber's Salesman* and *The Electragist. Mill Supplies* was added to these in 1929 and the company was operated for several years as a subsidiary. McGraw-

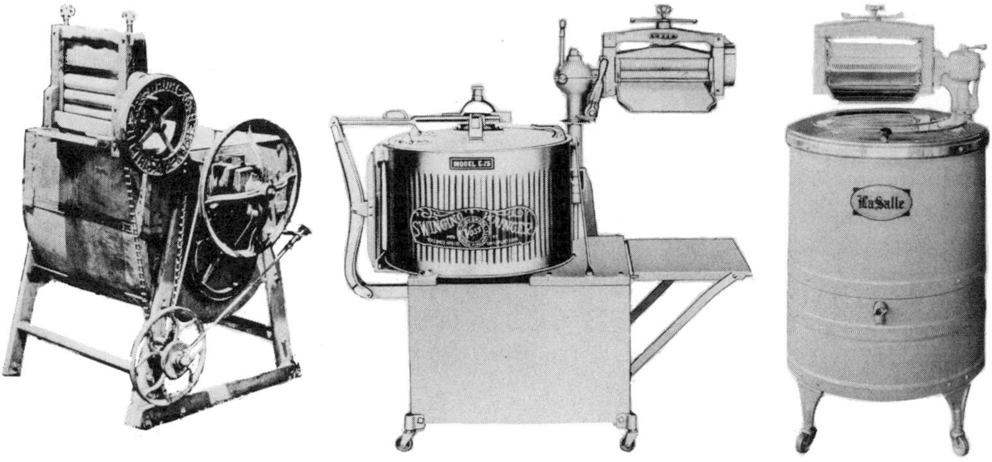

Left, a washing machine of the 1890s; center, of the 1920s; right, the 1930s.

Hill eventually changed the titles of the magazines to *Electrical Wholesaling, Electrical Construction and Maintenance,* and *Industrial Distribution* and sharply defined their fields. So, by the time the depression ended, five electrical papers [7] marched proudly abreast under the McGraw-Hill banner (with the sixth, the trolley journal,[8] trailing behind); and so meticulously had the path of each been drawn that they rarely stepped on one another's toes.

For the uninitiated, it is hard to imagine that five fields of electrical business activity could be so distinct. To see this more clearly let us go back first to *Electrical World* as the horizontal paper covering all the fields and emphasizing especially the generation of power for all purposes and the sale of kilowatts by the utilities. *Electrical Construction and Maintenance* (then called *Electrical Contracting*) dealt editorially with the work of erecting transmission lines, powerhouses, and wiring, and its appeal was

[7] *Electrical Contracting, Electrical Merchandising, Electrical West, Electrical Wholesaling,* and *Electrical World.*

[8] *Transit Journal* (formerly *Electric Railway Journal*).

to the contractors who took on those jobs. *Electrical Wholesaling* dealt with the furnishing of supplies to contractors, manufacturers, and dealers, as well as appliances in quantity, and its appeal was to the middleman between those who made commodities and the ultimate consumer who used the finally fabricated products. *Electrical Merchandising* was for the dealer who sold products to the ultimate consumer; its concern was with appliances and its readers were mainly retailers. Appliances were first sold by house-to-house agents of manufacturers of utilities, then in electrical specialty shops, and finally also in hardware and department stores.

All these papers were able to pinpoint reader and advertising areas with accuracy and they continue to this day to operate on parallel lines with a minimum of overlapping and a prosperity which shows no sign of decrease. There is no competition with electric power by any other force and, even in an advanced atomic age, it is unlikely that any direct application of nuclear power can eliminate the flexible current.

5 In addition to those papers that were purchased in the transition years, several were split-offs from parent stems as specialization increased. In 1928, for example, it was noted that, especially on the West Coast, *Chemical and Metallurgical Engineering* had among its readers many food processors. This led to the suggestion that food processing become the subject of a new paper. Thus *Food Industries* was born and grew into a prosperous magazine. A quarter century later when the persons engaged in these industries attained the importance and dignity of engineers, the title was changed to *Food Engineering.*

Perhaps the most vitally needed specialized enterprise of the depression period was the adjunct to *Engineering and Mining Journal* issued January 2, 1930, as *E. & M. J. Metal and Mineral Markets.* Its material was not novel; for some thirty years the *Journal* had "compiled and released, at weekly intervals, quotations on the prices of the major nonferrous metals, non-metallic minerals, ores, and other products within its field." Through this service the magazine had acquired "a prestige without rival."[9] The figures had been used as the basis of contracts both in America and abroad and also by the courts as standard and authoritative. They were accepted by both buyers and sellers and by governmental as well as by private agencies.

But the tempo of business all over the world had been stepped up. Such data as these could not be allowed to get cold. *Engineering and Mining Journal,* being concerned with many other matters, was naturally subject to certain delays. Accustomed to ticker readings on exchange business, men were impatient, too, to learn of these metal and mineral markets. But the ticker was unreliable in this field. It could never be counted on as finally authentic by *E. & M. J.* standards. So the little eight- or ten-page supplement was designed. The announcement read:

> A separate publication, it will be mailed a few hours after the closing of the market on Wednesday of each week, or on Tuesday if Wednesday happens to be a holiday. . . . Untrammeled by the delay inherent to the printing and binding and mailing (as second-class matter) of a technical magazine, the new service has been designed to meet an urgent want among producers and consumers, and among buyers and sellers of raw, intermediate, refined and scrap products.[10]

The significance of this departure lies in the fact that it was a *service,* not simply a publication. As such it was a forerunner of several services, some of them daily as well as weekly, which have filled the intervals between the issues of various publications. With the taking on of services, the company assumed new obligations. Not only did the essential of scrupulous accuracy in this spot news demand a considerable staff for the research and the checking, but it required new communications facilities. Furthermore, the services brought a rearrangement of cost thinking because they were not directly supported by advertising. As costs have increased over the years, subscription prices have naturally grown

[9] *E. & M. J. Metal and Mineral Markets,* vol. 1, no. 1, January 2, 1930, p. 7.
[10] *Ibid.*

higher, reckoned as they are on quite a different scale from that of publications. The subscription price of *E. & M. J. Metal and Mineral Markets,* for instance, had quadrupled by 1957.

Another offshoot came in 1930 from *American Machinist,* intended to serve the engineers who design machinery, appliances, and other engineered equipment manufactured by the metal-working industry. This was called *Product Engineering.* It was bred of the same need that had fathered Hill's *Locomotive Engineer* back in the early days. That paper came, we remember, because the railroad field was becoming so large so fast that *American Machinist* could no longer cover it. In the first issue of *Product Engineering* an editorial stated that:

> . . . the product engineering function was developing so rapidly in the metal working field that it was no longer possible to meet its requirements through a paper that was also covering the highly complicated manufacturing problem. Hence . . . decision to separate the two functions and to publish *Product Engineering* as a separate monthly magazine. . . .[11]

6 By 1937 recovery had come in a new world. Eight years before, the curtain had come down on an era. Socially, economically, and technologically, the scene had almost totally changed in the interval. The enormously increased population had outgrown its environment. In many areas groups had replaced individuals. Mass production had brought a degree of anonymity not only among the workers but in management, too. It was becoming difficult to single out a true captain of industry. In the upper echelons one-man businesses had largely ceased to exist. New tax structures were putting a ceiling on individual fortunes. The vast accumulations of wealth of the past were finding resting places in foundations. There were no more "robber barons." Business, even the biggest business, had apparently become respectable; at least it was ceasing to be the butt of angry muck-raking writers.

[11] Vol. I, no. 1, p. 39, January, 1930.

In the new technological era invention had outgrown thc garret. The new devices that were crowding in on us were no longer the product of dedicated but starving experimenters. They came now not from garrets and woodsheds but from streamlined industrial laboratories. They were made not by lonely inventors but by teams of anonymous men and women; they bore the labels of G.E., of Westinghouse, of Du Pont, of the Bell Laboratories, of RCA.

Recovery in a New World

7 Even before the curtain went up on this new act, James H. McGraw had ceased to be active in his business. His failing health had sent him more and more frequently to the West: Arizona and especially California.

A two-page spread from the first issue of "Product Engineering," January, 1930.

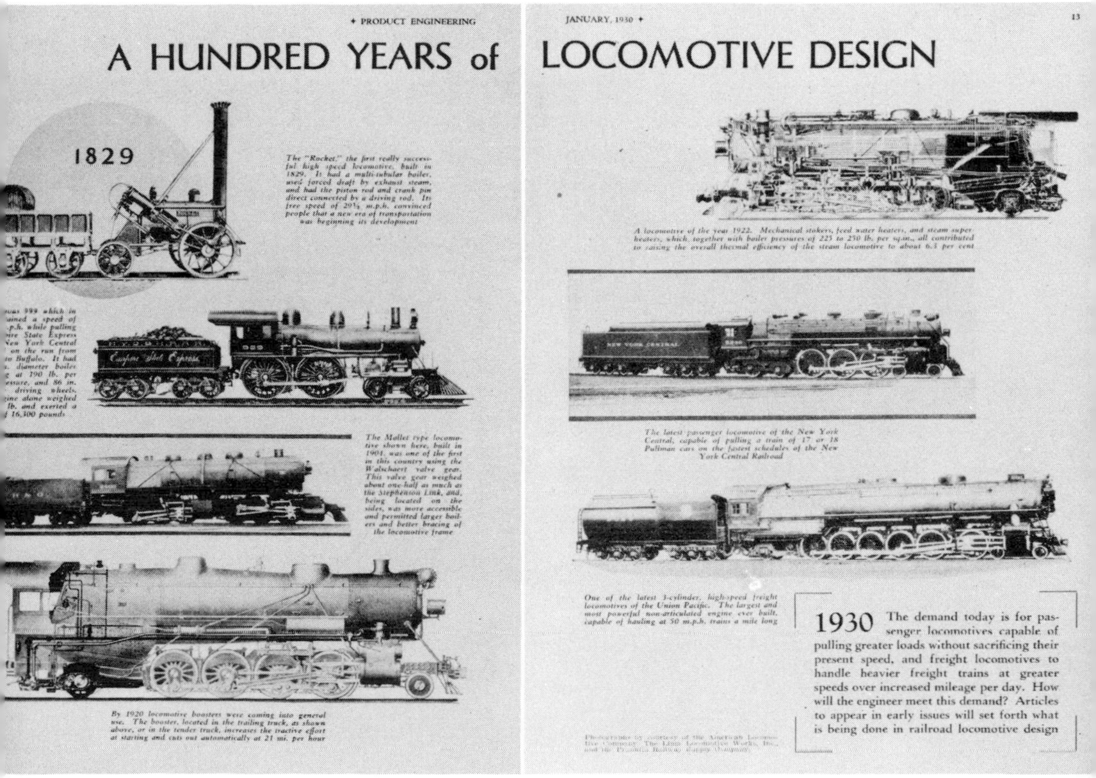

The Pacific Coast had long been familiar ground to him. Both before and after the McGraw-Hill merger, he had traveled widely over the country watching electrical development everywhere and had been determined to keep, as far as possible, a jump ahead of it in his papers. This exploration had shown him that California, Oregon, and Washington were still not highly industrialized, yet the potential in that territory for the development and use of electric power was high indeed. There were special features, such as extensive hydroelectric generation, high-tension long-range transmission, and much rural electrification which demanded on-the-spot observation. The Pacific Coast in those days was a far more specialized region than it has since become: there were question marks here and there on its industrial blueprint for the future which made it a peculiarly fascinating study.

In 1918 McGraw had found a publishing company in San Francisco which was putting out a regional paper called *Journal of Electricity*. For several reasons he had decided to buy this Technical Publishing Company. For one thing, he wanted a stake in the industrial future of the West Coast. Then, this regional paper was gaining national and international reputation because of its exciting revelations of the new far-western developments. Thus "it was something of a thorn in the side of [*Electrical World*] because of the tremendous editorial emphasis it placed upon these specialties which were germane to that area."[12]

He bought the company in 1919 and two years later changed its name to the McGraw-Hill Company of California. The paper became *Journal of Electricity and Western Industry,* and was "launched with 'the chief' as major-domo at a huge dinner at the Palace Hotel, with all of the industrial magnates from California and some from the Pacific Northwest."

He was a little bit ahead of his time [the editor and publisher remembers], perhaps fifteen or twenty years ahead of his time, with the Western Industry part of it.[13]

[12] George C. Tenney, recorded interview, pp. 4–5.
[13] *Ibid.,* p. 5.

It was, of course, routine for the chief to be ahead of his time. There are some who believe that his forehandedness made the times move faster. But the electrical manifest destiny of the Far West was precisely down James McGraw's alley. If it had been a civil-engineering manifest destiny or a chemical one he might have been less quick to recognize it.

In 1927 the paper's title was sensibly changed to *Electrical West,* a change which placed it properly with the fewest possible words. As such it prospered, especially when industry caught up with it. It is the only McGraw-Hill regional magazine today—that is, if we consider the international publications as not falling into that category.

There was, however, much to interest editors and managers of the other magazines in this developing region. Even before the merger, McGraw had established a small office in San Francisco operated by one man and a girl to which visitors from the New York headquarters could go for information about the area. But in the California McGraw-Hill Company all the magazines were more or less represented as well as the Book Company. The Book Company, indeed, started a retail salesroom in the San Francisco office where all the McGraw-Hill books were for sale.

In the early days of the California company there were some factors that are no longer operative. One was distance, dissolved now by airplane, telephone, radio, and television. For this reason the Pacific enterprise, though wholly owned by McGraw-Hill, was a largely independent, autonomous operation. It is difficult today to remember that the Far West was still a more or less isolated section.

There was this intensively developed area separated from the industrial Midwest and the industrial East by a couple of thousand miles of desert and two mountain ranges, with distant communications, totally different problems, a different way of life, different climatic conditions. . . . Remember that thirty years ago it was something of a trek to get from New York to San Francisco. . . . We didn't see very many Easterners, as a matter of fact.[14]

[14] *Ibid.,* p. 17.

One result of the distance from industrial centers was that only about 25 per cent of *Electrical West's* advertising was regional. It was natural for the developing Western region to be looked upon as a good market for Eastern industrialists. Another result was that the magazine's management received no harassing visits from the aging and ailing chief. *Electrical West* seems to have been the one electrical paper that he left alone. To editors and managers of the others he constantly aired his "standards of dissatisfaction," keeping them on their toes. This did not mean he was not interested in *Electrical West.* He sent messages, examined its financial reports, sometimes sent out his confidential representatives to inquire into its doings. But all this was very different from the direct personal contact with the chief. His scoldings, his inquisitions accompanied by the alarming penetration of the intense blue eyes, his classic dissatisfactions—these were missing for many years in San Francisco.

But then, after 1930 San Francisco was to see much more of James McGraw.

8 The Green Building is still alive with legends about the Old Man's life from this point on. There are old-timers, including former secretaries, who say that when Mr. McGraw officially retired he shut the door upon his business life. Others say that he returned but once from California at the bottom of the depression and then went away to make a new life for himself on the Pacific Coast; that, except when old colleagues came to visit him and talked of company affairs, he was shut off by a barrier of his own making from all his old associations; that he scrupulously kept hands off the business that he had expected his sons to carry on. There are suggestions that among the younger men he had become *persona non grata* and that he was aware of this. The interested outsider can hear all this and much more to reinforce his sense of this man's mystic qualities of genius, but if he examines the record, he will experience doubt and bewilderment.

The truth seems to be that McGraw-Hill's founder for some

James H. McGraw on Christmas day, 1943, at Saratoga, California.

time before his technical retirement had suffered in his mind a sharp conflict between his business and his health. He was, after all, beyond the conventional retirement age mandatory in many institutions. He had been physically tired by an uncommonly strenuous life. The number of miles of his travels to visit industrial chiefs, to attend conventions, to inspect newly acquired property, to launch new ventures ran into almost astronomical figures.

Concern over his fatigue had led him early in the 1920s to

think about his successors and he had turned the control of the company over to trustees. The trust included himself, his second son, James, Jr., and Malcolm Muir, an important figure in the business. Having done this, however, the business side of his mind returned to dominate the fears about his health, and through the twenties he had periods of intense activity alternating with long vacations in Arizona and California.

From his vacations he would come back, sometimes unexpectedly, to the office. This naturally confused those who had been carrying on the business in his absence. After he returned he would take an active personal part in the company's affairs without always knowing precisely what the score was or had been during his retreats. To some extent, therefore, it was apparently true that he caused considerable discomfort among the younger men who wanted him either in or out but not both. It is probable that this situation was far from unique with McGraw-Hill in the transition years when business in general was passing from individual to group control. If the history of many corporations which today make infallible gods of their founders were frankly examined, a good many skeletons in the form of restless ex-chiefs would be discovered causing havoc among their ex-subordinates.

But the record does not at all support a drawing down of the curtain. Late in 1930 McGraw went to California during a period of great pain due to an enlarged prostate gland. It took nearly four months after an operation in San Francisco for him to recover sufficiently to leave the hospital. After that the people in the office of the California company saw a good deal of him.

In 1933 whatever curtain he may have tried to draw down went sharply up again. The terrible news of the depression when McGraw-Hill had been hit harder than most publishing concerns, because of its close ties with hard-hit industry, convinced him that his people in the East needed him. In March Herbert Hoover remarked to him in a letter, "I was at first astonished at your again taking the helm, at this time of life, but I know what the old hand will do."

He came back to New York early in the fall of that distressed year by no means certain of what he could do to save his business but determined to put in his personal oar. If his return was resented, it is not in the record. It is said he was given a top-floor office that he hated—as if he were being "kicked upstairs." But it is also said that during his stay he quietly helped many individuals who had been hurt, and that into the meetings he attended he injected the old exciting stimulus of his personality. At the same time some of the older men remember that he was still battling with his health and would send for them to come to his apartment in 79th Street where he would be reading the financial reports of the papers in bed. To one executive who came just as he was reading the red-ink figures of *Business Week,* he is reported to have said, "How long are you going to continue that folly?"

The record, however, gives one extraordinary incident of the period. On November 29 he entered a washroom on the 32d floor of the Green Building and was set upon by two armed thugs who were hiding there. As the *Times* reported it:

> Two armed and masked bandits held up and robbed James H. McGraw, 73-year-old publisher, in a washroom adjoining his office. . . . Mr. McGraw . . . did not give up without a struggle in spite of the two pistols, one of which was pointed at his head, the other at his heart. . . .
>
> At about 3:30 o'clock he entered the washroom and was confronted by two husky young men with handkerchiefs bound across their faces. . . . One of them also had a hammer in a towel in his left hand.
>
> "Stick 'em up," ordered one of the robbers.
>
> Mr. McGraw calmly surveyed them and said: "What do you want?"
>
> "You know damned well," was the reply.
>
> The publisher, sturdy and vigorous, had about $90 in a wallet in a vest pocket, but he did not propose to give it up without a fight. Instead of reaching for the ceiling, he raised his hands and suddenly slapped aside one of the pistols. In so doing he managed to knock the hold-up man's mask from his face.

The other robber then swung the hammer at the publisher's head. Mr. McGraw dodged the blow and knocked the hammer aside with his arm.

His assailants both rushed him then and, pinning his arms, they tied him to a pipe with twine and gagged him with a towel. Then they searched his pockets, found the wallet, took the money, put the wallet back and fled.[15]

This account scarcely presents a picture of a feeble old man far gone in hypochondriasis. The story concludes with the statement that "it was said last night that he suffered no ill-effects from his experience."

He returned to the West Coast in May, 1934, according to those who remember seeing him go. But still the curtain would not stay down. A story in the New York *Herald-Tribune* in June said that "the white-haired publisher . . . seldom misses a day at his desk and has no thought of retiring," though whether the story meant a desk in New York or in San Francisco is not clear. The same story quotes a message from McGraw optimistically predicting recovery from the depression, but this might have been communicated from the Coast.

In 1935 the record shows him making a speech at the meeting of Associated Business Publications in Hot Springs, Virginia, on "Standards of the Business Press" and giving an interview to the Fafnir Bearing Company in New Britain, Connecticut.[16]

Again, in 1937, he spent a considerable part of the year in New York, living at his 79th Street apartment and working in an office on the thirty-second floor of the Green Building. He spent the winter of 1937–1938 in Tucson, Arizona, but in October, 1938, we find him back in New York, lunching with the editor of *Product Engineering* and inspiring an editorial which appeared in that paper the following month.[17] Then he spent his seventy-

[15] *The New York Times,* November 30, 1933.

[16] This interview was printed in *Teacher of Business. The Publishing Philosophy of James H. McGraw,* Advertising Publications, Inc., Chicago, 1944, pp. 85–91.

[17] "What Makes a Masterpiece," November, 1938, p. 421.

ninth and eightieth years in California. He had given up the winters in Tucson because he had survived all his retired contemporaries who had gone there for their health and it was too lonely for him!

But if, in his first octogenarian year, anyone in the Green Building supposed that their old chief was wholly out of circulation and that they had seen the last of him in New York, it was an underestimate of his true vigor. For, as World War II matured in Europe and the work of defense wiped out the last traces of depression, James McGraw found his way East once more.

CHAPTER TWENTY-TWO

Second World War

Although the site of the Green Building had been determined by the zoning laws against installing a printing plant in any structure between Seventh and Third Avenues, and although the building had been designed to accommodate such a plant, the presses were abandoned within two years after the building's completion. There were several excellent reasons for this and it would have saved a lot of expense if they had been considered sooner. But the long ownership of a so-called captive press had bred a sort of fixation in the top McGraw-Hill minds. This was difficult to lose. Pride in a self-contained organization was a normal emotion. But the publishing world was changing. Expanding periodical publishers were decentralizing their production.

Some of the largest of them were using several presses in different parts of the country because this facilitated the postal operations.

It took the upheaval of the depression, however, to shake the obsessive ideas loose from McGraw-Hill. As the company began to think about necessary economies, it made a careful analysis of costs in its captive plant. It found a considerable variation in seasonal loads. It was estimated that there was a 10 per cent difference in different months. A good deal of job printing was necessary to fill the spaces and keep the presses busy. In the depression years such orders were not forthcoming. Then there was the labor question. When cuts were necessary throughout the house, the organized compositors and pressmen were forbidden by union rules to cooperate.

But a printer who did nothing but print and who carried a number of accounts could spread his load more evenly. Also, as one of the chief proponents of the change remembers, that moment at the bottom of the depression was an especially favorable time for the change.

> 1933 was no banner year, as you know. At that time, printing could be purchased at less than actual cost and, therefore, cheaper than we could produce it for ourselves. Although the printer had quite an investment in printing machinery, he was forced by competition to accept work at almost direct labor costs sacrificing much of his overhead and depreciation, to say nothing of profit, hoping to keep his plant going until conditions improved.[1]

It was finally decided, therefore, to engage the services of a press in downtown New York. At the same time, all the press machinery and equipment in the Green Building was sold to the same plant. Careful, as usual, if it could possibly be avoided, not to throw men out in the street in this dismal year, an arrangement was worked out by which the purchasing press should also take over compositors and pressmen along with the equipment.

Printing contracts altered somewhat over the years. In the

[1] Donald C. McGraw, recorded interview, p. 7.

1940s McGraw-Hill conformed to the trend by taking on several printers, geographically dispersed. The periodicals were printed at New York, Albany, Philadelphia, and Chicago; books were printed at York, Pennsylvania, at Rahway, New Jersey, and at Binghamton, New York.

In the Green Building there is still a large production department which is the liaison between the editors and advertising managers of the various papers and their printers. Here, copy received from the editors is sent to the proper printer; proofs coming back are sent to the right editors. Here, advertising cuts are received from the advertisers; these are recorded, processed, and sent to the printer after checking by the different advertising departments. The scheduling system necessary for all this seems highly complex; actually it has been simplified enough to be virtually foolproof.

2 War broke in Europe while Jay McGraw was at the helm. The events preceding Hitler's jump-off in Poland changed a good many American minds. The leaning toward the Soviet Union stopped abruptly when the Stalin-Hitler pact was signed. Since 1938 when Hitler's anti-Semitism had forced a mass exodus of German Jews—among them the great scientists, Einstein and Haber—many German-Americans had turned against the Führer. The American people in general, however, were sharply divided on American intervention and, at least until the news of German conquests in 1940, the isolationist element showed great strength.

In 1939, indeed, whatever their sympathies, the majority wanted to keep America out. Many feared that against its will the nation would somehow be drawn in. But the mood changed and the phases of this change may be recalled by reading some successive editorials in *Business Week.* One in October, 1939, signed James H. McGraw, Jr. (and which appeared simultaneously in all the McGraw-Hill papers) read:

Dangerously widespread amongst our people today is the assumption that our participation in the European war is inevitable. Some mistrust the temper and program of the Federal government as likely to lead us into it; others fear that our sympathies will make us an easy prey for the propagandists; still others suspect that business and industry, in a blind greed for profits, may involve us in the conflict.[2]

In May, 1940, however, a *Business Week* editorial entitled "The Stock Market Goes Too Fast" used the exchange figures as barometric indices of the popular temper.

Clearly, [it stated] securities prices in recent weeks have been more responsive to men's emotions than to business facts. . . . Allied failures depress stock market sentiment. Each new German advance augments fears that the United States may be drawn in—on the theory that a German victory would be inimical to this country's national interest.[3]

By March, 1941, it was obvious that business facts as well as men's emotions had gone over to the belligerent side.

The lease-lend bill has been enacted and the President has asked Congress for $7,000,000,000 to start the program of building and lending materials to Britain. The United States is still a nonbelligerent; not a soldier is being sent to a battlefront; no planes threaten to bomb our cities. But on Mar. 11, American business entered the war.[4]

In the same issue the editors noted that Washington was looking not only toward Britain and Europe. Under a photograph of Singapore was the statement:

Washington wondered if Foreign Minister Matsuoka's departure for Moscow, Berlin, and Rome was setting the stage for Japanese action in the Orient, if first repercussions to our all-out aid to Britain would come on the Pacific front.

[2] *Business Week,* October 7, 1939, p. 51.
[3] *Ibid.,* May 11, 1940, p. 56.
[4] "Business Goes to War," *Business Week,* March 15, 1941, p. 15.

3 Throughout industrial America, however, regardless of the popular temper, the President's early call for defense measures had waked quick response. Inventories were taken of the nation's resources in plants, techniques, materials, and tools. The surveys revealed that one of the largest problems lay in the quantity manufacture of aircraft. For many reasons it was difficult to follow the line assembly used in automotive and other kinds of mass production. Fuselages were large and cumbersome and the elaborate handwork necessary to install the electric controls was not subject to acceleration. Standardization was hard to achieve because the actual performance of combat aircraft in the war uncovered many unanticipated "bugs" and the combing out of these required retooling in the midst of production. All these problems were closely followed through 1940 and 1941 by the magazine *Aviation.*

Week by week through the preparedness period, aircraft manufacturers got closer to the solutions until, in July, 1941, *Aviation* was able to report:

> Powered conveyor assembly line said to be the first in the industry, is credited by Vultee with halving final assembly time at the California plant and cutting floor space requirement by a third . . . assembly line has 46 stations.[5]

Meanwhile, back in the spring of 1940 while the Germans were swarming through France, *Business Week* was optimistic about our aircraft program:

> First thing on the docket is to expand airplane production from the current rate of 400 planes per month to well over 1,000 by the end of the year, and there will be no stopping then.[6]

By June, 1941, *Aviation* reported that the monthly figure of 1,476 had been reached. In that same summer *Aviation* presented a bit of history that was vivid against the war clouds. This was its

[5] *Aviation,* vol. 40, no. 7, p. 120, July, 1941.

[6] *Business Week,* May 25, 1940, p. 60.

twenty-fifth anniversary number[7] which reproduced some pictures from its first issue in 1916 and published some articles telling of the extraordinary aeronautical progress in the quarter century between the wars.

A month later the magazine pulled one of the few boners of its career. Three months before the Pearl Harbor disaster, an article entitled "Japanese Air Power" attempted to prove Japan's technical inferiority, her lack of machine tools, her inadequate industrial experience, and her shortage of pilots and stated that "even if Japan were suddenly endowed with a large airforce, she would not have the crews to maintain it."

> The Japanese fliers [the piece went on] are utterly inexperienced on the mass tactics of air war as it is being fought in Western and Eastern Europe. . . . Anyone familiar with aircraft losses of the past two years on Europe's Western and Eastern fronts . . . knows what a catastrophe Japan would be courting with her present manufacturing and manpower facilities if she grapples with any first-rate industrial power. . . . Numerically meager, obsolescent and qualitatively inferior, the Japanese air weapons would be matched in the Battle of the Pacific against a much stronger combination of adversaries than her formidable axis partner, Germany, ever had to face in Europe.[8]

A glance over the public prints of that pregnant autumn, however, will show that *Aviation* was only one of many to deprecate the Japanese potential. Some of the top experts, indeed, fell into the same error. On the very "day of infamy," for example, *The New York Times* carried a statistical article by Hanson Baldwin showing the superiority of Allied forces in the Pacific and one by Edwin James deducing from the talks in Washington that Japan was not "really looking for immediate trouble with the United States." The same issue carried a cartoon showing Japan tilting on a chair made of a swastika and juggling with his feet three objects labeled "China War," "Far East Expansion," and

[7] *Aviation,* vol. 40, no. 8, August, 1941.
[8] *Aviation,* vol. 40, no. 9, p. 148, September, 1941.

"Policy Toward the U.S." The title of the drawing was "If the Chair Slips—" [9] Less than a month before Pearl Harbor, *Time,* the Weekly Newsmagazine, had seen "a clear sign" that "jittery, encircled, embargoed Japan . . . still did not dare follow its sword-brandishing with sword-play" and that the "war threats in Japan's armory were getting rustier as time went on." [10] A piece in *American Mercury* stated:

> Most of Japan's five thousand planes are obsolete or obsolescent. Her fliers are poor. Their accident rate is the highest in the world. . . .
>
> But not only does Japan thus lack the physical resources to sustain a war with the United States, it lacks the necessary morale.[11]

In December, the specialized magazine, *Asia,* carried an article which optimistically explained:

> America's sea and air arms, fortunately, are now well enough entrenched in the Pacific to leave no doubt as to which side would have the upper hand in any Pacific war.[12]

Newsweek on July 7, 1941, said the "air power is Japan's greatest military weakness" [13] and on August 11, "Japan was learning that American economic biceps were strangling it." [14]

Business Week, though falling short of the mark, guessed better than many about future events. "What business must not fail to see," it warned on July 26, 1941, "is that Japan's next move . . . is but part of a bigger plan that will be fought out in the coming Battle of the Pacific" [15] and on August 2, "watch for a showdown in the Far East. Japan has issued her challenge to the Allies and all signs now indicate that Tokyo has no intentions to back-

[9] Editorial Section, December 7, 1941.

[10] November 17, 1941, p. 27.

[11] "Japan May Face Destruction," by James R. Young, November, 1941, pp. 571, 572.

[12] "No Man's Land between War and Peace," by Eliot Janeway, *Asia,* December, 1941, p. 664.

[13] "Japan's Worry: An Italy of the Orient," by Rear Admiral William V. Pratt, U.S.N., *Newsweek,* July 7, 1941, p. 41.

[14] *Newsweek,* p. 17, August 11, 1941.

[15] "It's Tokyo's Hour," *Business Week,* July 26, 1941, p. 52.

track." It added a word about Japan's "dream of a great Oriental empire to be ruled from Tokyo."[16] On November 15 *Business Week* said "the news which every American followed most closely this week was the flight of a diminutive Japanese diplomat across the Pacific. . . . On the outcome of these discussions between the President and Saburo Kurusu may hang war or peace. . . ."[17] But *Business Week,* too, finally fell into the prevailing error. While the Japanese planes were actually on the move toward Hawaii, a subhead on a news story read "United States plays key role by keeping Japan immobile on the Pacific front."[18]

4 One of the most instructive enterprises among McGraw-Hill publications during the prewar national-defense period was the August, 1940 number of *Factory Management and Maintenance.* Virtually the whole issue is an argument for less government interference with private enterprise, less bureaucracy, and less burdensome taxes on industries and individuals. Against the background of subsequent events the pleading may seem overzealous and the statements as to industry's mission for the welfare of the people overambitious, but this hindsight view does not detract from the value of the graphic statistical presentation. Nothing could show more clearly than its pictorial pages the progress of American productivity per worker in comparison with that of other nations as well as the then American living standard.

The editors tied in this material with the defense effort by the thesis that industry can:

> . . . create a better livelihood for the American people, and, at the same time . . . produce the materials for a national defense which will insure national survival.

The introduction explains that "these two tasks are really, at bottom, the same task."

> Today, as never before in our history, American industry must strive

[16] *Business Week,* August 2, 1941, p. 14.
[17] *Ibid.,* November 15, 1941, p. 81.
[18] *Ibid.,* Novmber 29, 1941, p. 68.

An illustration from "Factory Management and Maintenance," August, 1940.

toward an effective American economic system in the name both of prosperity and patriotism.[19]

The war, when it came, interrupted a part of the industrial "mission" and reversed some of the statistics, though other material was useful to the industrial war effort. But as a historical document reflecting the mood of American business on that 1940 threshold, it is as valuable as anything the company has produced.

When the war came to the United States, this same magazine wisely recognized the need to cooperate with government in the

[19] *Factory Management and Maintenance,* August, 1940, p. A1, vol. 98, no. 8.

regulation of industry, at least from the point of view of manpower supply. In 1942, therefore, it gave space and illustration to the promotion of the Manning Table Plan which had been developed jointly by the War Manpower Commission and the Selective Service System. This plan, intended to facilitate deferments from military service to fulfill industrial requirements was thus widely and quickly distributed throughout industrial America. *Factory's* presentation was, in the words of General Lewis B. Hershey, Director of the Selective Service System:

> . . . a lucid and easily understood explanation of a topic which may at first glance seem complicated. It should be useful not only to the industrial executives who will work with the Manning Table Plan, but also to the many others who will have to understand the Plan even though they are not engaged in its technical operation.
>
> For this reason I hope that *Factory's* presentation will be brought widely to the attention of industrial executives throughout the country. It will interest you to know that Selective Service System is forwarding copies to all local draft boards and State Directors as well as to a special list of manufacturers' and employers' associations.[20]

It was this function of getting government information into the hands of management that made the business press so useful in the kind of war that was being fought in the early 1940s. Nowhere were the lists of the key executives so complete and so selective as in the offices of the industrial journals where for years they had been carefully compiled, analyzed, and updated in the interests of readers and advertisers. Apart from this press, the government had no vehicle for reaching the men who were guiding the destinies of gun, tank, munitions, aircraft, chemical, textile, and other essential manufacture.

As it had in World War I, *American Machinist* had commenced this work from the very opening of hostilities in Europe. Its interest in machine tools was international. Since the turn of the century there had been a European edition and this had become

[20] Letter from Lewis B. Hershey to James H. McGraw, Jr., November 10, 1942, in McGraw-Hill Archives.

a separate publication entitled *The Machinist* in 1932. Though published in London, it had circulation not only in England but on the continent of Europe and throughout the British colonies. It had opened considerable overseas markets for American-made tools. It was natural then for it to follow the industrial progress of World War II from its start in 1939.

A series of five special articles gave shop-by-shop reports on armament manufacture. By the fall of 1940 reports on this subject were running in every issue. These were used by the Ordnance Department for specifications and by industry as methods manuals. With the approach of American involvement, *American Machinist* took special interest in the vital job of quick training for inexperienced persons in the use of metalworking power tools. Perhaps nothing was more valuable to the industrial mobilization than the country-wide inventory of metalworking machinery and equipment which this paper had been conducting at five-year intervals ever since 1925. Throughout the year that culminated in the Pearl Harbor attack, lathes, millers, drills, planers, and special-purpose machines were greatly in demand, and to know precisely where these things were located—often in obscure shops in small towns—was naturally essential. Agents were sent to the shops to buy such equipment for centralized war plants or the shops themselves were set to work on subcontracts.

Food supply presented one of the major war problems. Volume, weight, perishability, and availability in a variety of climates were some of them. From Alaska where engineers were working on the Alcan Highway to North Africa and the islands of the Pacific, the same food coming from the American supply must be processed and packaged in several ways. Here the magazine *Food Industries* was of practical assistance. In 1942 it published 103 articles and items on dehydrated foods and 97 in 1943. These were technological and how-to pieces. The paper was recognized as the standard source of information on the subject, and scientists in the Regional Research Laboratories used it as the liaison with the food processors. A special section was devoted to packaging. It paid particular attention to the shortages of packaging materials and the use of substitutes.

Chemical and Metallurgical Engineering distinguished itself by carrying in April, 1944, the first article ever published on the wide-scale plant production of penicillin, and in October, 1944, the first article on DDT. When the war ended it was first in the field with a description of the Oak Ridge and Hanford atomic plants. Four McGraw-Hill editors later were invited to witness the Bikini tests known as Operation Crossroads.

Engineering News-Record sent a correspondent to follow the construction of the Alcan Highway. He traveled the entire length of it and did a unique series of articles about it. He was the only reporter present when the road gangs working north and south met near the border of the Yukon. A correspondent was sent to cover air-base construction both on the Alaska mainland and on the Aleutian Islands. The Seabees were followed from the first training camp in Virginia in 1941 to their Pacific construction operation. In 1945 an editor was attached to the Chief Engineer's office of the European theater of operations to report for the paper on the rebuilding of ports and of highway and railway lines in preparation for the Rhine crossing. He was fortunate in being the only correspondent on the scene when the Ludendorff Bridge at Remagen collapsed. The *News-Record* here lived up to its old reputation as an accurate reporter on bridge failures when its two technical reports on the Remagen disaster were given official status by being used as texts in the Engineering Command Training School.

On the heels of the American landing forces in Japan was a *News-Record* correspondent. He went at once to Nagasaki to inspect the damage caused by the second atomic bomb. After war's end a *News-Record* editor was invited by Secretary of War Patterson to go to Germany to report on the work of Occupation Forces in the repair of Rhine bridges—a tour which enriched the paper by some twenty articles.

One of the most remarkable crystal-ball performances was the publication as far back as July, 1940, of an article entitled "Uranium 235—Power Fuel of the Future" in the magazine *Power.* The editors think this may have been the first article on this subject by a technical publisher ever printed in America.

These achievements were, of course, only a few of the McGraw-Hill wartime contributions. There were special magazines, such as the Spanish *En Guardia,* a good-will paper published for the government in the interest of Latin-American friendship, and *Wings,* sponsored by the Army and Navy Air Forces and distributed to aircraft-production personnel in the interest of increasing production. At the request of the War Department the McGraw-Hill *Overseas Digest* was established in 1944 and for two years was distributed to the armed forces overseas. It contained excerpts from articles in the current McGraw-Hill magazines.[21] The papers *Aviation News* and *Air Transport* were largely war enterprises. But there was not a single McGraw-Hill paper, including *Electrical Merchandising,* whose concern did not find a war application. As Donald Nelson, Chairman of the War Production Board, telegraphed James H. McGraw, Jr., in 1942:

> Your editors in a practical way are building understanding and teamwork between the management of war industries throughout the country and equally important they are helping to train war workers on the production front. . . . I hold the work of your men to be an essential contribution to the war effort at home on behalf of the men at the front.[22]

It is true, of course, that many phases of the war helped build certain of the papers. *Electronics* profited heavily from its attention to the whole new set of electronic developments which without war applications might have been delayed a decade or more. Of these radar was perhaps the most sensational. *Coal Age* which had been fighting an uphill battle with petroleum com-

[21] In 1946 McGraw-Hill established this digest as a commercial venture and it continues now as *International Management Digest.*

[22] Received October 9, 1942.

petition received a "shot in the arm" from the war demand for the mining, processing, and transportation of this older fuel. *Electrical Merchandising* was able to use the pause in the manufacture and sale of appliances to build up business for the future. Its prestige was greatly enhanced by its performance as "a main channel of information to dealers and distributors on government regulations concerning production limitations and price ceilings of major appliances and radio receivers."[23]

[23] *Know Power . . . in Action,* Associated Business Publications, Inc., 1954, p. 15.

This article, the first to discuss the actual methods of manufacturing penicillin, appeared in the April, 1944 issue of "Chemical and Metallurgical Engineering."

JOHN R. CALLAHAM *Assistant Editor, Chemical & Metallurgical Engineering*

PENICILLIN

Large-Scale Production by Deep Fermentation

At Terre Haute, on the banks of the Wabash, the world's largest plant for producing mold-derived penicillin has been in operation for several months. Engineered by E. B. Badger & Sons Co., financed and operated by Commercial Solvents Corp., this unit will process up to ten million gallons of fermentation liquid yearly to recover almost 500 billion units of penicillin. Yet a year's output will barely exceed one ton of dry product or less than one-half ton of pure penicillin. This process tapering, an extremely delicate fermentation, dehydration by high-vacuum sublimation, large-scale operations under the sterile conditions of a surgical operating room: such are some of the problems that were posed and have since been solved.—*Editors*

First large-scale plant in the world to produce penicillin by submerged fermentation is this Commercial Solvents Corp. unit at Terre Haute, Ind.

Photograph from an article on the Alcan Highway in "Engineering News-Record," March 16, 1945.

5 As President Roosevelt said, books, far more than in the first war were real "weapons." As James S. Thompson expressed it in 1942, the entire country had been turned into a "university of war."

The courses of study draw from every technological field. The classrooms include factory storerooms, millionaires' estates, corners of airplane hangars, suburban cellar playrooms, lonely "toughening" camps in the Sierra Nevada, training ships at sea. The students number millions. For this university of war it is up to the authors and publishers of technical books to supply many of the texts.[24]

[24] "The Technical Publisher in Wartime," an R. R. Bowker Memorial Lecture delivered in the New York Public Library by James S. Thompson. Transcript published by the Library, 1942, p. 4.

"Engineering News-Record" editor with Major William S. Carr on the Ludendorff Bridge the day before its collapse, which was reported in "Engineering News-Record" on March 22, 1945.

One of the training problems resulted from the enormous increase in workers employed in plants doing wartime production. There were plants which had expanded their working force from 2,000 in 1940 to 40,000 in 1942, and others which had less than 15,000 in 1940 were employing 150,000 in 1942. This meant that the promotion of skilled men was rapid indeed.

To guide this process, the Government organized what is known as . . . the Engineering and Science Management War Training Program. The ESMWT is administered by college professors and staffed by engineers and technicians. The Government appropriated $9,000,000 to this program in 1940, $20,500,000 in 1941, and in 1942, $30,000,000.

In this 1942 Bowker lecture, Thompson was able to report:

More than 500,000 men have been taught new skills through this program and "upgraded."[25]

Already before the close of 1942, the McGraw-Hill Book Company had published 167 books for the ESMWT courses; 64 more titles were added in 1943. Other technical publishers had also contributed many volumes, written, assembled, and printed in record time. An example of the speed with which these books had to be printed was Macmillan's feat of transforming 6,000 pages of manuscript into a series of eighteen volumes in a total of thirty-eight days. With all these books pouring out of the publishing houses, the ordinary marketing channels overflowed and even the department stores were handling them. In 1942, for instance, R. H. Macy in New York was carrying between 2,000 and 3,000 technical book titles.

In the summer of 1944 McGraw-Hill listed 304 new books that had been issued since January 1, 1941. The Book Company's promotion put special emphasis on radio and electronics, the two applications of science which had, perhaps, made quicker and wider advances than any others as a result of war needs. To compare communications in World War I and World War II is to see a revolution as total as that of any quarter century in the history of technology. The miles of telephone wire that were strung in 1914–1918 to keep connection between front and rear —vulnerable everywhere to interruption by the enemy— were no longer part of the picture in the 1940s. Now even the individual soldier could carry his walkie-talkie. The crude beginnings of ground-to-air radio transmission at the end of World War I had matured into a system of controls and intercom liaison that had changed flying from a haphazard adventure into a science. The bombsights that could penetrate fog and overcasts, the automatic aiming of antiaircraft guns, and the technique of instrument flying had produced a wholly new kind of warfare.

[25] *Ibid.*, p. 8.

All this required new, intensive, and difficult training of men. The new discipline of communications engineering had brought an upheaval of curricula. This in turn called forth whole libraries of new texts. Such subjects as frequency modulation, television engineering, radio navigation, and direction finders were being treated for the first time. Simultaneously books of the most elementary sort were necessary for the use of the thousands of novices being drawn daily into technical war service. Such primers as *Electrical Essentials of Radio, Understanding Radio, Fundamentals of Radio,* all written for the student with a limited mathematical background, were published parallel with handbooks for operators, such as *Practical Radio Communication* and *Radio Operating Questions and Answers.* Among these was the sensationally successful *Mathematics for Electricians and Radiomen* by Nelson M. Cooke, which had a curious history.

Cooke, who eventually rose to the rank of Lieutenant Commander in the United States Navy, had, in his high-school years, a deep aversion to mathematics. A passion for radio, however, plus a sympathetic teacher changed his views. Enlisting in the Navy at seventeen, he was appointed, eight years later, a Warrant Radio Electrician. Some five years after that he became an instructor in the Radio Materiel School at the Naval Research Laboratory in Washington.

Here a traveler from the McGraw-Hill Technical Education Department met him and tried to interest him in some of the department's mathematics texts. Cooke shook his head as he examined one after another. "Not for radiomen," he said. Finally the traveler said, "Well, why don't you write one yourself?" Cooke jumped at the idea and spent the next two years preparing the book. He had a unique opportunity to try out his material on the hundreds of students going through the school. They would work out and check the problems and questions. As a result the book had a ready-made market, for these students went on to become instructors in Navy schools all over the country, and they all felt they had had a hand in writing the book.

The book was published in January, 1942, and was reprinted five times during the year. In sixteen years it had twenty-seven printings and more than seven hundred adoptions. Its sale tops the 325,000 mark. In all that time no revision has ever been necessary.

For prospective aviators the series of books concerned with preflight training presented new opportunities for study. It included such subjects as aerodynamics and structures, aircraft engines, meteorology, air navigation, and orientation.

In the special catalogue of books on these subjects issued in 1944, the publishers evidently had one eye on the postwar period whenever it might come.

> Today, [read the announcement on the cover] the electronics industry is 100% at war, and is meeting the exacting demands made upon it. But tomorrow, many of today's wartime applications will revolutionize our peacetime lives. Electronics will invade every industry with totally new devices and machines. The future of the electronics industry is limited only by man's imagination.

In 1941, although the shooting war had not yet come to this country, while the training program was working toward its peak, there came the threat of a paper shortage. Such threats always turn what we have regarded as commonplaces into precious materials, and the outcry at that time from the war-educational field is evidence of the value placed on books as essential weapons.

> Your firm [wrote Gen. S. G. Henry, Commandant of the Fort Knox Armored Force School] furnishes about seven per cent of the total books in our school library and approximately thirty-three per cent of the engineering references. I sincerely hope that nothing will prevent your completing our present large order.

From Annapolis came an anxious letter from Commander Felix Johnson, Secretary of the Academic Board:

The Superintendent would consider any shortage of text books a very undesirable handicap in carrying out the curriculum of the U.S. Naval Academy.

The Coast Guard had found textbooks so essential that its officers believed their publishers should be given priority in case of a shortage. They were especially disturbed lest their order for J. W. Breneman's basic text, *Mathematics,* be held up.

Since we have your contract [an officer wrote McGraw-Hill] to supply this book until the end of the current fiscal year, June 30, 1942, curtailment of your ability to furnish this text would work havoc with our educational program involving U.S. Maritime Service and Coast Guard Reserve.

And the Navy Department wrote:

An interruption in the supply of technical information, in the form of books and magazines, will be very serious for the defense program and, undoubtedly, will cause false moves in certain instances which will prove very costly.

But fortunately word came from the Office of Emergency Management that:

. . . technical, scientific and engineering journals and books engaged in the dissemination of information directly contributing to the war effort have been included in the essential activity list. . . .

The list of these did not include magazines for general circulation. This assured paper preference as well as the deferment of "technical editors and managers" from service in the armed forces.

In May, 1941, a large cable order for technical books came from Tokyo. This was in continuation of extensive business which for years had been carried on by the McGraw-Hill Book Company with the Japanese house of Maruzen. In the past year or so this was only a part of the enormous business which Japan had been doing with the United States in vital war materials and which our government had not known enough to interrupt. But by May, 1941, the State Department had changed its attitude. It was not fear of a Japanese surprise attack that motivated the change; it was rather a sense of Japan's ambitions for an empire in the Far East to include all southeast Asia. This, although the cable read "owing to difficulty in getting books via Siberia obtained special import permit of American books" and followed with an order for several hundred volumes, Washington advised the withholding of shipment. While not in itself important, as there was a general stoppage of exports to Japan at the time, the incident shows that American textbooks and handbooks were of vital importance to our enemies as well as to ourselves.

6 With general rejoicing the war ended in midsummer, 1945. In the atmosphere of waving flags, descending ticker tape and confetti, and all the gay celebration of victory, there was no room for afterthoughts. Few worried about the chances of Russian betrayal or a long future of cold war. Few realized the repercussions that would be felt throughout the following decade from the bombs dropped at Hiroshima and Nagasaki. The bombs had stopped the war—that was enough—they had "saved millions of American lives." The impulse everywhere was the resumption of business, the picking up of all the dropped threads, and the progress through peacetime toward bigger and better things. Korea was but a place name on a map and hardly anyone in our part of the world foresaw the nightmare of communism sweeping across Asia.

But there were special echoes of the war's last days in the Big Green Building. There were men there who knew about splitting the atom and who had followed the nuclear approach, at least up to the time when the cover of secrecy had come down over the Manhattan Project. The moment the announcement of the bomb came on August 6, 1945, these men began thinking of a paper about atomic energy. Their minds were trained to click to a paper the instant there was something new in technology. Yet what paper that dealt with the dropping of bombs could be profitable?

But these nuclear-minded people, even in August, 1945, could see far beyond Hiroshima into a world of peace. They could see atomic energy as a force as radical as electric energy had been when it was first applied. They could see the dawn of a new industrial age. An established magazine dealing with this force could be profitable enough when that dawn grew into day. But meanwhile what if it made no money? What if it ran for years in the red? McGraw-Hill could afford it if those years gained for it the prestige that would make it an industrial necessity for the future. McGraw-Hill had got to the point where it could do that sort of thing.

McGraw-Hill, the parent company, was nearly thirty years old in August, 1945, and fully mature. The "child"—the Book Company—was nearer forty. Through a good many vicissitudes, not all of them happy, it had acquired a behavioral pattern. It had a sort of personality of its own apart from McGraws and Hills, apart from its directors and executives, that had recognizable features and character. Companies do that when they become institutions.

CHAPTER TWENTY-THREE

Milestones of the 1940s

Electrical World's reaction to the atomic bomb read:

> Last week the world was startled by the news of the atomic bomb and a sort of panic sprang up in the minds of men as they realized the awfulness of its power to destroy. . . .
>
> Because the first demonstration of this hitherto pent-up force which man has released is destruction, it naturally gives rise to the question —Has science striven all these years to find a way to wipe out civilization?[1]

The question has, of course, been asked, in some form ever since. But from the moment the news came, *Electrical World* and all its McGraw-Hill colleagues have insisted on the peacetime

[1] Vol. 124, no. 7, p. 104, August 18, 1945.

applications of the nuclear force and dwelt upon its immense potential for the future of civilization. This, to be sure, was the logical view for an industrial press. Yet from the beginning these magazines have been exceptionally thorough in exploring the potentials of atomic power as a source of energy for the normal uses of society. Thus they have provided a volume of week-to-week and month-to-month information which will one day be extremely convenient for historians of the epoch.

The news came to the Green Building on the afternoon of August 6. On August 7 memoranda went out from the executive offices on the thirty-second floor directing the appointment of an editorial committee on atomic energy to be composed of those men on the McGraw-Hill staff who had been so familiar with nuclear physics that the news had instantly clicked with their previous knowledge. This committee was to keep in close touch "with developments in the whole broad field of atomic energy and its applications." It would thus become the source of authentic information for every editor to draw upon. The memoranda also alerted the entire organization to the peacetime potentials of the force that had caused such immense wartime destruction. Obviously no time had been lost in furnishing both the Publishing Company and the Book Company with a directive to be applied across the board on the operating level.

On this same day, the first trial balloon was launched with the nine-page mimeographed paper entitled *Atomic Power*. It contained an article on uranium 235 and the chain reaction. On September 1, another of double the size was called *Atomic Engineering* to be "devoted to the design, construction, and operation of plants, equipment, and facilities for the development and commercial applications of atomic energy—in short, the engineering and industrial problem involved in putting together another great tool of science to the constructive uses of mankind." This announcement, of course, was shrewdly worded to attract not only the prospective reader but the potential advertiser as well, even in that atomic dawn when, for most of mankind, the bomb was still overshadowing other considerations.

In September every McGraw-Hill paper carried an insert: "The Atom—New Source of Energy." The Book Company later distributed many thousands of copies of this to colleges and universities as supplements to textbooks. In the eight pages, fission was explained in simple, nontechnical language with simplified drawings. There was a statement of the theory of nuclear physics, of the subdivision of the atom, once thought to be indivisible, and of the "solar system" each atom contained. While no one could attain anything approaching a detailed understanding of the scientific or technological facts from this demonstration, it was evident to every reader that the bomb had been a product of normal evolution from the revolutionized physical pattern, and not an accidental invention likely to evade human control. This awareness was supplemented in *Electrical World* and other papers with a step-by-step historical account of how the application of nuclear fission had been developed from the study of many scientists. Thus the hiatus caused by the blackout of the Manhattan District Project was briefly spanned.

On September 11 the McGraw-Hill Committee on Atomic Energy was appointed. There were four repesentatives of the Publishing Company and one from the Book Company. Soon after, the committee met with Senator Brien McMahon who was planning legislation for atomic-energy control. Late in November McGraw-Hill was represented at a dinner at the Mayflower Hotel in Washington at which Senator McMahon was host. This was an off-the-record affair with only thirty guests, including such key men as Irving Langmuir, H. D. Smyth, author of the Smyth report, James B. Conant, and Harold C. Urey. The dinner resolved itself into a conference which established the bases of the later McMahon Act.

2 In March, 1946, came the smallest trial balloon of all but the one which made the happiest landing. *Nucleonics,* in its first mimeographed issue, contained only five pages, most of which were devoted to the reprint of an article by Zay Jeffries in *Chem-*

Pilot issue of "Nucleonics" and July, 1958 issue.

ical and Engineering News,[2] the organ of the American Chemical Society. In the article, the word *nucleonics* was proposed to cover the whole of the new field.

From that point there was increasing impatience among the nuclear specialists in the Green Building to take the final plunge and put out a real magazine. The longer McGraw-Hill waited after its trial balloons, the more the company would be accused of indecision: this was the burden of some of the complaints at the delay.

It was decided, therefore, to prepare for the publication of a full-dress *Nucleonics.* It was a shot in the dark. Obviously no paper can endure unless it can be supported by advertising. Who would be the advertisers in *Nucleonics* no one could guess. But here was an exceptional chance to put the old McGraw theory

[2] Vol. 24, no. 2, p. 186, January 25, 1946.

of "readers first" into practice. Normally the advertisers should follow if the appeal to readers was successful. If they did not, after adequate trial, then the enterprise must be abandoned. This had happened in a few instances. But to the men who were planning *Nucleonics* there was no thought but of the potential army of readers. They must get to those readers before someone else did. Where they would go from there no one knew or even tried to speculate.

By 1947, after exploring at least the fringes of the vast territory, it was decided that the scientist was the person to aim at.

> At that time there was no organized, unclassified source of information on atomic energy. The people in the field, the people who were working for the Atomic Energy Commission, had no place to publish material they had developed. They had no single source of information to go to. There were then the beginnings of articles in professional society journals, very scattered journals, and if an individual wanted to keep up with the atomic energy field, as a field, he would have to read all these different publications.[3]

With the scientist as target *Nucleonics* began in 1947. Because it was on a high scientific level an editorial board of prominent scientists both in the United States and abroad was formed. An editorial board, by the way, must not be confused with an editorial staff. The board was an outside affair, advisory in its function, designed to give the paper prestige as well as technical counsel and criticism. The first full-dress issue in 1947 was highly technical, scarcely understandable by persons much below the level of the editorial board, and it carried no advertising.

The first years of *Nucleonics* were rugged. Feelings about the whole subject were running high. One faction wanted military control of atomic power. The scientists were bitterly opposed to this and organized political lobbies or pressure groups to induce the Congress to put the control into civilian hands. In 1946 the McMahon Act favored the civilian group. Then in 1948

[3] Jerome D. Luntz, recorded interview, p. 12.

Nucleonics seemed to get on the wrong foot as far as its elected circulation was concerned. In the July, 1948, issue an editorial appeared that criticized the McMahon Act and called for its revision in a way that was taken to favor the military-control advocates. One sentence, for example, stated:

While we agree that science cannot flourish under military domination, we do not feel that the military arts should be subordinated to the leadership of the natural scientists.

This sally into politics, out of character with the tenor of the magazine, was printed without consultation with the editorial board and caused an immediate reaction among its members against the magazine. At their insistence a statement in a box on the editorial page of the immediately succeeding issue changed the title of Editorial Board to Technical Consultants and denied these persons' endorsement of the offensive editorial. But the angry reaction was not confined to the board. Scientists generally were up in arms and, for a time, there was a manuscript boycott.

It was an instructive experience. Feeling their way in the dark, as it were, the editors could not be sure of what they were doing. Surrounded by a superheated emotional atmosphere, it is not altogether surprising that an incident of that sort should have occurred. But it showed the necessity of selecting a line and closely hewing to it. By returning to its nonpolitical, scientific character and by making itself indispensable through its editorial content to its scientist readers, *Nucleonics* regained their confidence and rebuilt its earlier prestige. Then, in 1954, the liberalizing Atomic Energy Act was passed and this permitted industry to construct nuclear power plants and opened a long, wide vista of the use of the nuclear force for peaceful purposes.

That was the milestone, the turning point, because since August 30, 1954, there's been a tremendous spurt in industrial activity.[4]

The engineer came in then, designing plants, machinery, and

[4] *Ibid.*, p. 25.

equipment, and *Nucleonics* turned from its exclusive scientific preoccupation into more practical fields. And this change brought the advertisers and a new, successful business compensated for the difficult beginnings.

3 In October, 1941, just before his eighty-first birthday, James H. McGraw had made his last visit to New York and attended the funeral of one of his favorite employees.[5] It was then and only then, when, on his return to California, he disposed of his New York apartment, that the door to the East was finally shut. Yet even then he never quite lost touch; he had many visits from old colleagues and he spent a good deal of time visiting the California home of the head of the San Francisco office. This friend was with him more than any other in his last years.

From California in the 1940s when he was past eighty, he wrote some revealing letters. He put a warmth into his handwritten letters that one rarely heard in his publicly spoken words. In 1944 he wrote to congratulate a former employee who had been close to him:

> I think you are the youngest and handsomest grandpa I have ever seen. Your picture is right here on my bed to prove it. . . . Please congratulate Jimmy for me. Tell him I am delighted at the fine news. . . .
>
> P.S. Tell Jimmy he and I have always been good friends since he was a year old.[6]

Jimmy had been one of the favorites among the children he loved. That love of children made one of the traits that contrasted oddly with his apparent austerity. And there is abundant evidence that they loved him back. Many stories are told of how they swarmed over him without fear or reticence, fighting for the chance to sit on his lap, stroking his beard. This and his love of nature—his extensive knowledge of birds, trees, plants, and flowers—are but two of the paradoxes that have made this man mysterious, to the outsider, at least. It is inevitable that such a

[5] Earl Whitehorne, editorial director of electrical papers, died Oct. 24, 1941.

[6] Letter to Edgar Kobak from Saratoga, California, dated August 16, 1944.

James H. McGraw in his suite at the Hotel Maurice, San Francisco, 1947.

person should become a legendary figure and it may be doubted if any final reality will ever emerge from the legend.

In San Francisco in the winters and Saratoga, some 40 miles to the south, in the summers, McGraw followed a strict health regime. He seems to have broken his doctor's orders only in the large-scale consumption of panatela cigars which his visitors brought him under cover. He had someone read to him for several hours each day. He read his favorite McGraw-Hill papers himself, usually quite thoroughly. For exercise, he daily followed an old custom. He would have his chauffeur let him out at a certain point, then drive ahead a mile or so. McGraw would then walk until he came up with the car.

His last years seem outwardly to have been serene enough, though no one knows, of course, what may have gone on in his mind. There are indications that he regretted having let his control of the company slip from his grasp. He said once to an old friend: "No one can whip a man except himself." Perhaps he was thinking then that he had beaten himself by quitting too soon. In his last year he had occasional intervals of wandering through old memories and then he would talk about his father on the old farm taking him by the hand on winter days and leading him out in the snow to some hillside to coast on his sled.[7] Such things are fondly remembered by those who were with him to the end but there was really nothing singular about them: they happen to most old men.

For the last six years he lived, except for his spartan diet, luxuriously enough. He kept apartments in several places so that at a moment's notice he might move from one to another in perfect comfort. Though he had not lived in it for many years, he maintained his home in Madison, New Jersey, in the style becoming a successful magnate's family.

He died at the Hotel Maurice in San Francisco on February 21, 1948. His body was brought to New York by the head of the San Francisco office and there were services at the Central Presbyterian Church.

Few men had been truly intimate with James McGraw and fewer had really loved him. Those who came nearest to it seem to have been people in the lower-than-executive ranks: women who had been his secretaries, obscure workers in the business whom he had pulled out of their troubles, persons who had known him outside the business. Those who knew him best tell how lonely he was, secretly eager for the warmth of close friendship but finding no way to reach it across the austere wall of his temperament.

But everywhere there was admiration and respect. Up and down the ranks of industry men wrote to speak of the loss to the business world; even those whom he had fought or stood up to in times when their sense of business integrity ran counter to his mourned his going. And there was awareness among the more sensitive members of the changing business society that along with McGraw's death, something personal had gone forever out of their world, something that was good.

[7] George C. Tenney, recorded interview, p. 34.

CHAPTER TWENTY-FOUR

Echoes and Memories

In the elevators of the Green Building you may still hear echoes of the Old Man's words. An editor with a suitcase will tell you that he will be in Chicago or San Diego or St. Louis tomorrow. "It's better," he will say with a twinkle "for an editor to wear out the soles of his shoes than the seat of his pants." This favorite that James McGraw reiterated over and over may not have been original with him and he may not have been unique in insisting on the practice, but it is probable that, more than any single factor, this perpetual editorial motion has been responsible for the success both of McGraw-Hill papers and McGraw-Hill books.

For advertising or subscription salesmen, travel was, of course, quite normal. But editors used to talk about their "easy chairs." There they sat, waiting for their publishing material to come to them. McGraw saw from the start that this would never do for an industrial paper. One of his earliest diatribes was against the editors who sat at desks with scissors and pastepot assembling their magazines from scraps of secondhand news. To him an industrial paper had to be identified with its industry and an industry could hardly be expected to come walking into an editorial office. That was why the McGraw editors were familiar figures on the sites of great construction projects, in mining towns, in power plants, in machine shops, in factories, and along lines of transportation. And that was why the men who worked in these places looked upon McGraw's papers as something they had a hand in producing.

Others had done this sort of thing in the past, as in the classic history of the Quebec Bridge failure;[1] and when it came to buying a paper, McGraw usually chose one whose editors had followed this pattern. When it became a McGraw-Hill paper, the practice would be stepped up. Money went into railroad tickets and hotel rooms rather than mahogany desks and Oriental rugs in the offices. And it was not a matter of the chief saying "Do this" and then sitting back in his own swivel chair. In his prime he wore himself out traveling. One executive who knew him well remembers never being sure at any given moment whether the boss was in his office upstairs, at a convention in Atlantic City, consulting with some electrical authority in Schenectady, or in a meeting of engineers in San Francisco. McGraw was never, himself, an editor, but when he would come back from his rovings, his mind full of restless ideas, he would put the itch into his editors until they had to go out and do likewise. And the habit grew until by 1957, with the vastly increased means of rapid transportation, editorial mileage in the United States and abroad reached three million.

Another favorite phrase that is still quoted was "Tiffany finish." To James McGraw every one of his products must have the same quality that went into some fine silver piece or setting

[1] See Chapter X.

of jewels that was made by the celebrated firm. He was quick to spot and condemn shoddy or unfinished work. His instinct for style surprised those who knew of his own rough farming background. That he became a perfectionist may have resulted from his normal-school training, for perfectionism is above all a teacher's trait. Many a man and woman remembers being exasperated as a youthful pupil at the relentless insistence by some since beloved instructor on nothing but the best. As one writer of a letter of condolence after James McGraw's death expressed it:

> Out of what many have considered his overmeticulous attitudes came the extraordinary high standards of style and effectiveness which are the hall-mark of McGraw-Hill publications. His insistent demands for accuracy and clarity came not in honeyed phrases, and he greatly scared the highly scareable, but at heart he was reasonable, and he admired and rewarded creative people.[2]

This about his admiring creative people is a point that is especially remembered about the founder. Not creative himself in the common sense of the term, he was a catalyst for the creative impulse. Men would leave the meetings at which he spoke with the urgency to get to work on some piece of design or writing: sometimes it was layout or illustration; often it would be an editorial constructed around new ideas picked up from the chief's talk. It was at these meetings that McGraw captured the confidence of his employees, however much they might have been upset by his private words. In his office when he called a man before him, he could be cantankerous and full of blame rather than praise, but when he addressed a group he could be patient, reasonable, and appreciative of the creative effort of his men.

He would give everyone a chance to talk, then make his decision. Occasionally he would reverse the group's judgment. But what is best remembered by those who were most often at these meetings was his summarizing of the individual editorial or

[2] Letter from Caleb H. Hodges to James H. McGraw, Jr., in McGraw-Hill Archives.

business achievements, mentioning each person by name. This perhaps was a demonstration of the adroit schoolteacher's skill in rewarding the doings of individual pupils.

2 For his editors, at least, his most endearing trait was his loyalty to them, which he carried so far as to appear to share the responsibility for their mistakes.

> He was perfectly wonderful [one remembers] in that respect. The mistake was not yours, and you did not get bawled out for a mistake. It was, "We have done this. We have made this mistake." Then he would help you try to rectify whatever you had done. . . . If you were in trouble he would defend you.[3]

In lifting these errors from the personal level to the plane of the editorial "we," he did something the offenders never forgot. In their moments of irritation at some seemingly captious conduct on the part of their chief they would remember an incident of this sort and it would calm their tempers.

Backing an editor who had been emphatic on his editorial page sometimes took courage for a publisher whose business depended largely on the good will of advertisers. There is a story about this in one of the recorded oral reminiscences which throws light on the Old Man's independence.

During one of the investigations of the electric utilities in the period before the 1929 crash, an editorial in *Electrical World* sharply criticized the operations of certain holding company chains. This "pyramiding," as it was then called, was, of course, later held to be one of the factors contributing to the financial disaster. But at the time it appeared such comment was certain to alienate a number of the key figures in the utilities industry.

The editorial was written by the late Earl Whitehorne who is still recalled as one of the great editors. Perhaps if the chief had been in the office, it would have been shown to him before it was printed. But he was on vacation at Lake Placid. So the then

[3] George C. Tenney, recorded interview, p. 28.

publishing director of *Electrical World* shouldered the full responsibility.

I read it, [he remembers] approved it, and it came out in the book. I said, "Well, it will be fun. We'll know whether there's anyone reading the book anyway. . . ." Comes Monday morning and I'm sitting at my desk. "Mr. McGraw calling from Lake Placid." He burned my ear off about this editorial. He had had complaints about it. He had had a call from Owen D. Young who called it to his attention. The old man really gave me the works. . . .

I said, "Mr. McGraw, nobody can bawl me out on the phone. I'll come up to Lake Placid, or you come down here, but we've got to do this face to face."

I always have to see a man's expression when I argue with him.

He said, "Come up tonight." [4]

Kobak spent a sleepless night on the train wondering what kind of job he could get after he had been fired from McGraw-Hill. McGraw met him at the station. They drove to the house and McGraw suggested that they wait till Kobak had had a bath and breakfast before they talked. After breakfast McGraw disappeared leaving Kobak unsatisfied and worried. In a genial mood, the chief showed up for lunch and then suggested that Kobak have a nap. Eventually he called the car and said, "Let's take a drive." Still the matter most on Kobak's mind had not been touched. Every time Kobak mentioned it, McGraw would change the subject. They drove to a cow barn where some new milking machines were in operation. They spent an hour there.

I didn't want to see any electric milking machines or any cows. . . . I'm still full of this editorial. Well, we get out of there and . . . back to the house. He disappears. A little later I said, "Mr. McGraw, I came up here for just one purpose, not a social activity. I want to talk about that editorial."

"Oh," he said. "That! That was one of the finest things that has ever been done."

[4] Edgar Kobak, recorded interview (edited), pp. 61, 62.

Well, here's what happened. Mr. [Samuel] Insull called Mr. Young and raised hell. . . . Mr. Young said, "You know we advertise in those books to sell our products, not to run the editorial pages of the magazines. I'll call Mr. McGraw though."

Mr. Young had not seen the editorial. Mr. McGraw had a tremendous respect for Young, and Young told him about this call. They couldn't discuss anything, though, because neither of them had seen the editorial.

Well the reason for the stall was that the paper had not reached Mr. McGraw until after lunch and he was stalling all that time . . . until *he* could read the damned editorial. . . .[5]

3 Opinions differ about the chief's sense of humor. There is, for example, this story, told in the same interview that contained the Lake Placid incident.

When our little Jimmy was about three years old, Mr. McGraw had him on his lap one day. Mr. McGraw loved to talk to little children. Jimmy was sitting there looking at Mr. McGraw with intense interest. . . .

Like all little kids, Jim was given to coming out with things that—well, you never knew what it was going to be, but it could make parents nervous when the boss was a guest. . . . Jimmy kept looking at Mr. McGraw's face, and then turned around to his mother and said, "Mama, how does Mr. McGraw wash his face—or does he?"

Well, the old man reared back and laughed, and then explained in great detail just how he washed his face and the importance of little boys washing their faces, too. Jimmy wasn't too impressed, and announced that when he could he was going to grow a beard because he thought that he would then not have to wash his face so often.[6]

Another story that is still told was put on record by an oldtimer. It suggests that the Old Man was not completely humorless. He had sent for a man to come to his apartment to talk to him about some phase of the business. The man sat there by

[5] *Ibid.*, pp. 62–66.
[6] *Ibid.*, p. 86.

James H. McGraw, 1935.

McGraw's bedside and talked. After a while he saw that the chief's eyes were closed and, assuming that he had dropped off to sleep, stopped talking. But then, without opening his eyes, McGraw said: "Go on, Jim. You haven't said anything yet, but maybe you will."

On the other hand, the Old Man could never laugh about anything that in any way touched the business. One who has been an officer of the company for many years has recorded this memory:

One of the advertising magazines was running a series of profiles of people in the advertising and publishing business, and they asked me to be the subject of one of these. I said I would, so they sent over an artist who . . . drew a very amusing caricature of me with a big nose, bull neck, sparse hair and all the things about me that are subject to caricature. Then they got one of our men to write a funny piece, picking on all my foibles.

When he brought it in to me . . . I read it over and said, "Look. I'll give you some more funny things about me that you haven't got here. . . ."

The article appeared. When it came out, the whole building was laughing at it. One day the old man sent for me. . . . I went to his office. . . . When I went in he was furious. He was white. He said, "Did you see this article. . . ?"

I said, "Yes, sir."

"Did you know it was going to be published?"

I said, "Yes sir."

"What are you doing about it?"

I said, "Well, I had not planned to do anything about it, Mr. McGraw. What do you think I should do?"

"Do you mean to tell me," he said, "that you knowingly permitted . . . a lampoon of this kind about a vice-president of this company to be published and printed and circulated. . . ?" I got my ears pinned back plenty. He never knew, and I never dared tell him, that the juiciest items in it that he was so upset about I had put in myself.[7]

To James McGraw, McGraw-Hill was always deadly serious. He could never bear to hear any part of it treated lightly; he frowned at wisecracks about any of the papers. Fortunately his austere view was balanced in other places, as many of the recorded interviews attest.

4 We have had glimpses of the McGraw publishing philosophy. Many of the tenets have persisted in the minds of newer men, men who never knew the founder. One principle which was less important in the formative years of the business because it had little opposition among business papers became of paramount importance in the chief's later years. This was the necessity of paid as contrasted with free circulation.

Free circulation in the early days was included by the less scru-

[7] Willard T. Chevalier, recorded interview, pp. 38, 39.

pulous publishers in the paid circulation figures. This practice, as we have seen, was stoutly opposed by the Associated Business Publications; and the Audit Bureau of Circulations was established to render it unfashionable.[8] But in the 1920s several business papers started with the avowed policy of unpaid circulation. They were given away free, like circulars, to their readers; but the readers presumably were carefully picked as the most likely prospects for the papers' advertising. Thus they used the term *controlled* rather than *free circulation.*

When these periodicals appeared in competition with the McGraw-Hill papers, it was obvious to the executives of the company that a basic tenet of the Old Man's belief was being openly violated. As one who has consistently carried the torch in this respect has stated:

It was a cardinal principle of his [McGraw's] philosophy that while a commercial press may derive its economic support from advertising it must never surrender to its advertisers the control of its editoral content or its circulation lists. Editorial space in McGraw-Hill publications was not for sale as a bonus with advertising space, and voluntary circulation was to be earned through superior service to the reader and not by sending free copies to an advertiser's mailing list.[9]

This cardinal principle was also a rule in the ABP and the giveaway papers were never members. In explaining its policy, the association writes of the value of a paper's contractual relationship with its subscribers—an impossibility without payment.

Each has a contract with its subscribers to deliver a *specific* number of issues of a *specific* editorial character for a *specific* length of time at a *specific* price.[10]

Obviously, say the champions of McGraw's philosophy, a person who voluntarily enters into such a contract and pays for it,

[8] See Chapter XII, p. 168.
[9] Willard T. Chevalier, recorded interview, p. 102.
[10] "The Plus of Paid Circulation," The Associated Business Publications, New York.

is likely to give the magazine more attention than one who gets it in the mail along with his other circular advertising, without either asking or paying for it. Furthermore, the publishers of the free paper have no check on the reader's interest because the question of renewal never comes up.

It is true, however, that despite these arguments the controlled-circulation papers have had a measure of success and the controversy is still hot. It is not within the province of the historian to enter this controversy beyond the statement of the views strongly and universally held within the company and the importance of this legacy from James McGraw.

5 While the body of memories is built largely out of the Old Man's strengths, some of his weaknesses are also recalled, and the outsider will hear stories from his most stalwart defenders that reveal fallible moments. He would occasionally reverse himself quite startlingly. Sometimes this would be deliberate—then it might well come from strength rather than weakness—but oftener it was a case of forgetting an earlier stand. There was, for example, a long discussion over the color of the new building. At a meeting at which the architect submitted samples of colored terra cotta, McGraw, over other objections insisted on green. Others wanted black with orange trim. But the chief was emphatic. He made a speech in favor of the green. He talked down the orange and black because his sons were Princeton enthusiasts and he said, "There's too much Princeton around here." He even cited his Irish ancestry as a reason for his choice.

A year later when the building was half up, he saw it from his Tenth Avenue office. He had been away in the meantime in California. He was standing, as he looked out the window, with one of the people who had wanted black with orange trim. He pointed to the green terra cotta and said, "Who picked that color?"

His associate was amazed.

"Why, you did! I was there. Don't you remember, I was for black, but you convinced me so I voted as you did."

McGraw-Hill building under construction, as seen from Tenth Avenue and 36 Street.

NO.
342 WEST 42ND STREET BUILD
NEW YORK, N. Y.
VIEW FROM southwest

"But it's not the green we picked."

They went and held the sample against the terra cotta.

"It's awful," said McGraw. "Perfectly awful. I must have been sick that day."

Several things, to be sure, had intervened. One was a year of worsening depression in which the burden of debt caused by the new building had been thrown into sharp relief. Another was the difficult time McGraw had been through after his operation. In time, however, the chief reversed himself again and came to love the building, color and all.

Another trait that sometimes riled his associates was his adoption of others' ideas as his own—a habit not uncommon among high executives. One day he said with pride to a vice president, "You know, it's really a great aggregation of papers." "No, Mr. McGraw," said the other. "It's an aggregation of great papers." A few days later someone said to the vice president, "Have you heard the Old Man's latest? He said to me, 'What we have here is not a great aggregation of papers. It's an aggregation of great papers!' Pretty smart, isn't it?"

This habit became an accepted thing, however, and men grew accustomed to hearing their aphorisms or *mots* turn up in the boss's speeches and writings. It is a mistake, perhaps, to call this trick of the mind a weakness. One of the talents for which James McGraw was celebrated was the flair for giving practical applications to other men's ideas. This, indeed, is what a publisher is for.

His occasional failure in the appraisal of men was due largely to emotional impulses. When he took a sudden, strong fancy to a man, he would overrule all the objections of his less impulsive employees and take the person into the company, often on a high level. Many an editor or manager saw danger signs in these curious attractions, because they knew facts about the candidate that would eventually work against him. Also they were likely to feel a sense of injustice at someone being brought in from outside and set over them. But nothing they might say could change the Old Man's whim.

They seldom had long to wait, however. Once a man who had appeared to have such great gifts when seen from afar had gone to work as a McGraw-Hill high officer, his close contact with the Old Man revealed all his defects. Sometimes even in a few months, McGraw would have to go into complete reverse in his estimate of a man's capacities. One of his otherwise great admirers said, "He could hire, chew up, digest, and spit out a vice president in a couple of weeks."

6 Apart from his preoccupation with his health, James McGraw was probably a good deal of an extrovert. It is true that his thinking focused almost wholly upon the institution of which he was an integral part. But he never pointed at McGraw-Hill, saying, "See what I have done; I, James H. McGraw, have built this thing." He forgot that he had built it or even that he owned it; rather, sometimes, he seems to have felt that it owned him. It was permanent; he was mortal; his concern for its continuance actually led him to withdraw from it when he thought his powers were failing. If he was dictatorial, it was because he truly felt the company needed dictatorship, not from any desire of self-aggrandizement. Even those who hated him—and there were some who did—could not accuse him of personal conceit. His pride was in the institution, not in the prowess of James McGraw.

There are tycoons who fear the rising power of their subordinates, who will transfer men who come too near the throne. There are bosses who cannot bear to hear their associates praised. The founder of McGraw-Hill was not one of these. He welcomed ability where he saw it no matter how high a man might climb. Perhaps such a man, he thought, such a group of men, could carry on when he was gone.

Whatever his faults, self-centered egotism was never one of them. He was restless, searching, unsatisfied. He was fond, it is said, of quoting Browning's lines:

> "Ah, but a man's reach should exceed his grasp,
> Or what's a heaven for?"

CHAPTER TWENTY-FIVE

New Directions

By mid-century certain trends in science and technology had become definite in America, and the words *research* and *development* had become shibboleths. In every major industrial installation there was some sort of research laboratory. In 1955 about 4 billion dollars was spent on research and development. As the editors of *Fortune* in their instructive book point out, "roughly 95 per cent of the $4 billion goes into exploiting previous scientific breakthroughs; perhaps 5 per cent into expanding the storehouse of fundamental knowledge."[1] The authors deplore this disproportion and point out that the United States is behind Europe in

[1] *The Mighty Force of Research* by the Editors of *Fortune*, McGraw-Hill Book Company, Inc., New York, 1956, p. v.

"inquiry into the fundamental secrets of nature." This has always been so, however. Since Franklin's remark that "a discovery which can be applied to no use, or is not good for something is good for nothing," Americans have concentrated on using the results of foreign basic research for the material enrichment of life in the New World.

But in the future, think and hope these writers, this will change; already, indeed, there are signs. They cite, for example, the work being done by General Electric in what they call "uncommitted thinking":

> Today, so independent of practicality is much of the G.E. Lab's work that C. G. Suits, its present director, points to a fascinating reversal of ordinary cause-and-effect that often confronts him: "From basic research we achieve what appears to be an answer to a problem; *we then search through our complex technology for the problem.*"[2]

It is interesting to note here the complement the Book Company has made to the activity of the Publishing Company by producing this book. The McGraw-Hill magazines have concentrated on technology, on scientific applications. Here now comes a McGraw-Hill book to tell us that Americans must think about the background as well, that we should not let the spectacular highlights of our inventions blind us to the need of exploring what is behind them.

These inventions resulting from the research on which we have spent so much money are peculiarly spectacular from the rapidity with which, in a mere handful of years, they have been developed, and because of the great alterations they have wrought in our economic, political, and social life. The "committed research" has given us, for example, such valuable technological end products as nuclear reactors, jet transport planes, antibiotics, silicones, atomic weapons, cheap television sets, polio vaccines, high octane gasoline, synthetic drugs and textile materials, computers, instruments for control, or "automation" technics, and a

[2] *Ibid.*, p. 14.

thousand devices for making life easier, as well as innumerable more or less useful gadgets.

The more important of these developments have brought significant additions and changes to the McGraw-Hill Publishing Company. Some of the publications changed their titles to indicate more accurately developments in the fields they covered; for example, *Chem and Met* became *Chemical Engineering; Mill Supplies* (acquired from the Electric Trade Publishing Company in 1935 along with *Electrical Wholesaling* and *Electrical Contracting*) had its title changed to *Industrial Distribution* and expanded its coverage of "industrial sales, product application and current news of industrial distributors and of manufacturers selling through them." *Aviation Week* emerged in 1947 as the one McGraw-Hill publication designed to cover the aviation industry which had suffered a sharp cutback following World War II. During the peak aviation production in the early forties McGraw-Hill had three publications to follow closely all phases of aviation: *Aviation* (monthly), *Aviation News* (weekly), and *Air Transport* (monthly).

2 In these burgeoning years, technologically enriched by discoveries and inventions the war had made necessary and possible, no phase of industry advanced more widely and quickly than the chemical. For if we include here, in addition to the chemical industry proper, whose field was the mere production of chemicals, the chemical processing which had entered into almost countless other industries, the horizon seems to recede into infinity.

According to an analysis made by its editor after the time-honored McGraw-Hill chemical publication had become *Chemical Engineering,* there were twenty-one industries apart from the ones producing chemicals which employed chemical engineers, consumed chemical raw materials or reactants, and used chemical equipment in their production operations. The editor listed these as follows:

Coke and coal products	Nuclear energy
Dyes	Paints, varnishes, and pigments
Explosives	Petroleum refining
Fats and oils	Pharmaceuticals
Fertilizers	Pulp and paper
Food processing	Resins and plastics
Glass and ceramics	Soap and detergents
Leather processing	Synthetic fibers and textile processing
Lime and cement	Synthetic rubber
Minerals and metals	Miscellaneous process products

In 1950 these industries had more than 10,000 plants having 20 or more employees and spent more than 40 billion dollars a year for chemicals, raw materials, equipment, fuels, electricity, and new plants. Their capital expenditures were 45 per cent of the total for all manufacturing. Since 1947 the value of the output of the chemical-process industries, exclusive of nuclear energy, had increased 67 per cent. Its increase since 1936 was an almost incredible 567 per cent.

These figures suggest the extent of the field into which the paper, after half a century of growth, had moved when the simpler title *Chemical Engineering* was adopted. Most of its 40,000 carefully selected subscribers were either chemical engineers by education and training or others whose function, whether their degrees had been in mechanical, electrical, or whatever branch, had become chemical engineering. Obviously the paper was a good advertising medium.

It was, however, necessarily technical. Its staff was largely made up of graduate engineers. Their knowledge and understanding had kept pace with the changes and the mushroom growth of the industry. But with all this technical growth had come, naturally, a large business growth; problems of management and marketing, of finance and organization peculiar to the industry, had arisen. Could *Chemical Engineering* reach all the people in that part of the enormous chemical complex as well as the engineers? Perhaps. It might be better, however, to design a new paper for the businessman who was an administrator but not an engineer, who need not follow all the technical details of his chemical or chemical-process business, and who had not the training to make such attention possible. Some of these already subscribed to *Chemical Engineering.* Would not many more welcome a paper wholly devoted to their interests?

Whenever such possibilities appear, it is the practice of McGraw-Hill to search for an existing paper to buy and convert to the new purposes rather than to start a new paper from scratch. In this case, a periodical called *Chemical Industries* was purchased; part of its staff came with it; it became *Chemical Industries Week.* The word *Industries* became smaller and fainter on the cover and in June, 1951, vanished entirely.

Chemical Week, as its name suggests, was a news magazine. It reported business trends and noteworthy events in the field. It also reported, omitting the technical detail, the technical developments. It was an immediate success and stands high today among the most profitable McGraw-Hill enterprises.

3 Closely allied at many points with the chemical and chemical-process industries is that giant that is turning most of the wheels of the world, petroleum. Starting without benefit of engineering or science, with rough and ready, highly wasteful operations in the field, and with swashbuckling business methods that brought it into the courts, split it, and invited competition, the American oil industry has now become the object of intensive research, requiring the applications of the best professional brains and education. The rise of such technologies as the automotive and aeronautical has caused chemists and chemical engineers to study means of increasing the power and efficiency of gasoline fuel. The resulting techniques, like the cracking of molecules, were undreamed of in the days when the first oil papers were born.

All this progress has come about in something less than fifty years; the scientific applications to refining are matters of extremely recent times. War needs, the increase in the use of large diesel motors, the incidence of jet planes, the conversion to oil of heating units, and all the changes we have noted in the use of prime movers—all these and other factors brought the kind of concentration on petroleum that we see today. In addition, there is the field of petrochemicals. Such products as synthetic glycerin and synthetic rubber bring the alliance between the petroleum and the chemical industries closer than ever.

The first oil magazine in which we are interested is *National Petroleum News,* a monthly established in Cleveland by Warren Platt in 1909. To put that year in its proper technological context, we must remember that the airplane was then only six years old, that the model-T Ford had been designed only the year before, and that, in the rural districts at least, the most useful petroleum product was kerosene for lamps and stoves. Five years before, Ida M. Tarbell's sensational two-volume *History of the Standard Oil Company* had shocked the American people into a new fear of monopoly.

Against the early operations of Standard Platt was a crusader. *National Petroleum News* was frankly started as a crusading paper, carrying on its cover the line "Representing the Independent Oil Men." This was later changed, when Platt thought it committed him too narrowly, to a statement that the paper "Prints the News for the Independents." Platt maintains that in those days nothing was printed in newspapers or periodicals except the doings of the Standard giant. Although it is too much to claim that Platt's paper was instrumental in breaking the trust, it is surely true that his crusade raised the morale of the independents.

It is amusing to look over the early volumes of NPN, as it was generally called, to observe what a pygmy the industry was in comparison with today's colossus, yet at the same time to note its overgrowth beyond the facilities of the time to handle it. Even then, when the automotive industry was still scarcely out of its infancy and aviation in the early experimental stage, oil transportation and marketing were little organized. Refineries, for ex-

Oil-tank wagon, 1911.

ample, had no sales departments, and marketing was done through irresponsible brokers and jobbers who set their own prices according to their individual notions of what the traffic would bear. The pictures of little horse-drawn tank wagons and of street-side gasoline dispensing stations—often without pumps so that the cars were fueled by buckets—and the descriptions of the waste at the center of production: all these show the revolution that has taken place between that day and ours.

In NPN's first issue was a piece on a report by Dr. David T. Day, petroleum expert for the United States Geological Survey to the National Conservation Commission, as to how long the country's oil supply was likely to last with current methods of production, storage, etc.

The crude supply will be exhausted by 1935, he declares, fixing that supply at 15,000,000,000 barrels, five billion barrels above the minimum estimated by himself and his assistant experts.

At the outside, warns Dr. Day, and allowing for the present rate of development in its use, the supply cannot last longer than 1943 when the maximum estimate of the nation's oil resources of 24,500,000,000 barrels, determined by the most optimistic of figures, will be gone.[3]

And Dr. Day could hardly have envisioned the impending automotive and aeronautical revolutions, the diesel developments, or the progress in internal-combustion prime movers, not to mention two world wars!

A born crusader, Platt was always using his paper to champion a cause. When the Standard Oil Trust was legally dissolved in 1911, at which time it controlled about 90 per cent of the nation's refining business as well as much of the production, NPN was on the watch for every evasion of the law. When the decision was handed down designating pipelines as common carriers, he fought the attempts to bypass it. He was especially vehement against the railroad-rate discriminations that were so notorious at the time. But he was equally eloquent and active on the positive side. He promoted the Independent Oil Marketer's Association at a time when marketing methods, outside of Standard, were primitive indeed, and he instigated all sorts of improvements in distribution. He was particularly interested in the drive-in filling stations when they began to replace the curb pumps. As one of his editors remembers:

> We supported that movement in every way possible. We ran programs, campaigns to beautify stations and make them attractive with floral decorations, and gave prizes and tried to stimulate the oil companies to doing the most for their stations. . . .
>
> Then, of course, the station rest room came into being. The station operators, by and large, who probably were used to pretty good facilities at home, didn't think that they had to supply them to the public for free. They were pretty filthy. We got into that subject, and Warren Platt enlisted the services of his wife and my wife and other females in other families to go around and check the women's rest rooms. . . . We got out some numbers which we hopefully could call clean rest room numbers.[4]

[3] *National Petroleum News,* vol. 1, no. 1, p. 5, February, 1909.
[4] Virgil B. Guthrie, recorded interview, pp. 12, 13.

The editorial trend of *National Petroleum News* was from the beginning toward the marketing phase of the industry. It began, to the consternation of the maverick oil brokers and jobbers, to publish current prices of crude oil and its products. Platt took on here a large responsibility. Had he been less honest or less insistent upon scrupulous accuracy, a successful suit against him could have put him and his paper out of business. This, however, never happened.

The move to publish prices brought the end of the high, wide, and handsome days of the oil industry. Men who had made fortunes by setting their own independent prices according to a local urgency of demand could no longer operate in the face of such publication. At the same time the refineries began to develop their own sales departments and the whole industry settled down to more efficient and regulated operations.

In the period following World War I, the industry developed such huge proportions that the tempo of marketing was greatly stepped up. Even a weekly paper could scarcely keep up with it, at least on prices and other spot news. It was then that *Platt's Oilgrams* were started as a daily service—one for prices, the other for news. As these were services rather than publications in the ordinary sense of the word, they carried no advertising; they carried high annual subscription prices: $150 for the price *Oilgram,* $185 for the news *Oilgram.*

Finally, however, late in its career under Warren Platt, NPN carried a technical section dedicated to refining rather than marketing. This began during World War II. The year after war ended, the section blossomed out into a new magazine, *Petroleum Processing.* We see, therefore, that this amebalike practice of reproduction by splitting was by no means confined to McGraw-Hill. By mid-century Platt's venerable paper had spawned three offspring, all of them destined to considerable prosperity.

4 To the casual observer it may seem odd that James McGraw managed to stay so long out of this immensely im-

This 1910 gas station is claimed by many to be the first real drive-in.

portant field. The delay was, however, in accord with his publishing policy. He did not enter a field that was already strongly held unless he could purchase one of its leading papers and convert or absorb it. No industry had as extensive a business press as that dedicated to petroleum. By the time of his death, some thirty publications covered every phase of oil activity.

There is reason to believe that the only papers McGraw would have liked to add to his list were those owned by Warren Platt. The two men were friends and saw each other often. Platt, whose attachments and loyalties have always been as strong as his antagonisms, had an unbounded admiration for McGraw. He used to go out of his way to meet him at conventions or other assemblages.

> Many such a meeting [he afterwards wrote] I have attended only in the hope that this pioneer educator of business and technical minds would be there and be aroused to deliver his forceful lessons in business paper publishing.[5]

[5] Editorial in *National Petroleum News,* Vol. 45, no. 9, p. 41, March 4, 1953.

At the same time, during McGraw's lifetime Warren Platt had no thought of selling his papers to anyone. To him they seemed like part of himself. He was still extremely active in their editing and management. He wrote the leading editorials in NPN. In 1949 he got out a fortieth-anniversary issue in which he wrote a thirty-two-page historical article entitled, "40 Great Years—the Story of Oil's Competition." This piece, with its photographic illustrations, its charts, and its graphs, is a valuable contribution to the industry's archives.

Early in the fifties, however, as Platt neared seventy, his doctor warned him that his work was too strenuous and that the time would presently arrive when he must entrust the papers to other hands. As he had no male heir and was naturally reluctant to see his lifework carried on by any but the most competent hands, his thought turned toward the heirs of the man he most admired. Curtis McGraw was then president of McGraw-Hill and by 1953 negotiations were completed. In March of that year, Platt wrote his valedictory editorial:

> I have just sold [he told his readers] . . . this publishing business, the product of which some of you have been reading for as long as 44 years. In my . . . years with the industry, I have seen it develop from the rough pioneering operations of its infancy, from a period where it had no science or worthwhile technology to speak of, where geology was known as "crackology" and refineries operated solely in "batches" of crude just as the proverbial "teakettles" to which they were likened. I have seen the industry grow until its refinery equipment stands like the tall buildings of large cities. . . .
>
> Managing this now great industry . . . are hundreds of thousands of men nearly all of high education. These men are developing a great wealth of new knowledge . . . but so fast is the development of the industry that this information must be gathered quickly, accurately reported and distributed . . . in the shortest possible time.

Platt then explains his reasons for choosing McGraw-Hill to carry on. When the negotiations were finished, he told Curtis McGraw:

. . . of one thing I was sure, that I never would have to apologize to my friends in the oil industry for my successors in ownership and management of this publishing business.[6]

These friends were, however, surprised at what McGraw-Hill did with NPN and were even more so when they discovered that the new owners were about to add it to what they considered an already overcrowded publishing field. The astonished question was echoed back and forth in offices, refineries, advertising agencies: "What! *Another* oil paper?"

What McGraw-Hill did followed somewhat the pattern of the chemical group. The success in three years of *Chemical Week* had shown the possibility of a news magazine dedicated to management. But there was also the need for the longer, more leisurely articles on marketing that NPN's effort to keep up with the news made it difficult to handle. The industry had leapt ahead of its journalistic facilities. So McGraw-Hill changed NPN from a weekly to a monthly and turned over the news gathering and publishing to *Petroleum Week,* a brand-new paper started from scratch in 1955.

Editorially, *Petroleum Week* was streamlined. It adopted a typographical trick designed to help the busy man skip what to him might be nonessentials. In boldface type at the head of each paragraph or section, was printed the condensed gist of what followed, so that the person searching for the material that vitally concerned him could find it without superfluous reading. Then, when he found it, he could read the detail.

This operation with the petroleum papers illustrates one of the publishing practices that has often proved successful: the expansion of one or two papers into two or three for special coverage of an industry which has many facets. But in another field in the late 1940s exactly the opposite technique was adopted when three McGraw-Hill aviation papers were boiled down into one. The choice of methods results from intensive study of the industry and of the publications that serve it. It has been found worthwhile to spend time and money on this sort of research. The

[6] *Ibid.*, pp. 41, 42.

company has learned through much trial and occasional error over the years to bide its time until it is reasonably sure: first, that there will be no duplication of papers; second, that no paper will be published unless there is an urgent present or future industrial need for it. The future needs must, of course, be guessed at but machinery and techniques have been built up within the organization that make that guesswork increasingly informed.

5 The peaks and valleys of aviation activities have been created in the periods of war and peace. Perhaps more than to any other industry, war has brought enormous expansion; the cease-fire has brought virtual collapse. This is natural enough since aircraft have become the principal military weapon. From the technical viewpoint, the variety, the experimentation, and the abundance of maintenance techniques made necessary in war are greatly in excess of the peacetime needs. As aviation settles back into commercial status a uniformity comes to it that requires less specialized journalistic treatment.

At war's end McGraw-Hill found itself overexpanded in this field. The old monthly, *Aviation,* was the nucleus. But there were also *Air Transport* for commercial flying and *Aviation News,* a weekly devoted to the reporting of current events. None of these papers was doing well in 1945. Studying this condition, one of the company's publishing experts wondered if the average businessman in the industry could need more than one paper, provided that paper covered every phase of the industry. Would this be an impossibly large order for a single paper? Not, this student thought, with the relative uniformity peacetime had brought to the flying business, especially if the one magazine were a weekly.

When the study was completed, therefore, this publisher boiled up the three papers together and out came *Aviation Week.* The new magazine set out to:

> . . . tell our readers all the current news about aviation or about airplanes, whether it is related to military aircraft, or commercial aircraft,

or personal aircraft; whether it had to do with new technical developments, or the social consequences of the airplane and so on. The magazine was departmentalized to accommodate this kind of treatment. We no longer treated technical stories as timeless prose. We treated them as straight news.[7]

The publisher did not have to wait long to see the results of his informal guess. Perhaps never in McGraw-Hill history was there such instant response as to this answer to a wide but half-conscious and hitherto inarticulate need.

What happened was that very quickly—so quickly that it almost scared us to death—everybody in the industry wanted to read this magazine, everybody from the president down to the starry-eyed office boys who clipped the pictures out because they were making collections of new airplane pictures.[8]

This unusual but successful experiment has shown that it is sometimes possible to saturate a field completely with a single magazine. But it also shows the flexibility of thought in planning publications that has come with long experience so that each new problem is now approached with a fresh mind, a mind purged of past prejudices and settled ways. The attitude is: "This isn't working so let's try that—even if 'that' has never been tried before." But the trial is not made until "that" is looked at from every side.

We come now to that classic in planning of which the company is especially proud: work that took ten years and involved the costliest research ever undertaken to obtain a preview of a McGraw-Hill paper.

6 Soon after the mid-century mark was passed, the lay public was surprised by the appearance of a new word in the language. Some thought the word ugly; some thought it hybrid; to many of those who knew something of the subject it attempted

[7] Robert F. Boger, recorded interview, pp. 11, 12.
[8] *Ibid.*, p. 12.

to describe, it seemed a lazy, makeshift, and inexact term. The word was *automation.*

Only the word, however, was new. Even the lay public had heard something of the technology that was being built around various instruments designed to replace the human mind and hand in the control of processes and machine sequences. A number of laymen had struggled with Norbert Wiener's book *Cybernetics*[9] and had got as far as Chapter 2, in which the language gave way to mathematical symbols, and the author used such terms as *feedback* and *servomechanism* with confidence that readers understood them. A larger number had read the spectacular article published two years before in *Fortune* on the automatic factory[10] and had begun to speculate as to whether these new developments were about to make the human race unnecessary.

Actually, instrumentation had long been used in specific phases of industrial processes. Such simple devices as the thermostat using the feedback principle had already become a commonplace of the American home. Certain chemical processes used automatic controls of heat, pressure, flow, liquid, and gas. In the mechanical sphere there were safety controls, automatic switching, automatic inspection of work, and devices for the turning on and off of electric or hydraulic equipment. In communications there was machine switching. Some of these go far back in technological history, but they were on the road toward this so-called automation.

During World War II great advances were made in the military uses of instrumentation. Automatic aiming of guns, instrument flying, monitors to check an aviator's oxygen needs, and many other inventions were developed which were far more precise than the human eye and hand. It was during this period that several editors of technical papers began to wonder if their papers touched this new technology.

[9] John Wiley & Sons, Inc., New York, 1948.

[10] E. W. Leaver and J. J. Brown, "Machines Without Men," *Fortune,* November, 1946, p. 165.

In 1944 an editor of *Electronics* presented a memorandum suggesting a paper to be called *Industrial Control Engineering.* The editor explained that *Electronics* could not adequately handle the subject, because certain controls were outside its province, that they were in the hydraulic, the optical, or some other engineering field. The new magazine—if and when—should cut horizontally across the whole of engineering. Following up this memorandum a trial balloon was launched, a little four-page multigraphed sheet. This was issued at intervals for two years and mailed to people in industry or in the armed forces who were likely to be interested. Then, however, it was dropped. Its promoters found that in those years so much of the information was classified as secret or confidential that editorial material would be inadequate.

Once started, however, the idea gained momentum. Certain important instrument manufacturers had become interested. They wrote to company executives. There were luncheon meetings at which the suggestion was discussed. But the men who had to decide remained skeptical. Such a paper, they thought, might compete unduly with other McGraw-Hill publications.

Then in 1952 *Product Engineering* editors quite independently and knowing nothing of the 1944 memorandum, suggested a new magazine. Later another independent note came from one of the new editors of *Food Engineering,* a man who had worked for an instrument company. Then the chemical papers came in with ideas. As a result of all these separate internal and external pressures, the top management decided to mobilize the company's research forces.

Never before in McGraw-Hill had so intensive a survey been conducted. District managers in Philadelphia, Detroit, Cleveland, San Francisco, and elsewhere were instructed to send out task forces to survey their regions. Interviewers went to key people in various industries. Elaborate questionnaires probed out opinions and guesses. Do you need such a paper? Why? Don't you get all the information you want from other papers? The first results were far from decisive. There were many "don't know" replies. Yet when all the answers were tabulated and analyzed, there seemed to be a sort of uneasiness out in the field, a half-articulate groping toward broader sources of information than any that existed. The most definite fact the first results established was that instrumentation, or automation, entered into not one or two but all branches of engineering, and that no vertical paper dedicated to a specific industry and no horizontal paper for a particular branch, such as electrical, chemical, mechanical, or construction, could do the job.

The editorial research aimed at circulation estimates was followed by an equally intensive survey of potential advertising. This was even more difficult. It had to cover not only the markets for instrument makers but those for every sort of component or material entering into what turned out to be a vast and still vaguely coordinated field. The details of such a survey are far too complex to be included in our story. It is enough to say that a glance at the tabulations demonstrates that the most highly trained research and statistical experts were at work for long, arduous stretches of time.

It was at last decided to print a pilot issue. A publisher was picked for it, and he was handed the complete file of material collected over nearly ten years: memoranda, correspondence, suggestions from every quarter, and all the research reports. The file, he tells us, was about 3 feet thick!

The publisher decided to make the pilot issue look exactly like an issue of a going magazine. It was not to be a dummy put together with pastepot and shears full of pieces clipped from other papers. The pilot editors:

> . . . went out with their cameras, with their notebooks, and they got the articles for this pilot issue. They were all new articles which they had dug up themselves. . . . We had to work out a format for the magazine, what would be the flow of editorial material, what typography would we use. . . . Then we had the idea that . . . we'd better make this look like a going magazine with advertising in it. We dreamed up

the idea from our list of what we considered to be the major prospective list of advertisers. We contacted these people and asked them whether they would send us an advertising plate on a product that would fit in this issue, that we would run this just as a sample advertisement, and it would be so indicated. Naturally they were all delighted to do this. The ads were not paid for. The idea was that if you were going to test a magazine, you had to have more than just the editorial content going out to a reader.[11]

New Directions

Only 2,000 copies of the pilot issue were printed and these were mailed to carefully selected lists of company executives and engi-

[11] W. W. Garey, recorded interview, pp. 48, 49.

Cover of the first issue of "Control Engineering," September, 1954.

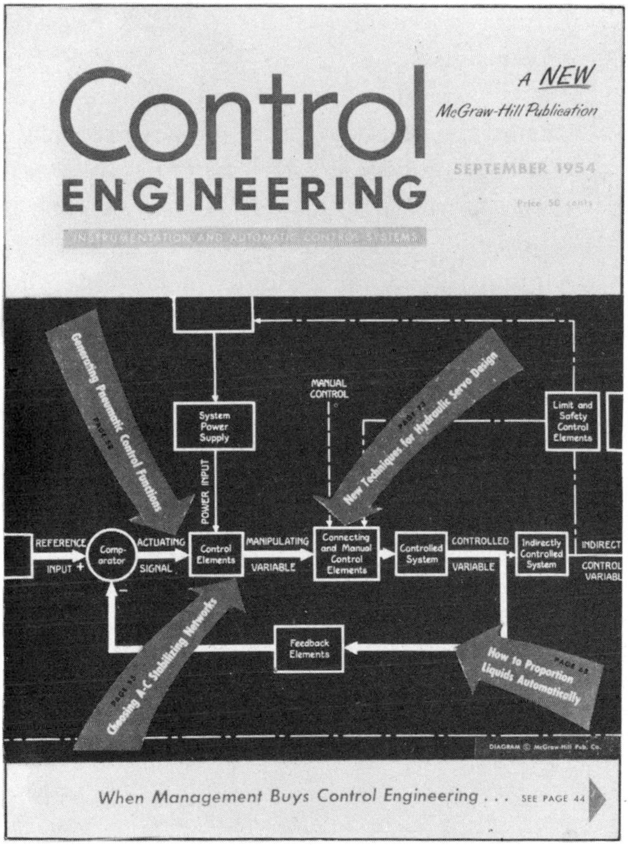

neers or, in many cases, taken personally by a research man into offices with the request that they be examined and certain questions answered. The results were conclusive. With the concrete evidence in their hands, the more or less vague ideas of these people crystallized. Letters full of praise and suggestions poured into the publisher's office. Out in the field salesmen began to sell subscriptions and advertising space—still with the proviso that the paper might not be published. But at a meeting in March, 1954, the Board of Directors of the McGraw-Hill Publishing Company approved the project and the first regular issue was scheduled for September, 1954. This was ten years after the first prospectus had been presented and two years after the intensive research had begun.

In this period several experimental titles were discussed. The word *automation* was discarded even for use in the subtitle. The final decision was for *Control Engineering*—and so it has remained.

It would be hard to find a more impressive demonstration of how expert research has come to replace guesswork in business-paper publishing. The pattern, however, has evolved through much trial and error. In several cases in the past, papers which have looked bright in prospect have not realized their potential. This was so, for example, of *Photo Technique,* a paper dedicated to the camera. *Operating Engineer,* an outgrowth of *Power,* was an experiment which had to be abandoned; it was merged with *Power* to give engineer-readers a full editorial service and to provide advertisers more economical coverage of this market via one large medium, instead of two with smaller circulations. *Bus Transportation,* though successful for twenty-five years, fell a victim to changing times; the U.S. public's use of this form of transportation shrank steadily in the 1950s to a point where this field could no longer support a vigorous publication.

The most costly experiment of all was *Science Illustrated.* Early in 1946 McGraw-Hill entered a new area—the general publishing field—with this magazine. Its editorial concept was the treatment of "life from the science point of view," and, as its name implies, it was largely pictorial. The factors that led to the discontinuance of this venture are many and complex, but to those who know the economics of publishing it is a familiar story. After a little more than three years of trying to build advertising revenue sufficient to get ahead of expanding circulation and the rapidly rising production costs of those postwar years the company could not foresee a return on its investment within a reasonable period of time. Reluctantly the decision was made to cease publication with the July, 1949, issue so that the company's resources and efforts might be directed into more profitable channels.

All these tries, however, were profitable enough in the long run, through the lessons they provided, to compensate for the temporary losses to the company. Today *Control Engineering* seems to be justifying the long experience that drew the blueprint of its planning.

Contemplation of the new automatic production with which this paper deals takes our thought far into the future. Many thinkers and writers are speculating on the industrial, economic, and social effects it may have in years to come. But certainly the vision of long sequences of machines in continuous production without human guidance suggests how far our story has carried us from the horsecar and gaslight age in which it began.

3 • TODAY AND TOMORROW

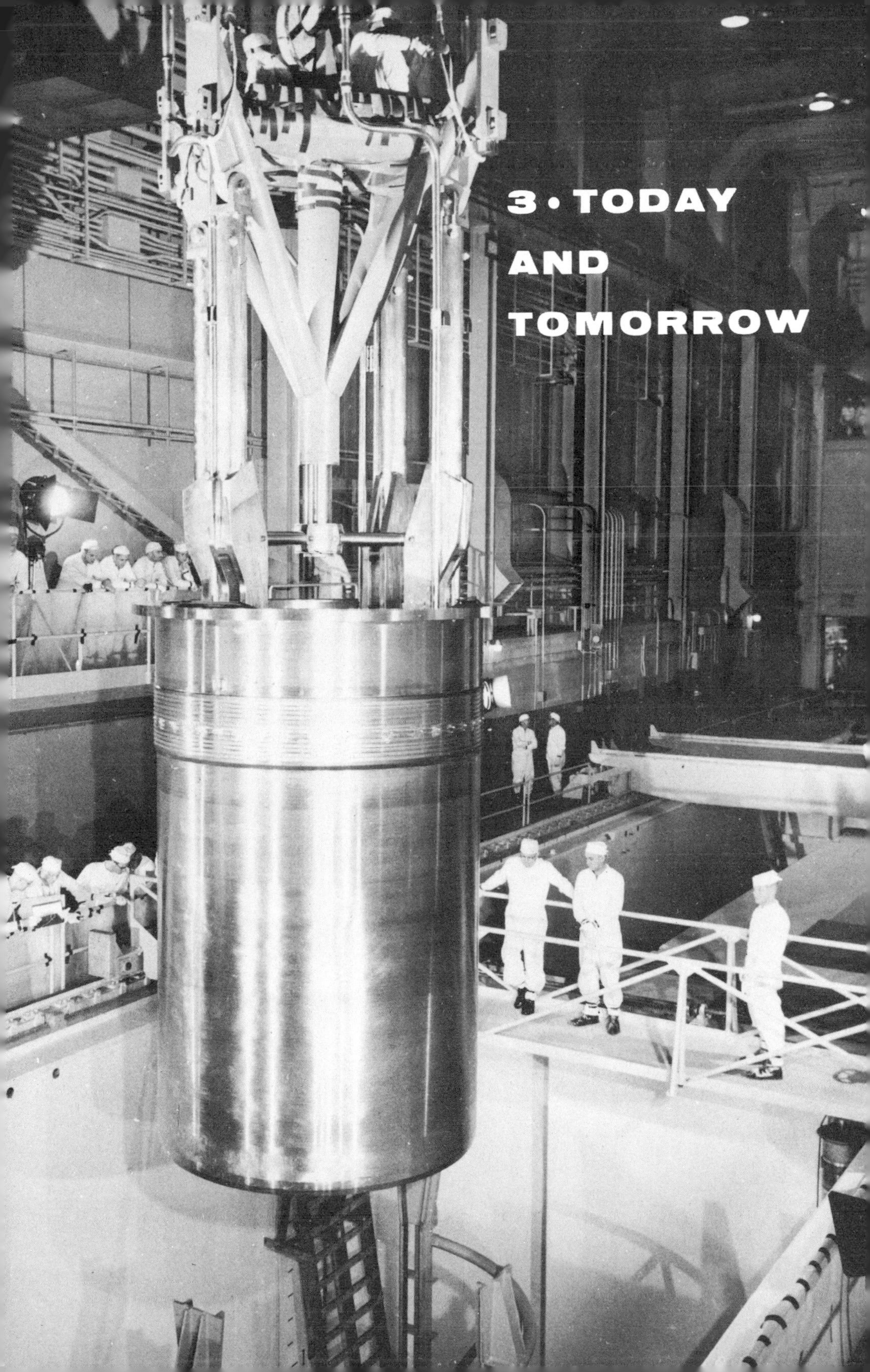

CHAPTER TWENTY-SIX

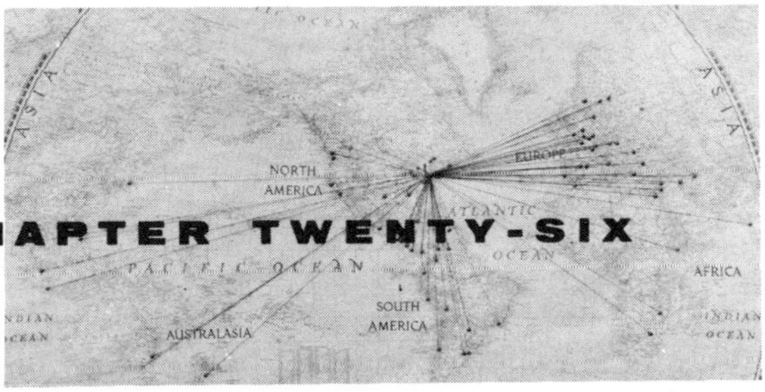

International

At mid-century the culture of many free-world nations had begun to seek and find a common level. With almost instantaneous communications it was inevitable, except in those countries where the door was shut against it, that the flow of knowledge, of information, and of spot news should become continuous. Where any degree of international good will prevailed, schools exchanged students across frontiers, libraries exchanged books, research centers exchanged data on new discoveries, and even individuals exchanged hospitalities. Boys and girls from foreign lands are entertained today in American homes and our young people visit families abroad; industrial teams from Europe and Asia are invited to inspect American factories, and our welcomes are returned overseas. There are even on occasion breaches in the iron curtain for such purposes.

Comparing a global view in 1955, say, with that of twenty years before, the whole face of the earth seems to have taken on a different social and cultural color. It is natural enough that with so rapid a change there have been perilous conflicts and much blocked understanding. Whether all this interchange will lead toward an eventual international harmony or whether some background struggle for power will interrupt the good intent, there can be little doubt of the magnitude of the effort or of its constructive purpose.

Our story is concerned with the part played in all this evolving drama by the power of print. Various agencies have been engaged in releasing this power. UNESCO, the Point Four programs, and the United States Information Agency are a few of the major ones. Below them the network of cooperating offices has thus come to depend very largely on the aid given to them by the free world's publishers. Fortunately the best publishers have built up machinery over the last score of years by which this aid can be given. It is true that the equipment for the task developed mainly out of self-interest with the motive of increased business; yet the effect of it has been to raise the international cultural level.

Every sort of American publisher has taken part in this activity. Special editions of *Time, Life, The Reader's Digest,* the *New York Herald Tribune,* to name a few, have become familiar sights on foreign newsstands everywhere. The American book-publishing houses have constantly increased their export sales and their sales of translation rights, but their special service has been their cooperation with the United States Information Agency which, for propaganda purposes, has placed translations of American books in all parts of the world. From Norway to Burma, from Spain to Japan, translated American books may be found in nearly every first-class bookshop.

It is logical that the technical press should be particularly active in the international field. In nearly every area there has been some new industrialization. Not only in the rapidly growing industrial complexes of India, Japan, and Latin America, but in the military installations of the Middle East where American aid has been administered, there has come a hunger for technical knowledge such as has never before existed. It would be natural to expect, therefore, that the McGraw-Hill Book and Publishing Companies, with their special experience and techniques in publishing this kind of material, should be leaders in the export field.

2 The Book Company had begun exploring the international book markets in a hot war year. A Good Neighbor mission had been sent to Latin America by the State Department in 1943 to discover the extent to which books published in the United States had penetrated there. Executives from five publishing houses—Macmillan, Silver-Burdett, Pocket Books, Doubleday, and McGraw-Hill—composed the exploratory team. Traveling by plane they visited Mexico, Peru, Chile, Argentina, Uruguay, and Brazil. In their six-week tour under United States Embassy auspices, they met publishers, education officials, librarians, book dealers and importers, literary agents, and local government representatives.

The North American publishers were appalled at the European dominance of the book markets. In most schools, for example, British and German technical textbooks prevailed. They were read either in their original language or translated into Spanish. At the moment of the mission's visit, however, the supply of such books was being cut off by the war. It was, therefore, an excellent time for the five United States representatives to direct the attention of Latin Americans to the valuable books published by their good neighbor to the north. James Thompson, the McGraw-Hill delegate on the trip, was able to report to the Book Company a favorable response and, as a result, a [Book Export Department] was established "for the promotion of McGraw-Hill books in Latin America and the development of other foreign markets." [1]

The revelations of this mission indicated a trend which, during and after the war, spread over much of the world. At war's end it was evident that in the shortage of books from Britain and Germany reading habits among scientific and engineering students of Europe, Asia, Africa, and South America had been changed. These people had turned to the United States and were surprised at the amount and quality of available books. At the close of the war, therefore, a new trend had developed. American publishers of technological and business books began exporting more English-language volumes than ever before, to Africa and the Far East as well as to the Western world.

In 1946 executives in the McGraw-Hill Book Company were aware of the extent of the trend. Whether it would continue now that the world was settling back to normal was another question. When British and German textbooks could again be obtained in quantity, would the schools abroad continue to use the American ones? To discover this the Book Company sent on an exploratory and good-will tour one of its college travelers who had made a special study of foreign educational patterns.

> I went around the world, [he remembers] visited about twenty-five countries, talked with publishers, librarians, editors, educators, top administrators in education, our cultural and educational staffs in our foreign missions . . . ministers of education in various foreign countries. . . . Everyone with whom I talked felt that American books had the leadership so far as content was concerned and that that leadership might continue for a number of years.[2]

The survey trip was encouraging but it did not wholly answer the question. How long was "a number of years"? The reply to that one apparently must be made by the American publisher. At McGraw-Hill it was decided that the continuance of the trend

[1] *Book Company Notes,* vol. 1, no. 4, December 21, 1943, p. 2.
[2] Basil G. Dandison, recorded interview, I, p. 7.

would depend on whether the publisher promoted or neglected the new market. In furtherance of this purpose, that same year James Thompson visited eleven European countries and made arrangements in twenty cities for a McGraw-Hill Week.

At home the small international division of the Book Company was immediately enlarged. The first step was to establish an educational department for the cultivation of foreign university markets. It operated on the general pattern of the domestic department but had special circulars, special correspondence, and special selling techniques adapted, after much study, to foreign educational needs and customs. It built up a staff of skilled correspondents to keep in touch with the educators on a carefully compiled list to

> . . . cultivate the foreign educators, encourage them to write us whenever they had questions, to visit us whenever they came to this country in order that we might discuss their problems and exchange opinions, and at the same time learn from them new avenues which we should explore to distribute our books more fully overseas. . . .[3]

The Book Company then set up a review department which compiled lists of leading scientific, technical, and educational periodicals abroad, got in personal touch with their editors, and encouraged them to write reviews of the books in their field. They then developed a list of librarians throughout the world and kept these people documented with all of the company's promotional material.

In looking at this international picture it must always be borne in mind that McGraw-Hill had been dealing here with technical books and that the language difference in such books is of minor importance. Every advanced technological student is obliged at some time to read a text not in his own language. This is easier, of course, than reading general books—biographies, histories, or novels, for example—in which there are much idiom and subtle nuances of meaning. The technical book may deal largely with

[3] *Ibid.*, p. 9.

mathematical or chemical equations which use universal symbols. Or, if it is a book on physics or engineering, it is likely to use words with Greek or Latin roots such as *electronic* or *photometry* which are alike in most languages. Thus, while the ordinary trade book must be translated in order to have wide circulation in a foreign country, the technical textbook need not be.

In the decade since this large-scale, aggressive, international work was begun, some 1,300 McGraw-Hill textbook titles have been adopted by 435 educational institutions in 41 foreign countries. In late years total export sales come to a million copies of 3,500 titles a year. Today about 2,000 reviews of those books appear annually in some 25 foreign languages. The [export sales department] has offices or full-time representatives in Australia, Brazil, France, Germany, India, Cuba, Japan, Chile, Mexico, the Philippines, the Scandinavian countries, and part-time representation in 23 other countries.

In addition to the exporting of books the Book Company has developed a translation program of considerable proportions. The demand by publishers abroad for language rights for selections from the entire McGraw-Hill list—from scientific, technical, medical, and business books and also from trade books and juveniles—has grown steadily over the years. McGraw-Hill books have been published in twenty-six languages and a number of dialects from Afrikaans and Arabic to Serbo-Croat and Turkish. The most frequently recurring languages range in about this order: Spanish, Japanese, French, German, Portuguese, Italian, Swedish, Near and Middle Eastern dialects, Dutch, and Danish. The sale of translation rights has averaged about a hundred titles a year.

3 The Publishing Company's activities outside the United States have remote origins. In 1891 McGraw's Street Railway Publishing Company issued the first international number of the *Street Railway Journal;* from 1897 to 1904 it published digests of news in German, French, and Spanish. In 1899 John Hill organized the American Machinist Press, Ltd., of London to distribute

McGraw-Hill Book Export Exhibition in Turkey, 1957.

the European edition of *American Machinist.* In 1907 this became the Hill Publishing Company, Ltd., of London which three years later had a branch—Deutscher Hill Verlag, A.G.—in Berlin which translated and distributed *American Machinist* through Germany. The London office handled McGraw-Hill Book Company export business. In 1919 the name of the London Hill Publishing Company was changed to McGraw-Hill Publishing Company, Ltd. In that same year the New York headquarters of McGraw-Hill began the Spanish-language *Ingeniería Internacional* for Latin-American readers.

At this time the automotive field was strongly held by McGraw's old associate, Horace Swetland. In addition to several exceedingly important domestic automotive papers, Swetland issued also *El Automóvil Americano* in Spanish for Latin America and *The American Automobile (Overseas Edition),* an English-language version for world distribution outside the Americas. When

Swetland died, however, his company got together with McGraw-Hill and on a fifty-fifty stock-held basis formed the Business Publishers International Corporation to publish both the Swetland automotive papers and the McGraw-Hill *Ingeniería Internacional.*

This subsidiary corporation, jointly owned by McGraw-Hill and Swetland's United Publishers Corporation (later the Chilton Company), made several experiments between 1925 and 1947 with Spanish-language electrical, pharmaceutical, and industrial merchandising papers as well as the wartime good-will *En Guardia;* but these were all sold or dropped. In 1947 McGraw-Hill bought out the Chilton interests in the B.P.I.C.

This bit of detailed history shows that international activity in McGraw-Hill is not a new thing. But the scale is new. Before World War II no one dreamed, for example, that the London company would one day have 113 employees or the Canadian, 50, or that the total overseas staff would number more than 300 persons.[4] The London company now, in addition to handling books, puts out a magazine called *Metalworking Production,* an evolution from the European edition of *American Machinist.*

The American Automobile and *El Automóvil Americano* are edited for foreign manufacturers, dealers, distributors, service-station owners and mechanics, garagemen, fleet owners, parts and equipment importers, and other people in the automotive business. The papers contain suggestions as to how to meet various problems not encountered in the United States, such as shortages of high-octane gasoline. To improve conditions in certain backward countries many ideas are given about repair garages and service stations.

A typical issue of *The American Automobile* contains articles on servicing automatic transmissions with descriptions of major makes, diagrams showing how they work, and the relationship between engine tune-up and transmission performance, improved lighting in repair shops, truck maintenance, service of starters and ignitions, brake fluid, clutch performance on new trucks, and

[4] At latest count, 340, of whom 56 are part-time.

how good driving makes for economical operation.[5] There is a department in both papers called "News of the Industry." One article herein which must have interested many foreigners was on the beginning of a trend in the United States toward lower-powered and lower-priced cars. *The American Automobile* has about 15,000 paid subscribers; *El Automóvil Americano* has 19,000.

The Spanish paper *Ingeniería Internacional* split in two in 1942 because of developments in South and Central America where large road and dam construction projects were being undertaken. Retaining the original title, the words *Industria* and *Construcción* were added to distinguish the new magazines. The first is published for operating management men in manufacturing plants in Latin America, Spain, and Portugal; the second for Latin-American contractors, engineers, government officials, and importers of construction machinery and equipment. Circulations of both run about 15,000.

A late addition to the list of export papers is the *Management Digest* which digests the contents of thirty McGraw-Hill publications plus a selected list of thirteen other papers. A suggestion of the detail of its international coverage is given in a letter received from a Japanese whose invention of a precision riveter had been noticed in the *Digest:*

> . . . But what I was astonished at above all [wrote K. Tsujimura from Tokyo] is the attentiveness of your news-gathering facilities which did not miss even a small machine like this riveter in the Far East.[6]

4 What are these news-gathering facilities of which this Japanese inventor speaks in such astonishment and how have they been developed in response to the late widespread American interest in foreign business, politics, and technics? This story which from rugged beginnings has brought McGraw-Hill to third place[7]

[5] July, 1957. Vol. 34, no. 7.

[6] McGraw-Hill *International Management Digest,* July, 1957, Vol. 12, no. 7, p. 5. The *Digest's* overseas circulation is nearly 30,000.

[7] *New York Times,* first place; *Time, Life,* Inc., second.

among the noncooperative news services of the United States is perhaps the most romantic chapter in the whole history of the company's international picture.

In 1947 there were a few McGraw-Hill offices outside the United States for circulation sales purposes. Representatives of the company in those places, in South America and Europe, had occasionally sent in news to be printed in McGraw-Hill magazines but actually, except for *Business Week,* the domestic papers carried very little regular overseas material. At least until World War II most of the editors thought there was such an immense amount of industrial and business news in the United States that there would hardly be room for stories from abroad. During the war, of course, when there were such large American operations overseas, individual papers which, like *Engineering News-Record,* were especially interested, employed war correspondents in the European and Pacific theaters. When the war was over most of the editors settled back into the American scene.

There were, however, a few farseeing men in the upper echelons of the Green Building, the sort of men who can visualize a need before it has been articulated, almost before it exists. Among them were men who had traveled, who knew something about story values in Europe and Asia as well as in South America. As the war ended, interesting things were happening in the world. India was changing from a colony to a dominion. New independent nations were being born in the Far East and in Africa. Though much of Europe had been hard hit by the war, strenuous efforts toward recovery were under way or would soon be made. There was an almost infinite amount of reconstruction necessary after the bombings and this involved engineering problems. Also, there was promise of industrialization which would offer competition with the United States where none had existed before. Many of these things would open new export markets to American manufacturers. American businessmen would come to do more and more business abroad. There were more signs than ever before that American isolation was over.

McGraw-Hill World News office in Tokyo.

As the plans of these men of vision matured they encountered a good deal of apathy or opposition. This was natural enough. Publishers and editors felt that the cost of these plans would not be justified by results. These people could not be blamed. They had been deeply immersed in American business. Here in the United States, they believed, was where the profit lay. To them the economic status of most foreign nations was so far below the

American level that it seemed hardly likely that much gain would come from this sort of exploitation of the foreign scene. If, now, new plans were for such papers as *The American Automobile,* that would be different: the advertising by American companies in such magazines brought a direct return. But these designs were for a news service, pure and simple: an outlay of money with intangible resulting profit. The papers would be supplied with foreign news for which they seemed to have neither need nor room; what guarantee was there that this would bring in an increased income?

Certain editors were more easily persuaded than others of the value of such a service. *Business Week,* for instance, could not ignore overseas business. International loans, banking operations, foreign aid, among other things, affected American business. *Engineering and Mining Journal* had long depended on reports from abroad, and now that such important materials as uranium were being found in unexpected parts of the world, the ties with foreign mining had become closer. Highly technical magazines such as *Chemical Engineering* and the new *Nucleonics* needed scientific information from Europe. On the other hand, such papers as *Factory Management and Maintenance, Coal Age, Industrial Distribution, Bus Transportation, Fleet Owner,* and *Electrical Merchandising* seemed to need only domestic news. It was even dubious what benefit *Power* and *Electrical World* could derive, because American operations in their fields were presumably superior to anything that was happening abroad.

The visionaries went ahead nonetheless and established World News Service. The first correspondents went to London, Paris, Berlin, Bombay, and Shanghai (one was assigned as a roving reporter to cover all Europe). Then a pattern was established and when the stories came in from these people about business conditions, construction projects, standards of living, chemical processes, and what not in the various parts of the world, editors began to formulate plans about their individual needs. This provided a training basis for prospective correspondents and each of them thereafter went through six weeks of training before they left.

Sometimes they would take lessons in a foreign language. The bulk of the training consisted, however, in studying the operations within the Green Building. Prospective correspondents would visit every editor and talk with him about his needs. At first some of the editors were not greatly interested. But as stories came in and were printed here and there and aroused response among the readers and demands for more, the skeptics began to wonder whether the international interest might be growing. What was happening, in fact, was what had happened so often before: the men upstairs had guessed right about a latent need in American business, industrial, and engineering spheres. Finally, as advertisers increased their export operations they found new usefulness in papers that carried foreign news.

The correspondents were not technical men. They could not be, for each correspondent had to cover too many fields. They were journalists with a nose for news. Their noses were simply turned toward business and engineering happenings, not toward political events. They sent stories of new dams, new hydroelectric installations, new airports, new chemical plants, changes in foreign currency values, labor movements, prices, wages, living standards, supply and demand, marketing, or road building, with plenty of factual material, leaving technical analysis to the editors of the individual papers. The talents required of the correspondents were tolerance toward foreign ways, ability to meet emergencies, knowledge of how to find their way around, tact, ingenuity in circumventing bureaucratic red tape, capacity for taking tough living and traveling conditions in their stride, and stamina to fortify themselves against homesickness.

There were demands, too, on the correspondents' families. Men going to foreign lands for several years naturally took their wives and children along. One whose boy was with him for seven years—from five to twelve—tells that the experience gave the lad . . .

McGraw-Hill World News correspondent covering a construction story in Mexico City.

. . . a certain flexibility of spirit, we'll say, of approach to things; to him things aren't all black and white. People are people. . . . The last year we were in India, he went to a school in Bombay. There were twelve hundred students . . . and he was the only Anglo-Saxon boy. . . . He had a lot of trouble, but he picked up a lot of knowledge—that is, of getting along with people. Of course there was the overlay of somewhat the same experience in Brazil. It's incomprehensible to him, as a fourteen-year old, that there should be any racial prejudice whatever. . . . To be sure, he's forgotten all the Indian tongues that he ever knew, and substantially he's forgotten the Portuguese that he spoke fluently in Brazil after two years and a half. Nonetheless, I think the residuum is there so that when the time comes and he has to cope with another modern foreign language, he has the appreciation for the fact that anyone who says "the house white" instead of "the white house" is not perforce a fool who hasn't been exposed to the blessings of Anglo-Saxon civilization.[8]

Another correspondent who went to Argentina where his wife joined him had some amusing and some difficult experiences. He was lucky in finding a country place to live in that contained both a farm and a swimming pool. In the McGraw-Hill office at Buenos Aires there was a staff of three men and some eighteen Argentine girls. When he was established, he decided to throw an office party at his place and he invited all these people, but to insure a reasonable proportion of the sexes he had his secretary tell the girls that each of them might bring a friend. He supposed, naturally, that it would be a boy friend, as would happen at home. But he did not know the Argentine customs. To date a man for such an occasion would be quite improper.

. . . to my great amazement 'the friend' in the case of most of the girls turned out to be their younger sister, sent along as a chaperon. This meant our office party would have eighteen girl employees and eighteen girl chaperons, plus Jim Downey who had been representing McGraw-Hill in Argentina for twenty-five years, the office boy, and myself. I told my wife this would be a deplorably dull party for the girls, and asked what suggestions she had to make it more interesting. Having just arrived in Buenos Aires on a Moore McCormack ship still sitting in the harbor, my wife had the brilliant idea of inviting the officers and some of the crew who had been especially nice to her on the trip down to Buenos Aires. The girls were delighted with the party, and the Captain and his officers arrived, and we thus introduced to the gauchos of Argentina that great American custom, the office party.[9]

This sort of friendly dealing with people in a foreign country reflected the wisdom of choosing men with flexibility and an absence of provincial bias. The party stood this correspondent in good stead when later he had to deal with hostile elements under

[8] Joseph K. Van Denburg, recorded interview, I, pp. 25, 26, 27.
[9] John Wilhelm, recorded interview (edited), pp. 33, 34.

the Perón regime who thought correspondents were spies.

Sometimes correspondents got into real trouble. Soon after the war a blanket assignment went out from the Green Building to study the underground factories that were being built in various parts of Europe to protect industry against bombing in a future war. The correspondents in such countries as Sweden were able to work with full cooperation from the government. But in Moscow the unfortunate McGraw-Hill man was instantly accused of espionage and summarily ousted!

Some of the work involved perilous undertakings. In Mexico one correspondent did much traveling in his own car over mountain roads that were little more than trails, and he had many hair-raising experiences. He also accompanied the Mexican president on the first train of a railroad which had just been completed through a once impenetrable jungle to the Yucatán peninsula. The train had an old-fashioned system of air conditioning, or rather refrigeration, consisting of fans blowing air over blocks of ice under the cars. In the middle of the jungle the ice gave out. As the trip was a three-weeks' journey, the appalling heat truly tested the correspondent's endurance! But the story of the railroad was important to *Engineering News-Record.*

Some of the news the World News men were asked to cover had human interest. There was, for instance, a blanket assignment to get material for a story about coal miners around the world. Miners were interviewed in various countries not only about their wages, hours, and technical details of their work, but about their home life, their families, their recreations, and what they ate. Another world-wide story did the same thing for truck drivers. Sometimes more than fifty countries were studied in the large surveys. A correspondent remembers that on one occasion:

> . . . they asked us [all the correspondents] to do a feature story on factory personnel around the world, to compare the hours, the lot, the wages, the duties, the income, and the standard of living of the people in thirty or forty countries. They picked as their standard a screw ma-

chine operator, and our job was to . . . see the screw machine operator on the job, and later to go home with him and see the way he lived, the size of his family, the facilities he had, all about his way of life.[10]

The World News Service expanded as new papers appeared. When the petroleum papers were acquired, there were additional geographical requirements. As the oil crisis came in the Middle East, *Petroleum Week* and the News *Oilgram* had to have quick news about the situation there. Cairo, Beirut, Baghdad, and other areas to which little attention had been paid before had to have strong correspondents.

The World News people learned not only what to send as stories but also what not to send. There might, for instance, be a flood in Holland which would have plenty of coverage in the newspapers but only certain aspects of it would be worth the correspondents' notice.

To McGraw-Hill a flood as such wouldn't be of direct news interest, but the performance of dikes and roads would be interesting to *Engineering News-Record* as well as plans for rebuilding; while *Business Week* could well be interested in an article on the economic aspects of the flood, such as its effect on world markets; while *Chemical Week* would be interested in any suspension of operation of chemical plants, etc.[11]

In areas where full-time correspondents are not necessary, stringers are used. Stringers are men or women who work part time and are paid for the stories they write. There are occasional stringers who earn more in this way than the salaried correspondents. As to compensation for all kinds of correspondents there are, of course, differences in the value of money depending on cost of living in various countries. For example, a man might be able to live well with a house and servants in some Latin-American spots whereas, for the same amount in Caracas—said to be the most expensive city in the world—he would have next

[10] Joseph K. Van Denburg, recorded interview, II, p. 7.
[11] John Wilhelm, recorded interview (edited), pp. 82, 83.

to nothing. All these things have to be considered in the Green Building.

As a result of all the international activities the name of McGraw-Hill has become well known in most parts of the world. A correspondent tells, for example, of registering at a hotel in La Paz, the remote and not easily accessible capital of Bolivia, and being told that he was the fourth McGraw-Hill man who had registered that day.

World News people have been useful to the Book Company as well as to the magazines. Correspondents are often used as book representatives in areas where the Book Company has no staff. Sometimes special developments call for their aid.

> For example, [tells one of the book export executives] quite recently we heard of a large development of research libraries in Korea. We don't have an office in Korea, and our book representative in Japan was too busy there to leave. Therefore we asked our overseas correspondent in Tokyo to spend several weeks in Seoul until McGraw-Hill had placed its catalogue and all related literature in the hands of all book-sellers, educators, librarians, publishers, and all persons from the United States who had official connection with the United States information and foreign aid programs.[12]

In general the people in international work seem to enjoy it. It is full of novelty and excitement. There is a constant flow of unexpected problems. Nothing, according to men who have been in it since it started, ever stands still.

[12] Basil G. Dandison, recorded interview, I, pp. 14–15.

CHAPTER TWENTY-SEVEN

Education by Text and Film

By mid-century the changes that had come in the American technological and business scene had wrought a radical change in the pattern of American education. The technics of automation, of television and radio, of radar, of artificial refrigeration and air conditioning, of thermal control, of processes of synthetic manufacture—to name only a handful—had spread the need of technical education far beyond anything dreamed of in the early years of the century. And that need had come to penetrate a lower level than ever before. The old apprentice training no longer sufficed to fit men for jobs of installation and maintenance of machinery and equipment that could once be handled by the all-round rule-of-thumb mechanic. Even in the period between the wars, the apprentice system and the old-time trade school had begun to decline; after World War II they were increasingly replaced by what is known today as the technical institute and the vocational junior college.

From the technical institute—a two-year terminal school—emerged the technician who was on a level well above the mechanic or machine operator but still below the graduate engineer. It has been said that the technician is to the design engineer what the nurse is to the doctor. His job is to install and maintain the machinery or process that the engineer designs. The increasing complexity of such equipment requires of the technician an understanding of physics, chemistry, and mathematics that cannot be learned through apprenticeship. He needs books, teachers, examinations, a curriculum of study.

This level of skill-plus-knowledge has entered other realms than industry. The physician, for example, no longer takes electrocardiograms or x-ray photographs himself; he leaves that to the medical technician who is not a doctor. Laboratories of all kinds employ many useful men and women who earn a good living but do not aspire to be chemists or doctors.

At the same time in business offices there has come an urgent demand for educated personnel. The old high-stool bookkeeper who had little more than a grammar-school education is no longer evident in the business picture. Business machines which can be operated by semiskilled persons have partially replaced him, but a large intermediate stage has also grown up analogous to that of the technician in industry. Persons on this subexecutive plane require education which is no longer mere instruction or training; they must enter at least the fringes of economics, psychology, sociology, or some other social science to supplement drill in the basic disciplines of shorthand, typing, filing, or related routine office procedure. To supply these things, the high school years may not be enough, whereas four years of college may be more than a boy or girl with these intermediate business ambitions can afford. Into the gap has come not only the more advanced business or commercial school but an institution known as the junior college or community college. And such developments must inevitably be reflected in the nation's book-publishing houses.

2 In 1941 the McGraw-Hill Book Company took official cognizance of the trend. Actually certain persons in the company had been aware of it before this and had urged the formation of new and revised departments to exploit the markets that the movements were opening. As it turned out, the definite establishment of such a department in 1941 was fortuitous, for within a few months of its founding the nation's entrance into World War II greatly enlarged the picture.

As one who was in on the ground floor of this Technical and Business Education Department remembers, business

> . . . just skyrocketed. The deeper we got into the war, the faster was the rate of growth. The more we published for this field, particularly books in industrial training, the faster the department developed. . . . The aircraft industry alone . . . was a fabulous thing and a great source of revenue. . . .[1]

More significant, however, than this war boom was a change of attitude on the part of industrialists which materially affected the long-range program of the department, for it was the war urgency which awakened in industry the recognition of the need for technicians. During the period of hostilities, the colleges started, with federal funds, to train persons to fill thousands of gaps that had suddenly opened up in the intermediate phases of industry due to stepped-up production.

> These programs, in level, were certainly less than the traditional four-year engineering programs and, of course, in time they were much shorter. . . . They were offered on a very wide scale, and out of those programs developed a number of books that have subsequently become standard at this level. But the more important development . . . was the recognition on the part of industry as well as the recognition

[1] Edward E. Booher, recorded interview, pp. 5, 6.

on the part of engineering educators . . . that this person called a technician . . . was a necessary part of the "technical team."[2]

When the war was over, quantities of men who had been exposed to various programs of training filled the existing technical institutes to overflowing and posed an urgent need for more. These schools were a natural for veterans who were unable to get into colleges and universities or whose formal education had been so interrupted that they no longer felt they could give the time to long courses. The GI Bill of Rights, however, provided ample funds for the two-year technical institute curriculum. The result was that these schools multiplied almost overnight. When this period ended, the movement had gained enough momentum to compensate for any temporary drop in activity.

The demands of these schools taxed the ingenuity of the Technical and Business Education Department's editors to the utmost. They not only projected individual books; they planned series of books for whole courses of study. The books ran the gamut from practical mathematics to engineering English. They were written on a new pattern.

> Usually these schools are not looking for a college text, and they don't want a high-school text either. Therefore, a whole new text literature has to be developed especially for the two-year technical-terminal type program because the first year student in these schools isn't planning on going on for four years. He's going to be starting on a job at the end of two years.[3]

In other words, tempo must be speeded up and great selectivity must be used in order to eliminate superfluous material. In general, a new set of authors was sought because the authors of college engineering texts, for example, produced too long and exacting a book, whereas the high-school author turned out one that was not sufficiently advanced. So eventually the editors went to the technical institutes themselves for manuscripts.

[2] *Ibid.*, p. 10.
[3] H. Walter Shaw, recorded interview (edited), p. 8.

Three publications of the McGraw-Hill Technical Education Department: "Technical Education News," the quasi official publication of technical institute education in the United States; the annual "Special Issue"; and a twenty-page guidance booklet, "The Engineering Technician."

As time went on, however, through the postwar years, these institutes were not the only market for the intermediate texts. The United States Armed Forces Institute, a sort of government correspondence school for the services, provided another. A third was training within industry, an important activity that has developed in recent years. Many large corporations offer schedules by which workers may "learn while they earn." As the general manager of McGraw-Hill's Technical Education Department has stated:

About twenty per cent of our sales in recent years have been to training programs sponsored by business and industry for their employees. There has been a change in the philosophy, in the attitude of business and industry in respect to employee training. Twenty-five or thirty and more years ago, most firms had employment departments, and you came equipped with your skills and your knowledge and they hired you for what you knew or could do.

The recent change in basic philosophy is that business and industry now hire the individual who comes with a basic education and, either on or off the job, provide their own special training.

Employee education and training is not considered to be a frill any more by forward looking concerns. It is thought of as a legitimate cost of doing business. The cost of training the worker, the supervisor, and the executive is put on the books right beside the cost of maintaining the machinery. This shift, of course, is something we are following and developing texts for and promoting where we can.

We try to show business and industry how they can use our texts to do the training job they have to do. We try to sell them our texts because they are authoritative, they are easy to teach from, and they are easy to learn from. We show those responsible for training that using our texts is much less expensive than to try to write, design, and manufacture their own. We also show them how to prepare their own study and lesson guides or other supplementary material to adapt our central core text to their specific needs because training is done on the job.[4]

The business part of the department's title eventually dropped out. For the first seven or eight years of its existence, what with the war and the GI programs, the technical books greatly predominated. The higher reaches of business education were in the hands of other departments of the Book Company. The so-called Technical and Business Education Department was concerned, on the business side, mainly with practical books. These, as we shall see, were later merged into the list of the Gregg Publishing Division.

[4] *Ibid.* (edited), pp. 9, 10.

These four college books were recently selected by the American Institute of Graphic Arts as among the fifty best textbooks published in the year May, 1957–May, 1958.

3 The oldest educational-book department of the Book Company is dedicated to college textbooks. We have seen the beginnings of this College Department back in the days before the McGraw and Hill publishing companies merged. Many of the texts then and for many years afterward were for engineering or science courses. The first departures were into industrial management and business administration. Most of the texts were adapted to study in the later college years; there was relatively little for freshmen and sophomores. The social sciences were hardly touched.

During the 1930s a strong publishing effort in new fields resulted in the department's being firmly established in the social sciences by the end of this decade. After World War II strong emphasis was placed on the further development of freshman and sophomore texts in all the areas in which it published. This enabled the department to reach the large markets in these introductory courses and the many students who did not continue study beyond the first two years of college. This, in turn, supported a rapid growth of the staff of representatives of the department from ten to forty-five.

A key figure in the college department of any book publisher is the so-called college traveler. His title derives directly from his activity. His work is just that: *traveling to colleges.* But what makes his position especially interesting is that he both promotes and procures. A McGraw-Hill college traveler visits the important professors on every campus in his territory, talks about old and new McGraw-Hill books in each professor's field, and at the same time inquires about the professor's own production. Is he doing any writing? Is he planning a textbook? What are the gaps in his field, what textbooks are needed?

The fascination as well as the unique importance of the college traveler's job comes from the fact that his client, the professor, is a potential author as well as a potential instrument of sales. By adopting a textbook, he may bring about the purchase of hundreds of copies, but he may also become an important future producer. For the traveler, therefore, the promotion and merchandising of his company's books is no more essential than the discovery of books and authors on the nation's campuses. He must keep his ear tuned to the talk of bright young faculty members, of this book or that which is being written behind some closed study door. Then he must find a way to open that door and ultimately suggest to the professor that McGraw-Hill is his ideal publisher.

One editor has described the perfect traveler as "a good part dilettante." He has got to get around the campus. He must have a talking knowledge of many subjects. He must be able to draw out the professor until suddenly he is talking about the book he's been writing secretly for five years or thinking about for twenty-five.

Editors in the College Department are not editors in the usual sense. They go after manuscripts, often dreaming up the kind of book they want before they go. But they do not edit the manuscripts that come in. They choose an outside editor, usually a professor of high standing in the particular subject. McGraw-Hill, as always, is strong on series of textbooks—books which follow a college curriculum through to completion—rather than single separate volumes. There is, for example, the McGraw-Hill series in psychology which covers, in addition to general introductory texts, clinical, abnormal, personality, developmental, experimental, and social phases of the subject. Such a series will have an outside editor and often a committee of experts to project and edit its texts. Today some forty series are published, most of them in the College Department.

The new provisions for freshman and sophomore texts resulting from larger enrollments in both four-year and junior colleges do not replace the traditional attention of the College Department to advanced books. They merely add emphasis to the department's activities. But the members of the staff maintain that along with this extra emphasis has come leadership in the social sciences that was not a part of the company's early activities. They confidently assert, for example, that McGraw-Hill is well in the van in sociology and one of the top handful of publishers in political science.

In late years the physical appearance of college textbooks has completely changed. The new design in illustrations, typography, and color is, however, a departure which has occurred in the entire educational scheme from bottom to top.

4 "From bottom to top" is a more accurate description of the progress here than the common phrase, "top to bottom." For it was with schoolbooks that the modern lively presentation began and the drab college texts were obliged to follow suit.

The book in the upper left corner is the first edition of "Mechanical Drawing" by French and Svensen, published in 1919; upper right, the 1948 edition; centered, the 1957 edition.

Today in most educational texts there is more animated writing than ever before, and more abundant illustration—half tones, line cuts, graphs, and charts—to complement the words, and color to replace the black and white.

A hint of the reasons behind this is in the changes that increased population and a parallel teacher shortage have wrought in American secondary education. A recent survey by the Ford Foundation showed that to keep up with the flood of children that is inundating the schools, 50 per cent of college graduates for ten years would have to enter the teaching profession. This

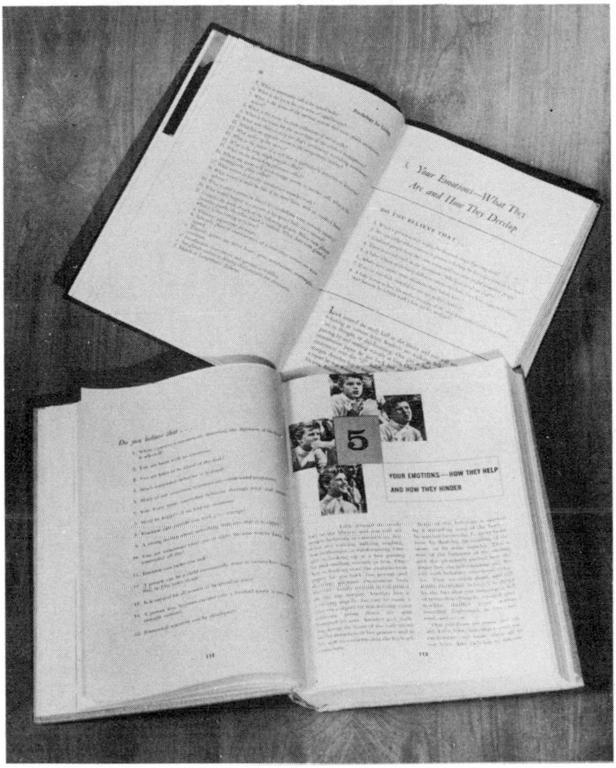

Above, the 1948 edition of Sorenson and Malm's "Psychology for Living"; below, the 1957 edition.

is obviously impossible. Indeed, the percentage is certain to fall far short of this, even if, as the Ford Foundation people hope, teachers' salaries are raised and their work is made more attractive. Meanwhile those who do elect teaching as a vocation will be under such pressure that it will be extremely difficult for them to do adequate jobs.

This situation offered a challenge to the publishers of schoolbooks. Would it not be possible, they wondered, for the new books to have what our vernacular calls a "built-in" teaching skill? Could not the book be made to do what the teacher could no longer do? In the old days, when the student got stuck over a passage in a text, the teacher was able to clarify it on the blackboard or to take the student aside and work it out with him. Today with overlarge classes this is no longer possible. But cannot the writer and editor of the textbook *anticipate* the student's questions and difficulties and thus ease the teacher's burden?

This sort of thing has come to permeate American society. From prefabricated buildings to precooked food, skills are passing from the interpretive to the producing units. The modern housewife, for example, unaided by domestic help, no longer has the time or training for careful, elaborate cooking. But the art she lacks is now supplied in the processing of the food before it leaves the factory. Whole meals are cooked, frozen, and packaged, so that there is nothing for the home cook to do but apply heat.

While education can never be packaged in quite this way, the trend is necessarily in this direction. Perfectionists may deplore it and remind us that civilization's educational peak was reached when Socrates walked with his pupils in Greek gardens and drew forth their thoughts. But nowadays when millions of Socrateses in as many gardens are hardly available, the power of print must take over. And in the absence of such educators in the schools, much precooking, so to speak, must be done in the editorial offices where schoolbooks are projected.

The challenge of the altered high-school picture helped bring about a revamping of the McGraw-Hill School Department. This department had been called a stepchild of the Book Company. It had evolved out of the publication of vocational books for the old-time trade school—of late years gradually disappearing—and sold, too, to high schools which had vocational courses.

Between the end of World War II and 1952, however, the company began taking its School Department with new seriousness. The beginnings of books that had accumulated were weeded out and revamped according to revised concepts. In 1952 a great step forward was taken when the Book Company purchased the Harper and Brothers school list. It was a small list, mostly books for academic courses, but a good one, and with it came some of the Harper personnel. Soon after, the department acquired new management of broader experience, and from then on it has been revolutionized and is growing to keep pace with the other educational departments.

The first move to meet the new challenge was a more thorough editing and testing of every book before it was published. Experts in art and visual presentation went over the manuscript with the author and other instructors in the subject. Wherever a rough spot was discovered the art editor called in an illustrator who could make the text clear with graphic aid—often in color. Today textbook manuscripts are read and criticized by students as well as by teachers. It is not enough to have several instructors say, "Yes, this is fine; I can teach the subject easily with the aid of this text." Perhaps he can, say the editors, and perhaps the student will say he cannot. So a person is chosen who is a beginner in the subject and is asked to put himself in the place of the pupil. Then from that viewpoint he reads the text. Usually he will put his finger on a passage and say, "Here, I can't understand this." The editor then takes the book back to the teacher and says, "The student got stuck here." So the editor, author, and teacher confer about the passage and it is simplified or graphically elucidated.

Even with all this preparation, however, persons in the new enlarged and improved School Department felt that, in certain cases, the textbook alone could not wholly meet the newly harassed teacher's need. They turned, therefore, with much hope toward a new department of the company which, in postwar years was taking shape, exploring and experimenting as it developed. This department was called Text-Film.

5 During the war visual education was widely used in quick training programs. At that time when the requirement of speed was paramount, the people in command of training projects seized upon any device that could help quicken the instruction. Factory workers were taught by film how to use lathes or millers; men in the Army medical corps were shown films on first-aid procedures; soldiers were taught everything from machine-gun assembly to venereal prophylaxis by motion pictures. This was, in fact, both visual and audio training, because the sound track brought in the expert instructor's voice interpreting the films.

The result of all this widespread activity was that many came to believe that the film alone was all that was necessary to education. These extremists visualized enormous darkened auditoriums filled with students, with the world's greatest teachers lecturing on the sound track and pointing to charts, diagrams, photographs, and animated drawings on the screen. What price books in that Utopia? What price old-fashioned schools, incompetent, underpaid teachers?

More thoughtful persons were skeptical. In publishing houses the skepticism was somewhat compounded with alarm. Are we, they asked, going to admit the failure of the power of print and remake our houses into studios? McGraw-Hill people naturally shared this fear of the competitive chimera, but at the same time they wondered if collaboration might not be possible: if both book and picture might not be improved by working the two together. They began experimenting.

Then the visual-education enthusiasts calmed down somewhat and came round to the belief that they could tie in their films with the book publishers, and they approached several of them with various propositions. So while McGraw-Hill was actually starting to experiment in this direction, seven other publishers pooled together a considerable sum of money to do a research project on the publishers' use of audiovisual materials. After some six months they issued a lengthy report concluding that educational films were outside the publisher's province.

This report seems not to have worried the McGraw-Hill Book Company people who had already taken the plunge. Some of the reasons given by other publishers seem cogent enough as we review them in the light of the time they were given, when facilities for projection in the schools were few and far between and when film-selling techniques were so unfamiliar to book salesmen. From the point of view of these publishers, the arguments seem incontrovertible.

The large and varied McGraw-Hill organization, however, felt able to experiment even if the tryout took it for a few years into the red. This was one of the areas in which bigness counted, for, as one Book Company executive put it, this was a "blue-chip operation." There are many critics of McGraw-Hill's size and it is undoubtedly possible to build up a plausible argument showing the advantages held by smaller publishing houses. On the other hand, the sort of pioneering that was done by the Text-Film Department and many other experiments in the periodical end of the business[5] requires a large backlog of resources.

Motion-picture production is an exceedingly expensive business. New York producers are almost completely unionized and labor costs have skyrocketed. A camera man, for example, who gets $200 a day can quickly send up the cost of a film. As prices go today, $50,000 is not excessive for editorial and production costs of a single educational film of thirty-minute running time.

For a start the Text-Film people selected a highly successful text. When McGraw-Hill people look toward their mountains, they always see two books standing on the peaks. One is the *American Machinists' Handbook;* the other is Thomas E. French's *Engineering Drawing.* Obviously French's book was the first text choice. For the other projects they spent about a year in research. They finally decided to diversify the field as far as possible. They therefore chose Harold S. Diehl's *Textbook of Healthful Living* for college health and hygiene courses, Raleigh Schorling and Howard T. Batchelder's *Student Teaching in Secondary Schools* for teacher training and in-service training, and French and Svensen's *Mechan-*

[5] *Business Week* and the World News Service are examples of this. And, as we have seen, such ventures as *Nucleonics* and *Control Engineering* required the capacity for taking losses.

ical Drawing for high-school drafting classes. Thus they entered both school and college areas with the first four large projects.

For selling to schools and colleges, the editor makes up a package consisting of a book, a film, a set of filmstrips, and an instructor's manual; to be sold complete. The difference in volume of copies of books and films is, of course, very great. A teacher will want every student in his course to have a copy of the chosen book, whereas the institution buys only one print of a film.

In its eleven-year career, the Text-Film Department has produced many pictures. In addition to formal courses they have dealt with anatomy, physiology, psychology, marriage and the family and industrial human relations, to name only a few subjects. A film on human reproduction caused some outcries from the self-styled guardians of public morals, but in the end the picture won the most thoughtful recognition and wide use. One industrial film presented a case study of an argument between two factory foremen showing both sides of a question. Another gave a discussion between a supervisor and a foreman. At the close of the picture the viewer was asked: "These are the facts. Who's right? How would you handle the situation?" One film for high schools went right into the middle of an extracurricular activity. A group of boys and girls are shown sitting at a soda fountain discussing the actors in the school play that was produced the night before. As one who is familiar with the film describes it:

> The kids are kind of disgusted. . . . They keep saying "How horrible they (the actors) were!" The cast walks in at that moment and you see a complete flip-flop. "You were wonderful. You should be on Broadway," and the like. One kid says, "They weren't so wonderful." The other one says, "Yes, I know but you can't tell them." The other one replies, "I'm a reporter on the paper and I've got to say it." Then the little blonde who was the star of the show walks up to the reporter . . . and says, "Joe, you haven't said anything. What do you think?" The film ends at that point with the question, "What would you say?" [6]

[6] Albert J. Rosenberg, recorded interview, p. 27.

"Sh! here she comes now." In this scene from "The Honest Truth," school playgoers prepare to shower praise on the girl whose acting they have just finished ridiculing. The film, a McGraw-Hill release, is one of the "What Do You Think?" series, produced by the National Film Board of Canada.

Pictures that concern the intimate social relations of the children

. . . get some wonderful group discussions going. You can develop a film on honesty, or on the bully and how he operates. I defy anyone to find any way of doing it as conveniently. You can't act it out in class. You can read it in words but it doesn't have the emotional impact.[7]

This student of educational-film potential has briefly summed up some of the possibilities:

With visual materials . . . you can bring the whole world into the classroom. . . . You can take visits to museums, boat trips, airplane trips. By means of animation you can show processes, medical infor-

[7] *Ibid.*, p. 27.

mation, bodily functions that you can't show any other way. With time-lapse photography you can show a tree growing in seconds or a flower opening or any long, involved process. You can telescope an operation that usually takes a period of months into a few minutes. With slow motion you can show a hummingbird's wing which has . . . so many beats to the minute that the human eye can't see it. . . .[8]

The possibilities are infinite. The McGraw-Hill Book Company's Text-Film Department, now that it is well under way, seems to be making the most of them. Getting under way, however, has not been an easy process. So far the most lucrative developments have come in the colleges and other advanced institutions rather than in the secondary schools where money is hard to come by, as the teachers' salaries attest.[9]

[8] *Ibid.*, pp. 25, 26.

[9] On this subject a useful statistical summary is given in Beardsley Ruml and Sidney G. Tickton, *Teaching Salaries Then and Now* (Bulletin No. 1 of the Ford Foundation Fund for the Advancement of Education), New York, 1955.

CHAPTER TWENTY-EIGHT

Book Company Expansion

When the McGraw-Hill Book Company acquired the Gregg Publishing Company, it took over one of the two great shorthand systems of the English-speaking world. John Robert Gregg, an Ulsterman who first published his system in Liverpool in 1888, had come, five years later, to the United States, partly in the hope of escaping from the hot competition in England of his great rival Pitman, and partly to secure the American rights to his invention. Actually he found the Pitman system already in wide use here and for a time was scarcely able to break even with his shorthand schools in Boston and Chicago. Success came to him, however, with the tremendous advances in American business and industry as the century drew toward its close. The typewriter

A flashlight picture of Mr. Gregg's first shorthand class in America, at the Boys' Institute of Industry, Boston, Massachusetts, 1893.

came into universal use in those years and with the demand for stenographers that followed it, there was room for several shorthand systems. Meanwhile Gregg had started his publishing company, and his textbooks explaining and teaching his shorthand had wide circulation. But perhaps the decisive factor in his success was the repeated victory of Gregg writers in the international shorthand contests beginning in 1910.

In the forty-odd years between the establishment of the Gregg Publishing Company and its merger with McGraw-Hill, secretarial and stenographic work had come to occupy the great majority of the 20 million women employed in the United States. In every part of the country today there are scores of business schools in

A scene from the McGraw-Hill Text-Film series on the Gregg method showing a contemporary shorthand class.

which these women are trained. The enrollment in business courses, either in high schools, colleges, or private business schools, is close to 3½ million. Some 20,000 schools teach the Gregg shorthand system. The methods used are the results of Gregg's own personal educational effort. His whole career was devoted not to the instruction of the ultimate users of his shorthand but to the teaching of teachers. This concentration on teachers and teaching methods plus the fact that most teachers and students consider the system simpler than any other has won Gregg its success. That success, in the United States at least, may be measured by the fact that of all the schools teaching shorthand, 96 per cent teach Gregg.

A photograph from the Gregg magazine, "Today's Secretary," showing the "Typical Today's Secretary."

The system has also been adapted to more than a dozen foreign languages. The latest of these is one of the native Filipino tongues. The most popular of the adaptations is the Spanish. This is taught throughout Latin America. Gregg himself was known and admired by Latin Americans, and today in some Latin-American countries the schools celebrate an annual "Gregg Day."

By the time of Gregg's death in 1948, his company had built a very considerable body of practical business-education literature. There were not only the shorthand manuals. There were books on business law, business mathematics, general office training, secretarial practice, on spelling, and business English. Several periodicals were published by the Gregg company. Those which were circulated at the time of Gregg's death were *The Gregg Writer* (changed to *Today's Secretary* in 1950), *La Revista Gregg* (Spanish), *The Gregg News Letter* (changed to *Business Teacher* in 1949), and the *Business Education World.*

Book Company Expansion

When John Gregg died, the McGraw-Hill Book Company had two departments more or less concerned with business books. One was the Industrial and Business Book Department which published practical manuals and professional books, sold largely by mail, and was a direct descendant of that original program which we saw in the company's earliest days and which contributed so much to its earliest success. The other was the Technical and Business Education Department dedicated, as we have noted, to textbooks. In the immediate postwar years, the mushroom growth of terminal technical institutes had turned this department to a preoccupation with technical rather than business texts. In 1947, however, an effort was made to restore the balance.

As Gregg was one of the two organizations dominating the field of practical business education in the United States, one of the Gregg staff was persuaded to come over to McGraw-Hill to engineer the expansion of its business-education list. Then, a year later, the Gregg company lost its president, and the idea of combining the two lists was a logical one, especially as the organization to which John Robert Gregg had given such intimate personal attention for half a century was left without strong leadership.

In January, 1949, then, the Gregg Publishing Company became a McGraw-Hill subsidiary. Three years later it was taken into the corporate structure and became the Gregg Publishing Division of the McGraw-Hill Book Company, Inc. There was a repetition here of much the same sort of psychological tension we saw in 1917, when the intensely loyal Hill organization came under the control of James H. McGraw. The Gregg company had been the same kind of one-man institution that John Hill had headed; its people's devotion to Gregg had kept them united and happy and they dreaded the move into what they thought was a soulless empire. As an executive who took Gregg's place in charge of the subsidiary recalls:

> . . . it took about a year for that staff to realize—and I think this is wholly understandable—that we did not wear horns, that we were almost human over here, and their personal welfare was tied up completely with the welfare of the Gregg company and how well we did with it. I think we made a very wise decision in keeping the organization at 270 Madison Avenue, in their own home where they were in familiar surroundings, working with the same crew, and where I was the only intruder. I even kept Mr. Gregg's secretary so that I was the only McGraw-Hill person there. . . . They gradually met other members of the McGraw-Hill organization through social functions and through the natural course of business, and by the end of that year they were ready to come to this building. . . . That transfer, I think, was helped by a big house-warming party that the executives of McGraw-Hill put on for the entire New York Gregg staff. It went off exceedingly well. There was a big buffet supper and the Gregg crowd was able to see and meet all of the people they would be working with over here.[1]

At the end of that party, an old Gregg hand had dubbed the merger "McGregg-Hill."

The Gregg Division's first job was the complete revision of the shorthand program. There had been no new edition of the basic Gregg shorthand book since 1929. The new simplified edition published in 1949 swept the country. A second edition, revised, appeared in 1955. In it the learning of the system was eased

> . . . chiefly by reducing the amount of arbitrary learning . . . in particular by eliminating a large number of brief forms and simplifying the system principally through the use of a new stroke, the *rd* stroke which, in turn, led to the elimination of the reversing principle. As a result of the revision the learning load was made substantially easier.[2]

[1] Edward E. Booher, recorded interview, pp. 8, 9.
[2] Robert E. Slaughter, recorded interview, pp. 21, 22.

John Robert Gregg, 1940s.

It turned the magazine *Gregg Writer* into *Today's Secretary*, a paper with approximately 150,000 circulation, which has fascinated many a young woman with its advice about dress, manners, speech, behavior toward the boss, and what it calls "personality and grooming." In this connection, the managers and editors of the division are not worried by new machine techniques involving dictaphones or tapc rccorders which are sometimes thought to presage the obsolescence of shorthand. Too many men in the executive echelons are dependent on the *personality* of the secretaries or stenographers to whom they dictate for a cold machine ever to replace the human presence. They are accustomed to secretarial thinking, memory, interpretative ability, understanding of the boss's peculiarities, correction of the boss's mistakes, filling in his omissions. And executives are likely to be scared of gadgets, to have a sort of "mike fright" when the wheels start turning. That, at any rate, is what the Gregg people say and certainly the statistics show no deterioration of shorthand education.

In addition to this morale builder, efforts are being made in the field to add to the secretary's prestige. For instance, an institute for certifying secretaries has especially enlisted the interest of the Gregg Division. It has done this through examinations in business law, business administration, accounting, and other advanced subjects. A hundred colleges now give courses guided by these examinations. This has done much to counteract the reluctance of some college girls to become secretaries on the grounds that the work is thought to be menial.

The Gregg Division has been greatly enlarged since its establishment by the Book Company. It employs today 150 people and operates district offices in Chicago, San Francisco, Dallas, Toronto, and London.

2 Perhaps no province of applied science has broadened its scope or changed its emphasis more in late years than that of medicine. The shift in trend from curative to preventive medicine is one phase of this. Concentration on general health as a guard against disease has been enhanced by the new programs of health insurance. Another is the expansion in the direction of psychiatry, spurred by the current increase in mental illness. Again there has been a radical change in medical education, in the teaching, that is, of doctors and nurses. And in the discovery of the so-called miracle drugs and the new serums or vaccines, the horizons of the profession have vastly widened. All these altered trends have posed an urgent demand for new textbooks: new in kind and in quantity.

The Book Company entered this field with a department dedicated to medicine, nursing, public health, and pharmacy in 1944. The college department had already won a reputation and author relationship through its publication of biological books and other texts on subjects that touched medical territory.

These beginnings in the realm of medical education led to an ambition in the company to expand on a more advanced level. The hope was realized in 1954 when one of the oldest medical publishing companies in the United States fell, as it were, into the ample McGraw-Hill lap.

Blakiston was a name known to physicians everywhere. For more than a hundred years this proud Philadelphia house had been publishing books; for some fourscore of those years it had made medical and dental works its specialty. But by 1942 it had come upon unhappy days. The Blakiston dynasty had died out. The company had been inherited by Horace White, its top executive under Kenneth Blakiston. White expected a White dynasty to replace the Blakiston one but tragedy struck early in the war years. White's son, whom he counted on to carry on the business, died on his way to Iceland on an economic mission when the ship on which he was traveling sank. This blow broke Horace White's interest in Blakiston and he sold it to the large New York house of Doubleday, Doran, and Company.

Kenneth Blakiston had been one of those gentlemen of the old school who were still in command of so many conservative family businesses in the first decades of the twentieth century. He was apparently gentle, kind, honorable in every dealing. He was beloved by his employees in each one of whom he had a personal interest. Under him it was a one-man house operating in the leisurely Philadelphia ambience. Its relations with both authors and buyers were intimate. Yet for such a house it had a considerable volume of business in the medical field. It published, for example, all the Red Cross books. After Blakiston's death and during World War II, it issued 15 million Red Cross manuals: a factor said to be a reason for Doubleday's interest.

As Doubleday's foster child Blakiston did not greatly change.

Presley Blakiston, founder of Lindsay and Blakiston and of P. Blakiston's Sons and Company.

Its new owner left it in Philadelphia and it continued pretty much in the old tradition, living on its reputation, expecting its manuscripts to come in over the transom, or in more or less haphazard fashion from "friends of friends" in the medical profession. Its editors did not go out after the authors as McGraw-Hill people did, with a definite program in their hands, a program worked up in the office with the assistance of committees of experts and outside professional advisers. Actually Blakiston was not Doubleday's cup of tea at all, and this is probably why they left it so much to its own devices.

In 1952 Doubleday brought the company to New York. There it was soon in the field of the McGraw-Hill magnet. The more the Book Company people saw of it, the surer they became that its list would fit in admirably with their own slowly growing shelf of health, nursing, medical, and pharmaceutical books.

 So in 1954 the deal was consummated, apparently to the satis-

Kenneth Blakiston, son of the founder of Blakiston and successor to the presidency.

faction of everyone. Doubleday was relieved of an appendage they had not the facilities to improve; the Blakiston people were glad to be welcomed into a company which had specific ideas of how its kind of books should be cared for.

Medical books are in some ways a fascinating problem for a publisher. The doctor who is a practicing specialist or research man is an author who is likely to be both meticulous and sloppy, who cares nothing for royalties, who greatly enjoys the prestige that comes from book publication, and who is the busiest human being publishers have ever encountered. These men often know little about writing but resent the slightest editorial change in their manuscripts.

There are, nevertheless, compensations for the medical-book publisher. Dealing with doctors, both as authors and as book buyers, has been summed up as follows:

One must realize that the doctor as a person, especially the experienced doctor, comes to have a special psychology. After all, almost every day of his life, somebody's life is in his hands and he comes to have a . . . feeling of being . . . almost a rule unto himself. In its worst form, it becomes a terrific professional arrogance. In its finer form, it becomes a terrific professional devotion. . . . There is very little you can do to modify or change their expressions or their beliefs on professional matters. It's not too easy a field to sell, and yet, it is a very prosperous field, a book-respecting field, a book-buying field, and I would say that doctors as a class probably buy more books per capita than any other type of American citizen.[3]

Book Company people think that it is perhaps too soon to

[3] Frank L. Egner, recorded interview, pp. 5, 6.

These Blakiston dictionaries were published around the turn of the century. Early reviewers commended their handiness and low price; Dr. Gould's "A New Medical Dictionary," bound in leather with half morocco and thumb indexed, sold for $4.25.

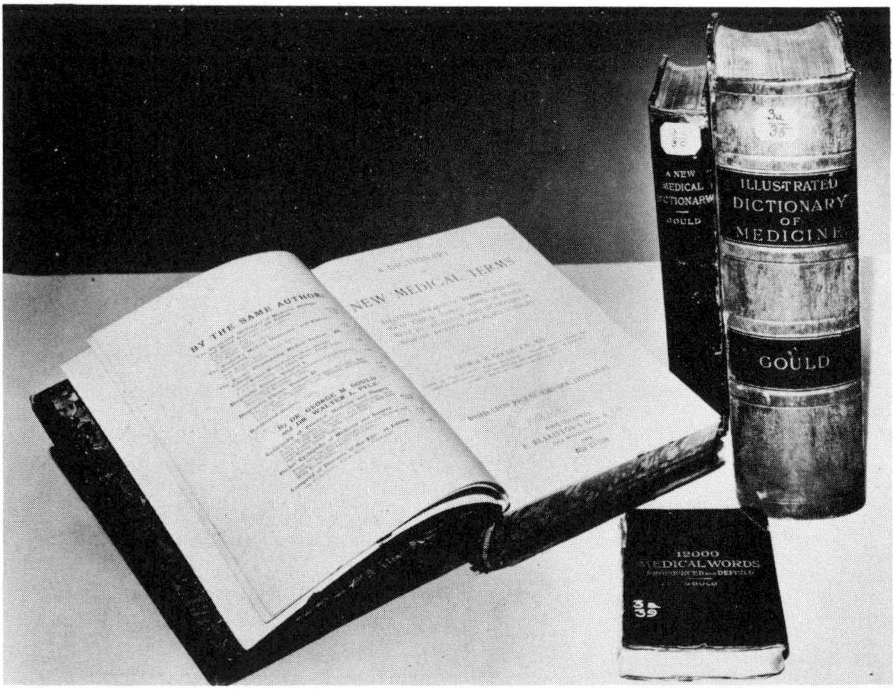

make positive statements about the future of the Blakiston Division. But there is an optimistic feeling that it

. . . has a chance of being the most important medical publisher in the country just because the power is here, the resources, the money, the drive, the will to do.[4]

3 We come now to a department of the Book Company that is not concerned with publishing in the accepted sense. Rather it is a service to industry and government. Occasionally books have been by-products of this department's projects; usually, however, its work has been of special or even confidential nature for an individual organization.

[4] *Ibid.*, p. 22.

An illustration from "Atlas of Eye Surgery" by R. Townley Paton, M.D., F.A.C.S., and Herbert M. Katzin, M.D., F.A.C.S., Daisy Stillwell, illustrator, 1957.

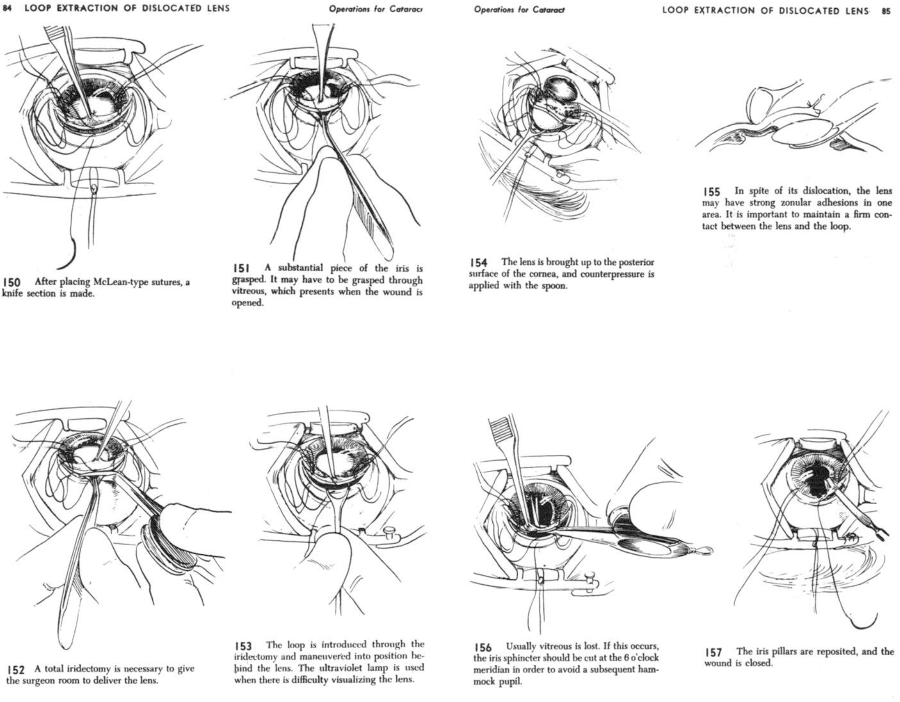
84 LOOP EXTRACTION OF DISLOCATED LENS
Operations for Cataract
Operations for Cataract
LOOP EXTRACTION OF DISLOCATED LENS 85
150 After placing McLean-type sutures, a knife section is made.
151 A substantial piece of the iris is grasped. It may have to be grasped through vitreous, which presents when the wound is opened.
154 The lens is brought up to the posterior surface of the cornea, and counterpressure is applied with the spoon.
155 In spite of its dislocation, the lens may have strong zonular adhesions in one area. It is important to maintain a firm contact between the lens and the loop.
152 A total iridectomy is necessary to give the surgeon room to deliver the lens.
153 The loop is introduced through the iridectomy and maneuvered into position behind the lens. The ultraviolet lamp is used when there is difficulty visualizing the lens.
156 Usually vitreous is lost. If this occurs, the iris sphincter should be cut at the 6 o'clock meridian in order to avoid a subsequent hammock pupil.
157 The iris pillars are reposited, and the wound is closed.

The Technical Writing Service idea is not original with McGraw-Hill. Several firms have performed it for a number of years. These have, however, usually done that and nothing else. The interesting aspect of our story is the way such a service functions as one department of a large and varied business most parts of which have something to contribute to its performance.

What such service does is this: it makes surveys or reports, statistical or otherwise, of some phase of industrial or government activity, such as the operations of the armed forces, management methods, or some new manufacturing or marketing system. It writes manuals on how to operate and maintain some new gadget in the armed forces or in a factory. It functions, in short, in almost every instance in which the power of print is necessary to a technical performance.

The first big job the Technical Writing Service took on was a project for the United States Navy which entailed the complete rewriting of a large body of doctrinal, tactical, and training material.

When this assignment got under way in 1951, it was probably the biggest single contract the Book Company had ever undertaken. It quickly outgrew the Green Building and occupied four floors of a building known as the Annex on 41st Street west of the McGraw-Hill building. It required, at the peak of activity, a full-time staff of 175 persons. In addition to the busy offices in the Annex, the company had to open an office in Washington to maintain liaison with the Navy Department. The work took three years to complete; it required some seventy volumes, and the cost to the government was approximately 1½ million dollars.

The satisfactory completion of this first large order (known in the company as CNO, from its origin in the office of the Chief of Naval Operations) established the service's reputation with the government. It was not surprising, therefore, that in 1955 the department received a call from a representative of the Atomic Energy Commission with a demand so prodigious that executives of the company still wonder how the responsible members of the staff were ever able to meet it. The order was to arrange, edit, illustrate, and prepare a typeset reproductible master for two volumes containing approximately 600 pages and 600 illustrations of highly technical information about the industrial handling of "Atoms for Peace," the raw materials of which were to be supplied by the Commission. In addition, there was to be an introductory volume complete with color pictures, describing these two books and six others that had already been prepared by the Commission, a booklet in color explaining the contents and physical layout of the United States technical exhibit at Geneva, and a booklet in color describing the operations of the "swimming pool" reactor that would be in operation at the exhibit. All of these latter publications were to be done in four languages (including Russian), the translators to be hired by Technical Writing Service. The Russian version, incidentally, turned out to be peculiarly difficult because the language had no known equivalents for some of the technical terms.

Now this, of course, was the kind of job McGraw-Hill was especially equipped to do, and the gentleman from the Commission was asked how long he would give them. The two technical volumes, he said, were required by June 1 and the other publications by July 15. It was then late in March!

This enterprise used almost every facility that had been developed over some fifty years, not only in the Book Company but in editorial offices of the publications as well and in the parent company's centralized services—such agencies as the production and illustration departments. It was a sort of climax to the whole history; a point at which all the long roads met. It is not surprising that this Geneva Package, as it is called, which fought its way through one of the most drastic schedules in publishing history and turned up on time at its appointed place should be an object of special pride in McGraw-Hill.

After the CNO job TWS became stabilized with an average force of fifty technical writers and editors. With some variations, its business became stabilized at a million dollars a year. It is a service for which there is a constant demand and it is likely to continue. The men in charge of it have learned the ropes; they have made an extensive study of government regulations—often extremely difficult to follow—and they have mastered the technique of administering the projects.

4 When the Book Company decided to publish nontechnical books for the general public to be sold through the nation's general bookstores, they called the department that produced these books Whittlesey House. The reason for this was, as we have seen and as an executive of that part of the business explains:

> We were afraid that there would be confusion as to discount, as to type of literature, if we had the same name.[5]

Later, however, they realized that the fear had been groundless and that the name had led to confusion rather than clarity.

> Whittlesey is a tough name to spell. People didn't associate it with McGraw-Hill, and we had greater chances for strength in the department allied with McGraw-Hill than we did being divorced from it in the public's mind.[6]

So the name was changed again and in 1950 Whittlesey House became the Trade Department of the McGraw-Hill Book company.

> We still retained the title Whittlesey House . . . for the junior books, feeling, just as we had felt before that trade books were different from technical, that junior books were different from trade and technical.[7]

Meanwhile, however, in the score of years before the change was made, there had been sweeping changes in the American book business. During World War II, the general bookstores had found technical books extremely profitable. This established a

[5] Harold W. McGraw, Jr., recorded interview, p. 2.
[6] *Ibid.*
[7] *Ibid.*, pp. 3–4.

trend which continues and the larger book retailers as well as the book departments of department stores find the technical book a necessary and a lucrative item. Thus the old rigid distinction has largely broken down and McGraw-Hill technical books are sold through the Trade Department, an operation which keeps that department in the black, regardless of the element of guesswork and gamble that is always a part of trade-book publishing in the strict sense of the term. Here, too, is another reason for putting the McGraw-Hill imprint on all books alike. Because of the large employment of all kinds of people, and especially women in industrial war work, technical books sold to what were really amateur workers—persons who had never read anything before but fiction or biography or, in short, *trade books.* This merger of reader interests has been of immense importance to our society.

Whittlesey House, as we know, began with a handicap. In the editing and selling of trade books other general houses had a far longer experience. One or two of them, indeed, had been in business for about a century before McGraw-Hill entered the field. The lucky breaks at the start, such as *Life Begins at Forty,* did not establish literary prestige equal to that of the older houses. The books with the highest standing were those that dealt with the social sciences, but here there is a twilight zone between the Trade and other departments.

Whittlesey House went gingerly into fiction. It did, however, hit the jackpot in 1945 with its first novel, Adria Locke Langley's *A Lion Is in the Streets,* a conspicuous best seller. Since then it has published, with more or less success, novels by Jesse Stuart, Mari Sandoz, Taylor Caldwell, Elizabeth Ogilvie, Kay Boyle, Mark Schorer, and others; but in the complete catalogue of McGraw-Hill books we find today only about a score of fiction titles—novels, that is, that are still in print—and few of these are of a very profound nature. The company has been reluctant to follow the custom of many trade-book houses which has been compared to horse racing. These publishers, it is said, put in a large number of horses at the beginning of a race with the hope

The late Peter Marshall with his wife, Catherine, and their young son, Peter John.

that a couple of them will break away. Through sheer force of numbers, they believe some success must come, and obviously that happens. Whether this apparently wasteful policy is a good one is debatable, but it is certain that each race leaves a certain number of also-ran authors unhappy.

Outside of fiction, however, the department has had some notable successes. Books with a religious or inspirational color, such as Catherine Marshall's *A Man Called Peter* (1951) and its successors, have attained sales figures that any publisher might envy. The same is true of Bishop Fulton Sheen's *Peace of Soul* and its successors. In prestige few books in recent years have surpassed the standard of the Boswell papers. Six volumes from the

As armed police stand guard, librarians at Yale University prepare to place the Boswell Papers, world's greatest collection of eighteenth-century manuscripts, in the Yale Library.

collection have been published and there will be many more to come. The negotiations for the rights to these papers were some of the most difficult and complex in the recent history of publishing and in them McGraw-Hill acted as liaison between the owner of the papers and Yale University which bought the papers from the owner. The owner was a night owl and would carry on no discussions until after dark. The McGraw-Hill editor was obliged, therefore, to spend two or three nights a week over a period of some four months talking to this gentleman before a sale could be consummated. Indeed, as this editor recalled, only on two occasions had he seen this man's face by daylight. One was on the day of the closing in New Haven, and the other was

. . . when I served as a pallbearer at his funeral. All my other meetings were in the dead of night and often in the very wee hours.[8]

There have also been some well-received biographies—of Florence Nightingale, of Robert Benchley, of Margaret Truman, Stonewall Jackson, Charles Darwin, Thomas Huxley, of Young Sam Johnson, and of Joan of Arc—certainly a variegated list. In history a high spot was reached with Cecil Woodham-Smith's *The Reason Why,* a real classic of the Crimean War. Two geographical titles of special interest are *The Coral Sea* and *Monsoon Seas* both by Alan Villiers, skipper of the *Mayflower II,* written for the Oceans of the World Series. In this the Trade Department has followed the example of other departments in promoting continuing publishing programs.

Whittlesey House entered the humor field early, first with Rosemary Taylor and her *Chicken Every Sunday* and later with such authors as Louise Baker and Richard Armour. The latter has achieved considerable success with his "It All Started With" series, burlesquing history.

Some outstanding gift books have also been developed by the department, including such titles as Richard Pratt's *Treasury of Early American Homes,* Floyd Clymer's *Treasury of Early American Automobiles,* and Robert C. Murphy's *Land Birds of America.* Of the several anthologies published, Charles Laughton's *Tell Me a Story* is perhaps the most successful.

Much of Whittlesey House's growth and development has been based on such how-to and reference books as *Betty Crocker's Picture Cook Book, The Singer Sewing Book,* Aaron Copland's *What to Listen for in Music,* Gilbert Chase's *America's Music,* Dorothy Baruch's *New Ways in Discipline,* and Roger Whitman's *First Aid for the Ailing House.*

One small but growing section of the Trade Department, whose products sometimes spill over into other departments, publishes what are called Junior Books. On these juveniles of many

[8] Edward C. Aswell, recorded interview, p. 49.

McGraw-Hill author Alan Villiers looks over a scale model of the original "Mayflower."

sorts for all ages, the Whittlesey House imprint is retained. There is a link here with the orginal McGraw-Hill effort before a trade department was thought of. This is the attention given books on science and technology for boys and girls: first rungs on the ladder toward the advanced publications that form the McGraw-Hill nucleus. Young readers of these volumes may well be stimulated toward technical careers.

The increasing interest of older children in geophysical facts, and in atomic, electronic, and biological directions is evident from the mounting sales of such books as *Exploring Earth and Space* by Margaret Hyde, *Electronics for Young People* by Jeanne Bendick (now in its third edition with a sale of 45,000 copies), *White Land of Adventure* by Walter Sullivan, *Horses and Their*

A few of the current Whittlesey House books.

Ancestors by William A. Burns of the American Museum of Natural History, and the volumes of the Children's World of Science Library.

Whittlesey House, however, has branched into many other fields, ranging all the way from picture books for children too young to read to novels, sports stories, and biographies for the teen-agers. *The Happy Lion,* published in 1954, achieved international celebrity, was given a German award for the "best picture book of the year," was translated into seven foreign languages, and started a series of Happy Lion books. It had the

An illustration from Gian-Carlo Menotti's "Amahl and the Night Visitors," 1952.

unusual distinction of being published in both East Germany and West Germany. The creators of this book, Louise Fatio and Roger Duvoisin, are expected to continue the Happy Lion sequence indefinitely.

For somewhat older children, the Miss Pickerell stories by Ellen McGregor, the Mountain Pony stories by Harry Larom, and the Anatole books by Eve Titus and Paul Galdone are successful repeaters. The junior book people are especially proud of Gian Carlo Menotti's *Amahl and the Night Visitors,* dramatized every Christmas by the NBC network.

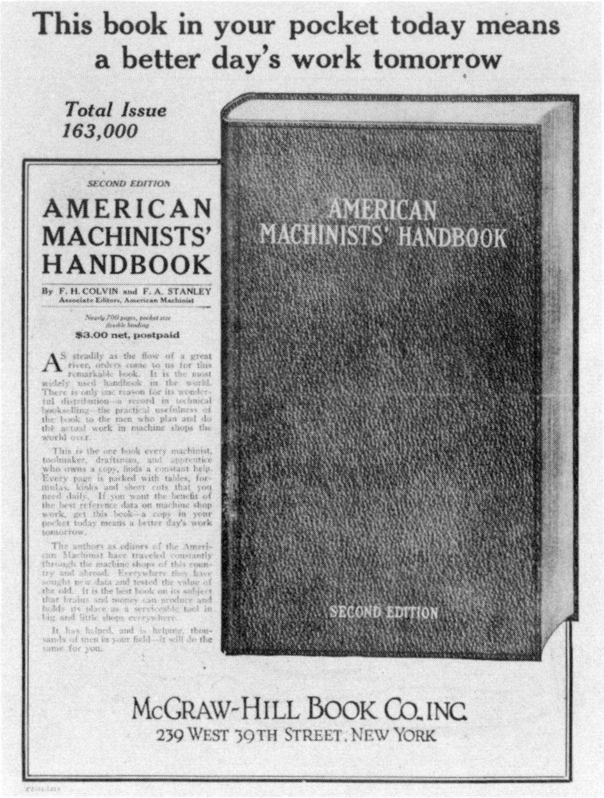
This book in your pocket today means a better day's work tomorrow
Total Issue 163,000
SECOND EDITION
AMERICAN MACHINISTS' HANDBOOK
By F. H. COLVIN and F. A. STANLEY
Associate Editors, American Machinist
Nearly 700 pages, pocket size flexible binding
$3.00 net, postpaid
AS steadily as the flow of a great river, orders come to us for this remarkable book. It is the most widely used handbook in the world. There is only one reason for its wonderful distribution—a record in technical bookselling—the practical usefulness of the book to the men who plan and do the actual work in machine shops the world over.
This is the one book every machinist, toolmaker, draftsman, and apprentice who owns a copy, finds a constant help. Every page is packed with tables, formulas, kinks and short cuts that you need daily. If you want the benefit of the best reference data on machine shop work, get this book—a copy in your pocket today means a better day's work tomorrow.
The authors as editors of the American Machinist have traveled constantly through the machine shops of this country and abroad. Everywhere they have sought new data and tested the value of the old. It is the best book on its subject that brains and money can produce and holds its place as a serviceable tool in big and little shops everywhere.
It has helped, and is helping, thousands of men in your field—it will do the same for you.
AMERICAN MACHINISTS' HANDBOOK
SECOND EDITION
McGRAW-HILL BOOK CO. INC.
239 WEST 39TH STREET, NEW YORK

Early advertising for McGraw-Hill handbooks.

5 More in line with the older McGraw-Hill traditions, is the Industrial and Business Book Department. We saw the beginning of this in the Book Company's earliest days when Foss and Caldwell started mail-order sales. The books sold in this way were generally highly specialized technical books which were intended as actual tools for engineers and technicians to work with. Through the years as more and more specialties arose, as well as entire new industries, the need for such books increased to a point where a publishing department became dedicated to them. As examples of this sort of publication we may pick at random the

The 1916 edition of "Mechanical Engineer's Handbook" by Lionel S. Marks and the 1958 edition.

titles: *Electronic Analog Computers, Motivation in Advertising,* and *Pump Selection and Application.* The books originating in this Industrial and Business Book Department are no longer sold by mail only; today both bookstores and colleges are channels for their distribution.

The department is especially proud of its handbooks. The distinction between a handbook and the examples just given of business or industrial books lies, among other things, in its authorship. The handbook is a collection of articles each by an expert in the particular phase of a general subject. It has an editor who picks the authors and arranges their contributions into a useful, comprehensive reference book. Handbooks range from those covering an extremely broad field, such as the *American Institute of Physics Handbook,* to the special *Handbook of Fastening and Joining Metal Parts.*

The long, profitable sequence of these books has developed through the half century of the Book Company's life, beginning, as we remember, with Colvin and Stanley's *American Machinists' Handbook,* the earliest venture in this direction and the longest-lived of all. More than fifty handbooks are in print today. They are on the average the largest of the McGraw-Hill books, running from 1,000 to 3,000 pages. As many as 100 authors may contribute to a single handbook.

The Industrial and Business Book Department is more closely in touch with the Publishing Company than any other. Editors of the papers are constantly consulted for advice as to authors and material and circulation managers provide prospect lists for circularization by mail.

6 A striking operational feature the Book Company has built, is its across-the-board program. This has broken down what in some houses are watertight bulkheads between the departments. Through interdepartmental meetings and broadcast memoranda the members of each department are told just what is being done in all the others and all are expected to feel responsible for the success of every product the company puts out. Thus a salesman for the College Department feels that it is up to him to tell his customers of any trade, business, or technical book that may interest them. If an editor of the Technical Education Department finds that one of his authors has a biography, a history, or a popular book on social science in the back of his head—or if a friend has one—no time is wasted in telling the Trade Department's editors about it. Let us suppose, for example, that a mathematician such as Lewis Carroll is amusing his children with such a story as *Alice in Wonderland* and one of these across-the-board people finds out about it. Certainly it will not be long before the head of the Junior Book Division of the Trade Department (called Whittlesey House) hears of it and gets after the versatile gentleman.

No sales representative, no matter how specialized his line, is allowed to go on the road without a general knowledge of projects and programs in other men's offices and without complete references that he may consult whenever questions are asked. Certain departments are so close that this information is often highly profitable. Take, for example, the large markets for juveniles that may be exploited by the traveler from the School Department. Again, there are very few college bookstores that do not sell the novels, biographies, or social science books that are extracurricular, yet always in demand among students.

What makes this across-the-board policy so successful at McGraw-Hill is the fact that each salesman and his department get *sales credit* and profit margin for every book sold in his market, no matter what department published the book. This incentive, though it causes a great deal of extra bookkeeping, results in hundreds of plus sales every day.

This cooperative practice brings us to the question of centralization and decentralization that has occurred at many points in our story. We have seen how autonomous these departments of the Book Company have been; yet there is this central magnet that draws them all together. Let us see now what sort of centralization is desirable in the parent company: what services, for example, or consultative bodies are useful or necessary to every function that is performed in the Green Building—whether it be the publication of book, magazine, film, or news letter. This sort of centralization, or "federal government," has been found, over the years and after much trial and error, to be highly economical under present conditions in our business world.

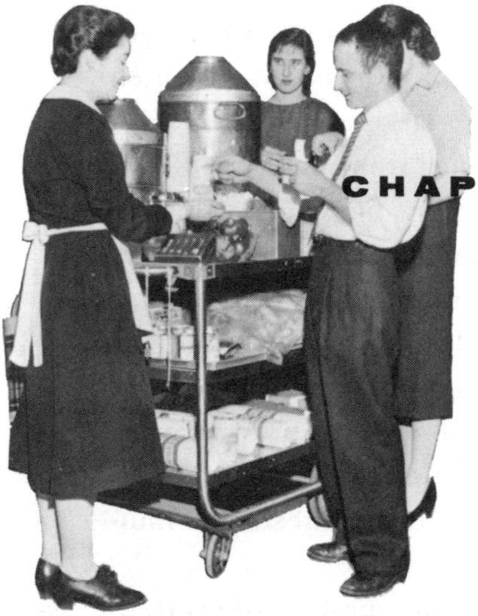

CHAPTER TWENTY-NINE

Behind the Scenes

Having observed the complexity of operations that the McGraw-Hill Company has come to perform, the question naturally arises: How is it done? What is the magic behind the curtain? What devices are there in the Green Building that keep so large a variety of machinery ticking in a synchronized rhythm?

We have caught glimpses of this. We saw how World News Service was helping to save the figurative editorial shoe leather. We have seen coordinating mechanisms in the Book Company. We have seen bold excursions into finance that have helped the organization as a whole in times of crisis. But certain aspects are still mysterious. What, for instance, keeps the editors uniformly abreast of the world's economic phenomena and advises them of the economic future? And how does it come to pass that, though the papers are so largely autonomous, those who work on them are constantly conscious of certain editorial, circulation, and advertising standards that must apply to them all? Somewhere behind the scenes there must be fountainheads accessible to all and, indeed, necessary to all.

Some of these are important not only within but outside the Green Building. People in business and industry have come to know that much of the statistical or prophetic material in the papers is not simply the result of a single editor's research but that behind him stands a trained body of experts engaged in full-time exploration. Advertisers have come to recognize something special in the approach of a McGraw-Hill salesman, something that carries a common hallmark regardless of any particular paper, a sort of brand that must have been applied at some central point.

This central machinery is not a late product. Gradually it has evolved to meet the contingencies of the times. By 1955 it had, however, acquired impressive proportions. Because much of it is unique, it will be useful to examine certain of the departments as an aid to evaluating this company in the large.

2 Independent, a law unto itself, and touching every phase of publishing in the Green Building stands an institution known as the Department of Economics. It is, in fact, a sort of liaison between the broad study of economics and the business world. It has been called a halfway house on the road that runs from the university to the offices of industrial management. More and more in late years the men in these offices have felt the need of knowledge of world economies; on the other hand, the editorial departments of all the McGraw-Hill publications—books and magazines—have wanted a medium for getting in closer, more permanent touch with the businesses and industries they deal with. The Department of Economics looks both ways. Its ultimate purpose, of course, is to amplify and refine the editorial output. In this way its work may be thought of as an internal service, but the impact of that service is felt far outside the Green Building, not only in all corners of industry but in the educational world as well. The results of its effort are imponderable in the sense that tangible dollars of income and outgo cannot be recorded upon a balance sheet. Yet its profits in terms of good will and usable information are such that publishers, editors, and business managers throughout the organization have come to think of it as an essential agency to whose cost they are glad to contribute.

The staff of the department consists of economists, university-trained in their discipline, many of them holders of Ph.D. degrees. Thus they have a broad educational background that extends beyond immediate business operations into economic theory. They are expected to keep in touch with developments all over the world: of raw-material resources, of supply and demand, of government controls, of means of finance, and of transportation; to translate this information into international terms and make it available to anyone whose business it affects. Thus they are able to talk to a manager whose thinking may have been confined within the circle of his own industry, about conditions in other industries or other places which may materially affect him.

Into the offices of the Economics Department comes a constant stream of industrialists, managers, businessmen, financiers and, indeed, educators. All these people are seeking the kind of information that can be assembled only by a research that extends, so to speak, across the board. Mostly they want to know what is going to happen tomorrow, next year. They are looking for crystal-ball gazers whose feet, however, are firmly on the ground and whose forecasting instruments are attuned to the probabilities by a volume of statistics and a careful study of trends. The steel man or the rubber man, for example, wants to know how far he should expand in the next few years. Each of these will have to discover the trend in the automotive industry before he can decide. The Economics Department can instantly supply figures showing trends over ten years or more plus a reliable estimate made after a study of all contributory conditions of collateral growth in the immediate future. One program which the department has especially emphasized is the compiling of indexes of industrial capacity.

An index is described as "a statistical tool, measuring the change in a series of figures—plus or minus—from a base period. The figure in the base period is expressed as equal to 100." The fifteen indexes calculated by the department—two weekly, nine monthly, three quarterly, and one annually—measure trends in production, income, prices, capacity, and new orders. These are published in various McGraw-Hill publications.

The visitors from outside are given the information they want free of charge. They do, however, pay in one sense for this, for they in turn give the department the information it wants about a particular area. In this way there comes about an accumulation of knowledge which, when analyzed, catalogued, and indexed, provides much of the resources the department needs. The industrialists are glad to cooperate in this way. In the end the ultimate purpose is reached: there is a reservoir from which every editor, and many a publisher as well, may draw. These people are becoming more and more dependent upon the Department of Economics every year to keep their publications accurate and up to date.

The monthly reports that emerge from this scholastic enterprise that sits in an office building which looks as if it were only concerned with commerce have an uncommon aspect. One would expect these economic explorations, heavy with statistics as they must be, to be dreary reading. They are necessary reading, to be sure; but you would expect to approach anything of the sort with a sigh, drawing your chair up to the desk, adjusting your glasses, and getting ready for an endurance test. Yet once you start on these, you find you could read them equally well in a hammock, for they are highly entertaining and even, in parts, relaxing. Running through the statistical matter is a vein of imaginative, creative writing. The reports are richly spiced with humor. In their heaviest parts, there are gay or ironic references to political blunders, popular prejudices, science-fiction trips to Mars, newspaper errors, haywire books, the shibboleths of bankers, the paradoxical utterances of pontifical economists, as well as Madison Avenue extravagances, or the comic-opera acts of the Kremlin.

To us [reads the introduction to a recent report] one of the more attractive aspects of the development of space travel along with an increasing weight of evidence that there are flying saucers, is that it will elevate to credibility the theory that our remote ancestors arrived on earth on an errant spaceship rather than crawling out of the slime. Aesthetically we would much prefer to think that our grandparents, in the nth power, arrived as first-class passengers on a spaceship rather than spending generations in the ooze as lizards, etc. It's getting to seem just about as reasonable, too.[1]

Another report speaks of a letter received from a steel company evidently written by a secretary:

As requested, I am enclosing a copy of the address entitled "The Outlook for the Steel Industry and its Complications for the Economy." We don't blame her a bit. Implications these days are usually complications.[2]

There is a "Note on inflation":

The Michigan legislature has raised from $50 to $100 the amount of money you must steal to commit a felony rather than a misdemeanor in that Commonwealth.[3]

A midsummer report begins with the relaxing news:

July is not the ideal month for weighty words about the outlook for business activity . . . when 30% of the industrial labor force is on vacation. And while we suspect that the vacation business is itself an industry of more importance than many . . . an accurate index of vacationing has yet to be devised.[4]

[1] Department of Economics, Monthly Report, June 25, 1957, p. 1.
[2] *Ibid.*, May 27, 1927, p. 1.
[3] *Ibid.*
[4] *Ibid.*, July 30, 1957, pp. I, 1.

In the same report "because of its seasonal appeal" are five pages on "Antarctica—or the Economics of Icebergs."

> The known economic resources of Antarctica consist of (1) ice, (2) whales, and (3) wind power. . . .
>
> Though man can freeze to death in Antarctica, oddly enough he doesn't catch cold. It's too cold for most germs to survive. When the Jet Age comes along, a trip to the South Pole may finally provide the perfect cure for the common cold.[5]

This whole piece is as fascinating a story as one is likely to find in, say, the *National Geographic Magazine.* Surely if some of the heavier articles and books on economics were occasionally salted in this way they would be more palatable.

It is not surprising, then, that these reports are eagerly awaited and read not only by the editors but by the salesmen, too, who often carry them on their travels and bootleg them into offices all over the land. But in addition to these reports, intended only for Green Building consumption, there are also elaborate printed brochures available to top management executives everywhere. They are in no sense promotional. One called *Business Plans for New Plants and Equipment: 1957–1960* gives predictions about prospective plants and equipment, industrial capacity, and growth for research and development expenditures.

One operation by the Department of Economics attracted special attention in the educational world. It has also helped promote a national cause which has long attracted the top aid of the top foundations.

This operation was a campaign to obtain funds from industry to raise the salaries of college teachers. The program was carried out through the medium of what are known as "company editorials"; editorials that are carried simultaneously in all the McGraw-Hill papers. The company editorial is an old institution formerly signed by the president but today accompanied by a statement that it is prepared by the Department of Economics "to help increase public knowledge and understanding of important nationwide de-

[5] *Ibid.*, pp. III, 1, 2.

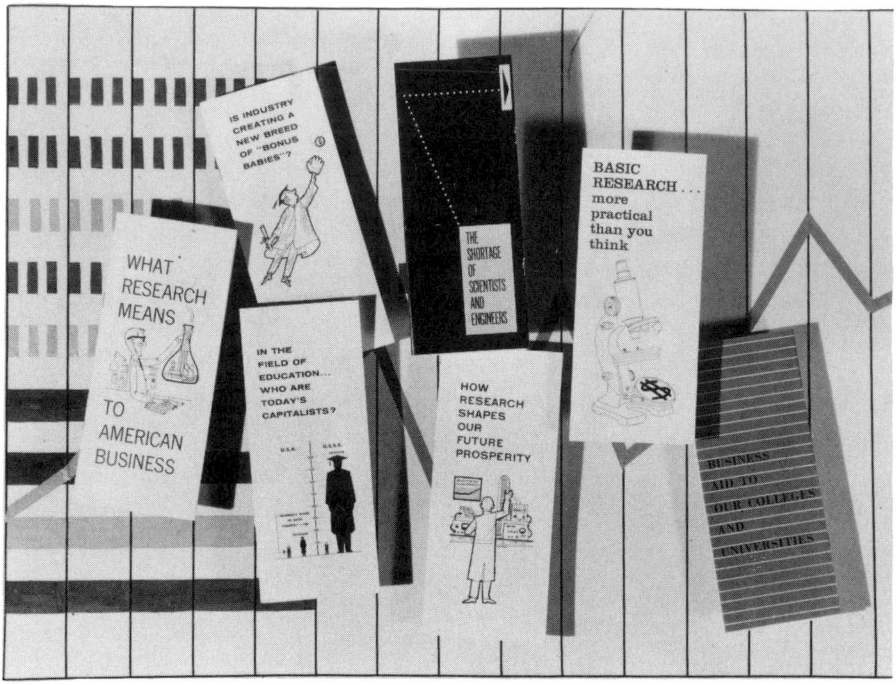

Reprints of some company editorials prepared by the Department of Economics.

velopments that are of particular concern to the business and professional community served by our industrial and technical publications."

The editorial that set the key of the college series was entitled, "Our Colleges and Universities Are Living on Borrowed Time . . . Time Borrowed from Underpaid Faculty Members." This revealed the shocking fact that, in the United States as a whole, college teachers were worse off in terms of their capacity to pay the cost of living in 1954 than they had been in 1939, whereas industrial workers were 48 per cent better off and physicians were 80 per cent better off.

There were seven of these editorials in the series and of them the head of the department says:

I should think that it would be correctly stated . . . that they had as a whole a tremendous impact, by far the greatest impact of any series of editorials we have run. . . . [6]

Obviously, such an effort for educational improvement is in the tradition we have observed dating back to the schoolteacher founder of the company. So, too, is the training through which the staff is constantly going in this department. Indeed, the excellence of this training sometimes works a hardship. Several times banks or similar institutions have turned when they needed an economist to McGraw-Hill instead of to a university, and occasionally one of the best men is lured away.

3 Although the Department of Economics is the highest of the McGraw-Hill "schools" in terms of the breadth of its scope, it is by no means the only one in the Green Building. There are, for example, editorial courses: courses in evaluation of substance and journalistic presentation, special training in writing, layout, arrangement, illustration, typography, and so on, to which every new editor is exposed.

So whatever one may think of the literary quality of the business papers, it is not accidental that they conform to certain standards that are company-wide. These are taught in centralized instruction periods and apply equally to *Business Week* and *Food Engineering*, to *Electrical World* and *Fleet Owner*. Clarity, simplicity, and directness are the watchwords in writing and the writing must cooperate with a graphic presentation that can be quickly understood by a reader with little time at his disposal. Nostalgic critics may deplore the disappearance of more leisurely, reflective articles of the sort that once gave value to bound volumes of periodicals but such things would be lost in the quick-moving world of today and McGraw-Hill editors know it. The business paper must, above all things be useful to its readers, and whereas businessmen were once able to put their feet on the desk and

[6] Dexter M. Keezer, recorded interview, p. 11.

lean back to a long, gas-lit reading of a literary presentation, the incessant interruption by new, hurtling events precludes any such study in this mid-century.

We have, therefore, the direct, almost telegraphic headline, the quick, topical first paragraph that leads the reader into the very core of the subject, the elimination of all superfluous wordage, the semantic precision, and the attention-getting-and-holding techniques that have come to prevail in all McGraw-Hill papers. These things are not easy to learn. Nor are they easy to codify into a formula. They have evolved through experience, been acquired gradually through the years of extremely intimate relationship between editor and reader. The new editor learns them from exposure to them rather than by having them drilled into him, and the so-called training courses are intended to intensify that exposure.

The larger classes are held in the company dining room, between meals, on the thirty-third floor of the Green Building; the smaller, more intimate ones are held in the penthouse. A recent comprehensive course running for four 2-hour sessions and limited to twenty participants to allow for good cross discussion covered:

1. Historical background—how research revolutionized illustrated publishing
2. Structure in layout
3. Structure in text
4. Display editing—heads, decks, captions, all-type articles

This fourth subject is given special attention. It is a curious fact that in magazines as well as in newspapers, heads and decks frequently do not belong with the pieces they top. Sometimes this happens because they are added by one who did not write the article and who has not read it carefully; again they are put on to give the piece a sensational look not justified by its substance. Even McGraw-Hill papers have by no means been guiltless

Editorial staff of "Electrical Merchandising" attending class on editorial presentation.

of this offense in the past and it has become a major effort to train writers to integrate the headlines with the text.

Editorial workshops have discussed such topics as "Why Johnny Can't Correct Page Proofs Effectively," "Making Timeless Stories Timely," "Legal Problems That Editors Should Know About," "How to Write Readable Sentences," "How to Work with Photographers Effectively," and "Marks of a Professional Magazine." The opportunity to ask questions and explore details makes these sessions educational as well as instructive. Other meetings bring editorial and advertising people together so that they may understand functions other than their own. Occasionally a film will be shown to point up the lectures.

From the number of editors the organization requires, it is evident that classes and workshops are kept busy. This number has now risen to the rather impressive total of 622. Then there are the schools for salesmen. Selling in America has gone through an evolution and a revolution. In an economy of abundance it has become increasingly difficult. The old-time, hard-drinking, loud-dressing, ungrammatical character who used to bore, bludgeon, or wheedle his prospect into buying could not get by today's receptionist. A McGraw-Hill executive who once dealt with such persons remembers a point of transition from the old to the new when a space buyer complained of one rough diamond who spit tobacco juice into the wastebasket all the time he was selling his magazine. Again there was the point at which the salesman no longer felt that he had to drink with his prospect.

Nowadays advertising managers prefer college graduates. They note how a man dresses. They will caution a salesman against wearing something unexpected or startling. A prospect, they say, may be so fascinated by a salesman's tie that he won't hear anything the man says. Did he buy that tie himself? the prospect will be thinking. Did his wife give it to him? A girl friend? Has he got a lot of other ties like that? These unspoken questions will so preoccupy the person he is trying to sell that not a word of the excellent persuasion about *Business Week* or *Engineering News-Record* will penetrate. Wear garters! one McGraw-Hill sales manager has insisted. Then the prospect will not be distracted by skinny or obese legs sticking out of what the manager calls "bobby socks."

The McGraw-Hill magazine sales force is built from raw material recruited largely from college and university graduating classes. This raw material is put in a training pool or reservoir from which men are drawn to fill positions in company research, classified advertising sales, and circulation sales. In this way, by the time a vacancy occurs, there is a person to fill it who has become thoroughly imbued with the company traditions and policy. It is then the practice to make as many of the sales staff as possible permanent employees destined, if they earn it, to promotion to executive positions.

To become a member of a pool, a man is as carefully examined

"Salesmen keep eyes and ears open for good prospects." Cartoon from McGraw-Hill Text-Film Department's series on salesmanship.

as if he were entering a government or a university position. After answering some penetrating questionnaires about his education, his family and community backgrounds, and his health record, he is given an aptitude test by an outside agency. It is because of this screening, company executives feel, that the people who sell McGraw-Hill circulation and advertising today are welcomed in so many business offices. And there is the further factor of *esprit de corps* within the company—something on which of late years there has been special emphasis.

4 Those imponderable qualities, loyalty and *esprit de corps,* cannot be synthetically constructed. They must evolve out of an infinite multitude of small actions and events over the years: a man forgiven, someone patted on the back and encouraged or given a raise without asking for it; an executive who remembers names, who inquires after an employee's wife and children, who helps a subordinate out of some desperate personal dilemma—all these build into a body of good will. It may never be forgotten, for example, that Old Man McGraw stood by an editor who had made a conspicuous mistake or quietly aided some victim of the depression or that Old Man Hill stopped each morning at every desk to give a friendly greeting or took a personal interest in the bereaved family of some faithful employee. A company, therefore, may be said to have a memory. Into that memory go hates and bitterness as well as loyalties and confidence; but the ultimate *esprit*—as it is called, because no Anglo-Saxon word quite does the job—arrives when the happier remembrances dominate.

Like every other organization McGraw-Hill has had its ups and downs of morale. There have been times when internal politics were rife, times of scattered discontents, years of doubt. As we have seen, the company was so hard hit by the depression that its survival is remembered in some quarters as almost miraculous. There seems to have been, however, even in the depths, a hard core of loyalty that has brought recovery or fresh change.

CHAPTER THIRTY

Tomorrow?

Men who have lived long with McGraw-Hill are sometimes asked: What of its future? What are the plans for expansion or change? The questions, they say, can only be answered by another question: What is the future of industry, of technology?

Whatever growth or revolution the coming years may bring in those aspects of our civilization—and it looks as if there will be plenty of both—McGraw-Hill will reflect. As we look back over its history, we see constant adaptation—more rapid as the tempo of the change has accelerated its pace. There has scarcely been a moment at which an accurate forecast could have been made for the publication scope of the succeeding five years: today a year may turn up something new. Such papers, for example, as

Nucleonics, may be projected suddenly by an event; others, such as *Control Engineering,* may have a slower gestation, nurtured by a trend.

But changes have come from other causes. In such an organization as this, where every editor's hand is on the pulse of his readers, there must be an adaptation to altering human and social tempers. Bombarded by pictures, print, and voices attacking him with news and opinions, the American businessman has built a sort of psychological wall about himself not easy to penetrate even by the news he needs. As we have seen, he has no disposition to read long, informative articles—even if he had the time. Thus even the information that is essential to him must be presented in a way that is not only attractive but compelling. We have observed this side of the coin in several individual cases. There is, however, another side.

The technical man, especially in his learning years, must have reading in large, often difficult doses. Before he arrives at the "harassed" administrative stage in management, as more and more engineers are doing every day, he must devote long, slow hours to the digesting of precisely the material the men in the top echelons can have no patience with.

Publishers of technical and business papers have had to take these diverse needs into account. They have come to know that they must adapt their magazines to one or the other; in the modern world they cannot do both. McGraw-Hill has chosen, for most of its papers, the quick, newsy approach the executive wants. But it has done this with the knowledge that other sources of information have come into our world to take care of the other need. And McGraw-Hill itself is creating many of those sources.

An anecdote sometimes told in the Green Building illustrates this. A manager of *Engineering News-Record,* a graduate engineer, met an old engineering friend of whom he asked, "What do you think of the job *News-Record* is doing?"

"Well," said the friend, "it's not the paper it used to be. I used to read Hill's *Engineering News* and McGraw's *Engineering Rec-*

ord religiously. Then with the merger I went on with the *News-Record.* I still read it. But it's not the old paper I used to read and I read it now for a different reason."

"And with the same interest?"

"I wouldn't say that. Once upon a time the *News* and the *Record* and a few other papers were the chief means available to the civil engineer to keep up with his profession. Together these papers composed a body of technical progress that was available nowhere else. Those bound volumes comprise the archives of the profession over a long period. The files of those papers are still essential in every engineering library.

"But times have changed. The more recent technical material has gone into books. It has appeared in the technical papers presented and discussed by the engineering societies and is published in their proceedings. At the same time a pressing need has developed for the news of the day-to-day, week-to-week developments in the profession and in the industries that are dependent on it. This function is just as important as the other and now it is admirably performed by your paper. I still feel that I could not keep up with the progress of the profession without *Engineering News-Record.*"

We see then that the periodical has come to fulfill the function it would perhaps have done all along if the other vehicles had been there. But they were not, or not in sufficient volume. The papers, therefore, tried to do both things: to give the news and to be a compendium of technical information.

McGraw-Hill, then, has adapted itself to the change by publishing both the news and the books. Much that was formerly carried by the periodical publications is handled by the Book Company. In this way it has been able to keep up with the enlargement of the various technical fields and the stepped-up tempo of their movement. At the same time it has come to serve the vast new area of management.

It is impossible, however, to generalize too broadly. In such new fields as atomic energy and automation, the magazines *Nu-*

cleonics, Control Engineering, and others are largely dedicated to basic technics and techniques, still in early stages of development.

As we come to the end of our story we may see the beginnings of new enterprises in the publications field. A new paper, *Purchasing Week,* is expected to fill a need long felt in a wide area. A year before the launching of the Russian satellite, Sputnik, the first issue of *Missile Engineering*[1] appeared. Here is a medium suited to deal with phenomena yet unexplored.

2 Editors in the Book Company are constantly taking the temperature of the reading public and preparing to meet its future needs. That public, incidentally, is behaving unexpectedly under the pressures of mass communication.

When motion pictures first came into their maturity, some publishers despaired about the power of print. Yet despite the progress of visual education and documentary record, the sale of books and magazines went up. This rise was not due merely to the increase in population but rather to cultural advance. When radio broadcasting arrived, obsolescence of the printing press was again expected. But nothing of the sort happened. On the contrary circulation of many of the general magazines grew to the point where, in view of rising production costs, it became a liability. At the same time the demand for paperbound books showed that the power of print had risen to a new high. Finally when television came and publishers were wondering whether they had better convert their shops into studios, it turned out that the new device was actually stimulating reading—at least in certain fields.

Documentaries, historical presentations, and quiz shows, for example, have sent thousands of people to the libraries—people who had never before read anything but the morning newspaper or an occasional magazine. Such vivid reconstruction of past events as "You Are There" and "Cavalcade" on television and

[1] Since February, 1958, this has been retitled *Space Technology.*

Tomorrow?

radio have excited viewers and listeners about the historic periods and their backgrounds. The rash of quizzes that followed "The $64,000 Question" has spread the notion that anyone may become well informed whether he be a taxi driver or a shoemaker and that his acquired knowledge may win him a fortune. On the heels of these things new dictionaries and encyclopedias have appeared on every side.

The McGraw-Hill Book Company has been fully aware of this trend and has projected a large encyclopedic program. A planned *Encyclopedia of Science and Technology* is expected to extend through ten volumes. There will be some 20,000 alphabetically

Cover of "Aviation Week including Space Technology," February 24, 1958.

Home office of The McGraw-Hill "Encyclopedia of Science and Technology" in Charlottesville, Virginia.

arranged articles by acknowledged authorities. A prospectus has announced that the volumes "will serve as a comprehensive reference work for the student, teacher, engineer, technician, scientist, and others seeking information on scientific and engineering subjects. Readability and comprehension, in general, will be at the college underclassman level."

Another encyclopedic project is the fifteen-volume *Encyclopedia of World Art* published in collaboration with an Italian publisher. The Italian-language edition will be published in Rome, and about a year later English-language editions will be published simultaneously in New York, Toronto, and London. The quarto volumes will contain some 10 million words of text, hundreds of maps and line drawings, and almost 7,000 plates of which more than 1,300 will be in color.

The signing of the contract for the "Encyclopedia of World Art" in Rome in May, 1957.

All these trends cannot help but encourage those who are concerned with the future American reading potential. There are, sure enough, possible pitfalls on the way. Costs of production which show no signs of decrease are certain to reduce the sale of general books in a depressed period. Trade books are regarded as a luxury. They are one of the things people stop buying at the first signs of a departing prosperity. This does not mean that Americans stop reading. Our extraordinary American free public library system offers this assurance. At the same time, the growth of libraries with their necessary purchases offers some compensation to the publisher for the occasional lapses of the individual buyer. Professional and practical books have greatly increased both in number published and copies sold.

Texts, which form the bulk of Book Company production, are,

of course, less affected by economic ups and downs. Educational institutions are likely to continue, at least until society falls into chaos. Thus there will probably remain a basic stability in the Book Company on the surface of which there will be room for whatever flexibility the times demand.

3 The McGraw-Hill policy, matured in recent years, of feeding the top from the bottom offers better opportunity for advancement than ever before. It is rare nowadays for important executive positions in the companies to be filled from outside. The care used in the selection of men and women to fill the lower positions has built a reservoir of talented persons well equipped to go up as soon as a vacancy occurs. Thus there is a constant upward movement within the companies and employees are encouraged to think of McGraw-Hill as a lifework with the ever-present possibility of substantial ultimate reward. This, at any rate, is the ideal, and if there are occasional exceptions to the pattern, they are fewer as time goes on.

A demonstration of how this policy has worked out in the last dozen or so years is in the past record of the twenty-five men who today have publishing responsibility for the papers. Twenty of these have the title of publisher; five are associate publishers. Of these, in 1947 three were already publishers, one an assistant publisher, six were editors, two were managers, three were advertising salesmen, one was in promotion and research work, and one was manager of an auxiliary service conducted by the company. Only eight out of the twenty-five were outsiders in 1947 and two of these were former McGraw-Hill employees, since returned. We see here a pretty rapid rise within the organization. It may be taken for granted that all these publishers have learned a great deal about the whole of McGraw-Hill, not merely the traditions and practice of their own individual publications.

Thus, though there is a high degree of autonomy in the conduct of each separate paper or group of affiliated papers, yet the publisher is likely to know what goes on in the rest of the organi-

An architect's sketch of the new McGraw-Hill Book Distribution Center in East Windsor township, New Jersey. This building is now under construction.

zation and is able to cooperate when necessary in other enterprises than his own. Also, from such a listing as has just been presented, we see that men have come up to the level of publisher from both sides of periodical activity, editorial as well as business.

4 It is believed by all of those who have the continued success of the whole McGraw-Hill enterprise at heart that complacency is the worst enemy of progress. Yet the temptation to pat oneself on the back for a particular triumph and then rest on the laurels is usually easier than to look for the mistakes that have been made along the road or to find out the ways in which the job might have been better done. Old-timers know that there is almost always some ground for dissatisfaction, because they learned that lesson from James H. McGraw.

The ghost of the Old Man still walks in the halls, in the aisles between the desks in the offices, and into the private sanctums of the top brass: restless, insistent, asking as he picks up a paper here, a book there, "Why isn't this better?" And men and women who never knew the founder in the flesh are well acquainted with his ghost. Publishers, managers, editors, and salesmen all feel the prodding, know that they are sitting too long in their swivel chairs, know that they must get up and pack their bags and get out on the long trail that he blazed, to find new places for McGraw-Hill to enter, new services to offer, and rich new material to bring home.

We shall see plenty of flux in the years to come, and perhaps in years to come the organization which has been the hero of this story may have quite a different look. The papers we know may not all be there; others may come to serve some new phase. But those who have had the privilege of seeing the core of the enterprise predict that there will be high "standards of dissatisfaction" as long as the Green Building endures.

APPENDIX

Chronology of Events

The following lists are intended to highlight significant events in the story of McGraw-Hill and to suggest the framework of historical and technological progress within which the company developed.

	SIGNIFICANT EVENTS	MCGRAW-HILL DEVELOPMENTS
1858	First cable message sent across the Atlantic.	John A. Hill born in Sandgate, Vermont (February 22).
1859	Comstock Lode discovered in Nevada.	
	First successful oil well sunk in the United States by Edwin L. Drake.	
	Darwin's *Origin of Species* published.	
1860	First repeating rifle produced by Oliver F. Winchester.	James H. McGraw born in Panama, New York (December 17).
	Abraham Lincoln elected President.	*Mining and Scientific Press* founded in San Francisco. (Merged with *Engineering and Mining Journal* in 1923.)
1861	Massachusetts Institute of Technology established; first classes met in 1865.	
1863	National Academy of Sciences incorporated to promote science and investigate scientific problems for the Government.	
1864	Abraham Lincoln reelected President.	
1865	Web printing press invented by William Bullock.	
	Abraham Lincoln assassinated; Andrew Johnson became President.	

SIGNIFICANT EVENTS	MCGRAW-HILL DEVELOPMENTS	
	American Journal of Mining founded. (Ancestor of *Engineering and Mining Journal*)	*1866*
First elevated railroad (Ninth Avenue El) began operation in New York. Purchase of Alaska.		*1867*
George Westinghouse invented the air brake. Patent for first practical typewriter issued to Christopher Latham Sholes who coined the word "type-writer." Open-hearth process for steel industry introduced from England; first used in Trenton, New Jersey. General U. S. Grant elected President.	*Industrial American* founded. (Ancestor of *Textile World*)	*1868*
First transcontinental railroad completed in the United States. Patent issued for process of making celluloid (Hyatt). Suez Canal opened.		*1869*
John D. Rockefeller organized the Standard Oil Company.		*1870*
First narrow-gauge passenger locomotive used on Denver and Rio Grande Western Railroad.		*1871*
General U. S. Grant reelected President.	John A. Hill became an apprentice in a print shop in Wisconsin.	*1872*
Cable streetcar first used in San Francisco.		*1873*
First electric streetcar successfully run in New York with current generated by stationary dynamo as result of invention of third rail by Stephen Field.	*The Operator* founded. (Ancestor of *Electrical World*) *The Engineer and Surveyor* founded. (Later called *Engineering News*)	*1874*

	SIGNIFICANT EVENTS	MCGRAW-HILL DEVELOPMENTS
1876	American Chemical Society founded. First U.S. patent for telephone issued to Alexander Graham Bell. Demonstration at Philadelphia Centennial Exhibition of Corliss 1400-horsepower engine. Rutherford B. Hayes elected President.	
1877	World's largest cantilever bridge constructed over Kentucky River. Heating system from central station installed at Lockport, New York, by Birdsall Holly.	*American Machinist* founded. *The Plumber and Sanitary Engineer* founded. (Later called *Engineering Record*)
1878	Thomas A. Edison patented the phonograph. Edison Electric Light Company (first electric light company) formed. First commercial telephone exchange opened. (New Haven, Connecticut)	John A. Hill worked on the Denver and Rio Grande railroad firing a locomotive.
1879	George Selden applied for patent for self-propelled vehicle. Thomas A. Edison developed the incandescent lamp. Arc-lamp system of street lighting installed in Cleveland and San Francisco.	James H. McGraw taught in a district school (Harmony, New York) during the winter terms, 1879–1881.
1880	American Society of Mechanical Engineers founded. James A. Garfield elected President.	James H. McGraw entered the State Normal School in Fredonia. During these years he also worked at teaching elementary school and at part-time jobs of book agent, subscription salesman, and contributor to the local newspaper and magazine.
1881	President Garfield assassinated; Chester A. Arthur became President.	
1882	Thomas A. Edison opened his Pearl Street (New York) plant for incandescent electric lighting.	*New York Review of the Telephone and Telegraph founded.* (Later called *Electrical Review* and acquired by McGraw-Hill in 1921.)

SIGNIFICANT EVENTS	McGRAW-HILL DEVELOPMENTS	
Electric flatiron patented by Henry W. Seely, New York. Electric fan developed by Dr. S. S. Wheeler. First hydroelectric plant in the United States opened at Appleton, Wisconsin. First railroad passenger cars lighted by electricity.	*Steam* founded. (Ancestor of *Power*) *The Electrician* founded. (Later called *The Electrical Engineer* and merged with *Electrical World* in 1899.)	
Brooklyn Bridge opened. First practical steam turbine built by De Laval.	*American Journal of Railway Appliances* founded (July 16). Its column on street railways became the basis for *Street Railway Journal* founded in 1884.	*1883*
American Institute of Electrical Engineers founded. Electric passenger elevator invented. George Eastman patented his invention of photographic film. Grover Cleveland elected President.	James H. McGraw became an advertising salesman for the American Railway Publishing Company (publisher of the *American Journal of Railway Appliances*) after his graduation from Fredonia State Normal School in Chautauqua County, New York, in June, 1884. In September, 1884, he returned to upper New York State to become principal of the schools in Corfu, Genesee County. *Steam* was acquired by the American Railway Publishing Company. A new magazine, *Power, with which is incorporated Steam,* was published (November). *Street Railway Journal* founded by the American Railway Publishing Company (November).	*1884*
Electric welding process invented by Elihu Thomson. Linotype machine invented by Otto Mergenthaler. First electric streetcars commercially operated in Baltimore.	John A. Hill contributed to the *American Machinist's* column, "Letters from Practical Men," with a letter signed "J. A. Hill" on the subject, "Oil Holes for Locomotive Motion" (May 23). He was then running a locomotive on the Denver & Rio Grande after a year as founder and editor of the *Daily Press,* Pueblo, Colorado. James H. McGraw went to work with Horace M. Swetland in Boston for the American Railway Publishing Company, then publishers of *Power, Street Railway Journal,*	*1885*

and the *American Journal of Railway Appliances* (August).

James H. McGraw became manager of the subscription department of the American Railway Publishing Company with New York offices in the Stone Building, 32 Liberty Street (November).

1886 Electrolytic method of extracting aluminum from its ore invented by Charles Martin Hall.

Alternating-current system of electricity for commercial purposes demonstrated by George Westinghouse.

American Federation of Labor organized.

James H. McGraw worked in Philadelphia as associate editor and manager in the Southeastern Office of the American Railway Publishing Company (January).

James H. McGraw borrowed $1,000 from James Knapp, wealthy farmer in Chautauqua County, New York, and loaned it to the American Railway Publishing Company. For this amount and unpaid salary of $1,500 due him, he was given stock of the company and became a vice president.

1887 Interstate Commerce Commission established.

Daily railroad service to Pacific Coast established.

James H. McGraw was spending half his time in New York, one quarter of his time in Philadelphia, and the other quarter traveling for the American Railway Publishing Company. By the summer of 1887 he was mainly in the New York office at 113 Liberty Street.

Pacific Lumberman, Contractor and Electrician founded. (Ancestor of *Journal of Electricity* later called *Electrical West.*)

John A. Hill published his first article in *American Machinist,* "Promoting Firemen," (vol. 10, p. 2) signed "J. A. Hill" (April 9).

1888 First successful trolley line began operation in Richmond, Virginia, built by Frank J. Sprague.

George Eastman put Kodak box camera and roll film on the market.

Invention of induction electric motor by Nikola Tesla.

Benjamin Harrison elected President.

John A. Hill became editor of the *Locomotive Engineer* with the first issue (January). It was published by the American Machinist Publishing Company at 96 Fulton Street.

Light-Line Phonography published in London by John Robert Gregg (May 28). This was the first Gregg shorthand book.

SIGNIFICANT EVENTS	MCGRAW-HILL DEVELOPMENTS	
	James H. McGraw purchased the *American Journal of Railways Appliances* (August 4). Brief partnership of Swetland and McGraw to publish *Power* and the *American Journal of Railway Appliances.* At the split of the partnership Mr. McGraw took full interest in the *American Journal of Railway Appliances* and Mr. Swetland kept *Power,* which he continued to publish until its sale to John A. Hill in 1902 (October 1–November 7).	
Oklahoma Territory opened to settlers. First electric sewing machine manufactured by Singer Manufacturing Company.	James H. McGraw made his first payment on the *Street Railway Journal* to Emerson P. Harris (April 15). The sale was announced in the May 15, 1889 issue. James H. McGraw formed a partnership with his father-in-law, Curtis E. Whittlesey, to publish the *Street Railway Journal* and the *American Journal of Railway Appliances* (April 17).	*1889*
Sherman Antitrust Act. Pneumatic hammer patented by Charles B. King.	Publication of Gould's *A New Medical Dictionary* by P. Blakiston, Son & Company, Philadelphia.	*1890*
Thomas A. Edison patented his motion-picture camera and radio. California Institute of Technology founded. First electric automobile designed by William Morrison in Des Moines, Iowa.	James H. McGraw formed the Street Railway Publishing Company with C. E. Whittlesey and C. E. Stump (January 8). Mr. McGraw was President. Offices were in the World Building, 61 Park Row, New York. *Engineering Magazine, an Industrial Review* founded in April. (Ancestor of *Factory*) John A. Hill acquired part interest in the *Locomotive Engineer* along with Angus Sinclair. The partnership of Sinclair and Hill was formed, with offices in New York at 912 Temple Court, corner of Nassau and Beekman Streets (October 1). James H. McGraw sold the *American Journal of Railway Appliances* (November).	*1891*

	SIGNIFICANT EVENTS	McGRAW-HILL DEVELOPMENTS
1892	Nikola Tesla developed the polyphase motor that could be driven by alternating current. Manganese steel manufactured. First gasoline automobile made in the United States by Charles and Frank Duryea. First acetylene manufactured. Grover Cleveland elected President.	
1893	Beginning of interurban streetcar service.	
1894		The offices of the *Street Railway Journal* were moved to the Havemeyer Building, 26 Cortlandt Street, New York (January). The printing offices remained at 113 Liberty Street, where they had been since November, 1886.
1895	X-ray discovered by Wilhelm Konrad Roentgen, German physicist. Hydroelectric power first developed on large scale at Niagara Falls by George Westinghouse. First patent for automobile driven by a gasoline engine issued to George Selden (applied for in 1879). Invention of multiple unit system, electric train control, by Frank J. Sprague, New York. First automobile race in the United States held in Chicago.	
1896	Henry Ford completed construction of first gasoline engine to run successfully and he road-tested the first Ford car. Model airplane (built by Samuel Langley), powered by miniature steam engine, flew 1½ minutes for ½ mile over the Potomac River. Discovery of gold in Klondike. William McKinley elected President.	John A. Hill and Angus Sinclair purchased the *American Machinist* (January). Mr. Hill became Treasurer and General Manager of the American Machinist Publishing Company. James H. McGraw purchased the Electrical Industries Publishing Company, publishers of *Electrical Industries.* The publication was retitled the *American Electrician* (April 22).

SIGNIFICANT EVENTS	McGRAW-HILL DEVELOPMENTS	
	James H. McGraw formed the American Electrician Company of which he became President (May 15). Offices were in the Havemeyer Building, 26 Cortlandt Street, New York.	
First subway in the United States completed in Boston.	John A. Hill acquired full interest in the *American Machinist* and sold his part interest in *Locomotive Engineering* to Angus Sinclair (May 27–June 3). Mr. Hill became President of the American Machinist Publishing Company.	*1897*
War with Spain. Discovery of radium by Pierre and Mme. Curie. First practical submarine (Holland No. 9) submerged off Staten Island. First diesel engine for commercial use built in the United States.	John A. Hill incorporated the American Machinist Press of which he became President and Treasurer (May 4). First international issue of *Street Railway Journal* published (January).	*1898*
Invention of loading coil, long-distance telephony. Peace treaty with Spain signed. High-speed tool steel invented by Frederick W. Taylor and Maunsel White.	James H. McGraw purchased the *Electrical World* from W. J. Johnston (February 10). James H. McGraw purchased the *Electrical Engineer* from Joseph Wetzler (March 11). The McGraw Publishing Company was incorporated (March 15). James H. McGraw was President. Offices were at 26 Cortlandt Street, New York. The publications of the McGraw Publishing Company were *Street Railway Journal, American Electrician,* and *Electrical World and Electrical Engineer.* *The Gregg Writer* founded in April. (Ancestor of *Today's Secretary*) The McGraw Publishing Company moved to 120 Liberty Street (May). "*Jim Skeevers' Object Lessons,*" the collected articles by John A. Hill signed "John Alexander" (from *Locomotive Engineering*), was published by the American Machinist Press, Inc. (October).	*1899*

SIGNIFICANT EVENTS		MCGRAW-HILL DEVELOPMENTS
		The American Machinist Press, Ltd. was incorporated in London at 34 Norfolk Street (November). The March 22, 1900 issue of *American Machinist* (*European Edition*) was the first to be distributed from this office. This publication was later called *The Machinist* and now is known as *Metalworking Production*.
1900	First quantity-production automobile factory established in Detroit by the Olds Company. Carnegie Institute of Technology established by Andrew Carnegie. William McKinley reelected President.	
1901	Assassination of President McKinley; Theodore Roosevelt became President. United States Steel Corporation established. Spindletop, first oil gusher in Texas, discovered.	James H. McGraw purchased, on July 17, *Engineering and Mining Journal* (Scientific Publishing Company) which he sold to W. J. Johnston late in 1902. This was not a publication of the McGraw Publishing Company, but was published by Engineering and Mining Journal, Inc., of which James H. McGraw was president for a time and later a member of the Board. *The National Electrical Contractor* founded. (Ancestor of *Electrical Construction and Maintenance*)
1902	Air-conditioning equipment installed in a printing plant by Willis H. Carrier. Flatiron Building completed in New York (20 stories).	The Hill Publishing Company was incorporated with offices at 218 William Street, New York (January 29). John A. Hill was President and Treasurer. John A. Hill purchased *Power* from Horace M. Swetland (February 2). *Electrochemical Industry* (ancestor of *Chemical Engineering*) founded in September by James H. McGraw who formed the Electrochemical Publishing Company to publish it (see 1913 item). James H. McGraw bought *Engineering Record* from Henry C. Meyer (November 1).

SIGNIFICANT EVENTS	McGRAW-HILL DEVELOPMENTS	
Henry Ford organized the Ford Motor Company. First Pacific cable opened. First gasoline-driven automobile traveled from San Francisco to New York in 52 days. *Shop Management* by Frederick W. Taylor published by the American Society of Mechanical Engineers. First successful man-carrying airplane flight made by Wright Brothers at Kitty Hawk, North Carolina.		*1903*
Ida M. Tarbell's *History of Standard Oil Company* published. New York City subway began operation. Russo-Japanese war. Theodore Roosevelt elected President.	The Hill Publishing Company moved to 505 Pearl Street, New York (May 1).	*1904*
New York Central and Pennsylvania railroads both ran trains from New York to Chicago in 18 hours. Albert Einstein published his special theory of relativity. Federation of Trade Press Associations (now called Associated Business Publications) founded.	The American Electrician Company, Street Railway Publishing Company, and Electrical World and Engineer, Inc. were merged with the McGraw Publishing Company (December 20).	*1905*
Eugene Lauste invented sound track on film. San Francisco earthquake and fire.	The Hill Publishing Company started to publish *Engineering and Mining Journal* (October 20). John A. Hill had purchased interest in the W. J. Johnston Company from H. M. Swetland in 1904.	*1906*
Crash of New York Stock Market and financial panic.	*Selling Electricity* established in January. (Ancestor of *Electrical Merchandising*) The McGraw Publishing Company moved to a new building at 239 West 39 Street, constructed especially to house the	*1907*

SIGNIFICANT EVENTS

Invention of audion radio tube by Lee De Forest.

Marconi system of wireless telegraphy opened between the United States and Ireland.

First electric washing machine marketed.

MCGRAW-HILL DEVELOPMENTS

publications and printing plant (September 7).

The American Machinist Press, Ltd. was renamed the Hill Publishing Company Ltd. at 6 Bouverie Street, London, England (December 18).

The McGraw Publishing Company published *Standard Handbook for Electrical Engineers,* its first engineering handbook (December 30). It is still being published by McGraw-Hill and is now in its ninth edition.

1908 *Lusitania* set speed record for Atlantic crossing.

Singer Building (47 stories) built in New York.

First Model T automobile manufactured by Henry Ford.

Harvard Graduate School of Business Administration established.

Two subway tunnels in New York opened to traffic; one under the East River, the other under the Hudson River.

William H. Taft elected President.

James H. McGraw purchased the *American Telephone Journal* (February) and sold it later that year (August).

Colvin and Stanley's *American Machinists' Handbook* was published by the Hill Publishing Company. This handbook is still being published by McGraw-Hill and now is titled *The New American Machinists' Handbook,* edited by Rupert LeGrand.

1909 Junior high school system inaugurated at Berkeley, California.

First production of Bakelite, invented by Leo H. Baekeland.

First airplane flight across English Channel by French aviator, Louis Blériot.

The Hill Publishing Company published Herbert C. Hoover's *Principles of Mining* which is still in print. Mr. Hoover's next work published by the McGraw-Hill Book Company was *The Ordeal of Woodrow Wilson* in April, 1958.

The Book Departments of the McGraw Publishing Company and the Hill Publishing Company were merged to form the McGraw-Hill Book Company (June 21). John A. Hill was President; James H. McGraw, Vice President; Edward Caldwell, Treasurer; Martin M. Foss, Secretary. Offices were in the McGraw Publishing Company building at 239 West 39 Street.

National Petroleum News was founded by Warren Platt (February). This was acquired by McGraw-Hill in 1953.

SIGNIFICANT EVENTS	McGRAW-HILL DEVELOPMENTS	
First American aviation meet held at Los Angeles. Barney Oldfield set record for fastest speed traveled by man when he traveled a mile at 133 mph at Daytona Beach, Florida.	The Hill Publishing Company established a German company, Deutscher Hill Verlag, A.G., in Berlin which published the first German edition of the *American Machinist—Der Maschinenbau*—in Germany (January). The Book Company published its first book on aviation—Brewer's *The Art of Aviation.* The Book Company's first series was established—Electrical Engineering Texts—under the consulting editorship of Harry E. Clifford of Harvard University.	*1910*
Glenn H. Curtiss invented the hydroplane. First transcontinental air flight made from New York to Pasadena—3½ days actual flying time. Dissolution of Standard Oil Company ordered by Supreme Court. *The Principles of Scientific Management* by Frederick W. Taylor published.	*Mill Supplies* founded in January. (Ancestor of *Industrial Distribution*) Book Company published *Engineering Mathematics* by Charles Steinmetz (January 4). The first edition of Thomas E. French's *Engineering Drawing* was published (August 14). Sale of all editions, through the eighth published in 1953, totals over 1,650,000 copies. The Hill Publishing Company purchased the *Engineering News* from George H. Frost, owner of the Engineering News Publishing Company (September 7). The Engineering News book department was merged with the McGraw-Hill Book Company (November). The Hill Publishing Company established *Coal Age* (October 14).	*1911*
Woolworth Building completed in New York (58 stories). Sinking of the *Titanic.* Woodrow Wilson elected President.		*1912*
Sixteenth amendment to the Constitution permitting Federal income tax passed. Ford Motor Company adopted assembly-line technique for manufacturing the Model T.	*Metallurgical and Chemical Engineering* (formerly *Electrochemical Industry* founded in 1902) became part of the McGraw Publishing Company, Inc. (February 6). This publication is now *Chemical Engineering.*	*1913*

	SIGNIFICANT EVENTS	MCGRAW-HILL DEVELOPMENTS
	World's largest hydroelectric dam, Keokuk Dam, opened on the Mississippi River. Development of permalloy by Gustaf W. Elmen at Bell Telephone Laboratories, New York. Federal Reserve System established. Invention of cracking process for gasoline.	Book Company published *Principles of Industrial Organization* by Dexter Kimball.
1914	Henry Ford established the $5-a-day minimum wage for an 8-hour day. Panama Canal opened to traffic. Outbreak of World War I in Europe. Audit Bureau of Circulations founded. Beginning of taxi or jitney service and intercity bus lines resulting from regular jitney service.	McGraw Publishing Company opened an editorial office in San Francisco (February). *Weekly Drug Markets* founded by D. O. Haynes & Company in September. (Ancestor of *Chemical Week*) The Hill Publishing Company moved into the new building at Tenth Avenue and 36 Street from 505 Pearl Street (September). The new building was constructed especially to house the five publications and printing facilities. Three air-conditioning plants in the basement provided cooled air to all floors.
1915	First transcontinental telephone call (New York to San Francisco) *Lusitania* sunk by German submarine. Einstein published his general theory of relativity. His special theory had been announced in 1905.	
1916	National Research Council organized by the National Academy of Sciences. Invention of gas-filled incandescent lamp (Irving Langmuir, New York). Woodrow Wilson reelected President.	John A. Hill died at the age of 57 while being driven to work from East Orange, New Jersey (January 24). His friend and attorney, Arthur J. Baldwin, became President of the Hill Publishing Company. James H. McGraw became President of the McGraw-Hill Book Company, Inc., succeeding John A. Hill (February 11). The McGraw Publishing Company purchased *Electrical-Merchandise and Selling Electricity* (F. B. Rae Company) and published it as *Electrical Merchandising*, beginning July 15.

SIGNIFICANT EVENTS	MCGRAW-HILL DEVELOPMENTS	
	Aviation and Aeronautical Engineering founded, August 1. (Ancestor of *Aviation Week*) The McGraw Publishing Company purchased *The Contractor* in December. It was merged with *Engineering News-Record* July 4, 1918.	
United States entered World War I. Bolshevist revolution in Russia overthrew Czarist government.	*El Automovil Americano* founded by Class Journal Company (January). The McGraw and Hill interests were merged to form the McGraw-Hill Publishing Company, Inc. (February 28). At the time of the merger, the McGraw Publishing Company published: *Electrical World, Electric Railway Journal, Electrical Merchandising, Engineering Record, Metallurgical and Chemical Engineering,* and *The Contractor.* The Hill Publishing Company published: *American Machinist, Power, Engineering and Mining Journal, Coal Age,* and *Engineering News.* The two companies were united in the Hill Building at Tenth Avenue and 36 Street; the McGraw Publishing Company building at 239 West 39 Street was sold to the United Publishers Corporation. James H. McGraw was President of the new company; Arthur J. Baldwin was Vice President. The first issue of *Engineering News-Record* was published, the consolidation of the Hill Publishing Company's *Engineering News* with the McGraw Publishing Company's *Engineering Record* (April 5).	*1917*
Daily airmail service between New York and Washington, D. C., established. World War I ended with Armistice.	*The Key* founded as a special supplement to *The Gregg Writer* (September). This became the basis for a later Gregg publication, *Business Education World.*	*1918*
Eighteenth Amendment (Prohibition) ratified.	*Ingeniería Internacional* was established by McGraw-Hill for foreign distribution.	*1919*

SIGNIFICANT EVENTS		MCGRAW-HILL DEVELOPMENTS
	Treaty of Peace signed at Versailles establishing the League of Nations; U.S. Senate did not ratify it.	(April). This split into two editions in 1942, and in 1947 became two separate publications—*Ingeniería Internacional Construcción* and *Ingeniería Internacional Industria.* *Successful Methods* founded (July) by Successful Methods, Inc. (Ancestor of *Construction Methods and Equipment*) The Technical Publishing Company of San Francisco, publishers of *Journal of Electricity,* was purchased (August1). This company was the basis for the formation of the McGraw-Hill Company of California in 1921. The name of the Hill Publishing Company, Ltd. in London was changed to the McGraw-Hill Publishing Company, Ltd. (September 16).
1920	Airmail service between New York and San Francisco established. Warren G. Harding elected President.	*Jobber's Salesman* founded by the Electrical Trade Publishing Company in February. (Ancestor of *Electrical Wholesaling*) The Newton Falls Paper Company was purchased in April jointly with the United Publishers Corporation (later called the Chilton Company).
1921	Nobel Prize in physics awarded to Albert Einstein.	The McGraw-Hill Book Company, Inc. moved from 239 West 39 Street to the Penn Terminal Building, 370 Seventh Avenue (31 Street). The McGraw-Hill Company of California was established (February). It published the *Journal of Electricity,* later called *Electrical West.* *Electrical Review* was purchased, its title changed to *Electrical Review and Industrial Engineer,* and published by McGraw-Hill in January, 1922. It now is part of *Factory.*
1922	Insulin discovered by Fred Banting and Dr. Charles H. Best.	*Bus Transportation* established (January). It was discontinued December, 1956.

SIGNIFICANT EVENTS

First commercially sponsored radio program broadcast in New York (Station WEAF)

First successful radar research conducted at U.S. Naval Research aircraft laboratory in Washington, D. C.

MCGRAW-HILL DEVELOPMENTS

Mining and Scientific Press was purchased from the Dewey Publishing Company of California and consolidated with *Engineering and Mining Journal* to form *Engineering and Mining Journal-Press* (March). In 1928 this name was changed back to *Engineering and Mining Journal.*

Pacific Mining News was established as a supplement to *Engineering and Mining Journal* in San Francisco (May). It was published by the McGraw-Hill Company of California until October, 1923, when it ceased publication.

1923

Ethyl gasoline marketed in Dayton, Ohio.

Du Pont Corporation began production of cellophane.

First diesel-electric locomotive built in the United States.

Lee De Forest introduced in New York a system for producing sound motion pictures.

Jacob Schick received patent for first electric shaver.

President Harding died; Calvin Coolidge became President.

First transatlantic short-wave radio broadcast.

The Rodger Publishing Company of Chicago was purchased (May). It published *Electrical Retailing,* which continued to be published in Chicago as a supplement to *Electrical Merchandising* until January, 1925.

Platt's Oilgram Price Service founded by National Petroleum Publishing Company (W. C. Platt) on June 9.

Construction Daily—Reports was established (August 1). It is published five times a week and reports on business conditions in the construction industry.

1924

Radio Corporation of America (RCA) demonstrated technique of sending photographs by transatlantic wireless photography.

Calvin Coolidge elected President.

The American Automobile (Overseas Edition) founded by Class Journal Company.

1925

Scopes trial on teaching evolution in schools.

Court-martial of "Billy" Mitchell who advocated greatly expanded air force.

Photoelectric cell publicly demonstrated in New York by Westinghouse.

Radio Retailing established (January). It was sold in 1942.

On August 13 the Business Publishers International Corporation was formed jointly with the United Publishers Corporation (later the Chilton Company) to publish *In-*

SIGNIFICANT EVENTS | MCGRAW-HILL DEVELOPMENTS

Dry ice commercially manufactured.

genieria Internacional, El Automovil Americano, and *The American Automobile (Overseas Edition).*

Edward Caldwell became President of the McGraw-Hill Book Company, Inc., succeeding James H. McGraw (November 30).

1926 Army Air Corps created.

Admiral Byrd and Floyd Bennett made first successful flight over North Pole.

The Book Company published the first of seven volumes of the *International Critical Tables* (May 1). This immense compilation of scientific data, sponsored by the National Research Council, was developed by 300 experts from the National Bureau of Standards and several foreign nations.

Successful Methods, the property of Successful Methods, Inc., was purchased (May) and retitled *Construction Methods* in May, 1927. It now is called *Construction Methods and Equipment.*

The McGraw-Hill Catalog and Directory Company, Inc., was formed (August). In April, 1938, it became the Catalog and Directory Division of the McGraw-Hill Publishing Company, Inc. When this Division was discontinued in 1952, the catalogs and directories were turned over to the various magazines to which they applied.

Martin M. Foss became President of the McGraw-Hill Book Company, Inc., succeeding Edward Caldwell (December 29).

1927 Commercial telephone service opened between New York and London.

Charles A. Lindbergh completed first solo nonstop flight between New York and Paris.

First successful demonstration of television took place in New York.

Electric respirator, the iron lung, installed at Bellevue Hospital, New York.

The Book Company started to departmentalize with the College Department as a separate publishing unit (April 27).

Purchase of the Engineering Magazine Company properties—*Industrial Management, the Engineering Magazine,* and *Industry Illustrated*—and of the A. W. Shaw Company property, *Factory, the Magazine of Management* (November 12). These properties are all part of the present *Factory.*

SIGNIFICANT EVENTS	MCGRAW-HILL DEVELOPMENTS	
Holland Tunnel opened: first underwater vehicular tunnel in the United States. First talking motion picture, *The Jazz Singer.*		
First autogiro flown. Mechanical cotton picker was built at Weatherford, Texas, by John D. Rusk. Herbert Hoover elected President.	The Electrical Trade Publishing Company, publishers of *Jobber's Salesman,* was purchased and operated as a McGraw-Hill subsidiary in Chicago (June). In November, 1928 *The Electragist* was purchased from the National Electrical Contractors Association and published by the Electrical Trade Publishing Company as *Electrical Contracting.* In June, 1929 *Mill Supplies* was added to this subsidiary. Purchase in July of the A. W. Shaw Company, publishers of *System, The Magazine of Business, Harvard Business Review,* and the A. W. Shaw business books. The A. W. Shaw Book Division was consolidated with the McGraw-Hill Book Company, Inc. (See November 12, 1927 item.) Purchase of Bragdon, Lord and Nagle, publishers of *Textile World, Textile Advance News,* and textile books (October). The books were added to the Book Company list. *Food Industries* (now *Food Engineering*) was established (October). James H. McGraw resigned from the presidency of the McGraw-Hill Publishing Company, Inc. (October 29) and continued as Chairman of the Board. Malcolm Muir became President.	*1928*
Stock market crash. Lieut. Comdr. Richard E. Byrd completed first flight over South Pole. Color television was demonstrated at Bell Telephone Laboratories, New York. Radio telephone ship-to-shore commercial service inaugurated. Polaroid glass invented by E. H. Land.	The Aviation Publishing Corporation, publishers of *Aviation* (now called *Aviation Week*), was purchased (March). *The Business Week* began publication on September 7. (Now called *Business Week.*)	*1929*

	SIGNIFICANT EVENTS	MCGRAW-HILL DEVELOPMENTS
1930	Institute for Advanced Study established at Princeton, New Jersey. First radar detection of airplanes at Anacostia, D. C. Smoot-Hawley Tariff Act.	*Product Engineering* was established (January). *Engineering and Mining Journal Metal and Mineral Markets* was established (January). *Engineering and Mining World* was established (January). In January, 1932 this was absorbed by *Engineering and Mining Journal.* McGraw-Hill Book Company established its West Coast office and book depository in San Francisco. The McGraw-Hill Book Company entered the trade-book field with Whittlesey House (now called Trade Division) on February 13. The first Whittlesey House book, *The World's Economic Dilemma,* by Ernest Minor Patterson, appeared in the fall of 1930. *Electronics* was established (April). *El Farmacéutico* was purchased by the Business Publishers International Corporation (April). Ground was broken for the new McGraw-Hill Building at 330 West 42 Street, New York (August).
1931	Discovery of deuterium (an isotope of hydrogen) by Dr. Harold C. Urey of Columbia University. Empire State Building, world's tallest building opened in New York. First round-the-world flight made by Post and Gatty. George Washington Bridge completed. Synthetic rubber (neoprene) commercially produced by Du Pont.	The Tenth Avenue offices of the McGraw-Hill Publishing Company, Inc. moved to the new building at 330 West 42 Street (October 10). The Book Company moved to the new McGraw-Hill Building from 370 Seventh Avenue (December 6).
1932	Reconstruction Finance Corporation established.	Pitkin's *Life Begins at Forty,* the first Whittlesey House best seller, was published (October 25).

SIGNIFICANT EVENTS

MCGRAW-HILL DEVELOPMENTS

Discovery of the neutron by James Chadwick.

Franklin D. Roosevelt elected President.

1933

United States went off the gold standard.

National Recovery Administration (NRA) established.

United States resumed diplomatic relations with Russia.

Twenty-first amendment to the Constitution repealing the eighteenth went into effect.

Electrification of the Pennsylvania Railroad between New York and Philadelphia completed.

First U.S. aircraft carrier, *Ranger*, launched at Newport News.

Century of Progress Exhibition opened in Chicago.

Recent Social Trends was published, establishing the Book Company as a major publisher in the social sciences (January 3).

The McGraw-Hill printing plant, consisting of all equipment and machinery on the fifth, sixth, seventh, and basement floors of the building at 330 West 42 Street, was sold to the Charles Schweinler Press (January 16).

1934

First practical cyclotron built by Ernest O. Lawrence of the University of California.

First streamlined steam locomotive put in operation: New York Central's *Commodore Vanderbilt*.

Establishment of the Securities and Exchange Commission.

First stainless steel streamliner diesel-powered *Pioneer Zephyr* put in service by Chicago, Burlington & Quincy R.R.

Platt's Oilgram News Service founded by National Petroleum Publishing Company (W. C. Platt) on February 6.

Book Company published *Chemical Engineers' Handbook* edited by John H. Perry.

1935

Works Progress Administration (WPA) established.

NRA invalidated by Supreme Court decision.

Establishment of Congress of Industrial Organizations (CIO) by John L. Lewis.

First sulfa drug, prontosil patented in Germany.

The publications published by the subsidiary Electrical Trade Publishing Company were absorbed into the McGraw-Hill Publishing Company, Inc. and moved from Chicago to New York (January 1). They were: *Electrical Contracting* (now *Electrical Construction and Maintenance*), *Electrical Wholesaling*, and *Mill Supplies* (now *Industrial Distribution*). The Electrical Trade Publishing Company was dissolved.

	SIGNIFICANT EVENTS	MCGRAW-HILL DEVELOPMENTS
	Aviation gasoline, 100-octane, produced commercially.	James H. McGraw resigned as Chairman of the Board of the McGraw-Hill Publishing Company, Inc., retaining the title of Honorary Chairman. James H. McGraw, Jr., became Chairman. Malcolm Muir continued as President.
1936	Hoover Dam completed. Franklin D. Roosevelt reelected President.	
1937	Golden Gate Bridge, San Francisco. Social Security Act. First industrial atom smasher built. (Westinghouse).	Malcolm Muir resigned from the McGraw-Hill Publishing Company, Inc. (June 21). James H. McGraw, Jr., became President, and continued as Chairman of the Board.
1938	Civil Aeronautics Authority established. Hitler invaded Czechoslovakia. Du Pont began commercial production of nylon. Fluorescent lamps introduced in the United States. Introduction of self-propelled combine harvester. U.S. Coast Artillery conducted radar tests.	
1939	New York World's Fair. German scientists split uranium 235 atom with bombardment of neutrons producing atomic fission. Frequency-modulation (FM) form of radio reception invented by Edwin H. Armstrong. Germany invaded Poland; start of World War II in Europe. First regular transatlantic passenger flight. Nylon stockings. First battleship equipped with radar: *U.S.S. New York.*	*Photo Technique* was established (June). It was sold December, 1941.

SIGNIFICANT EVENTS	McGRAW-HILL DEVELOPMENTS	
First successful helicopter flight in the United States. Franklin D. Roosevelt elected for third term as President. Massachusetts Institute of Technology set up Radiation Laboratory for radar experiments.	Publication in *Power* of an article on uranium 235 (July).	*1940*
Pearl Harbor attack; United States entered World War II.	The Business Publishers International Corporation began publication of the magazine *En Guardia* for the Coordinator of Inter-American Affairs. This continued until 1945 and was distributed in three editions, Spanish, Portuguese, and French, for circulation in Latin-American countries. The Technical and Business Education Department was started in the Book Company (August). This split into two departments—Technical Education and Business Education (January, 1948). The Business Education Department was merged with the Gregg Publishing Company in 1949.	*1941*
Opening of the Alcan Highway. First American jet plane (Bell aircraft XP-59 tested at Muroc Army Base, California). First continuous nuclear reaction (Argonne Project) demonstrated at University of Chicago.	*Wings* was published by McGraw-Hill as a wartime service for the Bureau of Aeronautics, Navy Department, and Army Air Force (May). It ceased publication with the September, 1945 issue. *Transit Journal* ceased publication (December). This paper had been started in 1884 as *Street Railway Journal,* purchased by James H. McGraw in 1889, its title changed to *Electric Railway Journal* in 1908, and to *Transit Journal* in 1932.	*1942*
	A Book Export Department was established in the Book Company (July). *Aviation News* was established (August 2). It was merged with *Aviation* (July 7, 1947) to form *Aviation Week.* *Air Transport* was established (September). It was merged with *Aviation Week,* April 5, 1948.	*1943*

1944

SIGNIFICANT EVENTS

Development of synthetic quinine by two Harvard University chemists, Woodward and Doering.

Streptomycin commercially manufactured by Merck & Company.

Franklin D. Roosevelt elected for fourth term.

Large-scale commercial production of penicillin began in the United States.

MCGRAW-HILL DEVELOPMENTS

A foreign-language translation office was started in the Book Export Department of the Book Company (February 15).

The Health Education Department was started in the Book Company for the publication of books in nursing education, medical science, and related fields (March 1).

The McGraw-Hill *Overseas Digest* was published for distribution by the War Department to servicemen overseas. It consisted of excerpts from articles in the then 24 McGraw-Hill technical and business publications and was published monthly (March, 1944–March, 1946). In May, 1946, it was launched as a commercial venture under the title *McGraw-Hill Digest* and now is called *International Management Digest.*

James S. Thompson became President of the Book Company succeeding Martin M. Foss (February).

The Embassy Book Company, Ltd., of Toronto, Canada, was purchased by the McGraw-Hill Book Company (September 1). This company was the basis for the formation of the McGraw-Hill Company of Canada Limited.

1945

SIGNIFICANT EVENTS

Death of Franklin D. Roosevelt; Harry S. Truman became President.

First atomic bomb dropped on Hiroshima, Japan.

End of World War II.

United Nations Conference, San Francisco.

MCGRAW-HILL DEVELOPMENTS

The Book Company published Adria Locke Langley's best seller, *A Lion Is in the Streets,* its first venture into fiction.

The Department of Economics was established to provide economic counsel and assistance for the entire company.

World News Service was established to provide news from abroad for all McGraw-Hill magazines (July 1). In August, 1945, the first McGraw-Hill foreign-news bureau was opened in London. McGraw-Hill now has news bureaus in eight foreign cities.

The Text-Film Department was started in the Book Company, mainly to produce educational films correlated with its leading textbooks (July).

SIGNIFICANT EVENTS	MCGRAW-HILL DEVELOPMENTS	
	The first issue of *Atomic Power* was published on August 7. In September *Atomic Engineering* began publication. These were forerunners of *Nucleonics* published on March 15, 1946. *Science Illustrated* was purchased (November 1), and issued under new format in April, 1946. It ceased publication on June 17, 1949. *Welding Engineer* was purchased (December). It was sold December, 1954.	
Atomic Energy Commission established. U.S. Army Signal Corps reported a radar beam had reached the moon.	Curtis G. Benjamin became President of the McGraw-Hill Book Company, Inc., succeeding James S. Thompson (November 29). *Petroleum Processing* founded by Warren Platt. (Acquired by McGraw-Hill in 1953.)	*1946*
Congress authorized the Hoover Commission on organization of the Executive branch of the government. Taft-Hartley Act. World's largest reflector telescope completed at Mount Palomar Observatory, California. First plane to achieve supersonic speed: Bell X-1 flown by Capt. Charles E. Yeager, USAF, Muroc Air Base, California. General Electric conducted rain-making experiment by "seeding" cumulous clouds. Department of Defense established.	*Pharmacy International* was established (January). It was sold with *El Farmacéutico* in January, 1955. After the purchase by McGraw-Hill of the stock held by the Chilton Company in Business Publishers International Corporation, the name of Business Publishers International Corporation was changed to the McGraw-Hill International Corporation (March 27). The Book Company published the first volume of the 28-volume MIT Radiation Laboratory Series, sponsored by the Office of Scientific Research and Development and the National Defense Research Council (June 23). *Operating Engineer* was established (October). It was absorbed by *Power*, April 1, 1951.	*1947*
Production of aureomycin at Lederle Laboratory, Pearl River, New York.	James H. McGraw died in San Francisco at the age of 87 (February 21).	*1948*

	SIGNIFICANT EVENTS	MCGRAW-HILL DEVELOPMENTS
	Atomic research for industrial development was inaugurated by partnership between the University of Chicago and seven corporations. Harry S. Truman elected president. Invention of the transistor by William Shockley, John Bardeen, and Walter Brattain of Bell Telephone Laboratories.	The *McGraw-Hill American Letter* was established (July). The Book Company published the first volume of the multivolume National Nuclear Energy Series for the U.S. Atomic Energy Commission (December 30). The Gregg Publishing Company was purchased by the Book Company whose Business Education Department was merged with it (December 31). After operating as a subsidiary for three years, this Company was merged into the Book Company as the Gregg Division.
1949	Discovery of cortisone announced. President Truman announced his Point Four program. Russia exploded an atomic bomb.	*Construction Daily–Newsletter*, an additional service for readers in the construction industry, was established (June 29). *Fleet Owner* (Ferguson Publishing Company) was purchased (August 24).
1950	President Truman ordered the development of the hydrogen bomb by the Atomic Energy Commission. Korean War began.	The Foreign Department of the Book Company (formerly the Book Export Department started in 1944) became the Book Export Division of the International Division (January). James H. McGraw, Jr. resigned as President and Chairman of the McGraw-Hill Publishing Company, Inc. (February 24). Curtis W. McGraw, his brother, became President and Chairman of the Board. *Chemical Industries,* a monthly magazine, was purchased from MacLean-Hunter Publishing Corporation (August 1). It was retitled *Chemical Industries Week* and issued weekly. In June, 1951, it was called *Chemical Week.* *Betty Crocker's Picture Cook Book* was published by the Book Company (September 8). In eight years 4,500,000 copies have been sold. The Technical Writing Service was established in the Book Company (October 10). The initial function of this

SIGNIFICANT EVENTS	MCGRAW-HILL DEVELOPMENTS	
	department was to supply training and operating literature to the military departments during the Korean conflict. The Book Company published the first volume of the Boswell Papers—*Boswell's London Journal, 1762–1763* (October 16).	
First electricity generated from atomic energy at U.S. Reactor Testing Station, Idaho. Transcontinental TV began with broadcast of President Truman's address at Japanese Peace Treaty Conference in San Francisco.	The Mail Sales Department was named the Industrial and Business Book Department to denote its publishing fnction (April 1).	*1951*
First hydrogen bomb exploded at Eniwetok Atoll. *S.S. United States* set transatlantic speed record. Opening of first jet-liner passenger service, London to Johannesburg. Dwight D. Eisenhower elected President.	The secondary school list of Harper and Brothers was purchased and merged with the School Department of the Book Company (January). Gregg College in Chicago, which had been acquired in 1948 along with other properties of the Gregg Publishing Company, was given to Northwestern University (June 1). It is now known as the Gregg Division of the School of Commerce of Northwestern University.	*1952*
Department of Health, Education, and Welfare created. Korean armistice signed at Panmunjon.	The National Petroleum Publishing Company, the W. C. Platt Company, and Platt's Price Service, Inc. were purchased from Warren C. Platt (April 1). These companies were publishers of *National Petroleum News, Petroleum Processing, Platt's Oilgram News and Price Services.* McGraw-Hill discontinued publication of *Petroleum Processing* with the September, 1957 issue. Curtis W. McGraw died suddenly at the Hotel Carlyle, New York (September 10). Donald C. McGraw, the youngest son of James H. McGraw, became President of the McGraw-Hill Publishing Company, Inc. (September 17).	*1953*

	SIGNIFICANT EVENTS	MCGRAW-HILL DEVELOPMENTS
1954	*Nautilus*, first atomic-powered submarine launched. U.S. Air Force Academy established. *U.S.S. Forrestal,* largest warship ever built, launched. Salk vaccine used for treatment of polio.	*Control Engineering* was established (September). The filmstrip library of *Popular Science* was purchased and merged with the Text-Film Department of the Book Company (October 1). The Blakiston Company, publishers of medical books, was purchased from Doubleday & Sons, Inc. and merged with the Health Education Department of the Book Company to form the Blakiston Division (November 1).
1955	Merger of AFL and CIO.	The Book Company established a Chicago office and depository at suburban Lincolnwood, Illinois (May 20). *Petroleum Week* was established (July 8.).
1956	First nonstop transcontinental helicopter flight. World's first power station to use atomic energy to create electricity for civil uses opened at Calder Hall, England. Dwight D. Eisenhower reelected President.	Book Company undertook production of ten-volume *Encyclopedia of Science and Technology*. Publication will begin in 1960.
1957	Atomic test at Yucca Flat, Nevada—most powerful nuclear explosion in the United States. Commercial air service over the North Pole inaugurated between Tokyo and Copenhagen. International Geophysical Year began. Transcontinental jet-plane speed record set Russia launched satellite into orbit.	Editorial offices of the Book Company were established in Charlottesville, Virginia, for the development of the *Encyclopedia of Science and Technology* (January 29). The Book Company made arrangements with Istituto per la Collaborazione Culturale of Rome for the translation and publication of an English-language edition of the *Encyclopedia of World Art* (May 4). Young America Films was purchased and merged with the Text-Film Department of the Book Company (June 1). The Book Export Division of the International Corporation became the International Division of the Book Company (December).

SIGNIFICANT EVENTS	MCGRAW-HILL DEVELOPMENTS	
United States launched satellite into orbit.	*Purchasing Week* was established (January 6).	*1958*
Alaska became the 49th State.		
Inauguration of jet passenger plane service between the United States and Europe.	*Electrical Newsletter,* a weekly service published by *Electric World,* was established (June 6).	
St. Lawrence Seaway and Power Project completed.	The Art Book Department of the Book Company was established (September 1).	
Nuclear submarine *Nautilus* traveled from Pearl Harbor to England by way of the North Pole.	McGraw-Hill Book Company Distribution Center at Hightstown, New Jersey, was opened (December).	
United States launched first successful intercontinental ballistic missile.	Book Company purchased Handbook Publishers, Inc. (December).	

Following are the sources used for the political, economic and scientific events listed in the chronology:

The Encyclopedia of American Facts and Dates, edited by Gorton Carruth and Associates, copyright 1956 by Thomas Y. Crowell Company, New York

Kull, Irving and Nell, *A Short Chronology of American History, 1492–1950,* Rutgers University Press, New Brunswick, New Jersey, 1952

Kane, Joseph Nathan, *Famous First Facts,* The H. W. Wilson Company, New York, 1950

Power, 75th Anniversary Issue, September, 1957 (vol. 101, no. 9)

American Machinist, 75th Anniversary Issue, November, 1952 (vol. 96, no. 4)

Transit Journal, 50th Anniversary Issue, September 15, 1934 (vol. 78, no. 10)

Haynes, Williams, *American Chemical Industry, Background and Beginnings,* Vols. I, II, III, IV, V, D. Van Nostrand Company, Inc., Toronto, New York, London, 1954

Encyclopedia of American History, edited by Richard B. Morris, Harper & Brothers, New York, 1953

Picture Credits

(All photographs that are not included in the following list are the property of theMcGraw-Hill Publishing Company, Inc.)

Cover Photo courtesy of Berenice Abbott.

Title page from *Locomotive Engineer,* Vol. 1, No. 1, January, 1888. Courtesy of Engineering Societies Library.

Page

3 Courtesy of Bettmann Archive.
5 New Haven Colony Historical Society.
13 Courtesy of the New York Public Library.
16 Klarwill, Victor von, *Fugger News-Letters, 1585–1605,* Series 1, John Lane, The Bodley Head, Ltd., London, 1924.
18-19 Bathe, Greville, *An Engineer's Miscellany,* Patterson and White Company, Philadelphia, 1938.
21 MacCurdy, Edward, *The Notebooks of Leonardo da Vinci,* Reynal and Hitchcock, New York, 1938.
33 Roe, Joseph Wickham, *English and American Tool Builders,* The McGraw-Hill Book Company, Inc., New York, 1926.
34 Bathe, Greville and Dorothy, *Oliver Evans,* Historical Society of Pennsylvania, Philadelphia, 1935.
35 Evans, Oliver, *Young Mill-Wright and Miller's Guide,* 1795.
55 Courtesy of Bettmann Archive.
56, 57, 59 Courtesy of William J. Howes, Panama, New York.
66 Courtesy of Horace M. Swetland's daughter, Mrs. Maurice J. Kane, Center Lovell, Maine.
75 Courtesy of American Transit Association.
83 Courtesy of Engineering Societies Library.
84 Courtesy of Fred H. Colvin.
86 Courtesy of Denver and Rio Grande Western Railroad, P.O. Box 5482, Denver 17, Colorado.
108 *Scientific American,* August 26, 1882.
127 Courtesy of Willard Chevalier.
155 *Mining and Scientific Press,* May 22, 1920: "A Chapter in Journalism," by T. A. Rickard.
160 Courtesy of Henry G. Lord.
165 Courtesy of Associated Business Publications, Inc.
180 Photograph by Bachrach.
197 Courtesy of George Eastman House, Rochester, New York.
201 Courtesy of John A. Hill's daughter, Mrs. Edward Quirk.
212 Courtesy of the Institute of Aeronautical Sciences.
223 From "Chemistry—The Key to Better Living," courtesy of E. I. Du Pont de Nemours & Co., Inc.
224 Courtesy of Standard Oil Company of New Jersey.
242 Courtesy of Edward E. Booher.
245 Courtesy of Hugh J. Kelly.
286 Courtesy of International Harvester Company, Chicago.
293 Courtesy of American Transit Association.
305 Courtesy of George Tenney.
310 Courtesy of the United States Navy.
332 Courtesy of S. D. Kirkpatrick.
347 Courtesy of Keith Henney.
354 Courtesy of The Carter Oil Company, Tulsa.
433 Photograph by the Dicksons, Plymouth, Massachusetts.
435 Menotti, Gian-Carlo, *Amahl and the Night Visitors,* illustrated by Roger Duvoisin, The McGraw-Hill Book Company, Inc., New York, 1952.
453 Official U.S.A.F. Photograph, released by Office of Information Services, Air Force Missile Test Center, Patrick Air Force Base, Florida.

END PAPERS

For permission to use photographs that appear on the end papers, the author wishes to express his appreciation to: Authenticated News for the photo of a steel transmission tower; Brookhaven National Laboratory for the picture of a cross section of a model of the Brookhaven Cosmotron; Columbia University for its photo of college students at commencement; The Ford Motor Company for its photos of the 1909 Model-T Roadster and of the 1914 Ford Assembly Line; The General Electric News Bureau for its illustration of automation in a modern factory; The Institute of Aeronautical Sciences for its photo of the Wright Brothers' airplane; and Wide World Photos for the U.S. Air Force picture of an Atlas ICBM launching at Cape Canaveral, Florida.

Index